ME AND MY HOUSE

Me and My House

JAMES BALDWIN'S LAST DECADE IN FRANCE

Magdalena J. Zaborowska

DUKE UNIVERSITY PRESS   *Durham and London*   2018

© 2018 Magdalena J. Zaborowska
All rights reserved

Designed by Amy Ruth Buchanan
Typeset in Garamond Premier Pro and Meta
by Westchester Publishing Services

Library of Congress Cataloging-in-Publication Data
Names: Zaborowska, Magdalena J., author.
Title: Me and my house : James Baldwin's last decade
in France / Magdalena J. Zaborowska.
Description: Durham : Duke University Press, 2018. |
Includes bibliographical references and index.
Identifiers: LCCN 2017042679 (print)
LCCN 2017048237 (ebook)
ISBN 9780822372349 (ebook)
ISBN 9780822369240 (hardcover : alk. paper)
ISBN 9780822369837 (pbk. : alk. paper)
Subjects: LCSH: Baldwin, James, 1924–1987. |
Baldwin, James, 1924–1987—Homes and haunts—
France—Saint-Paul (Alpes-Maritimes) | Baldwin, James,
1924–1987—Criticism and interpretation.
Classification: LCC PS3552.A45 (ebook) | LCC PS3552.A45
Z985 2018 (print) | DDC 818/.5409—dc23
LC record available at https://lccn.loc.gov/2017042679

Cover art: (*top*) Baldwin waving in front of his house.
Photo by Walter Dallas. (*bottom*) Baldwin's study
as he left it. Both images from the documentary film
James Baldwin: The Price of the Ticket (1989); courtesy of
Karen Thorsen, Douglas Dempsey, and the James Baldwin
Project.

Duke University Press gratefully acknowledges the support
of the University of Michigan, its College of Literature,
Science, and the Arts, and the Departments of American
Culture and Afroamerican and African Studies, which
provided funds toward the publication of this book.

To Gosia, Tracey, Sandra, and Paola

And in memory of Evelyn Grendell Jordan,

Thomas Jordan, Neil Lawrence Jr., Sedat Pakay,

Radhouan Ben Amara, and Brenda Rein

CONTENTS

ix   ABBREVIATIONS

xi   ACKNOWLEDGMENTS

1   **INTRODUCTION.** If I Am a Part of the American House, and I Am
Vitrines, Fragments, Reassembled Remnants

51   **CHAPTER 1.** Foundations, Façades, and Faces
Through the Glass Blackly, or Domesticating Claustrophobic Terror

85   **CHAPTER 2.** Home Matter
No House in the World, or Reading Transnational, Black Queer Domesticity in St. Paul-de-Vence

145   **CHAPTER 3.** Life Material
Haunted Houses and Welcome Tables, or The First Teacher, the Last Play, and Affectations of Disidentification

213   **CHAPTER 4.** Building Metaphors
"Sitting in the Strangest House I Have Ever Known," or Black Heterotopias from Harlem to San Juan, to Paris, London, and Yonkers

295   **CHAPTER 5.** Black Life Matters of Value
Erasure, Overlay, Manipulation, or Archiving the Invisible House

317   NOTES

351   BIBLIOGRAPHY

377   INDEX

ABBREVIATIONS

AD	"*Architectural Digest* Visits: James Baldwin"
CR	*The Cross of Redemption*
ETNS	*The Evidence of Things Not Seen*
GR	*Giovanni's Room*
IB	*If Beale Street Could Talk*
JAMH	*Just above My Head*
JB	*James Baldwin: The Last Interview and Other Conversations*
LM	*Little Man, Little Man: A Story of Childhood*
NKMN	*Nobody Knows My Name: More Notes of a Native Son*
NNS	*No Name in the Street*
PT	*The Price of the Ticket: Collected Nonfiction 1948–1985*
TMHL	*Tell Me How Long the Train's Been Gone*

ACKNOWLEDGMENTS

Like humans, books thrive both in the solitude of intense labor and within dense networks of social relationships that nourish and shape them in equally important, manifold ways. *Me and My House* villages reach from the United States to Poland, France, Turkey, and Italy, and they are populated by family and friends, colleagues and students, and all those who at one time or another offered assistance, wisdom, encouragement, and support, long-term and at the spur of the moment. There have been so many kind people aiding this book on its way to fruition that I am afraid I cannot possibly name every one of them. Let me begin this list of thanks due by offering my deepest gratitude and appreciation to them all.

At Duke University Press, Courtney Berger has been a model editor to work with and has patiently and gracefully encouraged this project since we first met. Her invaluable advice and guidance have helped it metamorphose into this final version. I also owe enormous thanks to Sandra Korn and Christine Riggio, who have overseen its production and patiently withstood my creative crises concerning the final choice of images, cover, and layout. I also thank the copyeditor, Christine Dahlin, and, especially, Duke University Press's anonymous readers, who provided sage advice and guidance as this project took shape from proposal to final manuscript.

My former student, Dr. Annah MacKenzie, was the first reader of the drafts and helped me to format the earliest versions of chapters, offering much advice and encouragement over the whole process. Dr. Danielle LaVague-Manty assisted with shaping the last drafts as they went into production, Dr. Jennifer Solheim was invaluable in crafting the index, while Janée Moses, Ph.D. candidate, helped with the bibliography. My many conversations with graduate students in American Culture and Afroamerican and African Studies, and my teaching of hundreds of undergraduates in both departments, have deeply enriched my thinking on this project. I also thank all my Ph.D. advisees—and especially Jallicia Jolly and Katie Leonard—whose enthusiasm and love of literature have given me daily boosts of energy, and especially warmly Dahlia Petrus, who assisted with teaching and learning to navigate the digital realm, not to mention providing references to the coolest films, documentaries, and scholarship I am counting on receiving well beyond this project.

Institutional support at the University of Michigan's College of Literature, Science, and the Arts has been steadfast and generous ever since I joined it: from funds to help with the publication of this book, ADVANCE summer writing grants in 2016 and 2017, and a Michigan Humanities Award that secured time for me to work on this project, through the Rackham School of Graduate Studies and my home departments of American Culture and Afroamerican and African Studies, which have given plentiful, reliable, and warm staff support as well as travel and research funding, to the Institute for the Humanities, and its past directors, Danny Herwitz and Sid Smith, where the idea for *Me and My House* first took shape during a fellowship year. I also wholeheartedly thank my departmental chairs and colleagues, as well as those in other units, who have encouraged my work, and whose scholarship, mentorship, collegiality, and intellectual powers have nurtured and strengthened my own: Profs. Sandra Gunning, Frieda Ekotto, Evelyn Alsultany, Alan Wald, June Howard, Fernando Arenas, Paul Johnson, Larry La Fountain-Stokes, Sara Blair, Abby Stewart, Marianetta Porter, and Mary Kelley.

While I first envisaged and then painstakingly researched this project, David and Pamela Leeming, Sedat and Kathy Pakay, Karen Thorsen and Douglas Dempsey, and Jill Hutchinson and her daughter Leonore have been reliable friends, supporters, and sources of unique information on and beautiful images of Baldwin, his life, family, and dwellings without which this book would be much poorer. Their pioneering representations and brave preservation of Baldwin's legacy as biographers, documentary filmmakers, and fierce guardians of his house archive continue to inspire and enlighten me. Aisha Karefa-Smart, Helen Baldwin, and Trevor Baldwin were generous in sharing the memories of their brother-in-law and uncle, as were Lynn Orilla Scott, Ken Winfield, Nikki Giovanni, Nicholas Delbanco, Roberta Uno, Pitou Roux, and Hélène Roux Jeandheur, who let me interview them for this project, offering moving personal accounts of their connections to Jimmy and his life in the United States and France. The late Lucien Happersberger, whom I interviewed in 2007, will always remain in my mind as an indefatigable interlocutor; I thank Prof. Boris Vejdovsky of Université de Lausanne for facilitating our meeting.

Scholars at numerous academic institutions and members of the worldwide Baldwin fellowship have chaperoned other publications of mine along the way, and all have been invaluable teachers and interlocutors over the years, especially Profs. Lynn Orilla Scott, Michele and Harry Elam, Nigel Hatton, Ed Pavlić, Douglas Field, Nicholas Boggs, Quentin Miller, E. Patrick Johnson, Brian Norman, Justin Joyce, John Drabinski, Pekka Kilpeläinen, Robert Reid-Pharr, Ernest Gibson, Bill Schwartz, Cora Kaplan, Jacquelyn Goldsby, Dwight McBride, Cheryl Wall, and Violet Johnson. Prof. Paola Boi Pisano of University of Cagliari in Italy and Prof. Claudine Reynaud of Université Paul Valéry in Montpellier, France, enabled summer research support as well as rich intellectual environments during key phases of archival work, while Dr. Tulani Salahu-Din at the National Museum of African American History and Culture at the Smithsonian has been a revelation in terms of her support for the Baldwin archives and encouragement toward my future project to construct a digital James Baldwin house-museum.

I dedicate this project to my sisters by blood and long-term friendship—Gosia Zaborowska, Tracey Rizzo, Sandra Gunning, and Paola Boi Pisano. They have been there for me whenever tough times came, and there were many, given that I was diagnosed with a disabling chronic illness while working on this book.

Like them, several family members and dear friends who have passed on during the last few years, and whose vision of home and literal hospitality in the homes of their own have helped me grow as a human being and push my work along, are the ones to whom I dedicate this project.

Lastly, and most of all, my son, Cazmir Thomas-Jordan Zaborowska, deserves the most singular gratitude. Born while I labored on my first book on Baldwin in Turkey, he has bravely helped me with archival research in France since the age of thirteen and cheered my writing on steadfastly, especially whenever my health and stamina fail me. His courage, intelligence, perseverance, beauty, and loving support make my every day a prize and our life together the best home in the world.

The living room with its mantelpiece assemblage. Photo by author, 2000.

INTRODUCTION

If I Am a Part of the American House, and I Am

Vitrines, Fragments, Reassembled Remnants

> If I am a part of the American house, and I am, it is because my ancestors paid—*striving to make it my home*—so unimaginable a price: and I have seen some of the effects of that passion everywhere I have been, all over this world.
> —"Every Good-Bye Ain't Gone"

THE MATTER: HOUSE

I first walked through James Baldwin's former house on the edge of St. Paul-de-Vence, an ancient town in the South of France, in June 2000, while having only the vaguest notion of how his works and life story would soon fill my life. Inside, the stone house was quiet, cool, and shadowy, with the partially shuttered windows letting in slender shafts of sunlight filled with dust motes. As I walked across the sunny stripes on the floor, the melancholy air of the place struck me, no doubt because I was thinking of those whose home it once was, when it was filled with creativity and life. They were long gone by the time I paid their space a visit: James Baldwin, of course, but also his beloved younger brother David, who inherited the house after his passing; the beautiful dancer Bernard Hassell, who was their friend and house manager and who died there of AIDS; and many others, famous or not, who came to visit and stay a while. It also made me think of those who once tended to its grounds, surfaces, and objects, like Jeanne Faure, its previous owner and a close friend of Baldwin's, or Valerie Sordello, who cooked splendid meals in the kitchen and served them to Jimmy and his guests at the table outside, under an arbor. There must have been gardeners or groundskeepers, too, whose names and identities I would never know (I recalled Mohammed, the Muslim groundskeeper from Baldwin's last play, *The Welcome Table* [1987], who was based on an actual person, "Baldwin's own onetime gardener").[1] Of all the spaces, I was especially mesmerized by what was then, thirteen years after Baldwin's death, left of his upstairs living room. Quiet, somewhat dusty, with hints of that omnipresent Mediterranean moisture that curled some of the photos tacked to the wall over the mantelpiece, that space beckoned for some inexplicable reason.

To my literary-critical imagination, that living room seemed to hold the most stories, memories, and traces of human habitation. At first glance, it appeared a simple-enough space containing objects one would expect—a rustic wooden table and three chairs (each different), an orange-brownish-pinkish throw blanket over the couch with puffy round pillows, a Turkish (perhaps) rug under the table breaking the pattern of the checkered tiled floor. On the walls were photos, posters, and framed art, not to mention a storm of pictures and objects adorning the mantelpiece in the corner, dominated by a green, yellow, and red Nelson Mandela poster. After a few moments silently taking it all in, my eye and ear, as if honed by my earlier passage through the other parts of the house, began to discern visible and invisible, audible and inaudible, imprints, images, noises, and sounds. One could not stand unmoved, after all, while being at what must have once been the very heart of Baldwin's vibrant home. To me, it seemed as if the dark brick fireplace, now blackened with brushstrokes of once vigorous flames, filled with cold ashes and irons, could roar back to life at any moment; a fire poker resting in the nearby corner seemed ready to tend to it. A lamp with a purplish glass base, left on the floor for a moment, looked ready to be lit up again; I imagined how its glow would help me to see what was inside a black, rectangular cardboard box on the well-worn tabletop. The longer I stood there, the more the room filled with possibility and wonder and, yes, with desire and need.

I was a polite, slightly timid, first-time visitor then, yet I was also dying to open that box. I would not dare do it, however, which I now admit with some regret (I just brushed my hand against it), for I behaved as if I were in a museum, no matter that the house was far from being one (and will never become one, having since been lost to developers). I also yearned to pick up and feel the weight of the blue-green ceramic ashtray in the middle of the table that may have belonged to Baldwin. I could not be sure of that, of course, but still had to resist a powerful temptation to ask, maybe even beg, to take it with me. (Imagine having that fetish in my study!) Or that plain wooden whistle or, if not, perhaps the white and red kitchen towel lying next to it in a casual grouping on the table. Just one small token . . . something material to hold on to, to bring back from my visit. That temptation shamed me, but while in its grip I realized, too, that I could not bring myself to take anything unless it was given freely. But there was no one to grant me that wish, just shadows, imagined voices, and golden dust motes.

An important discovery I did not register in that moment, not until some years later, was that I had been caught up in a powerful and collective Baldwin-related sensation (if not affectation) that would travel through time and space. I was merely a predecessor to, or perhaps also appeared after, some others who had come, and would continue coming, to the site of Baldwin's house to find that material something that reading his work alone could not provide. Those of us who were lucky and privileged enough to be able to make it to St. Paul-de-Vence were gripped by that same powerful need or longing to save something material from the site.[2] All of us—scholars, intellectuals, writers, readers, and simply those who love Baldwin—not only searched for a physical keepsake, but also yearned to fulfill a dream of being somehow connected to the writer in ways that go beyond the literary magic that takes place on the pages of his texts. On some level, we must all believe that the precious matter of that particular black life, which ended in that house in 1987, could somehow be salvaged and preserved, especially in light of so few remnants of his existence, and the conspicuous absence of a writer's house-museum devoted to him in his home country.[3]

A few years ago, Baldwin's great-niece, Kali-Ma Nazarene, a talented photographer, traveled to the house and took haunting black-and-white pictures after it had been emptied of furniture, books, and all but a few broken chairs. Her trip to France had been set in motion by a dream in which the writer appeared to her and asked her to "meet me in Paris in two weeks, I can't stand it here."[4] Others, like Douglas Field, Thomas Chatterton Williams, and Rachel Kaadzi Ghansah, have written about the undeniable pull of this particular place, which compelled them to jump over fences, dig up pieces of china from the dirt around the partially demolished structure, or search desperately for other remnants, anything they could carry to take with them. In all of their accounts, this material hunger is palpable, as is the fervent imagining, or even inventing, of Baldwin's past and his possessions on the basis of available evidence, hearsay, and that thirsty desire to be close to him.[5] Perhaps reading Baldwin makes one greedy for the matter related to his life, for we have nothing else left of him but his published works. Perhaps the preponderance of digitized photographs and recorded interviews with James Baldwin online only magnifies this yearning for objects, for the solidity of *things* whose weight and concrete endurance might afford us a connection with him that is more substantial, more intimate, more worked for than the impersonal touch of a keyboard or a fleeting image on a screen.

This need to link literary, or metaphorical, representations of Baldwin's person and life story to matter, or tangible and enduring objects such as an ashtray or pieces of china dug up from the site of his house, stems from what Ian Hodder refers to as the human "entanglement" with things that have the power to "stand in the way . . . [and] force themselves on human action."[6] "Human existence is thingly, irreducibly so," Hodder contends from the purview of archaeology, social sciences, and humanities. He adds that "spiritual energies flow through icons and relics and awaken our devotion . . . [and] familiar things are absorbed into our sense of identity. . . . [They] provide a psychological comfort after tragedy and loss . . . [and] stimulate our cognitive capacities."[7] Baldwin's absence has been a source of grief since his death at sixty-three in 1987, while the pilgrimages to the site of his house that so many have since made confirm his continuing power over his readers' imagination and desire. And if we think of objects and things as "stuff," as Daniel Miller does, we realize, too, that structural "relationships between things rather than the things themselves" matter most, and that "systems of things, with their internal order, make us the people we are," and that is because "culture comes above all from stuff."[8] Hence our desire and need to collect remnants of Baldwin's domestic life in the face of its gaping absence and irreversible eradication. What's more, we are driven to preserve the material site of his house, or simply set foot inside the structure as long as it lasts, for we need to constitute what is still missing in the United States and even in St. Paul-de-Vence: wider recognition and concrete reminders of one of the most important twentieth-century American writers—someone who continues to help us become "better than we are," as he says in a clip from Karen Thorsen's documentary *The Price of the Ticket*. So, yes, Baldwin is all about us as humans and thus attached to and as things, and matter, too.[9]

THE MATERIAL: LIFE

In his last interview with Quincy Troupe, recorded at his house in St. Paul-de-Vence not long before he passed away, Baldwin complains about the ways in which his life story has become someone else's tale: "It's difficult to be a legend. It's hard for me to recognize *me*. You spend a lot of time trying to avoid it.... The way the world treats you is unbearable, and especially if you're black.... And you are not your legend, but you're trapped in it."[10] At the end of his life, Baldwin sees himself as a "very despairing witness," estranged from "myself and my generation," who feels "more and more homeless in terms of the whole relationship between France and me and America."[11] Within the soundtrack to *James Baldwin: From Another Place*, a 1970 art-film gem that the late filmmaker and photographer Sedat Pakay made about him in Istanbul and released in New York in 1973, the writer rather optimistically acknowledges the profound advantages of his transatlantic location and optic: one always sees one's home better "from another place, from another country." No matter that many of his contemporaries did not appreciate or care for that vantage point; he uses it deftly to focus on the vexing social and cultural issues at the center of the national house that is the United States. What he discusses only many years later, though, is that, while sometimes enviable and in his case always prolific, that remote and exilic authorial vantage point is often a lonely, painful, and usually misunderstood location. Yet that location was also what he needed, for it allowed him to hide his private and domestic life from public view.

"I certainly have not told my story yet," Baldwin explained to an interviewer in 1984. "I know that, though I've revealed fragments."[12] His passing a mere three years later from a terminal illness confirms that this mysterious "story" of his had not had a chance to reach completion. By then his ailing body had been sending signals he should not have ignored, though he did exactly that, for he was full of plans and projects as usual. He had people to see and places to go, like the international summit organized to accompany Mikhail Gorbachev's "perestroika" in the Soviet Union in 1986, where he was a guest of honor and speaker on global race issues.[13] As he told another interviewer just a few years before, at the age of fifty-six, he had harbored great hopes for many

1.1. The empty upstairs living room at Chez Baldwin. Photo by author, 2014.

more prolific years of activity: "For a writer, I'm very young.... I've an appointment with the twenty-first century ... when I will still be under eighty."[14]

After being largely dismissed and out of popular favor in the United States during his late years, and following his death in 1987, Baldwin has recently come into vogue. As if in response to our culture's contemporary yearning for charismatic spokespersons and leaders who might offer more than expertly marketed sound bites and images of oafish politicians, he has been brought back from exile as a kind of black cultural superstar. In academe, this return comes in the wake of new scholarship that has largely overcome tired old approaches that cleaved the writer's career into a "commendable" period ending with the publication of *The Fire Next Time* in 1963 and the decidedly less commendable one that followed and was soon lost, if not erased, from view. These new academic studies that I will refer to throughout the chapters that follow embrace all of his works, all the places where he lived, and all aspects of Baldwin's identity, thereby forestalling another division that used to plague his representation as either a gay *or* a black writer.

The new twenty-first-century Baldwin has been celebrated through public events such as the "James Baldwin: *This* Time!" Festival held in April 2014 at the New York Live Arts Theater, which also inaugurated the "Year of Baldwin" with exciting events held in his honor at the Harlem Stage, Columbia University, and other venues, most of which I attended.[15] The writer has also finally been given a landmark in the neighborhood where he grew up; a stretch of 128th Street between 5th and Madison in Harlem has been named James Baldwin Place, while the brick house in which he lived from 1958 to 1961, at 81 Horatio Street in Greenwich Village, now dons a commemorative plaque affixed during a public ceremony on October 7, 2015.[16] The plaque explicitly credits the writer with having had a significant impact on "ideas about race, class, sexuality, and morality" through his portrayal of the Village in his "bestselling novel *Another Country*," as well as highlighting his participation in the Civil Rights Movement. Inducted into the American Poets' Corner at the Cathedral of St. John the Divine in 2011, and inaugurated as the subject of a new scholarly journal, the *James Baldwin Review*, at several academic conferences in 2014, the "Son of Harlem" is suddenly back in favor in his home country, though it was the twentieth-century American politics of race and sexuality that forced him to become a wanderer and exile in the first place.[17]

The popularity and appeal of Raoul Peck's recent art film *I Am Not Your Negro* (2016) confirm both the resurgence of interest in the writer's life and oeuvre and the need for new interpretations concerning both.[18] Based on

1.2. The last room, with Baldwin's bed. Image from the documentary film *James Baldwin: The Price of the Ticket* (1989); courtesy of Karen Thorsen, Douglas Dempsey, and the James Baldwin Project.

1.3. The James Baldwin Place naming ceremony in front of Baldwin's former elementary school, P.S. 24, on 128th Street, Harlem, August 2015. Photo by author.

1.4. James Baldwin Place street sign. Courtesy of Trevor Baldwin, 2015.

"Remember This House," a treatment of a project Baldwin was planning to write on the lives of his assassinated Civil Rights Movement friends and historical icons—Medgar Evers, Malcolm X, and Martin Luther King Jr.— Peck's film crafts its narrative in Baldwin's intimate voice-over. By mixing fragments of the manuscript of "Remember This House" that he was allowed to use by the estate with quotations from Baldwin's neglected later works like *No Name in the Street* (1972), *The Devil Finds Work* (1976), and *The Evidence of Things Not Seen* (1985), Peck crafts his own tale about Baldwin delivered in the actor Samuel L. Jackson's beautifully modulated voice. Deeply political and personal, this tale demonstrates Baldwin's brilliance and effectiveness in deploying autobiography and the genre of the essay as weapons of social justice. Accompanied by archival images from the 1960s to the 1980s, as well as more recent ones from Ferguson, where protests against police brutality have irrevocably confirmed that the twenty-first-century reality of U.S. black life has not changed that much from that of the 1950s, *I Am Not Your Negro* prompts one to marvel at the currency of Baldwin's diagnosis of the racist "problem" at the heart of American collective and individual history and psyche. It also inspires questions such as: What would Baldwin have said about the occupants of the current White House, or about the "Muslim ban"?

Those who read him with the attention he not only deserves, but also poignantly requires of his readers, agree, however, that he would be speaking out about it all: refugee crises, domestic terrorist attacks, thousands of drowned black and brown bodies floating in the Mediterranean (as if marking a twenty-first-century replay of the Middle Passage), "illegal" immigrants tortured and dying during their perilous passage through U.S. borders, trans kids deprived of bathrooms in their schools, not to mention the virulent revival of white supremacist, misogynistic, and homophobic narrative at the core of the U.S. national house. The perspective on Baldwin as a sophisticated, tough critic and theorist of identity, as a citizen of the world and a villager from St. Paul-de-Vence, where he in fact wanted to die and be buried, is missing sorely from Peck's film.[19]

The attention that *I Am Not Your Negro* pays to the political obscures and erases the political-as-personal: except for a mention, the vital role that Baldwin's sexuality and gender identity, not to mention his various domestic abodes away from the United States, played in his activism and art remains unacknowledged and suppressed. In light of this reduction of Baldwin's voice and person, Peck's film ultimately falls into promoting the "Baldwin brand" genre, where the writer appears as a race man, an ancestral sage devoid of sexual and gender identity, whose words, often taken out of context, seem to convey a much more simplified and, indeed, divided vision of humanity than his writings actually convey. Baldwin was an intellectual genius whose wisdom and lessons belong to all humanity, and so in forgetting that, or simply not seeing that in his works, Peck's film excises a vital part of the writer. Yet again, Baldwin's complexity remains omitted, marginalized, and in exile.

Baldwin's recent return to his home country as a black cultural icon indeed obscures tragic and personal reasons for his first trip abroad. While fragmentary revelations of his life story can be found in all of his writings, the scattered pieces are not easy to assemble into a coherent whole, which I believe was a deliberate aesthetic choice on his part. In his 1977 essay "Every Good-Bye Ain't Gone," which provides the epigraph for this introduction and begins, "I am writing this note just twenty-nine years after my first departure from America," Baldwin mentions being "a part of the American house" on the condition of the price for it having been paid by his ancestors' "*striving to make it my home*" (PT, 642). The divergent semantics of "house" and "home" could not be clearer, with the former referring to the state and nation that built its power and wealth on the backs of African slaves, genocide of Native Americans, and exploitation of immigrants, and the latter referring to the private spaces of one's familial and domestic spaces, which, as of that essay's writing, the author seemed to be still in the process of trying to locate. Indeed, as Baldwin recalls his first departure from Harlem for France on November 11, 1948, he was not happy, and was experiencing "rain, fatigue, panic, the absolute certainty of being dashed to death on the vindictive tooth of the Eiffel Tower," and those sensations and the weather overshadow any possibility of "feeling the remotest exhilaration" upon his arrival in western Europe.

He was compelled to leave the United States because of who he was, too, for he "trusted no one, and knew that he trusted no one, knew that this distrust was suicidal, and also knew that there was no question any longer of his *life* in America: his violent destruction could be taken as a given; it was a matter of time." As he explains his younger self, *"By the time I was twenty-two, I was a survivor . . . with murder in his heart"* (PT, 642, emphases added). In light of this turbulent mix of self-destructive emotions accompanied by physical dangers to his body, Baldwin's landing in France meant a blank slate and starting anew; as he writes, "there I was, in Paris, on my ass." But it also meant, "*My* ass, mister, *mine*: and I was glad" (PT, 644). He continues somewhat gloomily, somewhat humorously, commenting on having to reinvent himself in a new place and language. This unhappy yet fortuitous landing in a foreign city meant, then, that being finally away from the American national house, he was then free to figure out what kind of home he wanted to make for himself as a writer and black queer American who both chose and was forced to live in the world.

THE METAPHOR: BOOK

"Perhaps home is not a place but simply an irrevocable condition," Baldwin writes in *Giovanni's Room* in 1956, his narrator's voice metaphorically linking his literary characters' and his own experiences of exile to those of immigrants and migrants throughout the world (GR, 121).[20] David, the sexually conflicted and repressed white American, and Giovanni, a displaced southern Italian, meet in Paris, where they fall in love and cohabitate in a symbolically loaded "room."[21] For the American, in Europe supposedly to "find" himself, the room becomes a closet associated with homosexuality, from which he has tried to flee and which he cannot bring himself to embrace. For the Italian, who cannot ever return home, and who accepts his sexuality unequivocally (he calls it the "stink of love"), the room is a space of desire, liberation, and redemption. Because David and Giovanni share neither a story nor a spatial vision of their connection, and can neither understand nor see each other as products of the Old and New World cultures, their relationship is doomed from the start. Blind to the ways in which he has inherited from his ancestors—those whites-in-the-making who "conquered a continent, pushing across death-laden plains . . . to an ocean that faced away from Europe into a darker past"—American-bred tales of homophobia and racialized gender bipolarity, David loses his only chance for love and self-discovery and -acceptance. By breaking his heart and leaving him, he also causes Giovanni's tragic end (GR, 7). However sensational (and deliberately so, given its reliance on an actual event in New York), that novel's racialized and sexualized recounting of what Nina Baym has termed the "melodramas of beset manhood" is powerful evidence of the ways identity is undergirded, created, and represented in complex relation to both narrative and social spaces.[22]

More specifically, Baldwin's reliance in *Giovanni's Room* on tracing the ways in which social spaces, and private dwellings especially, tend to expose links between identity and its gendered, racialized, and sexual representations at home and abroad confirms his engagement with the "architectural features of narrative space."[23] Baldwin takes this type of spatial storytelling on a transatlantic journey in a scene where Giovanni counters David's naïve belief that one day he can simply go back home to America: "You don't have a home until you leave it and then, when you have left it, you never can go back" (GR, 154–55). When David continues to insist that his is a special case, that, as an American, he can avoid the consequences of his actions, Giovanni jokes, "You . . . remind me of the kind of man who is tempted to put himself in prison in order to avoid being hit by a car" (155). The metaphor of the prison is an apt one for the American national house and men like David, for its prescriptions for manhood have so fully colonized his mind and body that he cannot find "himself" anywhere because of the simple fact that he cannot envision or *accept* his identity in full. Thus imprisoned in/by his sexuality, he is left impotent as a subject—he simply *isn't*, though remaining a cliché as "an American." What David realizes at the end is that he will never be free of memories of Giovanni and their affectively loaded room, no matter how far away he manages to escape from both. Hence Baldwin's novel can be read as recounting the impossibility of white American male domestic desire.

David's homelessness—as a man exiled from American notions of patriarchal, thus heteronormative and white manhood because of his desire for sex with other men—can be read in the context of what Claudia Tate terms "the political desire . . . [for] the acquisition of authority for the self both in the home and in the world."[24] While Tate builds this paradigm for post-Reconstruction black female texts, it works surprisingly well for David's story in *Giovanni's Room* once we realize that this seemingly "all-white novel" is in fact all about race, gender, sexuality, and various domestic spaces that are both public and private, national and international. David's sense of exclusion from his home country, and especially from his father's rigidly defined "manly" house, is exacerbated by the impossibility of his ever truly "playing house." Try as he might (and as he did, for a brief time with his onetime American fiancée, Hella), he would never become a proper American "husband."

On the day David meets and falls for Giovanni, that discovery is juxtaposed with a fleeting image of a black man, or one who appears black to him, seen from a cab window. Looking "beyond . . . [Giovanni's] heavy profile," and contemplating the fog hanging over the city as they drive through it, David sees the otherwise pearly soft mist "clinging *like a curse to the men* who slept under the bridges—one of whom flashed by beneath us, *very black and lone*, walking along the river" (GR, 61–62, emphases added). That homeless black man—his absolutely dreaded other and the flip side of Giovanni—who may have stepped off the pages of Ralph Ellison's *Invisible Man*, is whom David fears he will become if he lets his secret out: "I was in a box for I could see that, no matter how I turned, the hour of confession was upon me" (64). The truth of one's identity cannot be escaped, even if one forces oneself to become a prisoner of a model version—and David's American whiteness so encages him that he cannot conceive of himself as free. As Baldwin explains in a 1984 interview with Mavis Nicholson, his protagonist's central failure is an inability to feel: "If you can't love anybody, you're dangerous."[25]

Read closely, like *Giovanni's Room*, many of the works throughout Baldwin's oeuvre can be seen as engaging various manifestations of domesticity: material and metaphorical, spatial and ideological, gender- and genre-related, religious and secular, and indeed literal and literary, as well as embodied and psychological. From the examination of African American home lives between the North and the South, and within the spiritually and erotically charged spaces of the black church and Harlem and New York City streets in *Go Tell It on the Mountain* (1953), through that city's landscapes infused with interracial desire, contingent on southern and French homoerotic domestic locations, as well as queer homelessness in *Another Country* (1962), to the portrait of an artist as a black man with no place to put down roots in *Tell Me How Long the Train's Been Gone* (1968), to examinations of black families' and artists' tragic negotiations of private and public spaces within and without the United States in *If Beale Street Could Talk* (1974) and *Just above My Head* (1979), all of his novels explore various manifestations of what could be called the black house and home—the theme I pursue at length in this introduction. Deploying his experience as a lower-class child of Harlem, and later an accomplished writer who had to configure his domestic spaces around the challenges of his writing, activism, travel, and economic need, Baldwin infused many of his essays with metaphors of domesticity that confirmed his commitment to the private being always political and vice versa. Last but not least, his three plays, including the still unpublished *The Welcome Table*, and the staged and published *The Amen Corner* (1954, 1968) and *Blues for Mister Charlie* (1964), dramatized powerful instances of desire for utopian domesticity, and of family conflict as the backdrop for gendered and racialized intergenerational struggle and national identity.

Baldwin's need to sort out the autobiographical meanings of his own national house and of personal home spaces in essays, novels, plays, and even the few poems he wrote at various points in his life arises as much from his desire to reconfigure his identity as a black queer American as from a larger intellectual project to reinterpret the concept and problem that W. E. B. Du Bois famously named the "color line." Along with that project, Baldwin's writings explored and exploded the meanings of "blackness" and "home" as historical, economic, social, and cultural creations and representations, products, and constructs located in social space. I read this project of his as rearticulating and redefining Du Bois's "problem of the twentieth century," or the "color line" from *The Souls of Black Folk* (1903), by means of what Baldwin refers to in the essay "Every Good-Bye Ain't Gone" as the "demarcation line" between the things that "happened to me because I was *black* . . . and . . . things [that] had happened to me because I was *me*," thus hinting at theoretical approaches to identity that would arise in U.S. and European academes in the decades following the publication of his works (PT, 642–43, emphases added).

In that essay, which is as "fragmentary" in its depictions of his personal life as he makes clear it must be in that interview that I mentioned earlier, his task as a writer is to disentangle the *black* from *me*. He sets out to "perceive, define, a line nearly too thin for the naked eye, so mercurial, and so mighty" (PT, 643), or that tenuous space between the *black* and *me*, one that makes him "study the hieroglyphics of my circumstances," as the only way to "decipher my inheritance" (644). Within the few pages of its intense, frenzied prose, this short essay illuminates the meaning of "Ezekiel's *wheel in the middle of a wheel*, with the iron, inescapable truth of revolutions—we black folk say what goes around, comes around" (PT, 644). That is, the essay arrives at the realization that has cycled and revolved for Baldwin for nearly three decades as he has written diverse works and searched for answers all over the world, the realization that brings *home*, *blackness*, and *me* together in terms of his authorial experience, its perceptions, and its cost:

> There *was* a demarcation line, to be walked every hour of every day. The demarcation line was my apprehension of, and, therefore, my responsibility for, my own experience: the chilling vice versa of what I had made of my experience and what that experience had made of me. . . . I have been in and out of my country, in and out of various cauldrons, for a very long time, long enough to see the doctrine of white supremacy return, like a plague, to the continent which spawned it. . . . *Every good-bye ain't gone*: human history reverberates with violent upheaval, uprooting, arrival and departure, hello and good-bye. Yet, I am not certain that anyone

ever leaves home. When "home" drops below the horizon, it rises in one's breast and acquires the overwhelming power of menaced love.... My ancestors counseled me to *keep the faith*: and I promised, I vowed that I would. (PT, 645–67)

Baldwin's national house, the United States, is where the larger history takes place and where he cannot live permanently ever again. Immersed in that history, a singular life like his has a cyclical quality of intimation, experience, and confirmation of thus extracted knowledge: "I suspect, though I certainly cannot prove it, that every life moves full circle—toward revelation: You begin to see, and even rejoice to see, what you always saw," he explains at the end of "Every Good-Bye Ain't Gone" (PT, 646). That first trip away from his native country and place of birth set up a pattern for the rest of his life.

Baldwin's lack of sustained domestic life in the United States, beyond his difficult childhood and youth, and his more successful attempts at it in other places, reveal that "anguish" is part and parcel of being homeless, in exile, and it follows one wherever one may travel away from one's birthplace: "[It] has your number, knows, to paraphrase the song, where you live. It's a difficult relationship, but mysteriously indispensable. It teaches you" (PT, 646). The U.S. national house, however hostile to black queer men with artistic inclinations like Baldwin, also contains the home where his family lives, and where he was born, where his people have made their place for better or worse for generations, where, indeed, one must keep the faith, and accept anguish as part of the bargain. Hence when the writer comes back "to the eye of the hurricane," he is still menaced and metaphorically homeless in the country of his origin, but he now has his craft—which he uses like a shield, and which enables him to stay a while. Now at last, having written works beyond his first novel, *Go Tell It on the Mountain*—"All my love was in it, and the reason for my journey" (PT, 646)—and having returned as an established literary figure, his personal story of "that dreadful day of November of '48 is redeemed" (646).

BETWEEN *HOME, BLACKNESS,* AND *ME*

In this book, *Me and My House: James Baldwin's Last Decade in France*, which explores the tremendous personal price of this authorial redemption and coincides with the thirtieth anniversary of the writer's passing, I bring together the three entities that undergird "Every Good-Bye Ain't Gone": *home*, *blackness*, and *me*. I do so in order to explore the domestic and intimate parts of James Baldwin's story, and places where he lived and wrote in his late life, and to link his national house-rebuilding efforts—his critique in virtually all of his works of U.S. national identity as exclusionary and divisive—to the complex politics and poetics of racialized, gendered, and sexualized social space. And while the three key terms that I plant as the cornerstones of this project—*home*, *blackness*, and *me*—easily apply to all of his oeuvre, and do so as much as the parallel, organizational triad of terms I have chosen for the first part of this introduction (matter, material, and metaphor), I am especially interested in deploying them all to read, as well as to read them *through*, the works that Baldwin created during the last and most underappreciated decade and a half of his life, the period of 1971–87. These works comprise the young-adult novel *If Beale Street Could Talk*; an essay collection on popular culture and cinema, *The Devil Finds Work*; his last novel spanning Harlem, the American South, and Europe, *Just above My Head*; an essay-reportage on children's murders in Atlanta, *The Evidence of Things Not Seen*; and his last unpublished but completed play, on which Baldwin collaborated with Walter Dallas, *The Welcome Table*. These later works, still underappreciated by critics and scholars, resulted from another prolific period in Baldwin's life that came after his Turkish decade of 1961–71, which was marked by creative experimentation and relative domestic stability.[26]

Baldwin spent the last sixteen years of his life living in a sprawling stone Provençal house in the village of St. Paul-de-Vence, then a rather remote and sleepy town, in the South of France. As the site of his late writing and the place where he donned the hat of homeowner and host to a rambling household, Chez Baldwin, as the house came to be called by local inhabitants and a multitude of visitors, became an organic part of the author's daily life. It was featured in autobiographic musings and letters, and inflected settings and characters in a variety of his published works, from novels and essays to magazine articles, and, most significantly, his last play. It also provided yet another healing location that, like Turkey before it, nurtured both the author and the man by offering a quiet haven in which to write and rest after the turbulent late 1960s, which were scarred by the assassinations of his Civil Rights Movement friends and his ailing health. The house also provided ample space(s) to entertain guests and host parties, and thus became a vibrant social hub that was as necessary to Baldwin as the long, solitary hours he spent at his typewriter in a secluded part in the back, which contained his study and living quarters.

Inspired by this space's material and metaphorical impact on the writer's life and works, *Me and My House* approaches Chez Baldwin as a central location and lens for reconstructing his biography during his final years in France, and for re-reading his late works that were created there. As the place where he finally put down roots, it also provides an indispensable context for reassessing the aesthetics and ethics involved in the representations of black domesticity in his works—themes that have not been explored at length and whose impact is key to recasting Baldwin's place in twentieth-century American letters from the vantage point of the second decade of the twenty-first century. It is in that house that Baldwin actually achieved what he identifies as his creative goal in a 1961 interview with Studs Terkel (marking his rising star as a black writer), gleaned from Bessie Smith's tragic and homeless "Backwater Blues," of "accept[ing] disaster" and "going beyond it." What is striking, too, is that by 1971, when Baldwin decided to move to St. Paul-de-Vence, as much as in 1948 when he first left the United States, this statement echoed his general situation as an African American writer who partially chose, and partially was forced, to live most of his creative life away from his homeland due to the doubled otherness of his race and sexuality.

According to Edward Said, who describes committed intellectuals as always having to contend with exile, Baldwin also owes his inability to reside in the United States to his "intellectual's consciousness . . . a spirit in opposition, rather than in accommodation." While saving his life, quite literally, as Baldwin claims in "Every Good-Bye Ain't Gone," his initial departure from his family in Harlem, his home life in various places abroad, and later his ambivalent arrivals in the national house on his trips back all marked him forever as a witness. According to Said, Baldwin's practice of "witnessing" as a black intellectual means he is in perpetual exile—in both *material* terms, due to his inability to live and work in the United States, and *metaphorical* terms, due to his dissenting mind and revolutionary writing—inhabiting a terrain that cannot be pinned down or domesticated. This kind of situation, Said explains, "grips me because the romance, the interest, the challenge of intellectual life is to be found in dissent against the status quo at the time when the struggle on behalf of underrepresented and disadvantaged groups seems so unfairly weighted against them."[27]

Said qualifies his rather romantic, heroic, and masculinized definition of Baldwin as an intellectual in exile with a detailed explanation of his practice of witnessing that is worth quoting at length for its accuracy in summing up

Baldwin's development and his late career, when he was out of favor with American cultural elites on both sides of the proverbial color line, no matter his vast accomplishments and intellectual prowess:

> Witnessing a sorry state of affairs when one is not in power is by no means a monotonous, monochromatic activity. It involves what Foucault once called "a relentless erudition," scouring alternative sources, exhuming buried documents, reviving forgotten (or abandoned) histories. It involves a sense of the dramatic and of the insurgent, making a great deal of one's rare opportunities to speak, catching the audience's attention, being better at wit and debate than one's opponents. And there is something fundamentally unsettling about intellectuals who have neither offices to protect nor territory to consolidate and guard; self irony is therefore more frequent than pomposity, directness more than hemming and hawing. But . . . such representations by intellectuals will neither make them friends in high places nor win them official honors. It is a lonely condition, yes, but . . . a better one than a gregarious tolerance for the way things are.[28]

Baldwin, whose origins (mere generations away from slavery), dire poverty, and complex family situation prevented him from ever attending college in the United States, was "relentlessly erudite" as a self-taught genius; as I show throughout *Me and My House*, Baldwin redefined the very meanings of "intellectual" and "exile" for the late twentieth century with his intense focus on identity as always forged at the crossroads of race, gender, class, sexuality, religion, language, and, indeed, domesticity and social space.

Key to that redefinition is the triad of terms at the center of my project: *home*, *blackness*, and *me*. Put more abstractly, alternatively, even alliteratively—the inextricable interweaving in Baldwin's life and works of *space*, *story*, and *self*—these terms help to explain the exorbitant price his vocation exacted from him as both a private individual and a public, transnational, black queer American intellectual. While his public persona has received much attention, his private and intimate battles and vicissitudes of domestic life have not been much scrutinized outside of the biographies. As *Me and My House* shows, it is impossible to fully assess Baldwin's long-term design and desire as a transnational, black queer witness to rebuild and refurbish—if not at times demolish and build anew—the racialized American national house, without a close examination of his private life and his longings for domestic havens, for a stable love life, and, at times, even for children and a partner/coparent, something he would admit to only the closest of friends.

That insistence on always connecting the public and the private, evident in "Every Good-Bye Ain't Gone," on always making the personal political, is clearly his invention and necessity as a survivor and exile as much as it may have been inflected by his reading of women writers, whose books filled his library in St. Paul-de-Vence. Coming as it does in his earlier works, which preceded the second wave of feminism by a couple of decades, and with even more force in his later ones, this approach makes his rhetoric chockfull of autobiographical, even autoethnographic, vignettes—an intriguing precursor to what feminist critics would later embrace as "feminine" modes of writing.[29] In that sense, Baldwin must be approached as a writer whose works engage with both genre and gender experimentation, and *Me and My House* explores this theme in relationship to the modes of domesticity that enabled and nurtured his art.

DOMESTIC AFFAIRS, OR WRITING BLACKNESS
THROUGH SPACE, STORY, AND SELF

> It is terror that informs the American political and social scene—the terror of leaving the house of bondage. It isn't a terror of seeing *black* people leave the house of bondage, for white people think that they *know* this cannot *really* happen. . . . What the house of bondage accomplished for . . . the classic white American was the destruction of his moral sense . . . [and] his sense of reality and, therefore, his sense of white people had to be as compulsively one-dimensional as his vision of blacks. . . . White Americans have been one another's jailers for generations, and the attempt at individual maturity is the loneliest and rarest of the American endeavors.
> —"Notes on the House of Bondage"

In the essay "Notes on the House of Bondage," which appeared on the front page of *The Nation* magazine on November 1, 1980, Baldwin speaks "as a black American." Given that he often alternates this point of view with deeply autobiographical approaches, *Me and My House* juxtaposes Baldwin's personal, and in some ways not at all representative (though in others definitely so), story with that of "black domesticity" broadly conceived. In doing so, it argues for the centrality to narrative representations of identity within and without the United States of what Baldwin's works articulate as the always-

1.5. *The Nation* magazine with Baldwin's essay "Notes on the House of Bondage" listed on the cover (1980). Photo by author, 2014.

racialized social space, and specifically the realm of the domicile, which is private and intimate, gendered, sexualized, and inflected by religion, class, and region. Historically complex and contested, and often unspoken, given the hegemony of mythic-heroic narratives of American democracy, the realms of the house and home—conceived both as material structures located geographically and as a metaphorically personalized set of meanings and sense of place—have had a significant bearing on larger narratives of twentieth-century U.S. (national and imperial, as well as private and intimate) notions of identity.

In the essay "Encounter on the Seine: Black Meets Brown" (1950), written as he was nearing his third year of exile in France, Baldwin passionately affirms that since black Americans' "blood is in their soil," they and their white counterparts are part of the same national family and home. He also sees them as on their way together, literally "in the same boat," to gain "their own identity" as a multiracial nation. At the same time, he emphasizes that the "American Negro" has a unique story to tell as well as a particular goal to "make peace with himself [herself] and the many thousands gone before him [her]." Baldwin cautions, though, that the whole nation must embark on the journey of self-discovery (PT, 39).[30] And while, given the American historical

INTRODUCTION 21

record, one cannot expect "overwhelming changes" very soon, the national house must be shared, and its inhabitants must embrace their divergent stories of arrival, and acknowledge and contest the separate and unequal spaces behind its mythic façade of democracy and freedom. By 1980, in "Notes on the House of Bondage," he identifies whiteness as shackling national mythology and individual self-understanding.

Since slavery, the brutal, white man-made history of over a century of Jim Crow segregation, black codes, lynchings, and mob rule that targeted black bodies (along with Native Americans, Jews, Italians, Asians, and Mexicans) in American cities north and south have been etching tragic, racialized spatial knowledge onto the bodies and minds of African Americans, and all bodies of color, as well as on those marked "other" due to gender or sexual identity.[31] In her essay on the complex engendering of the racialized grammar of American identity that originated in the Middle Passage, Hortense Spillers refers to the "undecipherable markings on the captive body [that] render a kind of hieroglyphics of the flesh whose severe disjunctures come to be hidden to the cultural seeing by skin color." Such erasure of humanity, cultural specificity, and, of course, individuality and visibility is part of what the Middle Passage brought about as the "dehumanizing, ungendering and defacing... project," in which "the human cargo of a slave vessel—in the fundamental effacement and remission of African family and proper names—offers a counter-narrative to notions of the domestic."[32]

Historically, in western cultures the rhetoric of domesticity has been embroiled with that of national culture, middle classes, affect, and life writing, and until fairly recently it was largely cast as the exclusive domain of women and the feminine. While the ways in which domestic burdens hampered female participation in political and social life outside of the home have been explored prodigiously by Friedrich Engels, they were also interrogated by Dutch-speaking Sojourner Truth, cosmopolitan Frederick Douglass, and anarchist Emma Goldman, not to mention Harriet Jacobs, Ann Petry, Gwendolyn Brooks, or Toni Morrison. More recently, they inspired the writings of the second wave of U.S. feminist and literary critics like Ann Douglas, Nina Baym, or Susan Gubar and Sandra Gilbert, to name just a few.[33] Following their critiques, scholars like Farah J. Griffin, Lauren Berlant, Melvin Dixon, Amy Kaplan, Ann Stoler, Brian Massumi, Ann Cvetkovich, Saidiya Hartman, Phil Deloria, Laura Wexler, and Kathleen Stewart, who toil in the fields of cultural, visual, and literary studies, history, or anthropology, have focused on the links among widely diverse domestic cultures and practices within the broad fields encompassing the U.S. empire, transatlantic slavery, Native American studies, settler colonialism, and African Diaspora travel writing.

In African American studies, black feminist scholars like Spillers and Barbara Christian, as well as Hazel Carby, Patricia Williams, Valerie Smith, Barbara Smith, bell hooks, or Deborah McDowell, not to mention Audre Lorde, Alice Walker, Nikki Giovanni, and Toni Morrison in their roles as poets, novelists, critics, and spokespersons, have argued for crafting new idioms and grassroots theoretical approaches to the dramatically different experience of domesticity's representation by slaves and their descendants. Often, as Christian does, they include warnings about the unequal gender representation, patriarchal machismo of Black Power nationalism, and mixed blessings of "the race for theory." The domestic sphere has also been interrogated in post-Reconstruction black women's writing by Claudia Tate; as pertaining to black geographies of struggle and women's literature by Karla Holloway, Katherine McKittrick, and Clyde Woods; and in terms of gender roles and dynamics, photographic representations across the color line, "safe spaces for women," and in relation to the emergence of house-based, racialized phenomenology and ontology by scholars like Siobhan Somerville, Shawn Michelle Smith, Charles Scruggs, Patricia Hill Collins, E. Patrick Johnson, and Robert Reid-Pharr.[34] All of these explorations—the vast number of publications on the emergence of the Victorian interior, white suburbs, or urban housing notwithstanding—confirm that interest and investment in all matters domestic are far from exhausted.

Surprisingly, however, the myriad roles that domesticity and its representations play in Baldwin's works have not yet been interrogated with any consistency.[35] One reason may be that he is a male writer, and thus part of African American literature's masculine "big three," along with Richard Wright and Ralph Ellison, and literary critical approaches, until recently caught up in traditional binaries of gender and separate spheres, were not expected to be concerned with that theme.[36] Another reason may be his queer sexuality or bisexuality, and the scarcity of work on nonnormative domesticities—a juxtaposition of terms that to some may sound like an oxymoron.[37] Most obviously, perhaps, while images of his childhood home life haunt many of Baldwin's published works, and his major fictional characters and autobiographical personae in the essays often speak about the meaning of home and familial spaces and a longing for domestic havens, there are no material sites directly related to him in this country or anywhere else.[38]

Apart from the house he purchased for his mother on 71st Street in New York City in 1965, still owned by the Baldwin family, and the partial ruin of the only house he considered home in his late life—Chez Baldwin in St. Paul-de-Vence in France—there is no place to locate, study, reenact, or even stage a simulacrum of this author's domestic life.

My examination of Baldwin's approaches to domesticity in *Me and My House* shows that he understood very well that architecture and social space were indeed all about race—the critical lens gravely missing from the most famous western accounts—though not necessarily about "race" understood as a synonym for "black." For the literary and theoretical milieu in which Baldwin wrote and theorized about blackness and domesticity in the 1940s through the 1980s was filled with discourses on social space, identity, and narrative by such philosophers and literary theorists as Gaston Bachelard, Henri Lefebvre, Michel Foucault, Walter Benjamin, and Michel de Certeau.[39] While often concerned with class and materialist approaches to history, culture, and identity, these men were in fact constructing spatiality, and specifically the private space of the home, as a manifestation of whiteness as a presumed modern, unmarked racial category.

As I show in chapter 1, "Foundations, Façades, and Faces: Through the Glass Blackly," and in the four chapters that follow, Baldwin was one of the earliest theorists of whiteness and its desperate need for blackness as its reverse—echoing such important African Diaspora intellectuals as W. E. B. Du Bois, Frantz Fanon, Aimé Césaire, C. L. R. James, or Édouard Glissant—and he also conceived of race as a complex site of difference, located experience, and subject of spatial politics and object of domestic desire decades before academics began articulating it in those terms. *Me and My House* carefully situates Baldwin's writing on domesticity in the rich, and often confounding and controversial, historical, social, and literary theoretical context of the international intellectual scene in which he moved between the 1940s and 1980s, at the same time as it refers to the latest work on race, geography, and social space by the aforementioned American and African American studies scholars, as well as those toiling in the field of architecture and architectural history (e.g., Darrel Fields, John M. Vlach, Dolores Hayden, Dell Upton, Mabel O. Wilson, Craig L. Wilkins, Dianne Harris, Lesley N. N. Lokko, Craig E. Barton, and William Gleason).

Steeped in this rich context of wide-ranging scholarship, *Me and My House* revolves around three large, loaded, and interlinked sets of concepts that illustrate the interdependence of cultural identity and the spatial and temporal contexts of home in which it unfolds as a process both material and metaphorical: matter, material, and metaphor / home, blackness, and me / *space*, *story*, and *self*. These three conceptual triads refer, broadly and with much literary critical license, to the intersections of race, sexuality, and gender with the politics, poetics, and practices of social space, language, and narrative forms, as well as to various representations of identity in literary and other cultural texts that compose the rich context of Baldwin's works and life story. They function as an animated, rolling triangle, with sometimes *space*, sometimes *self*, and sometimes *story* and attendant contexts appearing as a fulcrum, thus demonstrating that, like identity and language, the politics of social space are socially constructed processes that are always in progress and always have material consequences, from the spaces of the nation to those of the home, the bedroom, and the human heart. Given its immediate contiguity with visual culture, the triad of *space*, *story*, and *self* can be seen as well as an optical device or prism that helps us see through and beyond (and indeed makes it possible to reject and refract, the way prisms do with light) the reductive binary rhetoric that for too long has dictated how Americans conceive of their identities and surroundings, how they describe and represent them, and how they imagine and talk about themselves as minds and bodies.

All three concepts are powerfully implicated in Baldwin's essay "Me and My House," which inspired the title of this book and first appeared in *Harper's* in 1955. Later renamed "Notes of a Native Son," the essay, constituting his first artistic manifesto, took him a dozen years to gestate following the events of 1943 that it describes. Its elegant harmonizing of autobiography, or life writing, passionate political argument, and brilliant social commentary has made it one of his most often-read and discussed texts. It also anticipates Baldwin's later authorial comment to Studs Terkel on Bessie Smith's homeless "Backwater Blues" as carrying a *"fantastic kind of understatement* in it. It's the way I want to write." That later comment links the writer's earlier thoughts on exile from the United States that inflected "Me and My House" (he was living in France on and off during 1948–57 and was about to leave for Turkey in 1961) with the necessity of being an exiled artist, much like Smith's singing persona. By 1961, then, Baldwin embraces Bessie Smith's blues message that the black artist must follow her or his vocation, even if its price is homelessness, abandonment, and despair, the price he anticipates already in 1955 in "Me and My House."[40]

The opening paragraph of that essay, much quoted by scholars, demonstrates the narrative entanglements of identity with social space and its practices and representations:

> On the twenty-ninth of July, in 1943, my father died. On the same day, a few hours later, his last child was born. Over a month before this, while all our energies were concentrated in waiting for these events, there had been, in Detroit, one of the bloodiest race riots of the century. A few hours after my father's funeral, while he lay in state in the undertaker's chapel, a race riot broke out in Harlem. On the morning of the third of August, we drove my father to the graveyard through a wilderness of smashed plate glass.... The day of my father's funeral had also been my nineteenth birthday. As we drove into the graveyard, the spoils of injustice, anarchy, discontent, and hatred were all around us. It seemed to me that God himself had devised, to mark my father's end, the most sustained and brutally dissonant of codas. (PT, 126)

At this point in his career, having published a novel and a play, and about to publish his first collection of essays that opens with this inimitable piece, Baldwin masterfully brings together his *story*, or autobiographical references to his childhood, relatives, and coming of age in Harlem in a large and impoverished family dominated by an unforgiving patriarch, with representations of *space*, or laconic reporting on current events in his home country and native city that has just witnessed a race riot. All the while, he is also contextualizing his father's funeral and its effects on his family and, most important, articulating the contours of his new *self* as a budding writer.

In this essay, the narrator's development and self-expression as an African American and an artist, and as a young man who must understand his lifelong struggle with his church and religiously fanatical stepfather—with whom as he admits he "got on badly"—are all linked to a moment of rapture that has everything to do with blackness, domesticity, gender, and religion (PT, 128). Carefully foreshadowed in the opening, that moment comes at the end of the essay, with the narrator affirming his break from his father's religious dogma—from the paternal "house" defined by a biblical citation from Joshua 24:15: "'But as for me and my house,' my father had said, 'we will serve the Lord'" (PT, 144–45). Baldwin now claims a right to his own "house" as a writer, the right to a separate life and identity, and the power to author his own story. He recalls preaching the same biblical passage as a teenager in the pulpit, and "proudly giving it an interpretation different from my father's" (PT, 145).

The closing words of his essay become a motto for his works to come. The art that will issue from the "House of James Baldwin" will result in new mythologies of blackness, new stories, selves, and modes of dwelling in the world that the writer must forge on his own:

> It began to seem that one would have to hold in the mind forever two ideas that seemed to be in opposition. The first idea was acceptance, the *acceptance*, totally without rancor, of life as it is, and men as they are: in the light of this idea, it goes without saying that injustice is a commonplace. But this did not mean that one could be complacent, for the second idea was of equal power: that one must never, in one's own life, accept these injustices as commonplace but must *fight* them with all one's strength. This fight begins, however, in the heart and it now had been laid to my charge to keep *my own heart* free of hatred and despair. (PT, 145, emphases added)

The "acceptance" and "fight" Baldwin refers to in this brilliant coda to "Me and My House" may seem contradictory; yet like homeless despair and creativity in Smith's "Backwater Blues," they are also inextricably connected and, paradoxically, generative. It is through both accepting and fighting such a contradiction, or "intimation" as he calls it in the next sentence, that Baldwin's narrator can engage in his craft and the attendant labor of creating a separate self and new modes of dwelling through authorship. By embracing the contradictions of identity and finding a place to write about it, he is able to become "an honest man and a good writer," as he defines his mission in the "Autobiographical Notes" that open *Notes of a Native Son*, the first published volume of his essays.

EXPLODING THE COLOR LINE

By 1977, these ideas ripen into "Every Good-Bye Ain't Gone," where Baldwin returns to the paradox of "acceptance" and "fight," though he now sees it as "a demarcation line," or "my apprehension of, and, therefore, my responsibility for, my own experience: the chilling vice versa of what I have made of my experience and what that experience had made of me" (PT, 645). In both of these essays, spanning a dozen years, Baldwin rewrites and complicates for the late twentieth and early twenty-first centuries the spatial implications of Du Bois's famous concepts of "double consciousness" and the "color line." Baldwin is, of course, indebted to Du Bois's rhetoric concerning the "problem of the twentieth century" and, in a sense, continues the older writer's project of black (male) intellectual and artistic uplift while finding his foothold as a man of letters between the self-consciousness and hypervisibility forced upon his perceptions by the hue of his epidermis, or what Du Bois calls "this sense of always looking at one's self through the eyes of others."

At the same time, however, Baldwin complicates, questions, and ultimately explodes Du Bois's binary concept of "two-ness—an American, a Negro; two souls, two thoughts, two unreconciled strivings; two warring ideals in one dark body" by making that body located, spatially contingent, gendered, sexualized, queer or bisexual, and engaged in storytelling that entails rewriting and reshaping the story of his life as much as the story of his people.[41] By the 1960s, Baldwin increasingly explores being a black American as an overwhelming trial for the individual, and from that moment on he views blackness as a complex and ever-changing construct, representation, locality, and performance. From the race man, he becomes a "kind of poet," as he names himself in Pakay's film, one whose 1970s and 1980s works reshape Du Bois's double consciousness and color line, the former through the introduction of the located, dynamic, and ever-changing phenomenological "me" that complements, revises, and expands the "African" and the "American" of Du Bois's model; the latter, by insisting on the constructed nature, in both material and metaphorical senses, of the older intellectual's very space of the color line, which Baldwin sees as nothing more than a white invention, problem, and responsibility with all its grave and devastating implications globally, locally, and individually.

A superb example of how this works in both instances can be found in a fragment from "Every Good-Bye Ain't Gone," where Baldwin contemplates the relationship between his subjectivity as an African American and those of the French and African nationals, and where he declares the complex reality that things and people, not to mention our temporal and spatial interpretations of them and of ourselves, are never quite what they seem:

> I will owe the French a debt forever . . . because, during one of my passionately insane barroom brawls, I suddenly realized that the Frenchman I was facing had not the remotest notion—and could not possibly have had the remotest notion—of the tension in my mind between *Orléans*, a French city, and New Orleans, where my father had been born, between *louis*, the coin, and *Louis*, the French king, for whom was named the state of Louisiana, the result of which celebrated purchase had been the death of so many black people. Neither did any African, as far as I could tell, at that moment of my own time and space, have any notion of this tension and torment. But what I began to see was that, if they had no notion of

my torment, I certainly had no notion of theirs, and that I was treating people exactly as I had been treated at home. (PT, 645)

This instance of spatial-temporal, geopolitical, and historical analysis goes hand in hand with life writing and self-criticism, both mightily admirable in someone of middle age—Baldwin was fifty-three when that essay was published—and of established authorial stature and considerable international fame. The narrator's admission of humility and what seems to be alienation in his predicament as a black American in the (post)colonial world, and his insistence on constantly revising his subject position, is revolutionary in both its acceptance of the self as a function of change and its spatial-temporal flux. This brilliant passage also anticipates—in the magical way artists sometimes intuitively, sometimes concretely, do ahead of theorists—the notion of cultural identity as a complex process entwining Africa, Europe, and the Americas.[42]

The depth and focus of Baldwin's vision in "Every Good-Bye Ain't Gone" come from his intense scrutiny of the world around him, his voracious reading and autodidacticism, and his often punishing self-examination as a writer for whom the reinterpretation of his own story was an ongoing project. Baldwin's remark about the African in the scene of his "passionately insane barroom brawls" links his African American narrator with his paternal ancestral roots in New Orleans *and* separates him from the diasporic African witness in France. Because the nameless African does not share the narrator's affective state, or "at that moment of my own time and space, [he did not] have any notion of this tension and torment," they cannot really know each other or share anything purely on the basis of their epidermal hues. As McKittrick writes, "The geographies of slavery, postslavery, and black dispossession provide opportunities to notice that the right to be human carries in it a history of racial encounters and innovative black diaspora practices that . . . spatialize acts of survival."[43] The only bond the African American and the African share in Baldwin's essay is that they are both such survivors. They do not share anything else, not even the reaction to the immediate situation in the bar, for each sees it differently and cannot comprehend the other's vision. In this rich context, the narrator's realization that the Frenchman he is confronting is even more clueless concerning the narrator's "tension and torment," and "could not possibly have had the remotest notion" about his feelings, amounts to a breakthrough equal to that which Baldwin mapped out in the conclusion to "Me and My House." Once again, his self expands his story in the spaces of confrontation with its earlier incarnations.

This description of a situation in which Baldwin's narrator finds himself estranged from everyone else around him, and thus rediscovers the fact of his uniqueness and alienation from all others and even himself, can benefit from a reading in the context of Julia Kristeva's approach to the concept of foreignness as gendered difference. In *Strangers to Ourselves*, she describes it as located in the metaphor of historical representations, as well as the visceral experience of the "foreigner": "Strangely, the foreigner lives within us: he is the hidden *face* of our identity, the *space* that directs our abode, the *time* in which understanding and affinity founder. By recognizing him [*sic!*] within ourselves, we are spared detesting him in himself.... The foreigner comes in when the consciousness of my difference arises, and he disappears when we all acknowledge ourselves as foreigners, unamenable to bonds and communities."[44] Baldwin was certainly familiar with French existentialism and Albert Camus's famous novel *L'Étranger* (*The Stranger*; 1942), in which a white Frenchman kills an unnamed Arab man in Algiers, and whose intertextual echoes we may discern in Kristeva's description. Baldwin's take on the foreigner is closer to Kristeva's than to Camus's, though, for it triangulates among the black American narrator, the (postcolonial) African, and the Frenchman, who are all caught up in the shifting postwar world, where all binaries are suspect and challenged. Thus while Baldwin's narrator in "Every Good-Bye" may be alienated, he recognizes himself as part of a community at home, in the United States. As someone who has lived both there and in the world, he can also read other people along with himself; he can envisage new, alternative communities.

In a subsequent passage from that essay, space, story, and self come together again as Baldwin embraces this knowledge and experience as a tool that can make life better for the next generation, or "the children":

> I have been in and out of my country . . . for a very long time. . . . This is not a bitter statement. It comes . . . out of love, for I am thinking of the children. I watch . . . French and Algerian children trying to become friends with each other, reacting to, but not yet understanding, the terrors of their parents, and very far indeed from having any notion of the terrors of the state. They have no way of knowing that the state is menace and shaken to the degree, precisely, that they, themselves, the presumed victims, or at least, the wards of the state, make manifest their identity. . . . They cannot possibly know that they, ex-slave and ex-master, cannot be used as their fathers were used—*that all identities, in short, are in question, are about to be made new*. (PT, 645, emphasis added)

In blending the autobiographical and cosmopolitan viewpoints, this passage repeats the tenets of the one in which the African American, the Frenchman, and the African meet yet cannot connect as if caught up in a bad joke.[45] Baldwin's inexact mirroring of the barroom scene onto the scene in which his narrator observes the French and Algerian children playing together while, implicitly, recalling the children of his own family back in the United States, elucidates his faith in humanity and the redeeming power of love for "the stranger" in the larger, human home. If we approach this passage as an approximate rewriting of the dire conclusions of Camus's novel, it can be read as making a clean and deliberate break with nihilism and existentialism, substituting Baldwin's vision of black queer humanism, or complex love, one that has the power to work both in the United States and in France, where the Algerians struggle to claim their postcolonial citizenship just as black Americans have been trying to claim theirs.[46]

The two passages from "Every Good-Bye" also further explicate the ways social space functions for Baldwin as a "field of vision" or, as Irit Rogoff explains it in *Terra Infirma: Geography's Visual Culture*, a realm of visual culture that has been constituted in traditional western philosophy "out of processes of negative differentiation—that whiteness needs blackness to constitute itself as whiteness, that masculinity needs femininity or feminized masculinity to constitute its masculinity in agreed-upon normative modes, that civility and bourgeois respectability need the stereotypical, unruly 'others.'"[47] Baldwin's barroom scene shows, first, how that model of binarily racialized perception works and holds his African American narrator hostage, and, second, how that narrator realizes its workings and refuses to be its victim by imagining and accepting the unique perspectives of all the characters involved in the scene. His realization illustrates the ever-present differentiated nature of space, which is "always sexual or racial . . . always constituted out of circulating capital and . . . always subject to the invisible boundary lines which determine inclusions and exclusions . . . populated with the unrecognized obstacles which never allow us to actually 'see' what is out there beyond what we expect to find."[48] These obstacles can be surmounted, Baldwin's narrator realizes, when he is able to see the playing children both as the ex-masters and ex-slaves *and* as the children of the new world, whose imagination and capacity for love can break down historical scripts, indeed, can make "all identities . . . new."

Baldwin's astounding capacity to remain hopeful arises from his faith in and mastery of language, whose embroilment with spatiality is at the center of what the feminist architect Leslie Kanes Weisman defines as semantic mirroring of architecture and idiom: "Space, like language, is socially constructed, and like the syntax of language, the spatial arrangements of our buildings and communities reflect and reinforce the nature of gender, race, and class relations in a society."[49] This affinity between what Weisman calls the "man-made" environment and discourse describing and designing it can be linked as well to a broader concept of human geography as "bound up in, rather than simply a backdrop to, social and environmental processes," as Katherine McKittrick and Clyde Woods argue. As they explain in *Black Geographies and the Politics of Place*, as the "materiality of the environment is racialized by contemporary demographic patterns as shaped by historic precedents," it is clear that "black human geographies are implicated in the production of space"—a statement with which Henri Lefebvre might agree, no matter how little his own classically Marxist project of *The Production of Space* deals explicitly with the issues of race.[50]

The alliterative space, story, and self triad at the center of *Me and My House* avoids such omissions by celebrating Baldwin's rewriting of a spatially contingent self and highlighting how his oeuvre defies binary notions of mobile, transitory, and in-dwelled identity. By turning my multivalent analytic lens on the black domesticity that propels both his works and life story, I also hope to fill a gaping absence in twentieth-century American literary history.[51] Among many writers who have lived away from the United States, or traveled in Europe following World War II—Richard Wright, Frank Yerby, Ernest Hemingway, Chester Himes, Adrienne Rich, Edmund White, Audre Lorde, John Ashbery, and Samuel Delaney, to mention just a few— Baldwin's ways of dwelling seem the least examined, and his material legacy (places where he lived, his possessions, furniture, aesthetic tastes) the least known. While American culture has usually embraced the architectural and spatial manifestations of its rich literary heritage by either creating museums to visit or providing simulacra of spaces where the best of national literature was created, the preponderance of writers' houses open to the public today makes it strikingly clear that African Americans have not been counted as part of this heritage until very recently.

Frederick Douglass's house in Baltimore, Maryland, and Alex Haley's in Henning, Tennessee, are notable exceptions to this rule concerning American writers' house-museums. The American Writers Museum, which opened in Chicago in 2017, will perhaps change this perception by creating a space for Baldwin and other writers of color.[52] For now, however, the places that nurtured this black queer writer, the dwellings that nourished his many selves, "all those strangers called Jimmy Baldwin," have not been, and most likely will not be, preserved outside this book. *Me and My House* examines the reasons for such erasures of Baldwin's domesticity in the context of his stylistic innovations, theorizations of gender and sexuality, and the rich and exciting new scholarship on this writer.

AT HOME WITH BALDWIN STUDIES

Much has changed in scholarship on Baldwin during this book's gestation, with the second decade of the twenty-first century ushering in his so-called renaissance. Given this explosion of popular and academic interest, we must avoid Reid-Pharr's dire prediction that, "as a subject established *within* the practice of literary and cultural criticism, James Baldwin ... seems shockingly ... dead," engaging instead in contextualized, black aesthetics–focused, and rigorously methodological and contextualized analyses.[53] Most of the scholars whose work has helped me to think through this project agree that early critical approaches to Baldwin's works unhelpfully pigeonhole him as either a gay or black writer, a novelist or essayist, a civil rights activist or expatriate, thus demonstrating how fragmented and misunderstood he was by white and black critics alike, many of whom could not divorce their judgment of his works from their views on race, sexuality, or his lifestyle.[54] Among earlier works, of note and lasting value are Rosa Bobia's *The Critical Reception of James Baldwin in France* (1998); Horace Porter's *Stealing the Fire: The Art and Protest of James Baldwin* (1989), which anoints Baldwin as a Promethean descendant of Henry James; and Trudier Harris's *Black Women in the Fiction of James Baldwin* (1985), whose feminist readings pave the way for subsequent gender-, sexuality-, and queer studies–based scholarship.

Edited volumes as venues for diverse scholarship include the seminal *James Baldwin Now* (1999) by Dwight McBride and D. Quentin Miller's *Re-viewing James Baldwin* (2000), both reanimating Baldwin's oeuvre for the new millennium while employing cultural studies approaches.[55] *James Baldwin and Toni Morrison* (2006; edited by Lovalerie King and Lynn Orilla Scott) ponders his multivalent, ancestral influence on the younger Morrison and their ongoing dialogue and labor as pioneers who gained "a broad national and international audience for" the African American literary tradition,[56] while Douglas Field's *Historical Guide to James Baldwin* (2009) offers rich perspectives on his works and interdisciplinary resources for teaching him on all levels. Examining the significance of his transatlantic identity, involvement with the theater, religion, music, activism, and immigration, Cora Kaplan and Bill Schwarz's *James Baldwin: America and Beyond* (2011) and A. Scott Henderson and P. L. Thomas's *James Baldwin: Challenging Authors* (2014) offer exciting forums for transatlantic scholarly exchanges. Michele Elam's *Cambridge Companion to James Baldwin* (2015) provides indispensable evidence of diverse and nuanced approaches by deftly locating Baldwin in the contemporary cultural landscape and across multiple academic fields.

Among single-authored books, Katharine Lawrence Balfour's *The Evidence of Things Not Said* (2001) and Lynn Orilla Scott's *Witness to the Journey: James Baldwin's Later Fiction* (2002) delve into new areas—Baldwin's relationship with legal discourses and the profound significance of his neglected late writing—while Clarence Hardy's *James Baldwin's God* (2003) examines Baldwin's deployment of scripture and black church practices. My own *James Baldwin's Turkish Decade* (2009) links his most productive period to an unexpected, complex, and unexplored location, and D. Quentin Miller's *A Criminal Power* (2012) applies the rich context of race studies, critical law studies, and prison literature to his works. Matt Brim's *James Baldwin and the Queer Imagination* (2014) showcases the writer's embrace of and blind spots about his representations of black, gay love, while Douglas Field's *All Those Strangers* (2015) illuminates Baldwin's underresearched engagement with the Left, his FBI files, and his relationship to Africa. Edward M. Pavlić's *Who Can Afford to Improvise?* (2016) is a poetically realized reconsideration of Baldwin's improvisational style and musical influences by jazz greats, while Jules B. Farber's *James Baldwin: Escape from America, Exile in Provence* (2016) and Herb Boyd's *Baldwin's Harlem* (2008) appeal to nonacademic audiences with reminiscences from various celebrities and family members, interviews, anecdotes, and local events.

At times confounded by the sheer volume and versatility of the great man's output, these exciting studies nevertheless help us reassess the great complexity and richness of Baldwin's contributions, as well as his relevance today. Echoing them, Hilton Als wrote a vignette in the *New Yorker* about the impact that "Down at the Cross" (1962) had on that magazine, emphasizing Baldwin's profound devotion to his craft: "What sometimes got lost was an understanding of the sheer talent and imagination that had gone into the piece, the knowledge that change always begins with the word."[57] Positioned under a black-and-white photograph of Baldwin—sitting down, leaning over a table toward someone unseen, gesturing with open hands, the inevitable cigarette held in the right, his face both serious and on the brink of a smile; a glass of water and coffee cup in front of him, his body framed by the fireplace and furnishings of his upstairs living room in St. Paul-de-Vence—Als's praise of Baldwin's authorial mastery displaces the writer in time by using a photo from the 1970s to discuss his seminal work from the 1960s, when he was in fact living mostly in Turkey.

While Baldwin purists may be distraught by this temporal and locational inaccuracy, I like it for showcasing the writer in his favorite element needed to do his best work; as he does in his books, we critics, too, can sometimes take productive liberties with chronology.[58] Als's critique is important, too, because it praises the author's style as inflected by sexuality: "Writing this piece ["Down at the Cross"], with, at times, a kind of gay humor and slyness, allowed Baldwin to expose the church's smoke and mirrors, intended to keep black people on their knees, held down by piety and ghetto-think." Als writes that Baldwin's words promised that "the world would be white no longer, and there would be no forgiveness for those who have equated race with power at the expense of others." To Marlon Ross, he "proffered the most devastating critique of the racist heteronorm in a wide range of genres," through a highly performative gesture of "allowing his sissified intelligence to be staged for the public eye through the exhibition of his out-of-gender person."[59] I see such performativity in *Tell Me How Long the Train's Been Gone*, whose Leo Proudhammer becomes an alternative, radical American hero/antihero—someone whom neither the white establishment nor Black Power could support.[60] As Dixon argues, in their multivalent thematics, Baldwin's novels revise a wide swath of African American literary history, from "Harlem Renaissance authors like Jean Toomer and Claude McKay . . . [to] Ellison, Wright, Jones, and Hurston."[61] While I agree, I also see him devising a craft that was both receptive to influence and uniquely his own.

The literary force of Baldwin's craft pervades new African American writing. In *Citizen: An American Lyric* (2014), Claudia Rankine ponders the price one pays for existing as a black person within a racist society. Evoking the tragic deaths of Trayvon Martin and many other black men, women, and children at the hands of police and others, and the never-ending spectacle of these deaths on the Internet, she counsels her readers, "[A] friend once told you there exists the medical term—John Henryism—for people exposed to stresses stemming from racism. They achieve themselves to death trying to dodge the build up of erasure. . . . The researcher who came up with the term, claimed the physiological costs were high. You hope by sitting in silence you are bucking the trend."[62] In 2013, Ta-Nehisi Coates, copying the form and style of Baldwin's *Fire Next Time*, writes about living in Baltimore while black in his National Book Award–winning *Between the World and Me*: "The streets transform every ordinary day into a series of trick questions, and every incorrect answer risks a beatdown, a shooting, or a pregnancy. No one survives unscathed."[63]

Baldwin knew these costs well, and yet, as he told Yvonne Neverson in 1978, he had the capacity to imagine positive returns to the black artist's articulation of his or her own and their people's suffering, speaking of the "artist ... [as] a disturber of the peace." This statement negates Addison Gayle's 1967 appraisal of Baldwin's message, that "salvation is impossible," anticipating that critic's rereading of the American black writer's central task a decade later as being the "master of the word ... our most consummate politician," whose critics must devote themselves "not to spurious theories of art for art's sake, but to art for the sake of Black people everywhere."[64] Baldwin's vision's capaciousness accommodates political, moral, and aesthetic possibilities alike. He describes to Neverson "the beginning of the flowering which is something unprecedented" of the literary and visual arts by people of color all over the postcolonial world, thus confirming his interest in how their ideas of freedom, individuality, and creativity circulated outside the United States. That stance, as Ross notes, went both along with and against the separatism of some black nationalists who engaged in queer baiting.[65]

Though the likes of Eldridge Cleaver, Ishmael Reed, or LeRoi Jones / Amiri Baraka (until later) did not embrace Baldwin, he was in good company with African Diaspora artists active concurrently with him, such as Chinua Achebe, Gwendolyn Brooks, Ann Petry, Cecil Brown, Audre Lorde, Wole Soyinka, and Maya Angelou. Other writers who came of age around the time he achieved recognition and following his demise, such as Derek Walcott, Paule Marshall, Gloria Naylor, Nikki Giovanni, Quincy Troupe, Alice Walker, Toni Morrison, Jamaica Kincaid, Caryl Phillips, Zadie Smith, and Chimamanda Ngozi Adichie, were often critical of race-based nationalisms and exclusionary and separatist notions of identity.[66] Usually grouped as part of the "big three" with Richard Wright and Ralph Ellison, Baldwin lends himself to readings that not only place him as an outlier to this Olympian male trinity due to his class and sexuality, but also show him as deeply influenced by the writings and art of black women, whose visions of domesticity and the national house were often instrumental in crafting his approach.[67] And while it is impossible to prove that he read all the books by women writers, many of which I found in his surviving library, noting a few examples of such dialogic encounters makes it clear that Baldwin thought deeply about the typically feminine private and domestic spheres from the earliest moments of his career.

1.6. Chez Baldwin archive: Books by women writers (Morrison, etc.). Photo by author, 2014.

For example, *Go Tell It* and Gwendolyn Brooks's gripping novella tracing a black woman's life in segregated Chicago published the same year, *Maud Martha* (1953), read together exceedingly well. Opening up discussions on lower-class black masculinity in Baldwin's John Grimes, who tries to sweep and clean the omnipresent dust in his family's Harlem apartment, and femininity in Brooks's Maud Martha, who struggles against the mythic "roach," such readings help materialize the effects of never-ending dirt and poverty in segregated housing. In a similar vein, implying a need for a separate study, Ann Petry's *The Street* (1946) and *The Narrows* (1953) invite a reading with *Another Country* and *Beale Street*, while Gloria Naylor's *Women of Brewster Place* (1982) can be productively read in conversation with both *Beale Street* and *Just above My Head*. The protagonist of Toni Morrison's *Home* (2012) could be read alongside *Another Country*'s Rufus, as well as Hall and Leo from, respectively, *Just above My Head* and *Tell Me*.[68] Most important, in all of these works, Baldwin and his female contemporaries and descendants focus steadfastly on the realm of affect and emotion and its interactions with subjects who move in highly differentiated social spaces and fields of vision, whose perspectival access or lack thereof to domesticity often determines their demise or survival.[69]

Black writing requires heroic efforts, as Baldwin wrote about Lorraine Hansberry's strength and resilience in *To Be Young, Gifted, and Black* (1970), and he may have been describing himself: "It is not at all farfetched to suspect that what she saw contributed to the strain which killed her, for the effort to which Lorraine was dedicated is more than enough to kill a man."[70] Racism is deadly and spares no one; it is cruelly obvious why the name of today's civil rights movement group is Black Lives Matter.[71] Baldwin's strengths influenced many of his contemporaries and those who came to writing after his passing in addition to Rankine and Coates: Adrienne Rich, Amiri Baraka, Randall Kenan, Shay Youngblood, Alain Mabanckou, Brian Freeman, Suzan-Lori Parks, and many others.[72] His letter to his nephew and namesake in "My Dungeon Shook" (1963) can be read as a missive to the writers who followed him: "This is your home, . . . do not be driven from it; great men have done great things here, and will again, and we can make America what America must become" (PT, 336). Reminding the youth, "You come from a long line of great poets, some of the greatest poets since Homer," Baldwin reasserts the power of language and the power of art to change the world (albeit without giving women their due in this picture). And while his vision of America as a national house is far from optimistic, and his glimpses of private home spaces where those who do not fit normative narratives may find shelter are rarely lasting, we need his rhetoric and stubborn faith in humanity more than ever. For while he was never romantic about his fellow Americans of all hues, he had faith in what some of them were capable of attaining.

VITRINES, FRAGMENTS, REASSEMBLED REMNANTS

> We have come to the end of a language and are now about the business of forging a new one.
> —"Notes on the House of Bondage"

> It's one thing to be aware of Miles Davis and quite another thing to know *where he comes from* and what sustains him. . . . The book, my book, and others come as a direct opposition of *the myth by Americans of black life and black music*. . . . The books prove them wrong, so they ignore the books.
> —Baldwin, in Troupe, "Last Interview (1987)" (emphases added)

At James Baldwin's last house in St. Paul-de-Vence, the mantelpieces, walls, and desktops were filled with many visual and textural arrangements that inspired his writing and nourished his complex aesthetic. His friend and interviewer Quincy Troupe remembers one of them vividly in a republished version of his last interview with the writer that took place at the house in November 1987, days before Baldwin's death:

> The many paintings and pieces of sculpture . . . a black pen-and-ink drawing of Nelson Mandela against an orange background, accompanied by a poem . . . an assemblage created by Jimmy's brother David in his honor. . . . The centerpiece was the citation of the French Legion of Honor . . . a sword and an old hunting rifle, both pointing toward the certificate . . . a black-and-white photograph of Jimmy, an abstract steel sculpture of an Indian . . . two crystal inkwells, a figure resembling a guitar, and an oversize ink pen. (JB, 80)[73]

I saw remnants of some of these collections when I visited that house in 2000, when I commenced my research. I wondered what stories they could tell, what new languages they were forging, as Baldwin lived the last years of his fierce creativity. When I returned to St. Paul-de-Vence in 2014, the house was empty, but I was fortunate to see what remained of Baldwin's possessions, and I surveyed a trove of objects that had been salvaged from Chez Baldwin before its loss to developers. These objects—the only archive of

1.7. Stacked artwork in storage. Photo by author, 2014.

James Baldwin's possessions other than his papers, which until recently have been kept under lock and key by his estate—had been kept in storage by a determined woman who could not bear to see them discarded, and whose story is among many that have inspired this book.[74]

The image opening this section displays a close-up of an arrangement that could have been the one Troupe describes—or what was left of it by 2000 when I took this photo—and was thus also likely made by Jimmy's younger brother, David Baldwin, who was a gifted artist in his own right and whose work adorned the house. A print of Richard Avedon's photographic montage hybridizing his own face and Baldwin's hung nearby, its edges curled with age and humidity. A colorful painting of a pregnant woman, created by David's son Daniel, Baldwin's beloved nephew whom he liked showing off in the village, served as a screen for the fireplace in the living room upstairs.

These leftover objects, art pieces, and adornments—books, journals, magazines, files of Xeroxed pages, vinyl records, and clippings that spilled over shelves and desktops throughout the house—were the only material archive remaining after James Baldwin's death in 1987. I was astounded that no one in his family wanted to claim them, but, then, scholarly desires for material preservation are more often than not at odds with those of estates, lawyers, and kin, not to mention archives and libraries. I am incredibly fortunate to have been able to see and document some of these material traces in this book on the inseparability of Baldwin's domestic and creative imaginations.

The eclectic archive that has inspired this project weaves in and out of Baldwin's writings, biographies, testimonies of friends and relatives, unpublished letters, interviews in various formats (including those on the Internet), and whatever remains of his widely conceived and still largely inaccessible legacy. As part of that legacy, I also engage with photographs that I took and impressions of his house in St. Paul-de-Vence in France that I wrote during my first visit there in 2000, as well as the leftover objects mentioned above that I was allowed to research in 2014 and thoroughly document in 2017. I include these discarded objects in this project to save and document whatever we may have left of the matter of Baldwin's life, while also honoring the inseparability of the material and metaphorical in his writings and life story. As I show in these pages, his connection to things and spaces is important for reassessing his complex legacy, especially his contribution to writing and rewriting the conundrum of black domesticity, whose full impact we have yet to acknowledge.

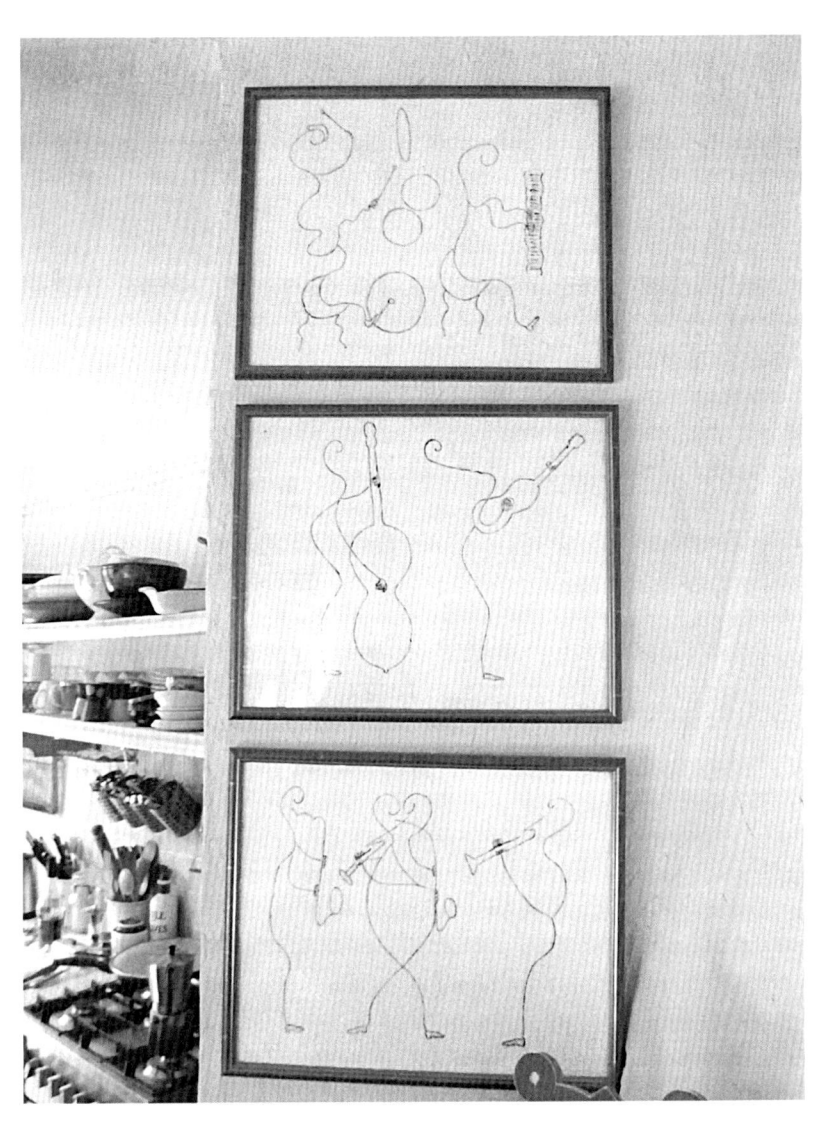

1.8. Daniel Baldwin's paintings in Jill Hutchinson's collection. Photo by author, 2014.

In doing so, this book also honors Baldwin's call to honesty and confession, celebrating him as an extraordinary person and artist whose legacy, however incomplete at the moment, should be recognized as every American's ancestral right. Closely reading his various fragmented impressions of moments when the self comes into contact with social space to tell stories, the five chapters that follow are divided into subsections that work both independently and in tandem as assemblages of thematically and conceptually linked vignettes. Such an arrangement helps me to keep the main tripartite subject of this book in focus through chapters 2, 3, and 4, which correspond to the central conceptual triad of space/matter, self/material, and story/metaphor. The complex thematic, analytical, critical, and biographical constellations contextualizing this triad are examined in chapter 1, which focuses largely on the scholarly and theoretical underpinnings of *Me and My House*. The sensitive and personal nature of some of the biographical, and occasionally autobiographical, accounts in the subchapters, and in chapter 5, reflects and responds to Baldwin's insistence on always putting his individual, family, and ancestral stories inside his texts, while respectfully paying heed to the writer's own late, improvisational style through their arrangement.[75]

On the level of composition, or the human story I tell here in sincere hopes that it will also be read outside of academe, the book's arrangement was inspired by a Polish material cultural practice. Perhaps more simply, its structure is rooted in a children's game—inspired by underground collages we made as kids growing up in Poland during the Cold War in the 1970s. Called *widoczki* ("vitrines" or "hidden vistas"), these assemblages were mostly the purview of prepubescent girls and consisted of colorful scraps of various discarded items (candy wrappers, tinfoil, flowers, leaves, paper, fabric) carefully arranged at the bottom of a hole dug in the dirt in a secret spot. As the culmination of this game, the final composition would be covered with a piece of glass and then carefully buried, its place marked with a sign that would be clear to its maker but illegible to others who might find pleasurable sport in its destruction. Each of us would create several such recycled treasures in different locations around the neighborhood and then visit them regularly. We protected them passionately for, once dug up, they opened a world of escape and offered us proof that we were capable of making something beautiful that belonged to no one else.[76]

I would like to think that Baldwin would approve of framing his story via this playful vitrine metaphor, given his own predilection for foreign locales,

1.9. Vinyl records from Chez Baldwin in Jill Hutchinson's collection. Photo by author, 2014.

his love of children, and his passion for the visual arts. His fondness for collage was clear in many of the places he occupied—he had various assemblages of images, clippings, objects, and sketches wherever he lived, especially in Turkey and France in the 1960s, 1970s, and 1980s. Many of Baldwin's friends with whom I have spoken in the decade and a half since my first visit to his house have confirmed that the writer was a consummate aesthete: he loved fine clothes, colors, and textures, quality fabrics, and interesting jewelry; his house was filled with tasteful furniture, rugs and throws, pillows, and knickknacks. His love of music manifested itself in a large vinyl collection that has survived both him and his brother David, who lived in the house until 1996. A corkboard in Baldwin's office that I saw reproduced in a magazine had the jackets of his last books—*The Price of the Ticket* and *The Evidence of Things Not Seen*—pinned next to photographs of friends and family; a white cast of Blaise Pascal's death mask leaned against the wall underneath the board. Like many of us, Baldwin liked to fill his dwelling spaces with comforting objects. In an unpublished letter to David Leeming, written from Istanbul on December 27, 1965, he referred to them as "little gimcracks, like mirrors, and ash-trays."[77]

While reflecting his aesthetic predilections, Baldwin's love for collages and assemblages also mirrored his writing style, especially those works he created during the underappreciated decades of the 1970s and 1980s. By that time, the visual and material inspirations introduced to him by his Greenwich Village mentor and surrogate father figure, the painter Beauford Delaney, along with the musical rhythms, improvisations, and avant-garde harmonies he admired in blues and jazz pioneers like Bessie Smith, Miles Davis, Nina Simone, or Charlie Parker, inspired mature, complex, and sometimes experimental narrative forms. These daring stylistic and compositional arrangements could be discerned already in his third novel, *Another Country*, and they certainly animate his later work—*Tell Me How Long the Train's Been Gone*, *If Beale Street Could Talk*, *Just above My Head*, *No Name in the Street*, *The Devil Finds Work*, and *The Evidence of Things Not Seen*. They are especially powerfully executed in the syncopated dialogues and call-and-response riffs propelling his play *The Welcome Table*, whose genesis goes back to Turkey and whose setting is literally within the very walls of his house in St. Paul-de-Vence. (I return to that important, haunting work in chapter 3.)

Me and My House places the juxtaposition between self and domicile, individual and social space, body and architecture at its center, while setting out to examine the material and metaphorical, or literal and literary, traces of this writer's domestic life within and without the United States.[78] Traveling between and among actual geographic and physical locations; the pages of his published works, interviews, and unpublished letters; the memories he left with friends and family; and an archive of objects salvaged from his house in St. Paul-de-Vence, this book shows how Baldwin challenged, revised, and at times exploded the conventions of racialized domesticity in the United States, and of national and African American cultural and literary histories.

Me and My House also taps into the longing and desire to preserve, to the degree that a project like this allows, what remains of the *matter* and *stories* of the domestic life of James Arthur Baldwin (1924–87). A pivotal and unique figure in American literary, social, and cultural history, Baldwin left a scarce material legacy that is only now beginning to be memorialized: a meager collection of his papers is available at a handful of libraries, and some of his works (and certainly his letters) remain unpublished or out of print. And, as noted earlier in this introduction, while there are a few historical markers honoring him in New York City's Harlem and Greenwich Village neighborhoods, there is still no writer's house or museum devoted to him anywhere. This absence and scarcity—not at all surprising given how few African American writers' houses are open to the public in the United States, and that, halfway through the second decade of the twenty-first century, the National Museum of African American History and Culture has only recently opened—only compound Baldwin's "homelessness." Much like those of countless other black Americans that the new museum honors without naming, his legacy remains in flux, the material traces of his life almost completely erased from his home country.

To this critic, Baldwin's literary mastery, in all its shapes and forms, and with all its demanding density and complexity, is unparalleled in twentieth-century American letters. As I show in this book, that difficult mastery was the result of a complex nexus of events and influences that would have taken a much longer lifetime than his to fully gestate and flourish. It came from a process that was seldom painless, often excruciating, and far from completion at the time of the writer's death from cancer in 1987, when he was only sixty-three. I have said this before, and more than once in my earlier work on this writer, but it bears repeating that Baldwin's writing life was a continuous fluctuating process, an ebb and flow of experimentation and honing of his style that repudiates the unhelpful cleaving of his oeuvre into pre– and post–*Fire Next Time* periods of ascendancy and decline that still, sadly, holds sway over some critics and scholars. At the center of this process, the part that took place over the last decade and a half of his life in 1971–87, stands his domestic abode in St. Paul-de-Vence. It is from that complex and materially and metaphorically loaded location that *Me and My House* sets out to reconstruct and prove the centrality of Baldwin's ideas on home, both to his writing and to his rich legacy as one of the greatest American authors, witnesses, and prophets.

CHAPTER SUMMARY

Subsequent parts of this book frame the movement of my argument from the *matter* of Baldwin's actual dwelling in St. Paul-de-Vence, through the *material* of his life story and coming of age that he recovers and rewrites in his later years, to his *metaphorical*, or literary, creations of domestic spaces in the late works that he composed at his beloved last house.

Chapter 1, "Foundations, Façades, and Faces: Through the Glass Blackly, or Domesticating Claustrophobic Terror," explains key terms and theoretical concepts that emerge from Baldwin's rich musings on the meanings of whiteness and blackness; domesticity and public space; individualism and national identity. These key terms are also cast against the Cold War and postcolonial, neocolonial, imperial, and transnational moments that provide the ever-changing backdrop for his works in the 1970s and 1980s. This chapter also shows how the majority of Baldwin's works engage two powerfully interlinked themes that are key to analyzing black domesticity in the twentieth-century United States: the necessity to survive *away* from one's home and difficult childhood, and the desire to create *alternative* kinds of domesticity and modes of dwelling for black bodies that do not fit normative gender, sexual, familial, religious, or social roles and designs. Against the backdrop of his complex biography, it examines some of the controversial terms qualifying his works and authorial persona, while also tracing the development of his late style and aesthetics and attending to past and recent Baldwin scholarship.

As the key location informing this project, Baldwin's last domestic abode dominates chapter 2, "Home Matter: No House in the World, or Reading Transnational, Black Queer Domesticity in St. Paul-de-Vence." While discussing the material remnants of the place, biographical information, interviews (including one with Lucien Happersberger, Baldwin's most important lover and his first domestic partner), texts he wrote about it, and the ways in which discourses on social space, race, gender, and sexuality interface with both fictional and life-writing narratives, this chapter also argues for approaches that deliberately blend the materialist and metaphorical aspects of the traces that Baldwin has left us as his complex legacy.

Chapter 3, "Life Material: Haunted Houses and Welcome Tables, or The First Teacher, the Last Play, and Affectations of Disidentification," explores the writer's home life in Harlem and his formative years as a student, budding reader, and writer coming of age as an artist under the care of his teacher, Orilla "Bill" Miller, with whom he corresponded until his death. It also considers his contributions to the rhetoric and theories of subjectivity in *Tell Me How Long the Train's Been Gone* and *The Devil Finds Work*, by highlighting how Baldwin continued to wrestle with and revise his ideas on racialized gender roles and sexuality, and especially late twentieth-century black masculinity, which he first critiqued in the essay volume *No Name in the Street* and continued to expand upon throughout his subsequent works, culminating with *The Welcome Table*. By locating the origins of recent theories of identity, such as José E. Muñoz's disidentification, in Baldwin's works, it focuses on his theorizing of the ways in which race and racism intersect with other aspects of national identity and nourish American popular culture.

By exploring his last two novels, *If Beale Street Could Talk* and *Just above My Head*, along with the last essay volume, *The Evidence of Things Not Seen*, and a children's story, *Little Man, Little Man* (1976), chapter 4, "Building Metaphors: 'Sitting in the Strangest House I Have Ever Known,' or Black Heterotopias from Harlem to San Juan, to Paris, London, and Yonkers," reads Baldwin's meditations on the national home, or what he called "the house of bondage," as well as on black queer, utopian domestic spaces that he offers as alternatives, where nonnormative identities find shelter, albeit temporarily, within and without the United States. The chapter's explorations of the writer's late aesthetics and thematic threads go hand in hand with examining his autobiographical and autoethnographic experience of homelessness and exile as a black queer artist. Baldwin found no place among *either* African American activists who embraced heterosexist black nationalism or Afrocentrism, *or* mainstream white cultural establishments. Disillusioned with American culture and politics by the 1980s, he was reinvigorated by his late-life articulations of androgyny and a growing interest in performances of the feminine inspired by his glamorous, black women friends.

The concluding chapter 5, "Black Life Matters of Value: Erasure, Overlay, Manipulation, or Archiving the Invisible House," brings to a coda the many thematic and theoretical strands of this project, as well as anticipating Baldwin's virtual house-museum, which I will undertake as a digital humanities companion project for this book. While reflecting the sequence of domesticating Chez Baldwin as a space of creativity and sociability that also yielded to Baldwin's black queer "manipulations"—as he refers to them in a 1987 *Architectural Digest* piece—this section also signals what I see as the urgent task of rethinking how we preserve the material legacy of black lives today. What we understand as the *matter* of black lives, its materiality, traces, remnants, and refuse, must be read differently from the matter of white lives that have so far taken historical precedence in the national house. Hence while Baldwin's home library and leftover objects have been abandoned as worthless, the *New York Times* reports that the Beinecke Rare Book and Manuscript Library at Yale University has recently bought Jonathan Lethem's entire archive, including "dead-tree artifacts" that are "charmingly weird," comic books, electronics, and a trove of drunken drawings of "vomiting cats."[79] (More about that in chapter 5.)

By contextualizing Baldwin's ideas within his biography, scholarship, and recent popular events devoted to his legacy, as much as in his complex literary works and my eclectic archive of objects salvaged from his dwelling, *Me and My House* offers an assembled portrait of a writer whose vision and passion for social justice filtered through all kinds of intellectual and imaginary spaces—from nation, to city streets, to the privacy of the bedroom. His personal contradictions, challenges, and struggles, which his essays, interviews, and brilliant letters reveal as being always unabashedly political, show us that regardless of any current theoretical vogue or idiom, Baldwin's proud domestication of our shared humanity and his fierce embrace of himself—"black, poor, and homosexual," as an interviewer once put it—may be his most enduring gifts.[80]

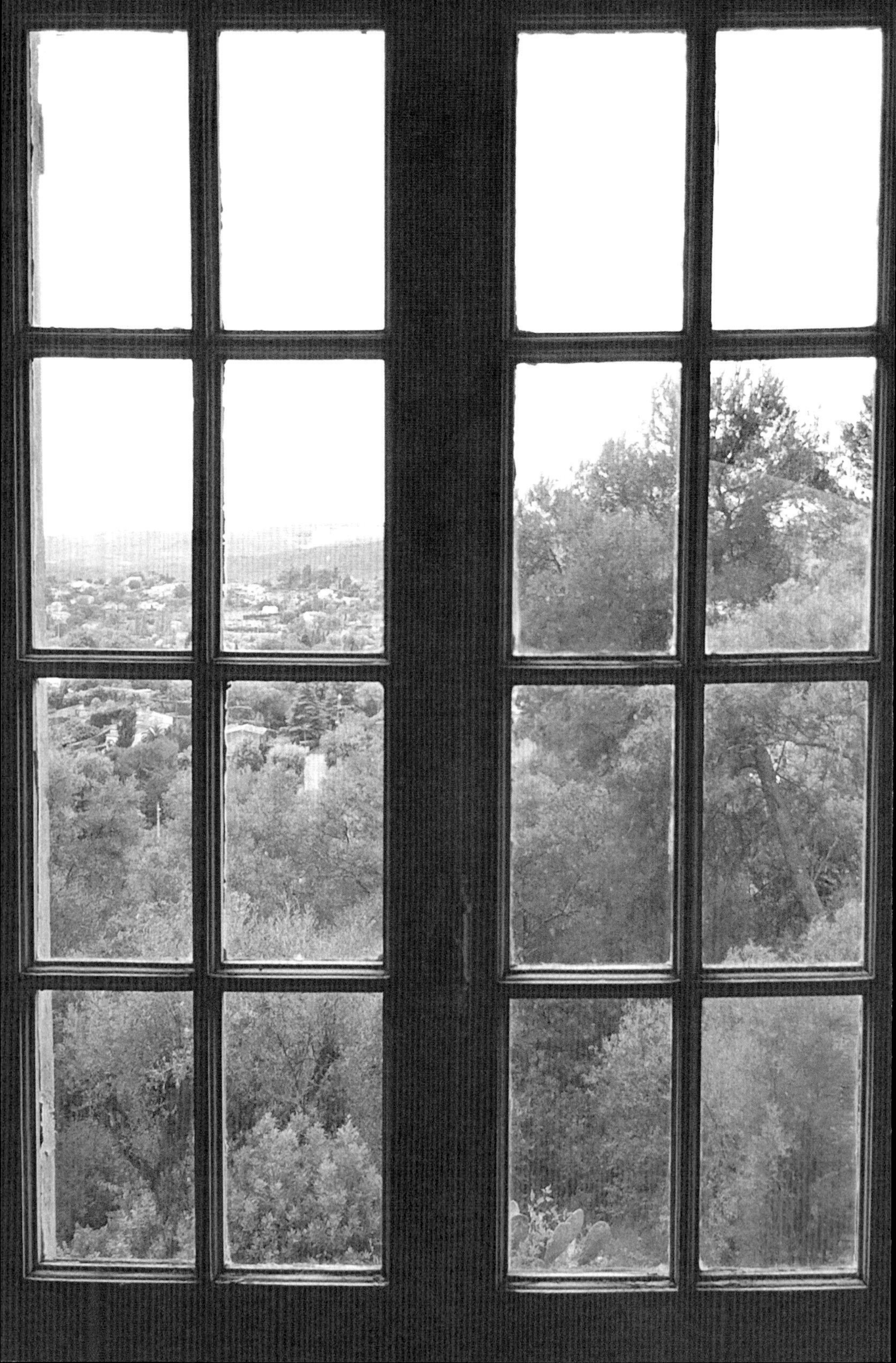

CHAPTER 1

Foundations, Façades, and Faces

Through the Glass Blackly, or
Domesticating Claustrophobic Terror

> I was not born to be what someone said I was. I was not born to be defined by someone else, but by myself, and myself only. . . .
>   No true account, really, of black life can be held, can be contained in the American vocabulary. . . . I don't see anything in American life—for myself—to aspire to. . . . Nothing at all. It's all so very false. So shallow, so plastic, so morally and ethically corrupt.
> —Baldwin, in Troupe, "Last Interview (1987)"

(*opposite*) View from an upstairs bedroom window. Photo by author, 2014.

About twenty minutes into the documentary *James Baldwin: The Price of the Ticket* (1989), the aging Baldwin, front and center in a black-and-white close-up, describes his condition as an African American writer who has spent the majority of his career away from the United States: "You don't ever leave home. You take your home with you. You better, you know. Otherwise you're homeless."[1] As he writes in "Every Good-Bye Ain't Gone" (1977), too, "when 'home' drops below the horizon, it rises in one's breast and acquires the overwhelming power of menaced love" (PT, 646). Baldwin's politics and poetics of home embody a vexed relationship between their material and metaphorical powers, occupying a contested terrain where affect, location, temporality, identity, and the stories they tell remain in constant tension, assembling and disassembling their own multiple configurations.

Baldwin's comments on home as baggage and unrequited love also cement a different, popular image of him as a cosmopolitan—a supremely confident artist and jetsetter, comfortable living and traveling throughout the world. By the 1960s, he had become a well-known writer, activist, and intellectual; by the 1970s, he was secure financially, living in France, his books translated into multiple languages and read all over the world. Yet, while his fame outside his home country seemed to have reached its apotheosis, his works were not selling well in the United States. From the late 1960s through the 1980s, his popularity declined and reviews of his works were predominantly negative. Never able to produce much during visits to New York City—the place of his birth, which he visited often to be with friends and his large, beloved family—Baldwin kept searching for writing havens outside his homeland.

A child of impoverished African American migrants from Louisiana and Maryland who sought better jobs and economic stability in the industrial North, Baldwin grew up keenly aware of his parents' desperate efforts to keep their large family housed, clothed, and fed in a city that offered only badly paid domestic work to women of color, and equally badly paid menial jobs to the men. Born in the Harlem Hospital to a single mother who never disclosed the identity of his biological father and later married a preacher named David Baldwin, young James was raised among those he calls the "truly needy," in housing projects situated alongside what he calls the "American Park Avenue," uptown in Harlem (PT, 680).[2] His elementary school teacher, Orilla Miller, who worked for the Works Progress Administration in New York City, often visited bearing clothing, cod-liver oil, and books for the sickly child. Young James was also his mother's right hand, helping to raise eight stepsiblings born in quick succession, who later became his homeland "tribe."

As he recalls in *No Name in the Street* (1972), the excruciating poverty and hardship of his early life affected them all profoundly, including his tyrannical stepfather: "Between his merciless children, who were terrified of him, the pregnancies, the births, the rats, the murders on Lenox Avenue, the whores who lived downstairs, his job on Long Island . . . and his unreciprocated love for the Great God Almighty, it is no wonder our father went mad. We, on the other hand . . . simply took over each new child and made it ours" (PT, 451). Baldwin never forgot his lower-class origins or his parents' southern roots: "You can take the child out of the country, but you can't take the country out of the child," he points out in the essay "A Fly in Buttermilk" (1958) (PT, 161). By the 1980s, he maps his genealogy thus: "My father was a son of a slave. . . . I'm really a southerner born in the North." His birthplace gave him a vocation as a way out of poverty: "I had to become a writer or perish," he explains, adding a transnational dimension to this process and confirming the position of international intellectual sage it subsequently earned him. "What we call the political vocabulary of this age cannot serve the needs of this age. . . . Europe is no longer the center of the world," he pronounces in an interview.[3] We must rethink how we choose our leaders, he writes in "Notes on the House of Bondage" (1980), combining being "Uncle Jimmy" to his nieces and nephews with being a politically engaged intellectual who has frightening relevance for our moment, amid ongoing wars, humanitarian crises, terrorist attacks, and the white supremacist tenor of the 2016 U.S. presidential election and its aftermath.

Having spent the majority of his writing life abroad, in France (1948–57), Turkey (1961–71), and France again (1971–87), with diverse sojourns in between, Baldwin describes himself euphemistically as being uprooted and living in flux, a "transatlantic commuter, carrying my typewriter everywhere, from Alabama to Sierra Leone to Finland" (AD, 122). Yet he clarifies that he did not so much wish to leave his home country in 1948, as he was driven out of it by desperation, racism, poverty, and homophobia, not to mention the desire to become a writer. In 1961, between travels that later led him to Turkey, he tells Studs Terkel, "I never intended to come back to [the United States]" (JB, 19). As he writes in the introduction to his last volume of essays, *The Price of the Ticket* (1985), two decades later, "There was not, then, nor is there, now, a single American institution which is not a racist institution. . . . The architects of the American State . . . decided that the concept of Property was more important—more real—than the possibilities of the human being" (PT, xvii, xix).[4] That Baldwin made human beings and their possibilities central to his works is well known. What is not, however, is how the ideas of home and homelessness and the desire for domesticity have determined these possibilities for his characters as citizens, family and community members, and complex individuals, and how all these factors affected him as an author who made his life story as a black queer American who lived internationally integral to his craft.

A 1961 interview with Studs Terkel contains an early articulation of Baldwin's authorial interest in domesticity as he describes how the famous blues singer Bessie Smith became his creative inspiration during the early 1950s. As the opening bars of Smith's "Backwater Blues" flood the air, images and sounds of ceaseless rain swirl around the singer's persona stranded in her house like a prisoner of the elements, waiting and wailing for a boat to rescue her, "'Cause my house fell down and I can't live there no more."[5] Somewhat breathlessly, in his still younger-sounding voice, Baldwin emphasizes how much both the contents of Smith's blues songs and her way of performing them shaped his desire to be a writer, or to master and domesticate a certain idiom and delivery that were uniquely her own.[6] What he longed to do was channel them into his work as an artist of the word:

> The first time I [ever] heard this record was in Europe, and under very different circumstances than I had ever listened to Bessie in New York. [And] what struck me was that fact that ... she was singing ... about a disaster ... which had almost killed her, and she accepted it and was going beyond it.... [There's a] fantastic kind of understatement in it. *It's the way I want to write*.... When she says "My house fell down and I can't live there no more"—it's a great ... a great sentence. A great achievement.[7]

Rescued by a boat and left "upon some high old lonesome hill," Smith's persona looks over the watery landscape overtaking her collapsing house. Stranded along with "thousands of people ain't got no place to go," yet feeling all alone, shocked, and stuck, she sings her story's conclusion: "Backwater blues done call me to pack my things and go / ... Mmm, I can't move no more / Mmm, I can't move no more / There ain't no place for a poor old girl to go."

A somewhat similar scene, and one of the most striking examples illustrating how the desire for writing the way Smith sang of home stayed with Baldwin for decades, appears in his last novel, *Just above My Head* (1979), located in Harlem, the American South, and western Europe. Although narrated by a man, and with a black queer male artist at its center, it features a complex black woman, Julia Miller, who is key to the book's several braided plotlines and who embodies the story from Smith's "Backwater Blues."[8] A former child preacher prodigy, Julia is so spoiled by her parents, and especially her father's desire for the material profit she makes in the pulpit, that her sanctified-brat refusal to let her seriously ill mother see a doctor until it is too late costs the mother's life. Orphaned at fourteen, with her younger brother sent away to live with relatives in distant New Orleans, she is left alone with her cruel, alcoholic father, who rapes her, usurps her wages, and keeps her a virtual prisoner in their apartment.

Like that of Smith's blueswoman persona, Julia's disaster is of biblical proportions: it obliterates her home and almost kills her, too. And while the physical structure of Julia's house may be still standing, her home and body have been shattered forever.[9] The trauma she must hereafter carry changes her, turning her into a horror-stricken pillar of salt akin to Smith's flood survivor, who is left alone, immobilized, surveying the apocalyptic landscape of despair surrounding her:

> Home was not the place she wanted to go, or to be: but she had no place else to go. She walked slowly because she dreaded getting there.... She would endure... feeling like something struggling at the bottom of the sea.... With all her heart, she wanted to flee—she could not move.... She was sitting still, watching everything crumble, and disappear.... She had to move, and yet, she waited.... With all her heart, she wanted to flee—she could not move. She could not move and yet, she knew she must. Soon it would be too late, she would begin to die. (JAMH, 237–38, 240)

Julia's tragic story is told on multiple levels: through Baldwin's elegiac rewriting of Smith's lyrics, cadence, and imagery; by means of other characters' tales about her; and through kaleidoscopic narrative strategies that I return to in chapter 4.[10] It also illustrates what Cheryl A. Wall calls the "blues-inflected line" of African American literary tradition that "insinuates itself at the beat," but also creates a safe space of improvisation, where "singers like Bessie Smith can sing ahead or behind the beat."[11] Most important for my purposes, Julia's story revolves around a tragic loss of home and lifelong efforts to survive and heal the trauma of her childhood by traveling away from the United States and forging domestic spaces and modes of dwelling where she can be safe, find peace, and accept the narrative of her origins and forge a new life.

Standing at the core of Baldwin's epic last and unjustly underappreciated novel, Julia's story is among many throughout Baldwin's oeuvre that offer moving, profound, even revolutionary alternatives to traditional mid-twentieth-century models of black domesticity and stock images of white-picket-fenced homes in dominant American national culture. The majority of Baldwin's works, I argue, engage two powerfully interlinked themes related to this conundrum-riddled subject in the twentieth-century United States: the necessity to survive *away* from one's home and difficult childhood, and the desire to create *alternative* kinds of domesticity and modes of dwelling for black bodies that do not fit normative gender, sexual, familial, religious, or social roles and designs. Foregrounding these themes, we can trace their presence and variations throughout Baldwin's novels, plays, and essays. They gain particular urgency and momentum in the works he wrote following his Turkish decade, having settled in the South of France by 1971: *If Beale Street Could Talk* (1974), *The Devil Finds Work* (1976), the aforementioned *Just above My Head*, *The Evidence of Things Not Seen* (1985), and his last unpublished play, *The Welcome Table* (1987).

That underexplored period, which Baldwin spent in his last home in the Provençal village of St. Paul-de-Vence in France, is as important to his artistic trajectory as was the Turkish decade that preceded it. His prolific output, experimentation with literary genres and styles, and bold engagement with black musical forms during that time could all be deemed characteristics of "Late Baldwin."[12] That underappreciated incarnation arises from his complex, if not conflicted at times, interrogations of various models of black masculinity in *No Name in the Street*, through much bolder explorations of genres and gender, as well as racialized sexuality, in the two novels that followed, culminating in *The Welcome Table*, in which the main character, or his *porte-parole*, is a black queer female singer.[13] He also began to think of androgyny and nonbinary subjectivity as uniting aspects of identity for all Americans, and he preached these themes in his much-quoted late essay "Freaks and the American Ideal of Manhood" (1985; later retitled "Here Be Dragons"). These late aesthetics and thematic threads go hand in hand with the writer's autobiographical and autoethnographic explorations of homelessness and exile as a black queer artist who could find his place neither among those African American activists and artists who embraced heterosexist and patriarchal black nationalism or Afrocentrism (and for whom he cared a lot), nor among mainstream white elite establishments that gravitated toward postmodernism and later poststructuralism (for whom he cared little).[14] The 1980s mark Baldwin's sharp turn inward, away from American culture and politics, and especially toward performances of the feminine within and without the United States. To this reader, that introspective turn had as much to do with his interest in nonbinary gendered and raced sexual identity pervading his late works as with his glamorous black women friends—Josephine Baker,

Nina Simone, Florence Ladd, Bertice Reading, Vertamae Grosvenor—whose company he often enjoyed at his house. His close friendships with French women, and especially Yvonne Roux, the owner of La Colombe d'Or in St. Paul-de-Vence, and the actor Simone Singoret, who lived nearby and was his frequent guest and close companion, helped him craft complex portraits of women characters. Baldwin's late novels, along with essays such as "Freaks and the American Ideal of Manhood" or "To Crush the Serpent" (1987), reflect these inspirations and his desire for sophisticated, nonnormative, utopian domestic spaces, while building up nonbinary models of the self through an interrogation and frequent disavowal of both white models of gay identity and also black nationalism and politics of respectability.[15]

The works Baldwin wrote during that late period also offer bolder autobiographical revelations concerning circumstances of personal pain and authorial anguish, reflections on his early childhood and family home and deep conflict with his stepfather, whose abuse left enduring trauma. They refer in more intimate detail to his coming of age as a young, bisexual, lower-class artist in Harlem and Greenwich Village, and they document his search for writing havens and modes of dwelling first within and then outside of his home country. However transitory, those domestic spaces he recalls, reimagines, and alternatively forges within and eventually outside the United States helped Baldwin script a new story that could accommodate his complex authorial and private identities—what we might call "black queerness" today, but what Baldwin perceived simply as a sum of his multiple, strange selves ("all those strangers called Jimmy Baldwin") as a black American man who loved "some men and some women."[16]

Arguing for the necessity to consider *both* the author, his public persona, private experience, and self-perceptions, *and* his works, located within complex contexts that surround their making, publication, dissemination, and reception, this chapter further unpacks the key terms and theoretical concepts that animate this project. My readings of blackness and queerness, as well as terms like *home, house, domesticity, nation, individual, author, artist, imagination*, and *creative process*, arise from Baldwin's rich musings on the meanings of whiteness and blackness, domesticity and public space, individualism and national identity, all conceived against the Cold War and postcolonial, neocolonial, imperial, and transnational moments that provide the ever-changing backdrop for his works in the 1970s and 1980s. Inspired by how Baldwin's introduction to Lorraine Hansberry's autobiography, *To Be Young, Gifted, and Black*, links dramatic representation to phenomenological experience of the material world and its power structures, I prioritize the interpretive instructions of my archive, in which literary works and literal objects, places, and bodies are in constant conversation, while identities and their representations, manipulations, and metaphorical and material remnants constantly inform one another.

As Baldwin writes in "Sweet Lorraine" (1970), "In *Raisin*, black people recognized that house and all the people in it . . . and supplied the play with an interpretative element which could not be present in the minds of white people: a kind of claustrophobic terror, created not only by their knowledge of the house but by their knowledge of the streets" (xiii). "Claustrophobic terror" is the key "interpretative element" to understanding Hansberry's groundbreaking play, *A Raisin in the Sun* (1959), its title dramatizing Langston Hughes's poem "Dream Deferred."[17] Having seen the play performed and having inhabited Harlem's housing projects, Baldwin defines this terror autobiographically and artistically, as arising from black bodies' affective experience and knowledge of the structures, proscriptions, and punishments of state-controlled social spaces—what he names synecdochically the "house" and the "streets."

Black people's ability to "recognize . . . that house and all the people in it"—and that their homes provided no safety—shapes their sense of national identity and individual self. It "could not be present in the minds of white people," who live in the same national house, not because of essentialized notions of racial identity or intelligence on either side of the color line, but because the social organization of space reflects, normalizes, and reinforces the class-, gender-, and race-related hierarchies undergirding the state and, accordingly, marks people's lives with material consequences meted according to their epidermal hues. Imprinting twentieth-century U.S. spaces that African Americans have been allowed to occupy, exclusions from those they have not—like the family in Hansberry's *Raisin*—and determinism to be locked into some others, such as prisons, housing projects, or ghettoes, that "claustrophobic terror" overshadows Baldwin's characters in *Beale Street*; *Little Man, Little Man* (1976); and *Just above My Head*.[18]

Like Smith's song, Hansberry's play—"suffused with the light which was Lorraine" ("Sweet Lorraine," xiv)—signifies an important female influence, especially visible in Baldwin's second play, *Blues for Mister Charlie* (1964), which stages the American nation as a southern town, house, church, and courthouse, all cleaved into exclusionary black and white zones that encapsulate the nation's racial, class, gender, and psychosexual conflicts.[19] Echoing Smith's beat, Baldwin's *Blues* unpacks Hansberry's Black Arts manifesto, "that art has a purpose, and that its purpose . . . [is] action: that it contain[s] the 'energy that could change things'" ("Sweet Lorraine," xiv). Both Baldwin and Hansberry prove Édouard Glissant's conclusion in the U.S. context, that "there is no theater without a nation at its source."[20] Baldwin's notion of "claustrophobic terror," then, elucidates not only the national scene, but also the deeply fraught and dangerous condition befalling those African Americans who would be artists in the United States, where the "concept of art and artist has the effect . . . of isolating the artist from the people" ("Sweet Lorraine," xiii). This isolation for black artists is "absolutely fatal," Baldwin writes, for "as a black American citizen" s/he "needs the support of . . . community from which . . . all of the pressures of American life incessantly conspire to remove" her. Deploying the language of segregation, Baldwin links the artist's social alienation to the death of creativity, and, importantly, to the waning of democracy: "when he [*sic!*] is effectively removed, he falls silent—and the people have lost another hope" ("Sweet Lorraine," xiii).[21] Baldwin's vision of his home country and himself as a writer in exile has as its center a transformative power of black identity and art, the art descended from slaves who, against tremendous odds, embraced newness and turned their tragic fate into what Glissant terms "a new set of possibilities."

Baldwin's and Hansberry's legacies as towering twentieth-century national artists stand on solid literary foundations of Black Diaspora writing by, among many others, Olaudah Equiano, Phyllis Wheatley, Jupiter Hammond, William Wells Brown, Frederick Douglass, Harriet Jacobs, Frances Harper, W. E. B. Du Bois, Charles Chesnutt, Nella Larsen, and Zora Neale Hurston, among others. These literary ancestors penned home as a conflicted, often fatal, space for enslaved Africans and their descendants whose black bodies determined their fate as chattel or subject to racist codes, laws, prejudice, and violence. Much more explicitly than any of them, however, Baldwin and Hansberry grapple with the ways in which racialized gender and sexuality inform and inflect spatially contingent identity, and how they determine multiple inclusions and exclusions both within and without black home spaces, those of the nation, and the wider world.

When asked about his sexuality in Sedat Pakay's film *James Baldwin: From Another Place* (1973), Baldwin explains that he felt so profoundly alone and singled out during his youth that it seemed as if he had no mother and no father, as if he had "no antecedents." The next three sections explore the painful process of shaking off this metaphorical orphan status, of becoming James Baldwin and claiming and naming his identity, no matter how different from what was accepted "at home." It offers a vitrine view of a singular genius, a complex and often baffling human being who now bears the role of *the* ancestor and antecedent, and whose works construct a capacious home for us all.

"THE LONELIEST AND MOST BLACKLY DISTRUSTED OF MEN" VS. KEEPERS OF THE KEYS AND SEALS

> Voyageurs discover that the world can never be larger than the person that is in the world; but it is impossible to foresee this . . . to be warned. It is only when time has begun spilling through his fingers like water or sand—carrying away with it, forever, dreams, possibilities, challenges, and hopes—that the young man realizes that he will not be young forever. . . . As long as his aspirations are in the realm of the dream, he is safe; when he must bring them back into the world, he is in danger.
> —"The New Lost Generation"

> People of color have always theorized . . . in forms quite different from the western . . . abstract logic. . . . Our theorizing . . . is often in narrative forms, . . . stories we create, in riddles and proverbs, in the play with language, since dynamic rather than fixed ideas seem more to our liking. How else have we managed to survive with such spiritedness the assault on our bodies, social institutions, countries, our very humanity? . . . My folk . . . have always been a race for theory—though more in the form of the hieroglyph, a written figure that is both sensual and abstract, both beautiful and communicative.
> —Barbara Christian, "The Race for Theory"

Among the remnants salvaged from the house in St. Paul-de-Vence that I was fortunate enough to research and document in 2014, I came across images of Baldwin's face in a brown cardboard box labeled "J. B. Miscel. Posters Pictures, Etc. Hold." The label was written in pencil, in large underlined script and handwriting that could have been Baldwin's (or his younger brother's), though a wide strip of worn-out, semitransparent tape with red lettering obscured some of the writing.[22] Among other items, the box contained black-and-white photos of Baldwin's face that had been pasted on the outside and inside of a paper folder. There were other, unrelated photos, floating loosely inside the folder, which I carefully set aside.

The close-up of Baldwin's gleaming eyes on the folder's cover caught my attention. With his pores, wrinkles, and every hair of his eyelashes and eyebrows clearly visible, it was accompanied by a title written in French, "Entretien avec James Baldwin" (Interview with James Baldwin). There was no information about who performed that interview or when or where it took

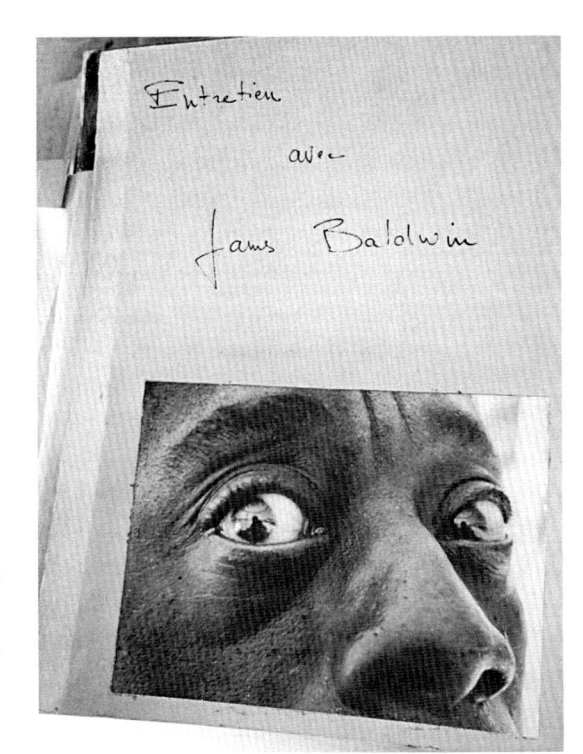

1.1. A folder with a photograph of Baldwin's eyes on the cover. Photo by author, 2014.

1.2. From the archive, the cut-up photos of Baldwin's face, within an open folder. Photo by author, 2014.

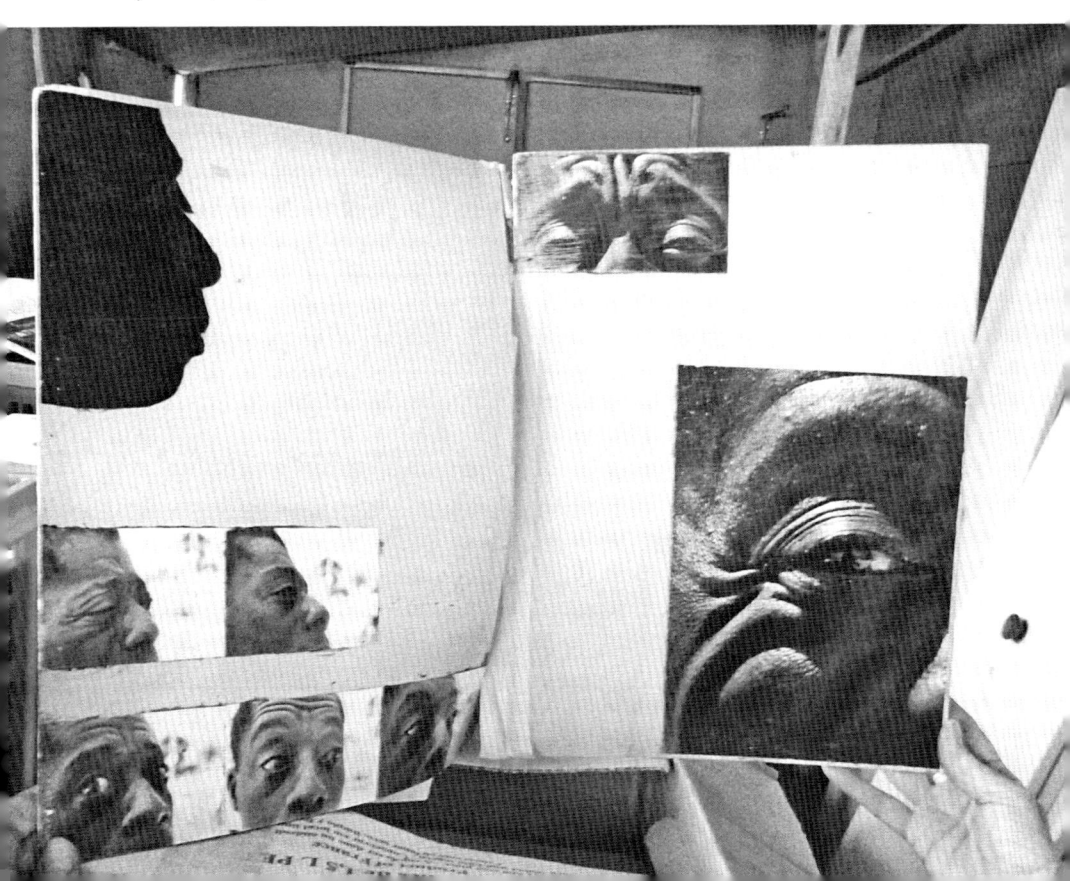

place.[23] Reflected in Baldwin's eyes in one photo is a blurry figure sitting across a table; he or she seems to be slightly inclined forward, and there is a bright spot to the left, perhaps indicating a window letting in daylight.

Inside the folder, on its left side, is a silhouette of Baldwin's face in profile, drawn in black ink. It looms over two rectangular strips of photos—the top one featuring two close-ups of the upper part of his face, and the bottom one with three similar close-ups. On the right side are two photos placed diagonally in corners: the top left one zooming centrally onto Baldwin's eyes and frowning forehead, the bottom right one framing his right eye centrally, and the topography of his partially visible face indicating that he might have been smiling or frowning. Whatever his eye reflects here cannot be discerned, but there is a dark shape in the eye featured in the bottom photograph. Fragmented in this way, the pieces of his physiognomy floating against the brown paper-bag-like hue of the folder, Baldwin appears as a disembodied, cut-up face enlarged for closer scrutiny.

This enigmatic project is all about his visage, which has been frequently photographed and extensively described, his large, protruding, expressive eyes its central feature. Convinced that he was ugly, given how often his stepfather battered him with statements on his looks, the writer was self-conscious about his appearance, swishy walk, and queer mannerisms, though he also learned how to use his physiognomy and hand gestures to great effect while speaking. In Pakay's film, there is a moment when we see Jimmy against the background of Taksim Square, his expression questioning and slightly worried, and then, having heard something from the person to whom that expression was directed, he suddenly breaks into his broad, gorgeous smile, and the whole scene brightens. That is the way Pakay saw Baldwin and wanted his viewers to apprehend and admire him. There are few such tender depictions of the writer captured by American photographers and filmmakers, for whom it seems as though he is a composition of fragmented blackness rather than a whole, complete person—a study in African features, a mask, an image, a visage as a cipher of difference.[24]

With these images of face/façade in mind, consider the insidious names Baldwin has been called regarding his racialized sexuality, some of which he supplies in an essay that clarifies that, during his youth, "the operative word was *faggot*, and, later, pussy, but those epithets really had nothing to do with the question of sexual preference: You were being told simply that you had no balls" ("Here Be Dragons," in PT, 681). In light of his late-life articulations of nonbinary identity, it seems clear why Baldwin did not embrace "queer" as a term or label for himself, though it was in popular use during his youthful years in Greenwich Village in the 1940s, as George Chauncey documents in *Gay New York* and Harold Norse in *Memoirs of a Bastard Angel*, prefaced by Baldwin.[25] As much as he did not like being labeled—he endured a particularly despised and well-known label of "Negro writer"—Baldwin also resisted the term "gay," which was widely employed in the 1980s, but which he did not feel resonated with his background or experience.[26]

Recalling his June 1984 interview with Baldwin for *The Village Voice*, the journalist Richard Goldstein remembers the writer in a brief introduction to a 2014 reprint of their conversation. Part of the Stonewall generation, who identified as gay and rallied for the civil rights of those who embraced same-sex desire in the 1970s, Goldstein describes their meeting as "the most powerful experience of my professional life." They met at the Riviera Café in the Village, "an old hangout" for Baldwin, and spoke frankly about matters relating to race, sexuality, and gay politics. Twenty years his junior, Goldstein sees Baldwin as a scarred survivor and sage, "a man who traced much of his acuity and pain to the nexus of racism and homophobia" (JB, 57). At the same time, he sees in him an intriguing combination of contradictory aspects: someone out of place, strange, yet strangely irresistible.

That experience of first encountering the writer, whose fiction was for him an "early vector of self-discovery," leads Goldstein to wonder if Baldwin has shed some of his Americanness, noting the way the man across the table is "watching the [local] exotica with that faintly distracted look Europeans cultivate." Echoing the impressions of many who met this charismatic figure in person, he adds, "What I remember most about that afternoon is the sight of Baldwin, gnomelike and far from serene, surrounded by passersby who recognize him, and just wanted to say, as I did, how full of him our lives will always be" (JB, 57). In his late years, Baldwin appears not only un-American, and thus out of place in the city of his birth, but also ill at ease and somewhat disturbed physically—shriveled in body and vulnerable, even while still projecting demigod power.

When asked about his sexual identity, Baldwin immediately notes the limits—indeed the *claustrophobia*—of available vocabulary: "We're trapped in language, of course. But 'homosexual' is not a noun. At least not in my book.... Perhaps [it is] a verb. You see, I can only talk about my own life. I loved a few people and they loved me. It had nothing to do with these labels. Of course, the world has all kinds of words for us. But that's the world's problem" (JB, 71). While some might say that he skirts the issue, or refuses to lend support to an important political movement that has embraced him as a forefather, what Baldwin is doing here is refusing to be theorized as

1.3. Chez Baldwin archive: Baldwin's caricature by David Levine.

much as refusing to have his desire and sexual acts labeled by someone else. In his stubborn insistence to be named "by myself, and myself only," Baldwin chooses his singular life story, his individual right to privacy, and the idiosyncrasy of his desire and sexual object choice, or "going the way your blood beats" as the only directive of whom to love or have sex with.[27] In this sense, he anticipates what in 1988, just a year after his passing, Barbara Christian declares as her black feminist method in "The Race for Theory," the fusing of language, knowledge, and semantics with subjective feelings, sensations, and affect that all inflect the body: "whatever I feel/know *is* . . . sensuality is intelligence . . . sensual language is language that makes sense."[28]

A year after the interview with Goldstein, in his *Playboy* essay "Freaks," Baldwin writes about finding himself in the "gay world," continuing his earlier meditation on terminology. Recalling his youth, when "the condition that is now called gay was . . . called queer," he claims that everywhere he went, he was deemed dangerous because of what others saw and sought in him as a black male: "I certainly had no desire to harm anyone, nor did I understand how anyone could look at me and supposed me physically capable

64 CHAPTER ONE

of *causing* any harm." He seemed a collective threat rolled into one slight body: "Men chased me, saying I was a danger to their sisters. I was thrown out of cafeterias and rooming houses because I was 'bad' for the neighborhood" (PT, 681–82).

Having had some bad relationships with racially curious "white girls" in the Village, which he dismisses as exploitative, he relates how "a friend found me—an Italian, about five years older than I, who helped my morale greatly in those years. I was told that he had threatened to kill anyone who touched me." Confirming, without naming it, the mundane designation interracial "bisexuality," the teenage Baldwin learns about sexual fluidity and power in gender relationships, as "our relationship never seemed to worry him or his friends or his women" (PT, 686). Describing his sexual history obliquely, without once labeling himself, his sex acts, or lovers, Baldwin shows how the aforementioned "gay world" exists as a separate entity in which he inadvertently "found himself," rather than a familiar space in which he willingly participated.

Two directives on sexual nomenclature from "Freaks" make clear why Baldwin's sexual ethics disallowed labels. Favoring Whitmanesque multiplicity and fluidity, first, "the object of one's hatred is never . . . conveniently outside but is seated in one's lap, stirring in one's bowels and dictating the beat of one's heart. And if one does not know this, *one risks becoming an imitation—and, therefore, a continuation—of principles one imagines oneself to despise*." Second, explaining why he never tried psychoanalysis, "it seems to me that *anyone who felt seriously that I had any desire to be 'adjusted' to this society had to be ill*; too ill, certainly . . . to be trusted" (PT, 686–88, emphases added). As an outsider whose blackness and sissy mannerisms make him excessively conspicuous, he has as little power over hegemonic terminologies as he does over how people see or classify him, and what they call him.[29] Yet he also gains knowledge unavailable to other participants in the same society: "I sensed, then—without being able to articulate it—that this dependence on a formula for safety, signaled a desperate moral abdication" or what he calls "the spiritual famine of American life" (PT, 688).[30]

Like Whitman, Thoreau, even Emerson, and later Wells, Petry, and Hurston, Baldwin chooses, somewhat romantically perhaps, an identity that is nearly anarchic when compared to omnipresent and stifling cultural norms in white and black. He elects life closely examined, and a sexuality that means more than "what comes naturally," that is an enigma until you come across it as located and embodied, for like love, desire is, he insists in "To Crush the Serpent," "where you find it." This approach stands at the center of Baldwin's humanistic project focused on persistent analysis of "the state and possibilities of the human being in whom the awakening of desire fuels imagination and in whom imagination fuels desire." Praising "imagination ... [as] perpetually required to examine, control, and redefine reality, of which *we must assume ourselves to be the center and the key*," Baldwin also gestures at claustrophobia "inherent in the limited space claimed by religious, sexual, or racial exclusivity" (PT, 678, emphasis added).[31]

His distaste for mindless sex—"There is nothing more boring ... than sexual activity as an end in itself, and a great many people who came out of the closet should reconsider"—reveals what may seem a puritanical streak. Yet, given that he was never in the closet, that he pursued sex with gusto, and was a diva and queen in his own right, this statement may signal yet another public performance of, and inherent contradiction within, his authorial persona (PT, 688–89).[32] The late Baldwin writes about his sexual coming of age with candor, without posturing, in his last published essay, "To Crush the Serpent," which juxtaposes sexual desire with fundamentalist Christianity, and elucidates teenage James's choice to "walk disorderly," or remain friends with a boy who "backslid" and with whom he was in love (CR, 162–63). The essay brands the national house—"the [black] minister and the sheriff were hired by the Republic to keep the Republic white"—as the guardian of racial purity, for blackness is synonymous with outlawed sex acts, miscegenation, and sin. The result is that white people may celebrate coming out as gay, as many did at the time, while people of color remain hunted by the state that criminalizes all aspects of their life, especially, Baldwin emphasizes, by attacking "the sexual possibility" and making "the possibility of the private life as fugitive as that of a fleeting nigger" (162).

This statement contextualizes another one from the earlier "Freaks," whose philosophical and prophetic elaboration manifests Baldwin's awareness of performativity inherent in gender and sexuality.[33] Taking on Boy George, Baldwin suggests that his model of black queer imagination not only is capacious enough for all kinds of androgynous play, if not trans identities, but also arises in stark opposition to what he defines as the American heteronormative "rage for order":

> Such figures as Boy George do not disturb me nearly so much as do those relentlessly hetero (sexual?) *keepers of the keys and seals*, those who know what the world needs in the way of order and who are ready and willing

1.4. (*opposite*) Chez Baldwin archive: Loose photos of Baldwin, Hassell, and friends. Photo by author, 2014.

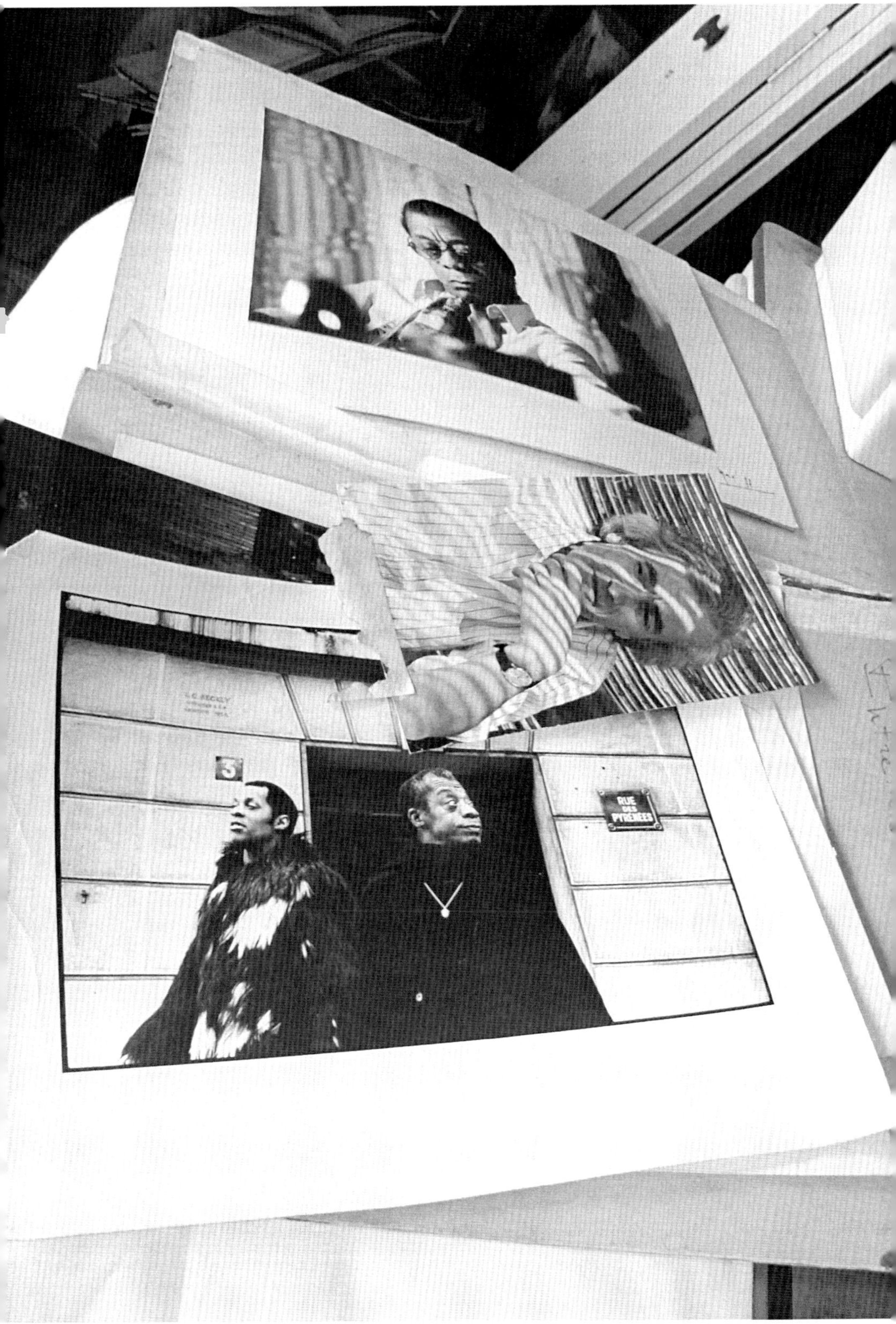
3
RUE DES PYRÉNÉES

to supply that order.... *This rage for order can result in chaos, and in this country, chaos connects with color....* All that noise is about *America, as the dishonest custodian of black life and wealth*; the blacks, especially males, in America; and the burning, buried American guilt; and sex and sexual roles and sexual panic; money, success and despair—to all of which may now be added the bitter need to find a head on which to place the crown of Miss America. (PT, 689, emphases added)

Sex, gender, and race cannot be uncoupled from national identity and economics just as black bodies' arrival on these shores cannot be uncoupled from them, and just as the continued black-white divide in idiom, experience, and history deeply mars the country that is more concerned with pageants than poverty, education, or hunger.

The racist rage for mythical order in the American national house also precludes, limits, and stifles the kinds of imagination and desire that Baldwin finds central to humanistic art. His essay, therefore, does not so much target the presumed "freaks" of its original title, as it does the manic, and truly freakish, ways in which the U.S. state and its cultural and social apparatuses handle and render safe, categorize, name, and thus manage and contain, all that they fear and cannot understand: "sex . . . sexual roles . . . sexual panic; money, success and despair." Referring implicitly to the first black Miss America of 1984, Vanessa Williams, who was stripped of her title and publicly shamed for having appeared in mixed-race homoerotic photographs, Baldwin hints at yet another woman's story confirming his reading of the U.S. psychosexual landscape, where black bodies are indispensable, yet are continually hunted down, threatened, traded, displayed, and reviled.[34]

Having dubbed himself the "aging, lonely, sexually dubious, politically outrageous, unspeakably erratic freak" in *No Name in the Street* in 1972, Baldwin had every right to be impatient that no one was paying attention to his changing vocabulary and grammar of American identities (NNS, 18).[35] He did not pay much heed himself, however, to how black activists and artists like Essex Hemphill, Joseph Beam, and Max C. Smith defined love among male African Americans: definitions that point to the spatial contingencies of then current nomenclature, such as the "gay black men," who live in predominantly white gay communities; and the "black gay men," who "view our racial heritage as primary and frequently live inverted, 'bisexual front lives' within Black neighborhoods."[36] The phrase "bisexual front lives" resonates in the context of Baldwin's frequent rhetorical references in his speeches and interviews to the heteronormative family, as in his conversation with Nikki

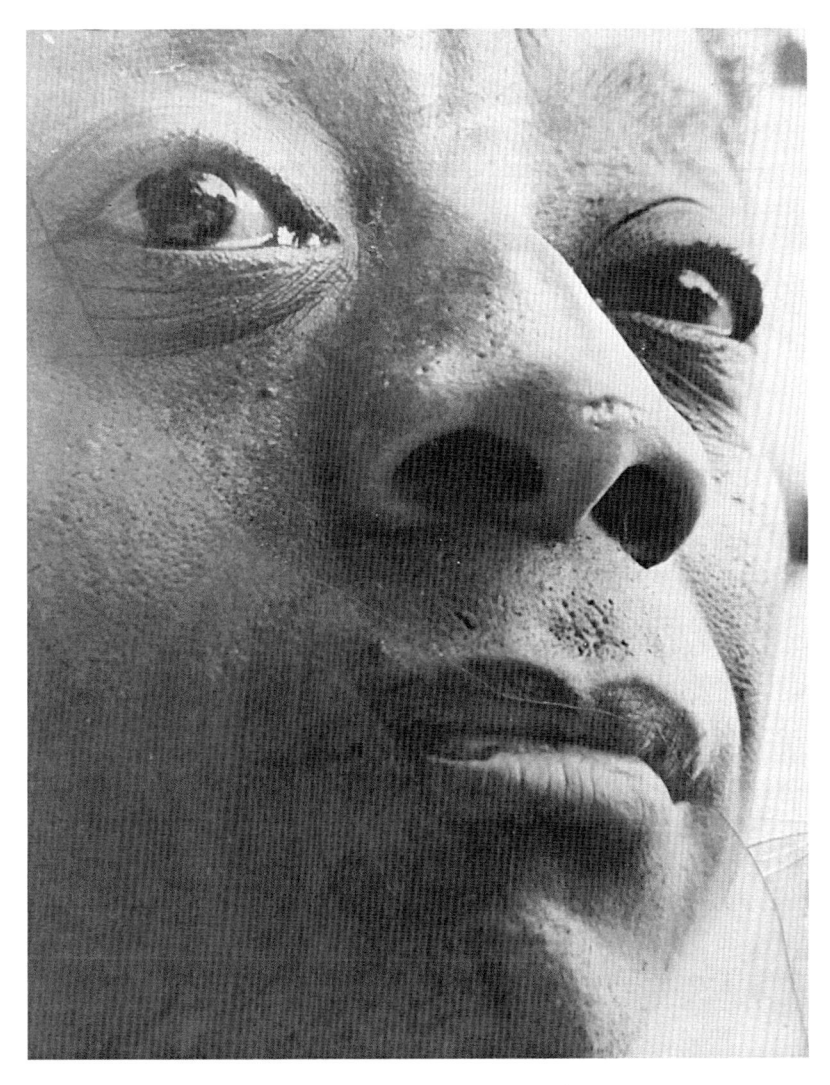

1.5. Chez Baldwin archive: James Baldwin's photograph, close-up. Photo by author, 2014.

Giovanni, later published as *A Dialogue* (1973).³⁷ Although they shared some physical similarities, not to mention a passion for literature, Baldwin did not engage with Hemphill or comment on the AIDS epidemic either. There may be multiple reasons for this silence, chief among them his ailing health and steady decline as the 1980s progressed.³⁸ Another, as Dagmawi Woubshet argues in *The Calendar of Loss* (2015), had to do with the fact that many black intellectuals thought of AIDS not as an isolated calamity, but rather "one in a series . . . that characterized their people and their country."³⁹

Black gays, gay Blacks, and black queers certainly needed an ancestor during his lifetime and Baldwin, albeit reluctantly at times, filled that role well, and he continues to do so to this day. He has been claimed as an important ancestral figure by the gay movement, and later queer studies, both of which have been coded white and see his second novel, *Giovanni's Room* (1956), as their foundational literary text, despite its explicit linking of whiteness with racism and homophobia.⁴⁰ Perhaps today Baldwin could serve as an anarchic, androgynous, maternal/paternal figure not only to these self-identified groups but also to all those queer and trans people who might embrace him as a pioneer of androgyny and label-free identities, like Janet Mock does in *Redefining Realness* (2014). In "Freaks," Baldwin theorizes, famously, what seems to be his final, all-encompassing vision of fluid identity and individualism where "each of us, helplessly and forever, contains the other—male in female, female in male, white in black, and black in white" (PT, 690).⁴¹ We are family.

Baldwin's notions of identity evolved alongside his late-life self-presentation as an increasingly feminine, or fashioned as androgynous, black queer man who wore silk scarves and jewelry. He cut a figure that may have seemed unmanly to some gay Blacks and black gays. In "Brother to Brother: Words from the Heart" (1989), a highly stylized rewriting of Martin Luther King Jr.'s "I Have a Dream" speech, Joseph Beam discusses masculinity by describing how the divided black gay and gay black communities are separating themselves not only from women but also from the realm of the domestic, by defining their space as *unlike* that of black women:

> We have few traditions like those of black women. No kitchen tables. . . . No intimate spaces in which to explore our feelings of love and friendship. No books like *The Color Purple*. We gather in public places: barber shops, bars, lodges, fraternities, and street corners, places where bravado rather than intimacy are the rule. We assemble to *do* something rather than *be* with each other. We can talk about the Man, but not about how we must constantly vie with one another for the scant crumbs thrown

our way. We can talk about dick and ass and pussy, but not ... competition for too few jobs and scholarships. We can talk about sporting events ... but not about how we are pitted, one against the other, as permanent adversaries.[42]

Beam's critique of black masculinity targets, at the same time as it embraces, its performances of power and anger—men must assert themselves regardless of sexual object choice. Hence, "My body contains as much anger as water. It is the material from which I have built my house ... blood red bricks that cry in the rain. . . . It is the face and posture I show the world," and such a performance of black masculinity also guarantees that "*I cannot go home as who I am.*"[43] This approach clearly resonates with Baldwin's own in *No Name in the Street* and "Freaks." I have no idea whether Beam had read them, though it seems reasonable to assume that he did, given his admiration for the older writer.[44] While Baldwin's *Just above My Head* could have served well Beam's communities of men, this book and its author may have made some of them uncomfortable, not by bemoaning the lack of kitchen tables, but by embracing women and their worlds and letting them transform his own, by having welcome tables open to anybody.[45]

While the jury may still be out on what to name Baldwin's complex sexual persona, for the sake of clarity throughout this project, I use the term "black queer" as I did in *James Baldwin's Turkish Decade: Erotics of Exile* (2009), or "bisexual" where needed.[46] My terminology harkens back to the groundbreaking *Black Queer Studies* (2005) volume, edited by Mae Henderson and E. Patrick Johnson, and its recent offspring, Johnson's *No Tea, No Shade* (2016), that insists on scholars of black queer studies embodying "the signifyin(g) tradition of African American arts and criticism—that of repetition and revision with a critical difference," as well as Siobhan B. Somerville's important early articulation of that tradition in *Queering the Color Line* (2000) and Roderick Ferguson's of the queer of color critique in *Aberrations in Black* (2003).[47] Recalling my favorite foundational definition of "queer" by Eve Sedgwick, Sara Ahmed's *Willful Subjects* (2014) excavates its etymology in the "Indo-European word 'twerk,' to turn or to twist, also related to the word 'thwart,' to transverse, perverse, or cross."[48] In *Queer Phenomenology* (2006), Ahmed also casts sexual orientation in relation to geography and location, as being about "feeling at home," considering "the work of inhabitance" part of queer experience.[49]

Queers and their ancestors by any other name have lived in houses and created families for as long as the rest of humanity, but as scholars have not paid much attention to this phenomenon, Baldwin's insertion of his sexual history, domestic practices, and representations of household into his works amounts to a pioneering, prophetic, revolutionary act.[50] Black queerness develops throughout his oeuvre as an ontological and epistemological process and project, mapping black male progression from childhood and adolescence, through adulthood, and middle age, with his poems, *Jimmy's Blues* (1985), anticipating the wisdom of old age. From *Go Tell It on the Mountain* (1953), whose teenage John Grimes confronts his homoerotic desire while traversing the spaces of home, street, and church, and who encounters cinema, masturbation, and love for a fellow parishioner, we move to *Giovanni's Room* (1956) and *Another Country* (1962), which interrogate hetero- and homosexual mores among men, and their experience and negotiations of gendered whiteness and blackness within diverse class systems and the expatriate and immigrant communities of Paris, New York City, and the American South.

Written in Turkey, *Tell Me How Long the Train's Been Gone* (1968) probes the inner life of an aging, uprooted, black bisexual actor caught up in a triangle of desire with a young, black male revolutionary and a white actress—their bodies and memories of his struggle with the racist American stage his only semblance of home. Tracing the lives of several African American men from childhood through middle age, *Just above My Head* celebrates black queer domestic desire where explicit sex and cooking rituals provide seductive alternatives to normative spaces and traditions of middle-class black families. As his later works demonstrate, Baldwin enmeshes affect with the politics of social space, and posits unexpected, nonnormative identities as generative and revolutionary so as to revise the ways in which domestic and national spaces are conceived, represented, and articulated. Inspired by Melvin Dixon, who traces in Baldwin a tension between "love" and "shelter," I see him deploying his multivalent concept of "love" rather than the American clichéd pursuit of happiness—as it requires more work, strength, and a leap of faith; he privileges "shelter" rather than one nation under god—as it requires familial collaboration and compromise in the face of conflict rather than the dogma of unity enforced by churches and armies. In short, his project is rewriting and repopulating both the national house and the intimate private home where sexual outlaws find shelter.

Baldwin's works help us articulate and redefine how sex, race, gender, and domicile construct an indispensable prism for the politics of home in our twenty-first century filled with new queer possibilities and political

1.6 and 1.7. Books from the Chez Baldwin archive: Altman and Goodwin. Photos by author, 2014.

dangers.[51] As a corpus of literature documenting evolving artistic practice and resulting aesthetics, they also script an ethics that interweaves a fascinating journey of self-discovery with a complex critique of national house enmeshed in complex relationships with the wider, interconnected world.

"[ME] HAS ALWAYS BEEN A LITTLE PAINFUL," OR EVERYTHING IS PERSONAL

> I think my exile saved my life . . . it . . . confirmed something which Americans appear to have great difficulty accepting. Which is, simply, this: *a man is not a man until he's able and willing to accept his own vision of the world, no matter how radically this vision departs from that of others*. . . . This country resembles nothing so much as the grimmest of popularity contests. . . . It puts a premium on mediocrity and has all but slaughtered any concept of excellence. This corruption begins in the private life and unfailingly flowers in the public life.
> —"The New Lost Generation" (emphasis added)

Baldwin's international movements and habitations shaped his life and vision of himself, and they also inflected his dynamic outlook on the United States and its national mythologies.[52] Rather than explicitly naming the U.S. condition as immaturity or perpetual adolescence, the way D. H. Lawrence does in *Studies in Classic American Literature* (1923), Baldwin's essay "The New Lost Generation" (1961) instead links African American and European attitudes to white American culture, stating that they "refer to Americans as children . . . and for the same reason: they mean that Americans have so little experience—experience referring not to *what* happens, but to *who*—that they have no key to the experience of others." While this conclusion explains American exceptionalism and its underbelly of systemic racism, discrimination, and genocidal conquest, it also gestures at the impossibility of attaining a stable identity for individuals comprising the people. Baldwin concludes that his own greatest lesson in Europe has been "the sanction to become oneself. . . . No artist can survive without this acceptance." The American house precludes the attainment of artistic freedom for writers of color, as much as it does that of true self. One must leave the "house of bondage" thus designed; however, having done that, one becomes "upon his return to his own country, the loneliest and most blackly distrusted of men" (PT, 313).

Much aware of this paradoxical situation throughout the 1960s, by the 1970s Baldwin writes, "The mind is a strange and terrible vehicle, moving according to rigorous rules of its own; and my own mind . . . began to move backward in time, to places, people, and events I thought I had forgotten. Sorrow drove it there, I think, sorrow, and a certain kind of bewilderment" (NNS, 10–11). Referring to a period of depression after the murder of Martin Luther King Jr. in 1968, and his subsequent decision to leave Turkey, these words from the opening pages of *No Name in the Street* also mark a retrospective turn in his writing whose objective was a reassessment of black masculinity in the aftermath of the Civil Rights Movement and of his experience as a writer against the background of the U.S. national house.

Combining introspection with a focus on public self-representation as an aging black man, this volume also reflects his renewed interest in gender roles, constructs, and performances, spurred partially by his bashing by Black Power proponents, especially Eldridge Cleaver, and the rise of black feminism, some of whose main spokespersons, like Maya Angelou, Florence Ladd, and Toni Morrison, were his close friends. His 1970s conversations with the anthropologist Margaret Mead (published as *A Rap on Race* in 1971) and with the Black Arts poet and feminist Nikki Giovanni (in *A Dialogue*) provide rich contexts for his recollections of female ancestry in *No Name in the Street*, which are important to understanding his critique of American national identity in relationship to his embrace of himself as an artist and black queer man.

His former-slave grandmother, Barbara, and mother, Berdis, feature prominently in the opening pages of *No Name in the Street*, acting as direct inspirations, masterly users of signification through the metaphorics of fabric, sewing, spools, thread, and stitching, for young James's choice of vocation as the "artist of the word."[53] These women, along with his elementary school teacher, signify further important inspirations for Baldwin's gospel of all-embracing kinship—his recognition not only of shared humanity with people of all epidermal hues, but also of his own uniqueness as a person like no other. When he insists on being "defined . . . by myself, and myself only," he thus articulates both his childhood lessons gleaned from women and, however ironically, one of the key tenets (if not clichés) of Americanness, *individualism*, signaling all the while how embracing this idea was precisely what caused his irrevocable exile from home, and his subsequent entrapment in the legend of queer blackness and intellectual notoriety.

As David Adams Leeming, Baldwin's biographer, explains, Baldwin's sense of himself by the early 1970s, when "white Americans were complaining of his 'ingratitude,' and the black militants appeared to assume that he was playing up to them so as to be welcomed 'home,'" was yet again caught up in claustrophobic binaries. He felt trapped between "'the white fantasy' and the 'black fantasy,'" complaining poignantly to his younger brother, "Have you ever known me to kiss ass?"[54] Stubbornly clinging to his critique of identity, or what I term "black queer humanism," Baldwin crafts idiom and imagery that have irrevocably changed not only American but also international cultural and literary vocabularies on subjectivity, social space, and narrative representations of individuality, as his literary and intellectual projects have now traveled, in translation and as originals, not to mention by YouTube, throughout the world. Beginning with a revision of the myth of the American national house, Baldwin also crafts an authorial home for his alternative and ultra-individualistic (if not black queer exceptionalist) vision of twentieth-century African Americans, whom he posits as key to his humanist salvation project, or what in "To Crush the Serpent" he identifies as an alternative to religious faith: "Salvation . . . [seen as] not separation . . . the beginning of union with all that is or has been or will ever be."[55]

Baldwin refashions this vision of salvation, rooted in his childhood's Pentecostal and Baptist traditions, by means of secular ideas of equality, community, safety, and freedom of erotic desire and sexual choice. His new faith transcends national borders and rises up like a building: "a mighty fortress, even in the teeth of ruin or at the gates of death." Baldwin's edifice—individualism combined with cosmopolitanism—is necessary to confront American and western histories of violence: "The burning of the witch, the heretic, the Jew, the nigger, the faggot—have always failed to redeem . . . the mob."[56] Thus encapsulating European and American histories of slavery, religious and gender-based persecution, the Holocaust, Jim Crow lynchings, and violence against sexual minorities, this provocative essay also recasts his life writing, making clear that Baldwin arrived at his spiritually and erotically infused humanism by reappropriating and re-creating, and indeed by disidentifying from, the dominant idioms he denounced on both sides of the color line. As he concludes, "Complexity is our only safety and love is the only key to our maturity. And love is where you find it."[57] Coming two years after "Freaks," also in *Playboy*, "To Crush the Serpent" confirms Baldwin's commitment to radically rewriting the stories of (private) domestic life and (public) national history by placing black nonheterosexual bodies at the narrative center of the world he created in his works.

We can see the workings of this vision on the national scale in the conclusion of his essay "The Price of the Ticket," which offers one of the most poignant comments on the rhetoric of Manifest Destiny—that ur-script of domestic nationalism—in twentieth-century American letters. In it, Baldwin puts in conversation transatlantic journeys and literary traditions that have often been seen as incompatible. In a passage that considers the "real reasons for [the white American's] journey," he muses on the simultaneous interrelatedness and divergence of transatlantic slavery and immigration within the racialized vision of the national house: "I know very well that my ancestors had no desire to come to this place: but neither did the ancestors of the people who became white and who require of my captivity a song. They require of me a song less to celebrate my captivity than to justify their own" (PT, xx).[58]

In a 1980 interview, Baldwin declares, "'Manifest Destiny' in the United States is simply a way of saying, we have the right to slaughter everything in our path, because it is obvious that we will control this part of the world, *so that I became a thing, my father became a thing, and the Indian became a corpse*."[59] The followers of historical materialism, even Marx himself, could not have put the centuries of slavery, oppression, and systemic Native American genocide, driven by greed and attendant racism, eugenics, and man-made ideologies of white supremacy—they often join hands, as Baldwin reminds us—more succinctly.[60] Connecting the tragic fates of African slaves and their descendants to the Native American genocide, Baldwin puts bodies of color and their destruction at the center of the American nation-building project, thus facing squarely on, decades ago, what Mark Rifkin describes as the persistent critical deferment of the "discussion of the ways domestic space is constructed and maintained through a persistent institutionalized violence against the prior inhabitants of the land and an erasure of their varied modes of occupancy."[61] The various histories of passage and arrival in the New World that Baldwin enumerates in "The Price of the Ticket" clearly arise from his statement about Manifest Destiny as a license to kill off indigenous populations and enslave Africans, while also anticipating Rifkin's statement and some recent scholarly discourses in immigrant and Native American studies.[62]

Baldwin's condemnation of American exceptionalism echoes in more recent scholarly efforts to "develop a language of mixture and migration capable of decentering idealized versions of the United States constellated around an image of it as geographically and culturally enclosed."[63] In *The Evidence of Things Not Seen*, Baldwin puts it more bluntly: "The doctrine of White Supremacy... translated itself into the doctrine of Manifest Destiny, having returned to Europe... like a plague... infests all the cities of Europe—is all that now unites the so-called Old World with the so-called New." Such a geopolitical order has spatial and historical implications, as it "places the African American in a stunning and vertiginous place" (ETNS, 93–94). Being so positioned allows for an unobstructed view of the centuries of power relationships that have constituted the so-called West, which "quite fails to see the unforgivable enormity of Hiroshima" as a logical result of its history that has been "a hymn to White people" while "all us others have been *discovered*" (81, 82): "Neither the Europeans nor the Americans are able to recognize that they . . . enslaved each other before they attempted a passage to India, or hoisted sail for Africa. And all that has united Europe, as Europe, or Europe and America, until today, is not the color White but what they perceive as the color Black. They do not care about each other . . . never have . . . it is inconceivable that they ever will" (81).

The fact that not many readers or critics appreciated the radical boldness of this message during Baldwin's lifetime makes it clear that they were not ready to renounce the cozy binaries and myths of Americanness. In "Notes on the House of Bondage," he speaks about the "fall of . . . the so-overextended Western empire" (PT, 673), as he also recognizes capitalist continuities in globalization and domestic and international politics. His words about the "charged, dangerous moment, when everything must be re-examined, must be made new; when nothing at all can be taken for granted" (PT, 674) refer to a sense of history that few Americans possessed then, and perhaps even fewer possess now. Baldwin's idea of the national and global houses envisions humanity as constituting a family, no matter that "our former guides and masters are among the most ruthless creatures in mankind's history, slaughtering and starving one another to death long before they discovered the blacks" (PT, 674). In *Evidence*, having teased out of his geopolitical musings a vision of diasporic solidarity, he still evidences hope—"We are only, now, beginning to recover . . . out of the most momentous diaspora in human memory, to rediscover and recognize each other"—as he calls for all Others to enact a demolition of the "morality . . . [and] definitions, of the Western world" (83).

Baldwin's loneliness as a prophet crying out in the wilderness of his home country took its toll. Practically on his deathbed, he confesses to Quincy Troupe, "I don't see anything in American life . . . to aspire to. . . . It's all so very false . . . shallow, so plastic, so morally and ethically corrupt" (JB, 105). Baldwin certainly did not fancy himself an Ishmael, but as far as his country was concerned, that is where he ended up at the close of his career and his too-short writing life. Finally catching up to him, the international black queer prophet, we hear his words echo in Stuart Hall's invocation of the new politics of diaspora: "The future belongs to those who are ready to take in a bit of the other, as well as being what they themselves are. . . . It is because their history and ours is so deeply and profoundly and inextricably intertwined that racism exists."⁶⁴ As Baldwin writes in "Notes on the House of Bondage," such an approach is necessary because the American national story remains the same: "The real impulse of the bulk of the American people toward their former slave is lethal: if he cannot be used, he should be made to disappear. When the American people . . . revile the Haitian, Cuban, Turk, Palestinian, Iranian, they are really cursing the nigger, and the nigger had better know it" (PT, 669).

To Baldwin, the knowledge of the tragic loss of black Americans' ancestral home and of their resilience and survival in the New World and the diaspora stands at the heart of what the national house is and means. That deep and complex history is its cornerstone and narrative foundation, no matter how repressed, denied, or covered up by happy façades.⁶⁵ It evokes a sense of a common language and story in a country where a quarter of its presidents were slaveholders, and African Americans were held as chattel in the tellingly named White House, which they had also built.⁶⁶ As Baldwin writes, "White Americans have been one another's jailers for generations, and the attempt at individual maturity is the loneliest and rarest of the American endeavors" (PT, 672–73). At the same time, he celebrates the resilience of black people: "The irreducible miracle is that we have sustained each other a very long time, and come a long, long way together. We have come to the end of a language and we are now about the business of forging a new one. For we have survived, children, the very last white country the world will ever see" (PT, 675). Baldwin's mantra concerning the end of whiteness domestically and globally originates already in the 1950s, with "Stranger in the Village" (1953), and stands at the heart of his project of centering African American identity in his home country as much as in the wider world.

WHO DID HE LOVE? WHO LOVES HIM? LITERARY INFLUENCES AND LEGACIES

> Brother,
> just between me and you
> tell me if it's true!
>
> They say
> silence brings no anguish
> where only silence lives:
> negatives,
> affirmatives.
> —"Ballad (for Yoran)"

As if paraphrasing Baldwin's words that open the documentary *The Price of the Ticket*—"There are days . . . when you wonder what your role is in this country, and what your future is in it"—Joseph Beam's short essay "Making Ourselves from Scratch" describes how he "clings to [his desk and typing table] as if for sanity" and disguises himself every day as a black, gay man, "donning the costume that alleges my safety."[67] The private space of the home, though not free from the politics of the outside, seems the only place of safety. While describing the objects that fill his office space in Atlanta, Kevin Young justifies that "writers need their totems, their altars," and Colson Whitehead explains needing to "keep up the hunt by moving my desk around . . . looking for a mojo spot . . . you know it's there, but it's invisible."[68] Like these two younger men, Baldwin, too, had his inner writing sanctum in St. Paul-de-Vence, filled with objects he cherished. It allowed him privacy to work as well as proximity to the rest of his household, where his entourage lived and where he socialized with guests and visitors.

Written in that study at the back of the house, Baldwin's introduction to *The Price of the Ticket* begins with words from an old gospel song: "My soul looks back and wonders how I got over," followed by a statement on origins: "I find it unexpectedly difficult to remember, in detail, how I got started" (PT, ix). Baldwin is referring to his craft of writing, but he also casts a shadow over his early life and difficult childhood, which remained a source of recurring trauma. How Baldwin managed that fine signature balance of tragedy and redemption, suffering and kindness, how, indeed, he "got over" tremendous personal adversity to arrive at a vision and craft that must have been both comforting and painful to mobilize will remain a mystery. What we do know is that traces of his pain appeared in his works, among them his rarely discussed poems (collected in the recently issued *Jimmy's Blues and Other Poems* [2014], which inspired the epigraph for this section). As Kalí Tal reminds, "Traumatic metaphors—the stories of survivors—are always political, even when they are most earnestly intended (or pretended) not to be. . . . They are political, they are intensely personal . . . the personal *is* political, without exception."[69] Baldwin embraced this dimension of life writing full on, inserting flashbacks about physical abuse by his stepfather and violent encounters with Harlem police, not to mention an incident of groping by a white southern politician, into his essays and novels. His embrace of the personal being political manifested as well in the increasing attention he paid to women characters and their circumstances of pain that grew well beyond *Go Tell It*, *Notes of a Native Son*, and *Another Country*.

In his fifth novel, *If Beale Street Could Talk*, he ponders these issues through a first-person teenage narrator, Tish, a young pregnant woman, whose lover and father of her child was jailed for a crime he did not commit: "Being in trouble can have a funny effect on the mind.... Maybe it's because you see people differently than you saw them before.... Maybe you get scared and numb.... And if you ever did like the city, you don't like it anymore" (IB, 8, 9, 10). As Ida from *Another Country* and Julia from *Just above My Head* discover, in the mid-twentieth century the price of identity for black women is that you never feel at home in your country, city, even neighborhood, and your own house may devolve into a space of abuse, as it does for Julia, or a space of constant sorrow, as it does for Ida following her brother's suicidal death. As Nikky Finney explains in her introduction to *Jimmy's Blues and Other Poems*, to women writers who came after Baldwin, who read about Tish, Ida, and Julia, he was everywhere, for "the air of the Republic was already rich with him ... the most salient, sublime, and consequential American writer of the twentieth century." His "personal and relentless assault on white supremacy and his brilliant, succinct understanding of world and American history" were conveyed in a unique style that combined "prophetic understanding, harmony, and swing" to achieve writing "counter-metrically, reflecting his African, Southern, Harlem, and Paris roots." That style, as the chapters that follow demonstrate, was honed meticulously for all of his readers of all epidermal hues, lifestyles, (dis)identifications, and persuasions. As Finney contends of his prophetic insights, he "saw us long before we saw ourselves."[70]

Baldwin's fictional female characters and his appeal to the younger generation of black writers of all sexes and genders can be read as continuing, with a twist, the black intellectual tradition Robert Reid-Pharr describes in *Conjugal Union: The Body, the House, and the Black American* (1999): "a separate universe through constant reference to a black body that is itself mediated through domesticity, through households."[71] Looking to literature from "early national" and antebellum America, Reid-Pharr emphasizes the corporeality of the black body defined by "race ... on [a] black/white axis."[72] Baldwin's late works and domestic practices answer two important questions Reid-Pharr's argument poses for the twentieth century: "What worlds will collide if black bodies continue their promiscuous, self-interested longing? What catastrophes await the erection of *improper households*?"[73] Baldwin's "improper," black queer household in St. Paul-de-Vence not only establishes an alternative space of black queer creativity, but also, throughout his works, erects the imaginary "House of Baldwin" that contravenes his stepfather's household filled with punishment and trauma.

In addition to channeling his autobiographic experience through both male and female characters, Baldwin's later works contain an element of the unknown, "an act of faith, a leap into the dark," as he explains to the *Xavier Review* in 1985. Like many of his readers, I often marvel at how well he domesticated the anguish and hurt that attended his creativity, how he kept the faith in his experience and memory so as to mine them for literary material, how he made it all sing through his prose. Did he, as Nigel Hatton thinks, have in mind Søren Kierkegaard's ideas? Or Du Bois's and Hansberry's? I agree that he did, and that sampling gospel songs and the Danish philosopher's ideas, not to mention the brilliance of "Sweet Lorraine" in the same paragraph, is precisely the kind of literary magic that Baldwin creates in ways no one else can, or likely ever will, match.[74]

Toni Morrison's eulogy at his funeral on December 8, 1987, at the Cathedral of St. John the Divine in New York City, asks him rhetorically what everybody who has read him recognizes as the desperate need that his work has fulfilled—"You knew, didn't you, how I needed your language and the mind that formed it? How I relied on your fierce courage to tame wilderness for me?"[75] Importantly, the language he gave her, Morrison insists, echoing the literary-legacy-as-house metaphor, was a space to "dwell in, a gift so perfect it seems my own invention." And that feeling of being at home in American English transformed by him was possible because James Baldwin was its re-builder, because he was not afraid of the cost of the reconstruction project he set out to accomplish. He transformed the idiom, and he "made . . . [it] honest . . . exposed its secrets and reshaped it until it was truly modern dialogic, representative, humane." As Morrison addresses her departed hero intimately, he accomplished a powerful balancing act through his craft:

> You replaced lumbering platitudes with an upright elegance. You went into that forbidden territory and decolonized it . . . and un-gated it for black people so that in your wake we could enter it, occupy it, restructure it in order to accommodate our complicated passion—not our vanities but our intricate, difficult, demanding beauty, our tragic, insistent knowledge, our lived reality, our sleek classical imagination. . . . In your hands language was handsome again. In your hands we saw how it was meant to be: neither bloodless nor bloody, and yet alive.[76]

Like Morrison and so many others, I, too, have felt safe and inspired by Baldwin's idiom, and I found a home in his syntax, imagery, cadence, and tone, no matter how terrifying and daring his topics, no matter how angry—never bitter, as Maya Angelou reminds us in an interview glimpsed in the film *The Price of the Ticket*—and cutting his rhetoric often was. Baldwin's artistic gifts made his medium into a thing of beauty that inspired and comforted the reader and, yes, made him or her feel supported and recognized in the emotions it evoked, even as he or she raged along with Baldwin at the violence, racism, sexism, homophobia, and xenophobia that marred his time in the United States and abroad.

Today, his words help us to articulate outrage at dispiritingly similar calamities in our own difficult moment, from Ferguson and Charleston to Charlottesville, from San Bernardino to Orlando. We must read him more than ever and make sure our children can access both the works and the person who wrote them, his private and public life and their material remains in their challenging entirety and complexity. As Morrison ends her eulogy: "'Our crown,' you said, 'has already been bought and paid for. All we have to do,' you said, 'is wear it.' And we do, Jimmy. You crowned us."[77] Now, let us show that we are worthy of the black queer house of American letters that James Baldwin has bequeathed us.

Chez Baldwin archive: James Baldwin and Bernard Hassell dressed to kill.
Photo by author, 2014.

CHAPTER 2

Home Matter

No House in the World, or Reading Transnational, Black Queer Domesticity in St. Paul-de-Vence

The house was empty. . . . My brother. Do you know, friend, how a brother loves his brother, how mighty, how unanswerable it is to be confronted with the truth beneath that simple word? . . . Yes. No. Everything becomes unanswerable, unreadable, in the face of an event yet more unimaginable than one's own death. It is one's death, occurring far beyond the confines of one's imagination. Or, surely, far beyond the confines of my imagination. And do you know, do you know, how much my brother loved me? how much he loved me! And do you know I did not know it? did not dare to know it: do you know? No. No. No.

—*Just above My Head*

PROLOGUE: THE MOUNTAIN, THE VILLAGE, THE STRANGER

The small Provençal town where Baldwin moved in 1971 was an unlikely location for him, given his earlier predilection for large cities like New York, Paris, London, or Istanbul. When he arrived there, he found himself the sole black person in all of St. Paul-de-Vence and environs, a place so removed from the rest of the world then that in many ways it strangely mirrored the Swiss hovel in the Alps where he had finished his first novel, *Go Tell It on the Mountain* (1953), two decades before and where he had tried to make a semblance of a home with a partner for the first time in his life. The Swiss village that gave the writer a glimpse of happy domesticity between two men in love that he was to chase, unsuccessfully, for the rest of his life was Löeche-les-Bains. In the early 1950s, the simple and harsh rural life there had still been dictated by the rhythm of the seasons, hardly changed since the seventeenth century. (Its only tourist attraction, hot springs, brought in some visitors during the warm months, most of them in need of medical treatment.) Baldwin was invited there by his lover, the Swiss painter Lucien Happersberger, who worried that Jimmy was not getting his work done in Paris, and whose family owned a small chalet that they could use.

The complicated story of their on-and-off relationship and their attempts at building a domestic space together as either lovers or close—and at times quarreling—friends or roommates in Löeche-les-Bains, and later Puerto Rico, Turkey, then St. Paul-de-Vence, are among the key biographical puzzle pieces needed to fully understand the premier twentieth-century U.S. black queer writer. It begins in Paris about 1949–50, when they first met, and ends at Chez Baldwin, where Happersberger visited many times, and where he stayed in the fall of 1987 until James died of cancer, literally keeping watch at his deathbed and taking care of his friend's ravaged body as if he were a nurse. That story, of unrequited love and unfulfilled, or partially fulfilled, black queer domestic desire on the part of Baldwin, and of betrayal but also persistent platonic love for Baldwin on the part of Happersberger, is an important addition to the lager cache of narratives mapping transnational American cultures, the narratives in which longing for home as haven intersects with erotic desire, race and class, private and public social spaces, and African American and western European histories. It is also a story about the ways in which all these concepts affect and shape gendered and sexualized identities and their representations, artistic expressions, and scholarly accounts about them both within and without the United States.

Finally, it is a deeply private story that was entrusted to me by Happersberger when we met for an interview at a friend's house in Switzerland in 2007.[1] "After you ... no more interviews!" he told me on that occasion, thanking me for "putting me back where I was then," and telling me that I helped him reconnect with positive emotions from the past—"I feel free with you"—through our conversation.

Little did I know that he would die of cancer in August 2010, several years before I could dream of accepting his warm invitation to visit him and see his paintings at his house in Martigny, and even longer before I could dream of sharing this book with him.[2] I was able, however, to send him a copy of my *James Baldwin's Turkish Decade* (2009), and he responded with a lovely letter in which he complained that "[his] friend cancer got [him]."[3] I was thrilled to hear from him and know that my book reached him. I meant to write him back, but I was mired in my own health and disability struggles. Soon, as too often happens, I heard the news of his passing.

Baldwin and Happersberger met in Paris, soon after the "stolen sheet incident" that Baldwin describes in "Equal in Paris" (1955). "All Americans were stars then [in Paris] in [the] 1950s!"—Lucien reminds me during our

2.1–2.4. Lucien Happersberger during an interview with the author.

interview—"and I needed to learn English." He is tall, with receding gray hair and a cheerful manner. Born in 1932, he was seventy-five at the time, laughing loudly, recalling that he was only seventeen during the 1950s, "a young naïve kid . . . knew nothing of racism, Harlem. . . . I was very curious." He ran into Baldwin while wandering around Paris; they had a drink and spoke French, and then, perhaps without quite realizing what exactly he was doing, Lucien found himself the love of James's life, a role he could never fully embrace after the first couple of years. "We shared drinking and eating, when we could . . . we had some good friends who did some good cooking. . . . Talking about this, I am getting excited!" And he was in love, too, at least for a while, given his belief in what he now terms "male homo-sensuality" and a simultaneous refusal to be labeled as a homosexual that echoes Baldwin's: "Everything was natural in what we did," he tells me, "all of this was new to me, but I accepted it completely—his race, his homosexuality, [that] he was attracted to me." When I ask about any letters, photos, he waves his hand at the loss of "all that," having lived in "two suitcases for years . . . [keeping] only three to four of the last letters" that Baldwin wrote to him in Switzerland.

Our conversation proceeds in cycles, with much wine and many snacks. I learn that Baldwin "was a difficult friend and a difficult lover," and that the famous Giovanni-like photo of Lucien in profile that features both in David Adams Leeming's biography and Karen Thorsen's documentary was taken on a trip to Puerto Rico they took together; there is a piece of Jimmy's elbow in its frame. Another image, perhaps the only surviving one where they appear together, was taken in Paris in 1953 and features, in black and white, Baldwin on the left; his mentor and father figure, the painter Beauford Delaney, in the center; and Lucien towering on the right and slightly behind Beauford.[4]

When we get back to the subject of Löeche-les-Bains and their visits there, Happersberger tells me that after about six months of their hanging out together in Paris, Baldwin was simply unable to write. "I didn't know what I was doing. . . . I put him up there . . . in the chalet," he says, and I am guessing that he means both taking Baldwin there and his conviction that he could write better in that secluded mountain hovel. Lucien also managed to get a little "pension" for them, or some money from his father to help to pay their living expenses. Baldwin writes of his anticipation of the place in "Stranger in the Village" (1953), the essay describing his experience and lesson from several visits there: "It did not occur to me—possibly because I am an American—that there could be people anywhere who had never seen a Negro" (PT, 79).

As Happersberger clarifies in our interview—something the essay mentions only cursorily (PT, 80)—they in fact made three visits together to

2.5 and 2.6. Löeche-les-Bains. Photos by author, 2007.

the village: the first, for about two weeks in the summer of 1950 or 1951, when they took a hazardous two-day backpacking trip to Chemin in the mountains.[5] "It was hard! . . . Jimmy almost lost his life on a glacier," Lucien recalls, and then adds, so I notice the connection to Baldwin's first novel's title, "The mountain was there," and how he couldn't forget the sight, "when they walked up the ice on the glacier . . . [of] the sun hitting . . . [Baldwin's] face." It was altogether "a biblical metaphor and experience . . . that counted" for him. (I am not sure if he means Baldwin or himself or both, but settle for the latter, as they were still in the first bloom of their love; Lucien's face lights up as he tells me that.) The second visit was over a three- to four-month period in the winter of 1951, and they lived together and, at least for some time it seemed, Lucien's girlfriend was also there, as he makes sure that I notice. Baldwin managed to finish *Go Tell It* only on their third visit, in the winter of 1952, when he also worked on "Stranger in the Village" and began writing his first play, *The Amen Corner*. Lucien assures me that no matter how he felt about it, Baldwin always had "beautiful contact with people [there] . . . he charmed [them] . . . danced with a woman who owned a bistro there . . . he knew who they were . . . [and] he really got his work done." From his own vantage point, James writes vividly in "Stranger" about his third visit, when "everyone knows that I am the friend of the son of a woman who was born here, and that I am staying in their chalet. But I remain as much a stranger today as I was the first day I arrived, and the children shout Neger! Neger! as I walk along the streets."

He explains his ability to "charm" them with a black American clichéd performance that seems to work well:

> I reacted by trying to be pleasant—it being a great part of the American Negro's education . . . that he must make people "like" him. This smile-and-the-world-smiles-with-you routine worked about as well in this situation as it had in the situation for which it was designed, which is to say that it did not work at all. No one, after all, can be liked whose human weight and complexity cannot be, or has not been, admitted. . . . All of the physical characteristics of the Negro which had caused me, in America, a very different and almost forgotten pain were nothing less than miraculous—or infernal—in the eyes of the village people. . . . In all of this, in which it must be conceded there was the charm of genuine wonder and in which there was certainly no element of intentional unkindness, there was yet no suggestion that I was human: I was simply a living wonder. (PT, 81)

These moments of contact between Baldwin the black American and the white Swiss villagers in the essay differ from Lucien's account, undergoing a transformation in the course of Baldwin's text. The bistro owner's wife, with whom Lucien thought he saw Baldwin dance happily, in the writer's account "beamed with a pleasure far more genuine than my own" upon informing him that the village Catholic church's collections "'bought' last year six or eight African natives," a custom "repeated in many villages . . . for the purpose of converting them to Christianity" (PT, 82). Her ignorance incites Baldwin's musings on slavery and colonial history, and his own situation in "the West onto which I have been so strangely grafted" (PT, 83). While challenging, it also leads to the acknowledgment of his authorial powers: "Every legend, moreover, contains its residue of truth, and the root function of language is to control the universe by describing it," he acknowledges (84). With time, even the worst of the ignorance slowly dissipates, as Baldwin admits two pages later, stating that his perception of being a perpetual stranger in Löeche-les-Bains is "not quite true." Some people have become friends, some are indifferent, and some dislike him still. It is much as it has been in America, after all; he now almost feels at home here (85).

Much in love during one of those visits, James and Lucien successfully played house together as a "strange couple," as Happersberger jokingly states in an interview featured in Thorsen's documentary *The Price of the Ticket*. As Baldwin writes in "Stranger," their isolation from the distractions they loved in Paris was nearly complete: "In the village there is no movie house, no bank, no library, no theater; very few radios, one Jeep, one station wagon; and, at the moment, one typewriter, mine, an invention which the woman next door to me here had never seen" (PT, 79–80). Indeed, he apprehends his remoteness from the United States and other African Americans in terms of irreconcilable cultural difference and the simple fact of social and geographic space, or "a dreadful abyss between the streets of this village and the streets of the city in which I was born" (85).

Yet it was precisely that remoteness that allowed for a low-key household routine that guaranteed that Jimmy could write all day, while Lucien shopped and cooked, as he reminds me in the interview. In the evenings they would go out for walks and drinks or, as Lucien recalls fondly, "I would take him out." In Thorsen's film, Happersberger remembers vividly the moment when the novel was finished, as one day he was listening to Jimmy's punching out loudly its final six letters—"THE END." Amid the wintry alpine landscape, surrounded by the white faces of the villagers, Baldwin's typewriter, manuscript, and Bessie Smith and Fats Waller records were the only reminders of his U.S. home.

Again, that combination of estrangement, remoteness, and familiarity of sound and memories associated with his American blackness was what he needed to get his work done. He also managed to think hard about his position as a black American in the West in his essay that on the surface seems a travelogue, and deep down is a profound personal and political meditation on the exceptional place of African peoples in diaspora amidst the decolonizing world, and especially in the United States. As Happersberger tells me in 2007, as if summing up the surprising conclusion of "Stranger," "In [Löeche-les-Bains] he could see what culture and knowledge could do ... [that] these people are victims of their culture," given their custom of "buying" Africans for the Catholic church. He emphasizes that Baldwin "understood so well ... the little people as victims of their culture." Being there was a "key moment for him ... he saw how much he was a modern human being, and they were in the middle ages.... It was a fabulous experience for him." Interestingly and in ways that make me study him even closer, he seems not to have been as much aware of the struggle that Baldwin was going through there as the sole black body amid all that whiteness of faces and landscapes. To Lucien, this was never a question, nor was there doubt that his black lover was the intellectual and genius, who took measure of the "little people" around him, who wrote them up and used them as literary material, rather than being, at least in any way worth mentioning, sized up by them. All of these perspectives are present in the essay, which compares bodies and spaces between Harlem and Löeche-les-Bains.

When Baldwin walked the streets of Löeche-les-Bains, local children, always curious and uninhibited, would remind him of being a "living wonder" in their midst by surreptitiously touching his skin and hair. This notice taken of his body "by some daring creature" (PT, 81) made him reflect on their difference, now in terms of his irrevocably racialized national origins, "between the [village] children who shout Neger! today and those who shouted Nigger! yesterday—the abyss is experience, the American experience" (85). In Thorsen's film there is footage from a documentary featuring Baldwin's return to Löeche-les-Bains at some later time. These fragments show the writer smiling, a star returning to one of the scenes of his fame's making, walking through the white landscape in a chic thick sweater, sunglasses, and scarf, his step slightly swishy, with laughing, running village children milling all around him. "I knew that they did not mean to be unkind, and I know it now," he recalls, regarding their earlier reactions to him. Then, changing the tense, he also admits it as a challenging mental switch he had to master to manage his presence there: "it is necessary, nevertheless, for me to repeat this to myself every time that I walk out of the chalet. The children who shout Neger! have no way of knowing the echoes this sound raises in me. They are brimming with good humor and the more daring swell with pride when I stop to speak to them." Sometimes it does not seem to work, however, for "there are days when I cannot pause and smile . . . have no heart to play with them; when . . . I mutter sourly to myself, exactly as I muttered on the streets of a city these children have never seen, when I was no bigger than these children are now: Your mother was a nigger." He concludes with the words that now adorn the walls of the National Museum of African American History and Culture: "People are trapped in history and history is trapped in them" (81).

Luckily, at the end of the day, there is the cozy chalet to return to, a semblance of home as Happersberger describes it: "typical, rustic, with a little kitchen and main room with a stone oven (we were always sitting there), a little room next to it. Very small. . . . Under us [on the lower floor], there was a mother (unwed) with a child—a horror at that time; she wouldn't talk." Happersberger also tells me about the villagers' primitivism of which he is ashamed: "I'm sure they thought he was Satan. . . . You would see that very clearly on some faces. . . . He had a trick, he would open his eyes so . . . then he was himself. It was much more important than people think. Then he hated it," he admits, and I chalk up his change of attitude to having been able to access deeper recesses of memory. He looks pained and tells me vehemently, "And it's true . . . it's terrible, we are the Bushes, bosses, those clean banks!" he exclaims the last few words, and I know his agitation refers to the then fairly recent news about the Nazi holdings in his home country's famed financial institutions. So I had been wrong about his seemingly shallow perception of Baldwin's experience. He wanted Jimmy to feel well in Löeche-les-Bains, true enough, but he also could see his friend's anguish and never-ending terror as someone who not only carried the history of his people on his shoulders as an artist, but also dealt with the reality of being the dark Other all over the world. Perhaps it is only now that Happersberger can see all this fully and unequivocally; perhaps as an older man, having outlived Baldwin by nearly a decade and a half, he can finally approximate and try to express the pain of it.

A moment later he is very sad, telling me that, after Baldwin's passing, he realized that "if he'd lived, I'd help him to go on. . . . I must say, I left Jimmy alone at that time" (from the context, I gather he means the few years

2.7. Lucien with his son, Luc, Baldwin's godson. Photo by author, 2007.

preceding his death), when he was "sick and tired . . . [and] that's why he was thinking of suicide at times. . . . I think he had no hope for this world." But, he emphasizes, "I was there the last months, every day." Lucien was astounded that Jimmy went toward his end with no fight, that he clearly "didn't want to live . . . didn't want to go on . . . that was his way to leave." He tells me how quietly Baldwin passed away; he was "serene, reading [someone was, to him], couldn't talk. . . . We [Lucien; David Baldwin, James's younger brother; and Bernard Hassell, who managed Chez Baldwin], sat with him, saw him, and watched him go," he tells me in a low voice, with a sad smile, then laughs a low, choking laugh, and drinks a toast.

DANGEROUS DOMESTIC MANIPULATIONS

> The loft stretches the entire length of the top floor, halfheartedly divided by a clothesline with a sheet draped over it. Behind this sheet is the bed . . . close to the floor, covered . . . with a heavy dark blue blanket, and many loud pillows. There is the bathroom, and the rudiments of a kitchen. . . . In the front . . . are Arthur's piano, records, tape recording apparatus, sheet music, books. . . . There is a sofa, chairs, a big table. On the walls, photographs . . . and posters.
> —*Just above My Head*

The last pages of James Baldwin's sixth and last novel, *Just above My Head* (1979), glimpse a utopian domestic space occupied by two black men in love who are musicians in New York City. The older one is a singer named Arthur, and the younger a pianist named Jimmy. Artistic collaborators as well as lovers, they have created a home together and the loft is where they live and work. For hours, days, and months, the labor of music commands their time. It is their progeny, though it comes from the black church, where openly queer men are usually not welcomed.[6] The rituals and sounds that framed their childhood and young manhood in Harlem are now fodder for their creativity, work, and passion. The space they occupy is both home and haven, the only place where they can be themselves, where their love not only dares to speak, but also can sing, shout, and testify to its name.

The interpenetration of artistic, domestic, and religious spaces in Jimmy and Arthur's utopian refuge echoes Baldwin's own experience both as a budding writer from a lower-class African American family and as a youth in the Pentecostal tradition of storefront Harlem churches. Written largely in his house in the South of France, where he moved in 1971 following prolonged stays in Turkey in the 1960s, his last novel also reflects the more expansive, meditative, and improvisational approach to fiction that he turned to in the 1970s and 1980s, or what we can term his "late style."[7] As Baldwin describes this work in an interview with Clayton G. Holloway for the *Xavier Review* in November 1985, it arose from a series of short stories that made him realize that "within the last twenty years my attention has been on something which I can not handle in a short story.... I am involved with the big canvas.... And that has been a very big challenge—and a kind of terror."[8]

The challenges and gestation of his late style required that Baldwin not only embrace new, and indeed terrifying, approaches in his works— approaches that his happy domesticity in the remote part of France certainly enabled—but also confront himself as an older artist who must, as he explains in the *Xavier Review* interview, concur with the process that "begins with ... apprehension; ... alienation; the sense of being other and therefore doomed ... his work is his only hope."[9] As Leeming stresses, Baldwin's last novel, "the longest and most ambitious," served also as his "extended metaphor through which ... [he] could once again examine his own life and career as an artist and witness."[10] As the writer mentions in a letter to his younger brother, David, on February 6, 1979, the day he thought he had finished *Just above My Head*, he felt torn, haunted, and uncertain about this book—that he somehow "missed it," was not quite "equal to the song" he heard and wanted to sing, but at the same time felt that he "didn't cheat," and at the "bottom of [himself]" that it was his "very best book."[11]

Given the writer's tremendous investment in that novel, it is no accident, then, that the two artist figures who occupy the utopian, black queer home space in *Just above My Head* bear their author's first and second names. The room described in the epigraph contains furnishings that could have come from a room in Baldwin's own house; the colors are familiar, too, resembling the palette of the author's French abode. Hall Montana, the narrator and Arthur's elder brother, whose story begins with him imagining, post factum, his brother's death of a heart attack in a London pub, has an epiphany regarding his situation while looking at the ceiling of his bedroom, whose description fits exactly the one in Baldwin's house in St. Paul-de-Vence, specifically in his living quarters: "whitewashed . . . with the heavy, exposed, unpainted beams" (JAMH, 15). In that novel, Baldwin's French house becomes part of the physical setting, as well as making the writing of its plot and characters possible as the space of authorial labor.

In the writing process, material circumstances often follow metaphysical visions and vice versa, for the scene with the ceiling moving down "just above" the narrator's head was also inspired by an actual dream the writer had within his Chez Baldwin bedroom in 1975. On the same night, his brother David, who was staying at the house, too, dreamed of characters in search of an author.[12] The brothers' dreams, the house, and an old gospel lyric, "Up above my head I hear music in the air," came together to make something Eleanor Traylor terms in her review of *Just above My Head* "both dreadful and beautiful . . . a tale told consistently . . . [by] the Baldwin narrator-witness."[13] Quite fittingly, his last novel reveals that Baldwin was concerned more than ever with familiar elements of his writing—his own and his people's stories past and present that are often traumatic—but also increasingly with matters spiritual and esoteric (dreams, premonitions, revelations, allegories, and parables) that should be seen as important, albeit underexplored, signatures of his late style and central to his lost decade that is the subject of this book.

As Lynn Orilla Scott surmises, echoing Leeming, all the major characters in Baldwin's last novel are "a composite of the author's attitudes, experiences, fears, and hopes . . . [and] contribute to [its] self-reflexive quality."[14] No wonder, then, that Baldwin used images of his immediate physical surroundings, where he found refuge in his late years, as the stage set for some of the novel's action. By the time he finished *Just above My Head*, he had written plays and directed theater performances in the United States and Turkey. He sang regularly, anything from hymns, gospel, and jazz, to pop, and the improvisational form of his last novel was much inflected by these black musical genres and expansive social landscape of the mid- to late twentieth-century African America at home and abroad. Scott sums up the aim of *Just above My Head*, whose frank descriptions of gay male sex turned off many critics, as "part of Baldwin's ongoing effort to create a form of self-representation that does justice to the complexity of African American subjectivity."[15]

While that complexity, and the terror that it inevitably brought to his writing process, had been Baldwin's intense focus throughout his life, he insisted on making sexuality, and especially male queer sex, as important as the issues of race and class in his representations of black American subjectivity. Of all of his works, *Just above My Head* deals with black queerness, and sexuality in general, most openly, at the same time as it makes clear deep prejudice against same-sex desire in the community, country, and the wider world around Arthur and Jimmy. The domestication of their bond, however short-lived, also marks a turning point in twentieth-century American literary representations of blackness and queerness, one that academic theory has caught up to only fairly recently.[16] As E. Patrick Johnson and Mae G. Henderson define the field of black queer studies that claims Baldwin as its literary ancestor, it aims to "quare queer—to throw shade on its meaning in the spirit of extending its services to 'blackness.'" As they emphasize, both terms, *black* and *queer*, are "markers or signifiers of difference . . . so we endorse the double cross of affirming the inclusivity mobilized under the sign of 'queer' while claiming the racial, historical, and cultural specificity attached to the marker 'black.'"[17]

In this chapter, which closely reads Baldwin's last writing haven and glimpses some of his late works, I push the dyad of *black queer* further by giving it a socially spatial dimension and by modifying it with two terms that his work has commanded and inspired: *domestic* and *transnational*.[18] The former term arises from the literary focus of this project on Baldwin's black queer home spaces, and from its architectural focus on a series of images of Baldwin's own house in St. Paul-de-Vence in the South of France. The latter term, *transnational*, has to do with what some of his readers see as ironic and others as tragic, namely that the writer was unable to find a writing haven in his home country.[19] Exiled from the United States both by circumstance and choice, following his forays into European exile in France and Turkey, Baldwin found and founded the most enduring home life in the remote village of St. Paul-de-Vence. He spent the last sixteen years of his life there, establishing a vibrant household, known locally as Chez Baldwin. That domestic space allowed for a nurturing routine that helped him to slow down in order to take better care of his ailing health and to remain productive as a writer, academic teacher, and transnational public intellectual who continued to travel but always returned home to his Provençal abode.[20]

After Baldwin died at home in St. Paul-de-Vence in 1987, Chez Baldwin was left to his younger brother, David, who had been James's right-hand man for years, the closest to him of all his eight half-siblings. Following David's death and several lawsuits, the house was lost to developers in the early 2000s, emptied of the brothers' possessions and deserted, despite James's dying wish to preserve it as a retreat for African Diaspora writers.[21] Today, there is no trace of the famous American writer's presence in the area, no sign, no marker, no photograph in the guidebooks. As of early November 2014, large parts of the structure were demolished, including the ground-floor section facing the back garden that contained Baldwin's study and living quarters. What you see in figure 2.9, which was taken from the back of the property, or what is missing in it, is the part of the house where the writer lived and worked. The disturbed dirt on the right side of the remaining structure marks that place.

Although a partial shell of the house still endures, as I was able to see during my most recent visit in June 2017, it seems now as if James Baldwin, the famous African American writer, never set foot in St. Paul-de-Vence. That there is no place in this country one can visit to imagine Baldwin's writing life, to frame with material architecture and landscape the metaphorical, biographical, and literary knowledge we have of him today, is deeply poignant at a time when the United States boasts some seventy writers' houses that are museums open to the public.[22]

Part of this chapter's subtitle, "No House in the World," signals a preoccupation with this glaring absence, indeed, with the callous destruction of James Baldwin's domestic space. It reflects on the changing physical appearance of Chez Baldwin through time and on its literary representations in the writer's oeuvre. While documenting the process of the structure's dissolution and disappearance, I read into the erasure, destruction, and emptiness and tease out from existing material evidence—Baldwin's works, letters, photographs of the structure and objects salvaged from it, and plenty of imaginative speculation—traces of a black queer domestic presence that Baldwin, the transnational African American writer and one of the most important literary figures of the last century, has left as his legacy. The author, whose works touch upon domestic themes with some regularity, commented on the paradox of house and home as discourse, structure, and process in a short autobiographical essay published in *Architectural Digest* in August 1987: "A house is not a home: we have all heard the proverb. Yet, if the house is

①

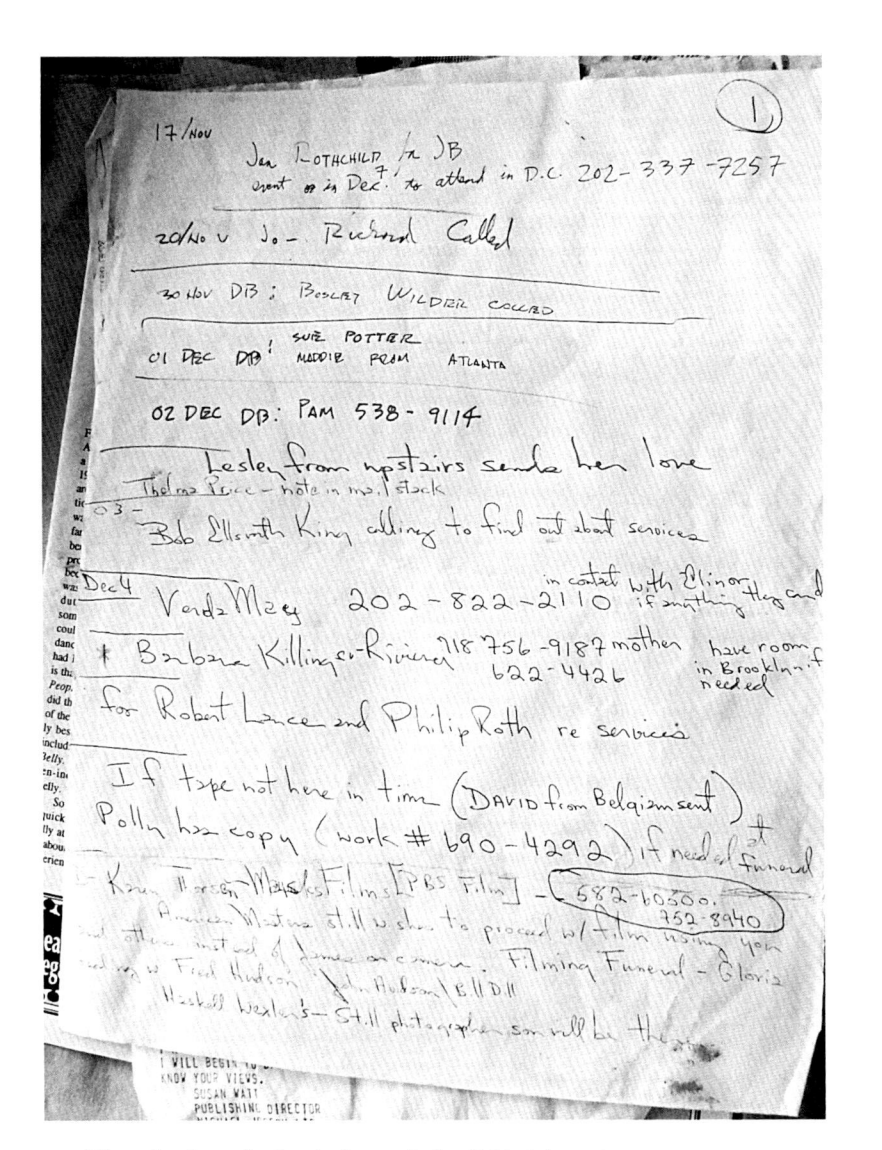

17/Nov — Jean ROTHCHILD /re JB
event op in Dec 7 to attend in D.C. 202-337-7257

20/Nov — Jo - Richard Called

30 Nov DB: Bosley WILDER called

01 DEC DB: SUE POTTER
          MADDIE FROM ATLANTA

02 DEC DB: PAM 538-9114

Lesley from upstairs sends her love
Thelma Price — note in mo.[?] stack
Bob Ellsworth King calling to find out about services

Dec 4 — Vanda Macy 202-822-2110 in contact with Elinor if anything they can

★ Barbara Killinger-Riviera 718 756-9187 mother   have room
                              622-4426   in Brooklyn if
                                                    needed
for Robert Lance and Philip Roth re services

If tape not here in time (DAVID from Belgium sent)
Polly has copy (work # 690-4292) if needed at funeral
— Ken ??? Maysles Films [PBS Film] — 582-6050.
                                       752-8940
American Masters still wishes to proceed w/ film using ???
??? instead of ??? on camera. Filming Funeral — Gloria
???? Fred Hudson ???Hudson\E\IDII
Haskell Wexler's — still photographer son will be the

2.9. Remnants of Chez Baldwin in St. Paul-de-Vence, with the wing that used to house the writer's quarters bulldozed and gone, November 2014. Courtesy of Jill Hutchinson.

not a home (home!) it can become only ... a space to be manipulated—manipulation demanding rather more skill than grace" (AD, 122). Appearing in print about three months before his death, this statement confirms the importance of his domestic abode to his late works and compels his readers and critics to engage in a rigorous search for the sources and effects of the domestic "manipulations" he implies in this little-known piece that I will discuss in detail in this chapter.

Putting into conversation glimpses of Baldwin's late works and those of his house in St. Paul-de-Vence, which I visited on research trips in 2000, 2014, and 2017, this chapter engages several questions that have shaped my thinking throughout this project. Are the house and property still, at least symbolically, Baldwin's? Do the remnants of the structure and the land around it remain the "writer's house," even though they physically and legally belong to someone else now? If so, what is it that makes a building that once served as someone's writing abode a viable and enduring site of literary and historical research? In other words, how does an architectural structure, a building or room, become a repository of a specific person's life, of his or her literary and material memory? How might it reflect such aspects of that person's identity as race, gender, class, or sexual orientation? Most important, what tangible traces, if any, could be imprinted on architecture by a black queer literary life?

I answer these questions in a somewhat impressionistic manner, compelled to such an approach by the phenomenology of imagination that animates Gaston Bachelard's *The Poetics of Space* (1958) and more recent work on social space, race, gender, and sexuality in the fields of architecture, history, anthropology, literary studies, and cultural studies. Hence, I specifically embrace Bachelard's focus on the imaginative interpenetration of material and metaphorical qualities of domestic spaces in both literature and architecture, but I am also deeply mindful of how all of these loaded terms, *domestic*, *space*, *literature*, and *architecture*, have been inflected by the brutal history of African Americans in the national house, and in private intimate spaces, since the times of slavery, black codes, Jim Crow segregation, redlining, and restrictive covenants, with some of these practices still persisting in many parts of the United States.[23]

As Darell Fields notes in his seminal book, *Architecture in Black* (2000), the very language we deploy as scholars is based in architectural concepts: "the literary (theoretical) descriptions of dialectic and semiotic structures are complex because they depict, indirectly, multivalent spatial compositions."[24] As he shows, signification as a mode of criticism, borrowed from Henry Louis Gates Jr.'s *The Signifying Monkey* (1988) and "based on mediation between seemingly insurmountable differences," helps to link W. E. B. Du Bois's famous concept of double consciousness to reading blackness in architecture, "its absolute presence and absolute absence in history ... the mirrored form of architecture in the negative ... a tradition all its own."[25] In another context, Toni Morrison brings signification together with the matter and metaphor of home as a literary representation when she compares her own fiction writing to "a racial house," which she had "to rebuild ... so that it was not a windowless prison ... a thick-walled, impenetrable container from which no cry could be heard, but rather an open house, grounded, yet generous in its supply of windows and doors."[26] She sees her authorial imperative much like Baldwin does—"to transform this house completely"—with the term *house* signifying both the country and national literary canon.[27]

Bringing into a broad interdisciplinary conversation approaches from literary, cultural, and visual studies, this chapter also rests on Fields's claim about the a priori nature of houses in collective and individual imaginations, that "the house's form ... is timeless ... a type ... not even a dwelling."[28] To this, I add Baldwin's observation from *Just above My Head*, which illustrates the types of readings I will often perform in these pages, that "any setting becomes [foreign] the moment one is compelled to examine, decipher, and make demands on it." This observation comes from Baldwin's composite narrator—part Hall Montana, part Baldwin—who makes it while contemplating transatlantic slavery and comparing the slaveholding castles, those antitheses of home and horrific preludes to spatial politics of the Middle Passage and American bondage, to a sickening global body: the "European outposts jutting, like rotting teeth, out of the jaws of West Africa" (JAMH, 550). While also taking as its foundation Morrison's description of a liberating home space of literature and its discourses, where binaries are breached to show the "inwardness of the outside, the interiority of the 'othered,' the personal that is always embedded in the public," I rely on Henri Lefebvre and Walter Benjamin's materialist theories of social space and the private interior, and especially their interlinking of the processes of spatial production with formations of identity and interpretations of history.[29]

In this expansive context, I employ Bachelard's literary critical formulation concerning our imaginary domain over places we inhabit: "Space that has been seized upon by the imagination cannot remain indifferent.... It has been lived in, not in its positivity, but with all the partiality of the imagination.... On whatever theoretical horizon we examine it, the house image would appear to have become the topography of our intimate being."[30] Thus Chez Baldwin can be seen both as a physical space of manipulation for its owner, as he claims in the *Architectural Digest* piece, and as a space offering a visitor the house/image as an intimate map of the self, one where, and through which, we can read our own versions of James Baldwin's "partiality of ... imagination," where, in the absence of any physical sites in this country, we can conjure up his black queer domesticity from what remains of his household abroad.

Following the glimpses of Baldwin's last novel in chapter 1 and in this chapter's epigraph, this part examines some of the contexts of its writing that are inextricably linked to the home site in St. Paul-de-Vence, but leaves its more thorough discussion to chapter 4. Similarly, a close reading of the house and its inhabitants as models for some of the writer's characters is important for reading his last play and completed work, *The Welcome Table* (1987), which I discuss in detail in chapter 3. In this home ground chapter, then, we begin a journey through Baldwin's last decade and a half at its end, as it were, with a close look at his last domestic abode and its materiality and imprint in his works. The no-longer-existing house and garden of Chez Baldwin emerge through descriptions and photographs, as well as Baldwin's own words, to provide a retrospective lens through which to reread this writer's late works and reassess the important, concluding chapter of his life.

Baldwin's late-life geography, as Katherine McKittrick would agree, arises from spaces that have been produced and their attendant meanings.[31]

In what follows, I discuss my first visit to Chez Baldwin, and I read closely Baldwin's *Architectural Digest* piece as a miniature photo-text that allows us to glimpse the writer's last public self-presentation in his most enduring domestic environment.[32] I also examine Baldwin's friendships with women, who enabled his relocation to the South of France, and who provided an extended family and role models as he settled into the last decade and a half of his life, the time that witnessed his growing interest in gender and female characters. I end the chapter with a report from my second visit in June 2014, which yielded an examination of the whole house and its material remnants—a hidden archive of salvaged objects—mere months before most of the house was bulldozed down; the chapter's coda glimpses my most recent visits to the site and Chez Baldwin's salvaged contents in June 2017.

My semi-autobiographical account of two house tours, along with a visual narrative about a haunting structure that no longer exists as Chez Baldwin, follows the writer's imperative to witness, which echoes and reworks Henry James's call to what Baldwin adopts as his artistic creed—"observing or looking at the situation," and approaching writing as a Kierkegaardian "act of faith, a leap into the dark," that is, "an attempt to look at where we are, what it means, and how we got to where we are."[33] The eclectic material this chapter comprises benefits from being placed in the context of Diana Fuss's emphasis on the dramatic role of writers' homes, which, as she describes it in *The Sense of an Interior* (2004), function as "theater[s] of composition . . . place[s] animated by the artifacts, mementos, machines, books, and furniture that frame any intellectual labor."[34] The theater of sorts we are about to witness in this meditation on Chez Baldwin requires not only a suspension of disbelief, but also a willingness to play along and embrace the elusive realms where literature and the literary take place, the mysterious spaces between the real and phantasmagoric, the seen and the imagined, the material and the metaphorical, word and thought, sensation and feeling.[35]

My framing of Baldwin's house as a material space that he manipulated and as a convergence of imagined and metaphorical spaces—a domestic theater—that organically enabled his creativity and staged the production of his works suggests an artistic collaboration. While that collaboration clearly unfolds between the writer and the diverse aspects, textures, artifacts, and grounds of his last abode, it also becomes an object of imaginative surveillance, if not obsessive projection at times, to visitors, readers, and scholars. Those who love literature take pilgrimages to places where favorite works were created, craving experience of landscapes and architecture recognizable from beloved poems, plays, and novels. We fantasize about "what it was like then" for our beloved writer; we take photographs and visit museums that were once his or her domicile. In doing all that, we cannot resist our own forms of imaginative, spatial manipulation and allow ourselves to be haunted by what Elisabeth Roberts and Avery Gordon term "the ghostly underside of reality" and its representations through images, memory, and storytelling.[36] My descriptions of Baldwin's domestic space are sensitive to such literary hauntings and affects, at the same time as they also deliberately echo his own descriptions in *Architectural Digest*, approaching Chez Baldwin as a character, much like the writer who occupied it, for such pairing and collaboration dominate his own narrative.

And while this way of interpreting the structure that was the vital setting for the writer's prolific late years might be read as an instance of what Anne Trubek's *A Skeptic's Guide to Writers' Houses* (2011) dismisses as "literary worship" confirming the obvious fact of "writer and readers . . . [being] already severed from the act of writing," my goal is not to elaborate on the acts of Baldwin's writing.[37] Rather, I explore possible processes of his writerly domestication in St. Paul-de-Vence, the processes of manipulation and imaginative transformation, and the processes of dreaming and staging to which he gives voice in his works, and whose traces and ghostly presence we can imagine by sifting through the elusive, haunting archive of whatever remains of his life in St. Paul-de-Vence.[38]

WITNESSING HOME

> It is virtually impossible to trust one's human value without the collaboration or corroboration of that eye—which is to say that no one can live without it.
> —"Here Be Dragons"

I first heard of James Baldwin's house in the South of France, which he called the "spread," during a summer research trip in 2000.[39] Chez Baldwin, as it was named by local residents, was just outside the city's medieval stone walls, in one of the world's most scenic locations—inland from Nice, overlooking the picturesque hills of Provence that slope dramatically to the bewitching waters of the Mediterranean. Instructed by a friendly bookstore owner in the postcard-pretty town, I found my way to the large, untamed property located along the sunbaked Route de la Colle, right outside the city's ramparts

2.10. Chez Baldwin: Entry and gatehouse. Photo by author, 2000.

and across from the famed hotel, the Hameau, where Baldwin stayed during his first visit to the area. I stood in front of a tall, locked, black iron gate. A two-story garage-gatehouse with a steep external stair slashing against its wall stood to the left of the gate. It looked unkempt, overrun with hot-pink flowering vines, but seemed occupied, as evidenced by a door left ajar and a red sports car parked in the street in front of the gate.[40] At first glance, the property seemed a typical, crumbling Provençal structure consisting of several buildings, with proud origins perhaps in the eighteenth century. A large garden tightened its grip on the stone and tile of the main building, which stood at the end of a crumbling stone pathway.

I arrived at that locked gate thirteen years after the writer's death, dreaming of coming across something exciting and inspiring; most of all, I hoped to see and absorb anything I could. Likely having noticed me peering into the property, a young woman appeared on the steps of the gatehouse. She was polite and friendly and accepted quickly that I, a holder of a small rectangle of paper, was indeed a professor from the University of Michigan who was researching James Baldwin in France. She gave me her mother's phone number and told me to call her for permission to see the house. By a mere stroke of luck, the young woman's mother, Jill Hutchinson, was available and let me see Chez Baldwin the next day, having explained that it remained largely in the state in which Baldwin's brother David left it in 1996. Removed against his wishes—he had wanted to remain with Jill and die in his brother's house, in his bed—David was taken to the United States in the final stages of a terminal illness. Hutchinson had been his beloved partner, a terrific woman who had helped the Baldwin family for years by taking care of the house and its many repairs, renting it out to generate income for its upkeep, and handling many official and legal matters. She not only gave me, a perfect stranger, a day of her time to let me see the house, but later took me to her own place in the nearby town of Vence to show me Baldwin's famed LP record collection that had traveled the world with him and the Legion of Honor medal given to him by the French president François Mitterrand in 1986. She had removed these items from Chez Baldwin after some burglary attempts convinced her that such valuable objects were not safe there.

Hutchinson assured me that over the years he had lived there, David Baldwin preserved the furnishings and layout of the house as much as possible in the way James Baldwin had left them at his death in 1987. She let me wander through the building, parts of which were unoccupied, and allowed me to take photographs.[41] (I did not find out much about her then, but managed to convince her to tell me a little more about herself upon my second visit in 2014.[42]) Although her friendship and later passionate relationship with David Baldwin did not begin until after Jimmy's death in 1988, and she never met the writer, she had read his novels as a young woman in England and "absolutely fell in love with *Another Country*," the first book of his she had read, and the book that "taught [her] how to really read." She credits her late-teen turn toward intellectual pursuits to the power of Baldwin's words: "I read all of his books I could get my hands on at the library," she told me. "[They were] my opening into the world I didn't live in.... I could not stop reading him." A former Olympic junior champion swimmer for the United Kingdom, she came from Scarborough, at whose library *Another Country* was considered "a naughty book, a banned book... like D. H. Lawrence's," and she felt self-conscious and shy to be seen with this "pornographic" volume. Later, she moved to the South of France, having married a Frenchman and for the sake of her young daughter's health. She became a self-taught businesswoman and still works as a sought-after bilingual real estate agent and gifted interior decorator. Filled with rare antique finds and art, her house in Vence is a space of refuge, where some of the remnants of Chez Baldwin have found badly needed shelter. She told me fascinating stories about Baldwin's residence and its inhabitants, passed on to her by David, who loved to talk about his brother and their life together as a family of men cohabitating in the house.

As we know from the biographies and documentaries, that family included Bernard Hassell, a beautiful dancer and choreographer who was "a black understudy at Folies Bergères" whom Baldwin met in 1952 at the Montana Bar in Paris during his first visit to France, "[and who] remained his close friend for life," as Michel Fabre recounts.[43] Later Baldwin recommended Hassell to his theater friends in Istanbul, who wanted to stage the musical *Hair*, which subsequently became a great success. Once James had moved into Chez Baldwin, Bernard came to live there and manage the household while taking the gatehouse as his living quarters. He can be seen in photographs with Baldwin at the restaurant La Colombe d'Or in St. Paul-de-Vence and being interviewed in Karen Thorsen's documentary; Beauford Delaney painted two portraits of him in the 1970s. Hassell was also one of the trustees, along with Baldwin, appointed to take care of Delaney's affairs when he was institutionalized and after his death.[44] His relationship with Baldwin was never sexual, and they weathered many stormy times. One of their fights in the summer of 1974 ended up with Bernard being fired; he was brought back to restore order in the increasingly chaotic household in 1976–77.[45] He died at the house several years after Baldwin, a victim of HIV. Nicholas Delbanco offers an unforgettable vignette of Bernard, arriving as part of Baldwin's entourage to a dinner that Delbanco and his wife, Elena, gave for their colorful party in their rented cottage in a nearby Provençal village in the mid-1970s. They drove up in style, in Baldwin's Mercedes, Delbanco recalls, "dark brown and substantial, just short of stretch-limousine size. . . . They were dressed for the occasion, grandly. They wore boaters and foulards. Their boots gleamed." And Bernard "especially was splendid," dressed to kill: "he emerged [from the car] twirling his scarf and waist-sash of pink silk. He did a few dance steps and flung his hat high and extended his hands for applause."[46]

David Leeming, who had known Baldwin since 1961 in Turkey and lived as part of his household on and off throughout the writer's Turkish decade, took care of his papers and correspondence and was entrusted with producing an authorized biography. He came to Chez Baldwin often, sometimes accompanied by his wife, Pam. He was there in late November 1987, just before the writer passed on, and he remembers that time movingly in the biography. Lucien Happersberger, along with his wife and children (Baldwin was his son Luc's godfather), visited as well and, as noted earlier, was there through the last weeks of the writer's life in 1987. Engin Cezzar came several times from Turkey to discuss screenplays for film projects that they started working on while Baldwin lived in Istanbul, which were never realized and cost them a falling out that was never repaired.[47] Friends, artists, academics, and celebrities passed through or stayed for a while, as did lovers, most of whose identities have been protected in the biographies. Among the visitors were Baldwin's close friend and possibly onetime lover Mary Painter; Cecil Brown; Henry Louis Gates Jr.; Josephine Baker; Nina Simone; Yves Montand and his wife, Simone Signoret; the writers Maya Angelou, Toni Morrison, Nicholas Delbanco, and Caryl Phillips; the artists and intellectuals Bill Cosby, Miles Davis, Eleanor Traylor, Louise Meriwether, and Florence Ladd; and many others.

Family members came, among them David's son Daniel, whose first visit took place when he was two or three years old, and who later became an artist who displayed his early paintings at the house. Daniel's mother, Carole Weinstein, came often, and spent many an afternoon with her young son splashing in the pool by La Colombe d'Or, where James Baldwin held court practically every afternoon.[48] Helen Brody Baldwin, who married James's half-brother and David's brother Wilmer (otherwise known as "Lover"), came too, and traveled the region and parts of Italy. Gloria Karefa-Smart, the writer's half-sister, who later became the executor of his estate, came as well, as did her daughter Aisha, a talented dancer. Helen and Lover's son, Trevor, visited briefly soon after his uncle's passing. Years later, Kali-Ma Nazarene, Aisha's daughter and James Baldwin's grandniece, whose paternal grandmother is Toni Morrison, visited the empty house in St. Paul-de-Vence and took haunting black-and-white photographs of the decaying structure and landscape around it as a tribute to her great-uncle, whose house was a key part of her journey of discovery as a black woman artist.[49]

While mostly known for managing his brother's affairs, David Baldwin, a veteran of the Korean War and a former Harlem bartender at Mikell's, was also a gifted visual artist. His works—paintings, collages, mixed-media pieces—have never been displayed publicly and remain with Jill Hutchinson, who has decorated her place in Vence with many of her favorites, keeping those her house could not accommodate in storage. After James's death, David took care of the house and tried living there on his own, with visits to the United States to take advantage of his veteran's health benefits. David's passing in 1996, also from cancer, which came in the wake of a rapid decline following a surgery in New York, halted his efforts to organize and secure the contents of the house, whose parts were subsequently rented out to provide income for its maintenance. When he became ill, he asked Jill to take care of the house for him. Jill, who was not allowed to accompany David on his final trip to the United States, was left alone to manage these matters while grieving her lover's death and her inability to be at his side. In addition to the sisters Hélène

Roux Jeandheure and Pitou Roux, who inherited some Baldwin artifacts from their mother, Yvonne, after her death, or were given some by him, Jill Hutchinson was the only person desperately trying to preserve whatever remained of James's and David's lives under Chez Baldwin's roof.

That roof, by the way, was old and leaky, so she hired her brother to provide affordable repairs. When I first walked around the property, tools and bags of cement attested to these efforts. Jill told me she worried that the makeshift repairs would not last, as there was no money to have the roof replaced to protect the interiors. Desperate to save the house, she tried enlisting help from anybody who showed concern. (Of course, I very much hoped I could help her make James's and David's wishes for their beloved house come true. I have contacted academic institutions and celebrities for funding, but to no avail.)

I am very grateful that Hutchinson told me the Chez Baldwin stories that David left with her, as well as some of those they made together in that house as a couple whose symbolic wedding was commemorated in one of David's collages that hung on the living-room wall. Her openness and generosity were a badly needed gift at a time when I felt the project I had undertaken was impossible to execute, with no real access to Baldwin's archives or papers, and no writing site I could research in the United States. After a rather emotional tour of the house, we sat at James's surviving welcome table under an arbor. That specific piece of furniture and the one in the living room were the actual objects that, besides an old hymn and Turkish parties with friends in the 1960s, inspired the writer to title his last play *The Welcome Table*. While in the lush garden, we wore Jimmy's "guest" straw sun hats, which Jill picked up from the hooks by the side door; she explained that they were necessary in the Provençal climate and that we ought to wear them to honor Jimmy. Bathed in dappled sunlight, surrounded by the breathtaking views of the area, with the ancient crumbling house looming behind, we may have made a picture worthy of an impressionistic painting (see plate 8).

Inside the house, the walls were generously decorated with David's artwork and photos of Baldwin and his friends and family, posters, and, in some of the upstairs rooms, peeling frescoes that may have been a few centuries old. Atop mantelpieces, desks, and tables were stacks of James's and David's photographs, files, books, journals, piles of Xeroxed pages, folders, and loose clippings in folders. Bookshelves overflowed with volumes. David may have contributed books and records to the sizable collections that were left at the house. For years after James's death, he answered letters from individuals and institutions hoping for permission to stage the writer's plays,

2.11. Side view of the house, with Baldwin's study obscured by vegetation. Photo by author, 2014.

2.12. Exterior of Baldwin's study. Photo by author, 2000.

look at his papers, publish news releases, or quote from his works.[50] Though uninhabited for some time, the interior seemed eerily full of life, as if vacated seconds ago. It seemed to be awaiting the return of the brothers, who had stepped outside for just a moment.

I lingered in front of the study on the ground floor at the back of the house (I could not look inside as it was rented out at the time), where Georges Braque had once had his atelier, and where Baldwin had his writing study, or "dungeon" and "torture chamber," as he called it in a letter to David dated March 8, 1975.[51] This letter, full of details about James's daily labors, talks about "sweating out" *The Devil Finds Work* (1976), about him being "scared shitless" about finishing it, and about his being "about to turn it in." The letter reveals an insecure and terror-stricken writer, who muses about always having to discover, when the "book [*Devil*] is almost over," that he is in his own eyes the "world's worst" author and has "no talent at all." He frets, in a diva mode, that he cannot imagine "anybody ever" reading his book, but is certain that at this crisis point, "either it, or I" will be forced to "leave this house." Echoing what, in an interview included in Thorsen's *The Price of the Ticket*, the late William Styron referred to as Baldwin's "schizoid wrenching" of his writing process, these thoughts on authorship reveal someone never fully secure in his talent, who approached every writing task as a terrifying challenge and every completed project as an occasion for crippling self-doubt.[52] The section of the letter devoted to *Devil* ends with an affirmation, however, that acknowledges that, even though the book is not "like anything" he has done before and "I just don't know," his lover, "Philippe," thinks it "very good."[53] The book was composed inside the study whose external view is shown in figure 2.13; it consisted of the workroom and the writer's living quarters, a suite of rooms, and a bathroom. Baldwin liked to take breaks to read or edit on the patio, sitting at a round wooden table in front of it.

The teeming garden, which embraced the house on all sides, was filled with places to sit and take breaks; it also held Baldwin's famed welcome table under an arbor, which features in some footage in *The Price of the Ticket*, and whose photograph, with the writer sitting at it all alone, appears in his *Architectural Digest* piece. A pathway festooned with dense greenery was adorned with colorful light bulbs strung over a metal frame that supported the vines—a remnant from Baldwin's fiftieth birthday party on August 2, 1974, "an occasion long talked about.... More lights than ever were strung in the little orange grove, the food and wine 'never stopped.'"[54] I walked through the now-overgrown, densely green tunnel and could easily imagine it all lit up at night, framing the many guests' laughter, conversation, and jokes.

On a wall by an arched passageway that led to the back of the property on the left side of the front of the house, a small, immured mirror blinked. Jill told me that Jimmy, always a sharp dresser and meticulous about appearing "impeccable," would check his looks in it before joining his visitors in the garden. As I wandered around, the never-realized plans, Baldwin's deathbed wish to transform the property into a retreat for African Diaspora writers, made a lot of sense. Despite the many loud parties, arguments, and fights it once witnessed, the peaceful and nurturing energy of the house and its surroundings was palpable, and the main building and adjoining structures were spacious enough to accommodate at least a dozen guests in separate studio-bedrooms.[55]

I stood for a while in the room on the main floor, the former living room with fresco-adorned walls, where Baldwin had been moved once he became too frail to walk down to his study and where he died on the night of November 30–December 1, 1987. It contained the artist's bed, a bookshelf filled with volumes, and a table with a mess of books and papers. I wandered through the rest of the house, peered through windows, took more photographs, and wondered how these spaces would affect my future reading of Baldwin's works.

Almost a decade and a half since that visit, I cannot give a conclusive answer to this question, although the lessons of my overawed tour of Chez Baldwin in 2000 later led me to Harlem, Paris, and especially Istanbul and other parts of Turkey, and Baldwin's nomadic home sites there, from which I have come back full circle to his house in France, where my work began. One of these lessons is always to look for the material as the context for the metaphorical, for the literal as the context for the literary, no matter how scant the archive. The attention that readers and scholars pay to places where important works have been created, and to structures, cities, and landscapes that inspired memorable lines of texts, stems from the need to anchor in the material and tangible what is elusive and impermanent about literature, and from our hope to share in imagination and inspiration. The need to see the places where writing happened emerges from the desire for closeness to one's subject. What better place to feel inspired than within the walls that once housed the admired writer?

Ardent desire for such inspirations, however commendable, may lead to overblown expectations of accuracy. As Trubek comments, curators of writers' houses often "try to get as close as possible to the real, to historical accuracy," whereas the "best realism realizes its own conceit; it nods to itself, aware of its status as fiction."[56] When visiting writers' houses we do not want to be "overly

2.13. Outside the writer's study. Photo by author, 2014.

2.14. The wing of the house where Baldwin's study and quarters were located on the ground floor. Photo by author, 2014.

2.15. The welcome table under an arbor with Baldwin and guests. Image from the documentary film *James Baldwin: The Price of the Ticket* (1989); courtesy of Karen Thorsen, Douglas Dempsey, and the James Baldwin Project.

sincere . . . [and] take the concept of historical preservation too literally and too far."[57] It is more important to use the space to trigger imagination and understanding of the writing process than to try re-creating what we will never know exactly as the precise placing of that desk or framing of that view through those study windows. For example, when visiting Marcel Proust's bedroom in Paris, Diana Fuss notes that its arrangement helps her to think of his acclaimed novel *À la recherche du temps perdu* as being as much about the search for lost time as about the search for lost space. Fuss's discussion of how, in Proust, "involuntary memory" triggered by a sudden recalled sensation often brings about "a forgotten place . . . the inverted mirror image of traumatic memory" applies also to Baldwin, no matter how different his circumstances are from Proust's.[58]

My visits to Baldwin's house in St. Paul-de-Vence—the place no one will ever curate as a "writer's house"—and interviews with his friends and lovers convinced me that, like Proust's, this African American writer's last novel, *Just above My Head*, should be read through his last domestic space, too, and that it, along with the play *The Welcome Table*, provides an "inverted mirror image" of some of his traumatic memories: having grown up poor in Harlem, being beaten and verbally and psychologically abused by his stepfather, experiencing widespread racism, homophobia, and police brutality. There was also the bottomless loneliness that he experienced as a black queer artist and voiced in his letters, the love for his mother and stepsiblings, and the sympathy for and understanding of the plight of black women that grew and deepened as he became older.[59]

As extended, literary reckonings with his life story and the larger history of his family and kin, both works deploy traumatic memories that affected individuals and entire groups and whole regions, too. Some arise from the writer's personal experience and imagination, triggered by visits to parts of the United States that he found terrifying—for example, when traveling to the South, he fears racist violence and envisages his own body hanging lynched from a tree (*Nobody Knows My Name* [1961]); he reports on the murders of the Civil Rights Movement leaders and random black, and some white, men and women by white supremacists; he visits prisons in Europe and the United States (*No Name in the Street* [1972]); and he comments on wars in the Pacific and on poverty in the unincorporated territories of the United States, such as Puerto Rico (*If Beale Street Could Talk* [1974]). As Fuss insists, in writers and their works, memories and imaginings, whether lived or experienced as the life of others we meet through literature, have the power to transport us to a new place, and they "effect . . . an immediate temporal and spatial

2.16. The upstairs living room. Photo by author, 2014.

dislocation that suspends not only then and now but also here and there."[60] Literature does make things happen in our heads, minds, and bodies. It is part of who we are as humans, and stories are political-personal weapons simply by the virtue of their form and content, as Mohsin Hamid, another admirer of Baldwin and a fellow writer-descendant, states eloquently.[61]

How the power of place affects fiction, and fiction in turn helps the readers transcend and reimagine places, resonates with Eleanor Traylor's perceptive review of *Just above My Head*. Traylor sees it as a novel about lifelines of families and specifically exploring the lineage of "blues boys ... [who] must become blues men." Echoing some of the points Bachelard makes about houses and literature inviting the mingling of often disparate elements, in Baldwin, Traylor insists, opposites meet in "the struggle to achieve blues manhood [that] ... engages the union of the sacred and the secular, of mind and feeling, of lore and fact, of the technical and the spiritual, of boogie and strut, of street and manor, of bed and bread."[62] Such a pairing of male writers with spheres domestic and affective also touches upon an important gendered dimension that, I believe, the two aforementioned, unlikely literary bedfellows—Fuss's Proust and "my" Baldwin—share, albeit with a twist.[63] As Fuss writes, for Proust, his intense domesticity resulted in conspicuous, if not at times contorted and desperate, attempts by his critics to (hetero) masculinize him by distancing him, the great French writer and "the man in time," from the sissy (my term) domestic sphere of an agoraphobe, who "wrote from her bed."[64] Unease with Proust's homosexuality manifested as a covering and remasculinizing of his legacy, even of his house-museum, so as to place him, however pretentiously, in the hetero-patriarchal national pantheon.

For Baldwin, the pairing means something quite the opposite. First, when he was still alive, and for a while after his death, not many cared to place him in a national pantheon of any kind, given his race and sexuality; neither could he be put back in the closet or de-sissified. He articulated his fierce individualism just days before his death, in his last interview with Troupe: "I was not born to be what someone said I was" (JB, 92). Second, he leads into this statement having remembered his cruel stepfather and what his abuse taught him—"how to fight ... [and] what to fight for." A survivor, he elaborates on the complex optics he desires applied to him and his legacy: "I was only fighting for safety, or for money at first. Then I fought to make you look at me" (90). From the safety of his domestic abode in St. Paul-de-Vence, Baldwin made the final demand to be fully seen, for his composite portrait to capture all of his complexity, contradiction, and challenge.

This explains, too, why he rather flamboyantly took on his Chez Baldwin domesticity with all of its sissy implications, claiming it and queering it in his own way through campy performances, rowdy parties, and long discussions of ideas, those rhetorical rehearsals of his that later found their way into his writing.[65] When ill and confined to his bed in the last stages of cancer, Baldwin turned the space around him into a musical soundscape and reading room, where Dinah Washington's songs were followed by readings from Jane Austen's novel *Pride and Prejudice*, which he appraised as "so economical, so devastating"; where his desire to be working on *The Welcome Table* and looking through drafts of his own works meant planning their completion against all odds; where men ministered to him like tender nurses whom "Jimmy and our love for him made . . . a community."[66] Baldwin entrusted men to be the "exceedingly clumsy midwives" of a new world order, for whom the "acceptance of responsibility contains the key to the necessarily evolving skill," in the epilogue to *No Name in the Street* that resonates clearly in his late essays on gender and sexuality (NNS, 196). Baldwin's achievement and message, combined with his black queer household and queenly persona presiding over it, are not only comparable to Proust's, but, indeed, remain in a league of their own. Among the many American national literary icons and their housemuseums, the haunting, fragmented remnants of Chez Baldwin provide a badly needed counterproposition to the several fetish-filled houses of white, macho "Papa" Hemingway.

These musings on Chez Baldwin serve the hope that his domestic traces will be preserved not only in his books but also in the places where he wrote them. As Fuss emphasizes, the point that brings me back to the haunting feelings that I experienced at Chez Baldwin in 2000, writers' houses invite us to enter "into conversation[s] with the dead," and the "recurrent interplay of subject and object in the space of writing reminds us that if the writer's interior is a memorial chamber, it is also a living archive."[67] While I first came to St. Paul-de-Vence looking for such an archive, I was keenly aware that I had no way of knowing whether Baldwin's last room looked exactly like the photograph I took of it in 2000, thirteen years after his death and four after David Baldwin had left it. What I could be sure of was that the house had changed physically and that, although no one could tell me what had been shifted, where and when, what was removed or added and by whom, spatial accuracy and verisimilitude were not as important as the fact that I was able to enter Baldwin's house and spend time there.

In the material-metaphorical triangulation of space, story, and self, again, what mattered was that I could see its interiors, note its textures and smells,

2.17. Storage area with the salvaged Chez Baldwin archive. Photo by author, 2014.

touch furniture and books, feel the light as it came through the windows, observe how angles of walls, staircases, and corners embraced and directed inhabitants and their movements. In contrast to visiting a famous writer's well-advertised and -appointed museum, where one might see a tidy desk artfully displayed behind a velvet rope just "as she or he left it," I encountered what remained of Chez Baldwin's messy, private processes of everydayness. As the cultural anthropologist Daniel Miller remarks, studying materiality of houses involves an invasion, "a willingness to step inside the private domain of other people."[68] At the moment of my visit, the ever-changing "memorial chamber" of Baldwin's domesticity seemed to reflect nothing more and nothing less: a collection of objects enclosed within walls to which my visitor's eye would attach meaning in the process of understanding. That process, though, as Nick Sousanis illustrates, is a complex mobilization of the senses, materiality, and energy; "understanding, like seeing, is grasping this always in relation to that."[69]

My experience echoes both Sousanis and Miller, with the latter posing a "challenge to our common-sense opposition between the person and the thing, the animate and inanimate, the subject and the object."[70] At Chez Baldwin as I saw it in 2000, that opposition was clear-cut nowhere at all, and the overall effect was indeed challenging, haunting, and paradoxical. I had an impression of a stage set, yes, and a sense of having tasted and tried on someone else's domestic atmosphere like a show or costume. My physical presence there was necessary to incite feelings and images that corresponded to my projections of what it might have been like to live and work in that place. I left with the understanding that, whatever stuff was left in the house, it mattered and had a vibrancy that was important to imagining how the writer manipulated his domestic space and how it collaborated with him.

According to how we understand traditional archives, that leftover stuff, or the surviving contents of the house—books, records, knickknacks, furniture, photographs, paintings, phone logs, posters, and files of papers and clippings—did not mean as much at all as the manuscripts and letters that were painstakingly removed soon after Baldwin's death by David Leeming.[71] In the economy of writerly remains, the documents created in the author's hand take apocryphal precedence and value above everything else. Their monetary appraisal means that they can be sold or auctioned off; their price may appreciate with time similarly to art, and thus become capital. Whatever else remains might attain decorative or didactic value, should it happen to be used as part of a simulacrum of a writer's study inside a museum, but why should anyone care whether a book came from the library at Chez Baldwin or not? Like many, I do care about that and consider the writing process a much more material, embodied, and located affair than a manuscript alone could elucidate, no matter its price in the traditional archival value system.

My satisfaction with my first visit to Chez Baldwin may have something to do with the fact that I am an interdisciplinary literary scholar and hence partial to what Bachelard terms the "activity of metaphor," as well as the ways in which all kinds of materials and "images [must] be lived directly . . . taken as sudden events in life." Bachelard's house poetics relies on the assumption that meanings and their material inspirations cannot be divorced from the realm of the metaphor and image that belong to the writer and reader equally. It is thus possible for the actual "house [to] acquire . . . the physical and moral energy of the human body," to be an agent, however ephemeral, in the texts it has inspired. This approach is particularly applicable to Baldwin, who acknowledges his dwelling's subjectivity in the *Architectural Digest* piece, or that his house "found me just in time." For a writer, Bachelard claims, "from having been a refuge, [the house] has become a redoubt . . . a fortified castle for the recluse who must learn to conquer fear within its walls."[72] Or, as bell hooks would have it, "home is a site where oppressed and disenfranchised people restore their spirits, and continue the process of self-recovery."[73]

Baldwin's house certainly became such a redoubt, self-recovery space for him, and it is clear that it would be impossible to understand his late life and writings without a close reading of it and of its contents. In a way, this ancient house recalled and transformed the village life he once shared with Happersberger in Löeche-les-Bains, allowing for the familial, homosocial setting he always desired, no matter that he never found a lover to become a long-term companion. As Jules Farber recalls, St. Paul-de-Vence was "a tranquil setting for his sexual expression. . . . Partners came, stayed, left or were chased out. . . . Doctors on a sick call . . . nonplussed when the bed was filled with another male body. . . . Nothing was said."[74] To the overawed scholar I was then, the place appeared to contain tangible traces of Baldwin's presence and desires; in the absence of any site in the United States, seeing the majority of his household possessions within its walls, including his library and visual assemblages on mantelpieces, felt powerful, as close to what Fuss terms "a conversation with the dead" as one could possibly get. The remaining objects constituted a sizable archive that no one had studied before, and they were deteriorating in a house that was slowly falling into disrepair. Confronting my literary research with the material structures and objects that enabled and framed Baldwin's creative process, as well as his daily life, became pivotal for my future research and writing.

Having been inside Chez Baldwin also helped me to understand the writer's late-life transformation into the steward and homemaker that he appears to be in one of his last published pieces, the short house tour in *Architectural Digest* in August 1987 and in the interviews he gave in 1985–87. Bachelard's phenomenology of the imagination elucidates an organic connection between material structures, the human body, and the images and dreams of those who live in, visit, think, or write about houses that pervades Baldwin's account. Once inhabited, a house enables a "geometrical object" to undergo a "transposition to the human plane," making the experience of material space become an extension of our humanity and endowing meaning making with transformative power: "Come what may the house helps us to say: I will be an inhabitant of the world, in spite of the world.... A house ... experienced is not an inert box. Inhabited space transcends geometrical space."[75] Whether standing or not, as a framing for and extension of the embodied writer, Baldwin's house has evolved its own complex poetics. Along with a politics of homelessness he developed before settling down, his material and metaphorical houses can be read as intriguing spaces of writerly manipulation in the context of the tour that he offers in *Architectural Digest*.

REPRESENTING HOUSE

> The key to one's life is always in a lot of unexpected places.
> —Baldwin, in Troupe, "Last Interview (1987)"

Baldwin's 1987 interview with the journalist, poet, and editor Quincy Troupe was recorded at home literally days before he passed. As Leeming reports, by that time he was very weak and unable to leave the house, having been moved "from his 'dungeon' downstairs, where he for many years lived and worked" to the upstairs part of the house, or "Mlle Faure's living room, with its ancient faded frescoed walls, Provençal tile floor, and deep fireplace [that] was turned into the bedroom, where ... he stayed for the rest of his life."[76]

This last known and published oral account of his life and career, "The Last Interview," constitutes Baldwin's reckoning with a rich and complex artistic and intellectual trajectory, while echoing profound paradoxes of his life and literary legacy with which we must contend today. It also provides an important context in which to read his self-presentation as a host in the *Architectural Digest* piece.

Troupe had come to St. Paul-de-Vence at the invitation of James's younger brother, David, who knew that the writer's days were numbered and wanted him to have a last chance to speak to his audience. Troupe recalls being shocked by the profound deterioration of Baldwin's appearance due to quickly progressing terminal cancer. His observations, however specific to the last moments of the writer's life, also indicate how many others apprehended the writer throughout his lifetime—as an intense and probing presence, a demanding interlocutor and keen observer, a sage filled with the power of prophecy, but also someone with a frail and fallible body and childlike presence in need of constant attention.

When Troupe greets Baldwin in the room to which he has been relocated, the writer "smiled that brilliant smile of his, his large eyes bright and inquisitive like a child." His voice sounds "very weak," but he promises to greet him "properly in about two or three hours." As Troupe takes leave of the sick room, Baldwin's "bright luminous owl eyes burned deeply" into his. "They probed for a moment and then released me from their questioning fire." Troupe feels relieved when David leads him out of "the darkened house," that relief coming at the same time as an indelible sensory memory of his visit burns into his mind: "that image of Jimmy weakly sitting there, the feel of his now-wispy hair scratching my face when I hugged him, the birdlike frailty of his ravaged body... large head lolling from one side to the other... as Lucien lifted him to put him to bed." That last image, of Baldwin cradled in the arms of Happersberger, the love of his life, reveals that which the writer often struggled to hide throughout his lifetime, but mentions at the beginning of Troupe's interview—his "extreme vulnerability" and emotional pain, and indelible sense of estrangement from his homeland (JB, 79).

The interview with Troupe confirms the importance of the author's last abode to the person he became at the end of his life and celebrates "unexpected places" in his life and oeuvre as key to understanding his journey.[77] As Wole Soyinka emphasizes in the foreword to *James Baldwin: The Legacy* (1989), in which the interview was later published, Baldwin's last work, the play he worked on until the day he died, *The Welcome Table*, owed its setting and plot to "an actual event... a late-night August dinner in the gardens." The play also had "Baldwin's intense, restive and febrile persona hover[ing]... over the pages."[78] In a somewhat similar vein, "*Architectural Digest* Visits: James Baldwin" (1987) uses the writer's name in a common metonymic fashion where it stands for his immediate milieu, thus making the man and house an entity. Unlike the play, this popular publication seems intended for coffee tables of homemakers rather than desks of literary critics. On a deeper level,

2.18 and 2.19. The last room: An upstairs living room that was transformed into his bedroom during the final months of Baldwin's life. Photos by author, 2014.

however, it seems part of the set of confessional life writings—essays, letters, diary entries, notes on new projects, interviews—that Baldwin produced in the last months of his life, and thus it calls for careful scrutiny.[79]

The text of "*Architectural Digest* Visits: James Baldwin" seems overshadowed by Daniel H. Minassian's lush photographs of the tranquil, sunlit Provençal garden and the simply furnished interiors of the old stone farmhouse. Of the seven photographs, only two depict the writer, who seems posed to complement rather than command the scene; it appears as if the piece is self-conscious about Baldwin's eclipsed celebrity in the United States. It is a "digest" piece, after all, meant to show rather than tell, or to showcase not so much the writer as the real estate he owns. On closer examination, however, it is a densely meaningful narrative that can be read as a photo-text that encapsulates Baldwin's last vision of himself, seemingly intended for a popular audience but suffused with what he sees as his larger literary legacy, and thus key to understanding his perception of that legacy.

Enabling his creativity, "the spread," as he called his house, allowed Baldwin to slow down in middle age and to embrace a life that included long-term household maintenance and growing into a community where he arrived as a perfect stranger. Having achieved, as he writes in *Architectural Digest*, the "age at which silence becomes a tremendous gift," he praises domestic work with the easy metaphor of "the vineyard in which one toils [with] a rigorous joy." Never one to tinker or engage in any serious physical labor, including gardening or housework, Baldwin was surely referring here to the upkeep and repairs on the house and its surroundings that some of the men in his entourage, or hired craftsmen, must have performed. His elegant metaphor of toiling in the vineyard, then, can be read as referring to his routine as a writer who, in his twilight years, sees his efforts as akin to physical labor involved in domestic labor and husbandry; he translates his work routine through the countryside metaphors of the lush land and real estate around him.

He elaborates on this train of thought, as this last house of his is "a very old house, which means that there is always something in need of repair or renewal or burial," yet the "exasperating rigor" of domestic maintenance "is good for the soul" and "one can never suppose that one's work is done" (AD, 124). This sentiment, indicating a deep satisfaction derived from being attached to one place and from observing its transformation with time, contradicts young Baldwin's belief, expressed in a 1957 letter written from Corsica to his childhood friend and editor Sol Stein, that his work is "my only means of understanding the world ... my only means of feeling at home in the world."[80] He beseeches Stein: "Please get over the notion . . . that there's some place I'll fit when I've made some 'real peace' with myself: the place in which I'll fit will not exist until I make it."[81] Thirty-three years old at the time, Baldwin casts himself as an eternal nomad "covering the earth," who believes that the best way to "escape one's environment is to surrender to it."[82] The moment for "making the place in which he fit" came when he approached middle age, after an exhausting decade and a half of writing and activism, as well as moments of despondency in the wake of the backlash against the Civil Rights Movement, the murders of some of its leaders (Medgar Evers, Malcolm X, Martin Luther King Jr.), and his waning popularity in the United States. At forty-six, he decided to anchor his work, to surrender to the house in St. Paul-de-Vence, even though this embrace of domesticity required that he surround himself with others who had to perform the physical tasks of its actual management and upkeep.

It can be said, too, that Baldwin as much "made it" his own as let the house "find" him. This signifies an important turn from being an exile and nomad to a homeowner, a turn not extensively documented that has inflected the works whose composition the house enabled.[83] Besides original footage of the place that Thorsen used in *The Price of the Ticket* and generously shared with me, precious few sources record details of his residence and its environs. A closer look at the photos and captions from *Architectural Digest* helps us contextualize the images that were presumably taken and arranged in collaboration with the writer.[84] The captions include snippets of Baldwin's speech, likely from a recorded interview, and provide detailed descriptions of key spatial elements of Chez Baldwin.

The first, extensive caption appears under the second photo in the series, which depicts the writer seated at an outdoor wooden table with a view of the village behind him. The text encapsulates his life story and legacy, identifying the first photo in the series, of the house from the back garden, which appears above the article's title: "'I first arrived in France in 1948, a little battered by New York because of my anger, my youth, and my pride,' recalls James Baldwin, whose debut novel *Go Tell It on the Mountain* began his exploration of social inequality and civil liberties"; "He is currently working on a new novel, *Any Bootlegger*"; "a bamboo-shaded table, where Baldwin and his guests eat lunch, is surrounded by the vegetation that he has let grow untamed." Two more images show the writer reading while seated on a stone patio under an umbrella, and they highlight the picturesque landscaping and architectural elements around him: "'An island of silence and peace' is how Baldwin describes the terrace directly in front of his office where he can take breaks from writing"; "Roses surround and climb over one of the oldest parts of the house, the back entrance with a shuttered door that leads into the kitchen" (AD, 124). The final page consists of three images that highlight the functionality of the interiors: "The corkboard in his office, where Baldwin often works till dawn . . . [p]hotographs of friends and family include one in the center of Baldwin with his brother David . . . two book jackets . . . of his most recently published works . . . plaster mask of Pascal"; "The living room . . . furnished with rustic Provençal pieces, in keeping with his preference for an unadorned environment"; "Photographs of . . . Baldwin, arranged along the living room mantel, and paintings . . . done by his friends."

As Baldwin writes about his "castle" in *Architectural Digest*, it became his redoubt in a process of gradually inhabiting it, spreading through it, but also being taken into it, becoming its integral part: "I looked around me and realized that I had rented virtually every room in the house. . . . It's a fine stone house, about twelve rooms, overlooking the valley and at the foot of the village. My studio is on the first floor, next to a terrace" (123–24). Between the lush photographs of the grounds and of the sparsely furnished interiors of the house, the writer's brief text narrates Baldwin and the house, as it were, in an abbreviated form familiar to readers of the journal in which it appeared. And yet, again, the piece both manages to be a digest piece intended for someone's coffee table and invites a deeper reading as a concise and complex, even intense, last glimpse of the writer's reflections on the history of his search for writing havens and a portrait of his most enduring domestic surroundings.[85]

By the end of "*Architectural Digest* Visits: James Baldwin," the portrait of the artist as an older black man ensconced in an idyllic and blissful southern French abode seems complete. But this is misleading, for Baldwin's sexual identity is never mentioned or even hinted at—not one bedroom photo appears; not one remark about his choice of lovers is made. The piece thus presents him as an unequivocally single, even solitary, man; an intellectual cultivating his talent in a remote location in his twilight years, he is comfortably desexualized, so that both he and his house can find their ways into middle-class living rooms. This portrayal stands in stark contrast to what he was writing about during his last years, especially in *Just above My Head* and *The Welcome Table*, which take place in the house that is Chez Baldwin, that employ characters who are clearly reflections of the writer and people close to him, and that ponder issues of gender and sexuality as openly as those of race and national identity.

The absence of Baldwin's black queer persona in the *Architectural Digest* piece, and later in accounts of his life, eulogies, and public acknowledgments following his death, and especially at his funeral, where the rhetoric excised his sexuality completely as if it were a shameful thing, are glaring vis-à-vis the accounts by his friends and biographers. Those who attended events at Chez Baldwin hail the author's legendary parties and entourages of visitors, lovers, and family who often filled the house and provided the social scene Baldwin needed as much as his solitary hours of work. Kendall Thomas writes that during Baldwin's very public funeral at the Cathedral of St. John the Divine in New York City on December 8, 1987, the silence about Baldwin's sexuality "cut me to the core, because . . . while Baldwin may have left America because he was black, he left Harlem, the place he called 'home,' because he was gay."[86] He adds, "In the years since Baldwin's death . . . his testimony as a witness to gay experience has become the target of a certain revisionist impeachment . . . [even though] we live in a world in which individual identities are constructed in and through constructs of gendered sexual difference." Referring to what he terms the "jargon of racial authenticity," which excludes non-normative sexualities from discussions of national blackness, Thomas sees Baldwin's black queer homelessness as a result of deliberate efforts to claim and domesticate him as a safely desexualized black writer, which attests to the exclusion of gay people of both sexes from the African American family.[87] His approach echoes the more general statement that Clayton G. Holloway made in the introduction to his 1985 interview with Baldwin, characterizing Baldwin as a "pariah," or "outcast at home and at school" who "struggled to achieve recognition and acceptance," before arriving at "celebrity status."[88] Again, Holloway never mentions the writer's sexuality, while implying a rather vague sense of his racial and class otherness, thus forgetting that Baldwin's message and vision throw such omissions into especially stark relief.

Baldwin's self-portrayal as a homeowner—we ought to admit the possibility that he was at least somewhat complicit in his representation in *Architectural Digest*—also omits his important connections to the local population, especially the women who welcomed him into their tightly knit village community; some of them were inspirations for characters in *The Welcome Table*. Baldwin suffered conflicting desires for home. On the one hand, he longed for domestic intimacy, safety, and the privacy of a monogamous relationship; on the other, he understood that his lifestyle of nighttime work, exhausting parties, often excessive drinking and smoking, not to mention strenuous travel and stormy love life, made stable domesticity virtually unattainable.[89] Finally, among the inhabitants of St. Paul-de-Vence, who cared little for his fame and notoriety, the activist-writer-traveler did become a homemaker-author. At one point in Thorsen's *Price of the Ticket*, we see him passing by the camera, inviting whoever is following with a theatrically sweeping gesture of hospitality, smiling his inimitable welcome.

This transformation is visible in the pages of the *Architectural Digest* piece, which juxtaposes his actions, achievements, and travels—"I had bought a building in New York . . . directed a play in Istanbul . . . visited Italy"—with the bodily and affective fallout of a whirlwind life that required a dramatic change of setting and pace—"I collapsed physically. . . . Friends then shipped me. . . . It was grief I had been avoiding, which was why I had collapsed. . . . Why not stay here?" (AD, 123). It was Mary Painter, an old-time friend, the woman whom Baldwin at one point "wishe[d] he could marry," who persuaded him to settle in her favorite location in Provence.[90] Once there, Baldwin could take time to heal his trauma. He spoke of the French women who became his friends as his guides and teachers, and he continued to enjoy the company of "sisters," or African American women whom he had admired and loved since his earliest years. Both became important inspirations for *The Welcome Table*. The material spaces of his house and the women who led him to them stand at the center of the next part of this chapter.

STAGING THE HOUSE OF WOMEN

> She was my guide to something else.
> —Baldwin, in Troupe, "Last Interview (1987)"

When Baldwin, ill and weak, came to St. Paul-de-Vence from Turkey in 1970, he was tired of moving around: "I have lived in many places, have been precipitated here and there" (AD, 122).[91] In Istanbul, he met Brenda (Keith) Rein, his assistant and typist, who became one of many African American and Turkish women—along with the singer Bertice Reading; the actors and singers Gülriz Sururi, Eartha Kitt, and Shirin Devrim (also an author); the journalist and critic Zeynep Oral; and the scholar and fiction writer Florence Ladd—who became Baldwin's close friends, confidantes, and enablers of his work, either directly collaborating, providing intellectual companionship, or inspiring ideas about femininity and gender roles, which he became increasingly interested in as his Turkish decade came to a close.[92]

Baldwin was also enamored of several black women, "sisters" like Rein and Ladd, including the writer and performer Maya Angelou, whom he met in Paris; the artist and cookbook writer Vertamae Grosvenor; the Caribbean American novelist Paule Marshall; the activist and writer Louise Meriwether;

and the scholar Eleanor Traylor. He also met and admired women writers, usually younger, who were his contemporaries and whom he often influenced while learning plenty from: the poets and activists Audre Lorde and Nikki Giovanni; the novelist Toni Morrison, whose son later married his niece; and younger writers like Suzan-Lori Parks and Shay Youngblood, both of whom studied with him when he guest-taught at several American colleges in the 1980s. Most important, from his earliest years, Baldwin was captivated by glamorous black women singers and performers like Bessie Smith, and especially by the international superstar Josephine Baker and the singer-activist Nina Simone, who both were guests at his house. Noting Baldwin's marked turn toward femininity in his self-presentation as an older man, Leeming claims that beyond his sheer admiration of these women, "there was a part of him that envied their style, their clothes, their gestures."[93]

By the publication of his fifth collection of essays, *The Devil Finds Work* (1976), on representation, cinema, and autobiography, Baldwin was confident in addressing the intersectionalities of race, gender, and sexuality, claiming that "identity would seem to be the garment with which one covers the nakedness of the self.... This trust in one's nakedness is all that gives one the power to change one's robes" (PT, 606–7). By the 1980s, "the female within the male ha[d] long fascinated" Baldwin, and the writer "not only enjoyed female company," but, as he had earlier in Turkey, also embraced camp and gendered performativity: he had "given in to a love of silk, of the recklessly thrown scarf ... the large and exotic ring, bracelet, or neckpiece. Even his movements assumed a more feminine character," as he succumbed to a "wish fulfillment or psychological nostalgia for a lost woman within his manhood." Inspired by female friends and visitors, he dreamed of "novels he could write about women who would convert the Jimmy Baldwin he still sadly thought of as an ugly little man into someone tall, confident, beautiful ... 'impeccably' dressed in silks and satins and bold colors," a "character" in whom "James Baldwin would be transformed into a Josephine Baker."[94] A village postal worker recalls fondly Baldwin's affectionate greeting every time he delivered mail: "He was ... like a grandmother to me, kissing me—and I'm not gay!"[95]

While he wanted to be like the black women he admired, Baldwin learned from the women of the town where his house stood how to feel at home away from his homeland. As Hélène Roux Jeandheur recollects, Baldwin truly lived his everyday life in the village, and he "was one of us." Her mother, Yvonne Roux, "adored him, and he adored her"; they spent hours talking every day and were very close friends. Her middle name, Clementine, served as an inspiration for Tish's given name in *Beale*; Yvonne helped him in crafting that young woman's narrative voice and character by always being there to discuss his writing with him. And, as her daughter asserts, "She was with him to the end." Yvonne, who dreamed of becoming an English teacher, translated *Blues for Mister Charlie* into French, and a piece that Baldwin wrote in French on the sculptures of the artist César into English. She introduced the writer, whom she proclaimed "the kindest man I have ever met," to her young daughters, Hélène and Pitou, who came to love him as a member of their family, and enjoyed his famous birthday parties at his house. As Hélène told me in an interview, to her the writer remains a genius and an internationally rooted humanist whose vision of identity was much ahead of his time; his life and works demonstrate that "nobody ever owned him."[96] She saw him last after his second surgery, and he told her that he wanted to die and be buried in the village, where his house stood. He also mentioned that he wanted his house to become a writers' colony after his death. She represented her family at his funeral on December 8, 1987.

Baldwin also became close friends with the "pied noir," Jeanne Faure, a "très a droite," or right-leaning local historian and author of a book entitled *Saint Paul: Une ville royale de l'ancienne France sur la Côte d'Azur* (1931). Faure was a French Algerian who considered herself exiled from her home country; Baldwin rented from her and later bought the house that became Chez Baldwin, where she had lived alone with her brother. Though their relationship was at first stormy, as she did not like Blacks, blaming them for the loss of the country of her childhood, and she even blocked the door between her part of the house and Baldwin's "with a heavy wooden wardrobe ... expressing anxiety about having a 'neeger' under her roof," as Farber reports, Mlle. Faure came to love Baldwin, and he cherished their friendship until her death, barely a year before his own, telling Troupe that "I truly learned a lot from her, from her European optic in regard to others ... she also had an optic that came from Algeria ... she was a hard guide" (JB, 99). Hélène Roux Jeandheur recalls Faure's strange relationship with him as completely out of character for a shrewish old lady who often scared the village children: "He was like a son and a lover to her. She totally adored him."[97] I found Mlle. Faure's photograph among the leftover papers during my visit in 2014; it is the same one that appears in the mantelpiece assemblage I photographed in 2000.[98]

The spacious house was just what the writer needed—"his kingdom with an open gate policy"—and provided a vibrant setting for meetings with friends and for family visits, creative collaborations, long discussions on poli-

2.20. Photo of Jeanne Faure, from the archive. Photo by author, 2014.

tics and art, and parties famed in the region.[99] Baldwin acquired the house bit by bit, paying Faure in installments when he received money for his books, talks, and smaller publications; later, Mlle. Faure and her brother moved to a smaller place in the village. She also agreed to have the house become his once she died. Never very organized about legal matters, Baldwin relied on his brother David to make sure everything was in order. On April 3, 1986, he wrote David, alarmed that Mlle. Faure "cannot possibly live much longer" and that with her death his house "becomes seriously endangered." The way out of the situation, where it seems final payments for Chez Baldwin were due, was to sell "the NY house at a loss"; he felt the situation was "very close to disaster." Clearly loath to endanger his domestic stability in France, he asks David to consider moving "before the end of the year," which meant moving his family out to another place in New York.[100] As for Mlle. Faure, she pinned "two pieces of paper with the amounts Jimmy still owed attached with a safety pin to her bedclothes" when she died.[101] By the time the house was lost in the early 2000s, Baldwin owed about $200,000 in taxes and back payments on the property, a sum that could have easily been raised then to save the house from destruction, thus fulfilling his wish that his beloved abode continue to serve as a writers' haven.[102]

In "The Last Interview," Baldwin makes a startling claim that further emphasizes his reliance on his domestic abode in St. Paul-de-Vence, telling Troupe the house and its environs enabled his reconnection with his ancestral American southern roots. He became a "peasant" in St. Paul-de-Vence "because of where I really came from . . . my father, my mother, the line. Something of the peasant must be in all of my family" (JB, 99). Baldwin's musings on his "peasant" origins—a remark that should be taken seriously, given that it was made on the eve of his death—came about because he suddenly felt that he fit in, albeit in a place and among people who were far from his birthplace, and while, of course, embracing peasant pursuits metaphorically rather than literally. The closest he came to such pursuits was when, "with childlike glee," as Farber describes, he "wandered barefooted in the groves, picking fruit and nuts."[103] This attitude won him a following among the townies, Leeming notes: "If people at first were suspicious of the newcomer with a reputation for an unorthodox lifestyle, they came in a very short time to love him as one of their own. Without having planned to do so, he had made a place for himself that he would consider home for the rest of his life."[104] Feeling at home, he built a close friendship with Simone Signoret, with whom he shared fierce commitment to political and artistic causes, while solidifying the unique bond he had with Yvonne and her large family.

Along with Faure, Baldwin became close friends with Hélène's grandmother, Tintine Roux, an older woman who ran the famous restaurant La Colombe D'Or and who "had picked herself to be my protector," Baldwin explains, and expands on this important connection to Troupe: "Both these women were watching something else besides my color. And they . . . loved me. . . . I miss them both terribly." What he meant is that he became legible to them, for they "recognized where I came from" (JB, 98–99). When Faure's brother died, she asked Baldwin to lead her at the funeral procession, to "stand . . . with her at the head of the family." The meaning of this act was "shocking" to the town, yet it symbolized the writer's full acceptance as not only a St. Paul-de-Vence inhabitant but also Faure's kin and thus a descendant of the town's elders: "what it meant . . . is that I was the next in line, when she died" (JB, 101). Indeed, by the time he was ill, Hélène told me, he was considered such a vital part of the town that the mayor of St. Paul-de-Vence wanted to bury him in its cemetery.

When Baldwin traveled to Paris to receive the French Legion of Honor medal from President François Mitterrand on June 19, 1986, he took Mlle. Faure with him, along with his cook, Valerie Sordello, to whom he had promised a trip to the big city, which she had never seen. Originally hired

2.21 and 2.22. Interior of La Colombe d'Or. Photos by author, 2000.

to clean and cook, Valerie became a "member of the family and was with Baldwin to the end."[105] Appearing briefly in the documentary *The Price of the Ticket*, Sordello remains a fleeting presence within the pages of Baldwin's writing, having inspired the character of Angelina, the maid, in *The Welcome Table*, in which all of the main characters are female and where the house emerges as both a setting and one of the characters—the theme that chapter 3 explores in detail.

The topic of Baldwin's female friends and their influence on his works intertwines with those of domesticity, queerness, homemaking, and homelessness and exile, while the vicissitudes that Chez Baldwin and its contents have endured since the writer's death offer a fascinating and heartbreaking material commentary. I present them all in the next section describing my return visit to the site in 2014, illustrated with images of the house and my impressions of how it changed over the fourteen years since I first saw it. Haunted by images of objects abandoned by the Baldwin family, but preserved and rescued with no little effort and expense by Jill Hutchinson after the house had been lost, I excavate a fragmentary archive of Baldwin's domestic remnants.

2.23. Valerie Sordello serving food to Baldwin and his guests. Image from the documentary film *James Baldwin: The Price of the Ticket* (1989); courtesy of Karen Thorsen, Douglas Dempsey, and the James Baldwin Project.

KNOW WHENCE YOU CAME

> Why aren't I a black nationalist? Because I don't believe it is enough to be black—one has to be human as well. We did not struggle for four hundred years just to become like the white man.
>
> —Baldwin, in Standley and Pratt, *Conversations*

After my first sighting of Chez Baldwin in 2000, I traveled to other places important to the writer—from the streets of Harlem and Greenwich Village to Paris, to Istanbul, Ankara, and Bodrum—and met many people who knew him and shared living spaces with him, and who all confirmed his paradoxical need for a frantic nomadic lifestyle on the one hand, and, on the other, his fervent desire to establish a stable domestic routine in multiple locations. Intrigued by his late-life turn to domesticity as well as the increasing focus of his works on families, female characters, and black queer home life that are prominent in *Just above My Head* and *The Welcome Table*, I returned to Chez Baldwin in June 2014. By that time I had published a book on the writer's Turkish decade and numerous articles about various aspects of his works.

I was not prepared for what I saw in place of the house that had been full of furniture, books, papers, photographs, and art when I first saw and photographed it. Now, I confronted an empty, disintegrating structure, virtually open to the elements, filling with vegetation and wildlife that had crept inside over the walls and windows. The back patio in front of the study, where Baldwin liked to take reading breaks at a round table under an umbrella, along with the brick and stone pathways through the garden were so overgrown with unchecked weeds that the crumbling structure of the house seemed to float on top of tall tan grasses swaying in the breeze. Full of sharp little burrs, this grassy expanse tugged at one's shoes, attached its tiny hooks to fabric and straps, and scratched one's skin as if attempting to deter movement. An occasional orange tree hung with bright fruit flashed amid the tangled greenery and dried branches, as if to recall the harmony between natural bounty and human husbandry that once existed here.

The writer's study, on the ground floor in the back, where Georges Braque had once painted, and which Baldwin called his "torture chamber," had broken shutters and windows, one missing glass entirely, and seemed especially exposed and pitiful.[106] When I visited the house for the first time in 2000, the study had been rented out to pay for the upkeep of the house, and so I was only able to photograph its well-kept exterior. Now the interior not only was wide open to view but also nearly blended together with the landscape, the boundaries between wall and garden nearly erased, and the writer's room had become a cavern that sported a fireplace filled with dry leaves. It seemed terribly significant that the very space that used to house the writer's creative labors was the most porous and open to the elements, the most vulnerable and deserted. There were traces of transient visitors, or laborers sent by the owner, some of whom left plastic bottles and food wrappers scattered on the floor. The trash mingled with leaves, twigs, dead bugs, and rodent droppings, creating mysterious organic/plastic designs on the stone mosaic floor.

The contrast between the interior images, shown in figures 2.27 and 2.28, taken during my two visits, speaks to the sad fate of Chez Baldwin. Once inside the study, easily accessible through low, open windows, I noticed the melancholy progression of time marked by the vines snaking over the chipped-tile floors, marking trails with no beginning and end. That part of the house consisted of three rooms linked together that ended with a small modern bathroom. The space of what used to be the heart of Chez Baldwin, that inner sanctum of the study, felt so eerie while we wandered around it that my twelve-year-old son, Caz, who accompanied me on that trip, picked

2.24. Outside the writer's study. Photo by author, 2014.

up a rusty hoe he found in the grass outside and told me he intended to protect us with it, "just in case." I tried to explain to him that the haunted feeling we picked up was simply that, a feeling our bodies generated, a normal sensation caused by the surroundings, a reaction to perhaps just a smidgen of guilt that accompanied our not-exactly-authorized visit to the property. I did have to engage in rather convoluted verbal gymnastics to explain to him that our entry was justified, indeed, was performed in the noble "interest of knowledge" and "for a good cause" of documenting a structure that might soon be gone.

As we wandered through the house and the grounds for over an hour, I found myself surprised by how emotionally fraught the confrontation between my past and present experiences of that space proved to be. I felt both sadness and anger that the house was let go by the Baldwin family following David's death, even though it was possible to hold on to it. I also felt frustration and despair about my own impotence to do anything, blaming

2.25 and 2.26. Baldwin's study and quarters. Photos by author, 2014.

myself for not having taken many more photographs in 2000 (who knew the house would be lost so soon?!), regretting that I never saw the writer's study furnished and inhabited. I kept circling around the structure, photographing frantically, getting annoyed as my son nagged me to leave. So much needed to be done, preserved, and documented; so much had been lost already. The obvious reason behind all this turmoil was the painful fact that the only viable writer's house for James Baldwin anywhere in the world was crumbling away before my eyes. It was not yet gone and could possibly be saved, but it was effectively out of reach of anybody who might want to preserve it by the sky-high price that real estate bidding wars had stamped on it.

Who could afford to pay thirty million euros for a writer's house that was falling apart? Would it be bulldozed to provide space for shiny new tourist quarters or a rich man's villa and swimming pool? Or would it be left alone, the lesser of two evils, waiting for the ravenous landscape to absorb the crumbling structure completely? By early November 2014, Jill sent me a distressed email and a couple of hastily taken photographs that provided glimpses of what was left of the house. Perhaps the reason why the first part of Chez Baldwin to go was the most vital—the writer's studio and living quarters—had

2.27. The ceiling in 2000. Photo by author.

2.28. The ceiling in 2014. Photo by author.

to do with razing to the ground any remnants of Baldwin's tenuous hold on the structure. I was not there when it happened, but I feel as though I had been: the disturbed soil smelled moist and cold, richly brown, loamy, and mineral, the day overcast and solemn.

After Caz and I saw the house, we met the owner of the famed local restaurant and inn, La Colombe d'Or, Madame Pitou Roux. As we chatted in the foyer of her establishment, which Baldwin visited regularly, she told us that the state of Chez Baldwin was a shame and proof of the meanness and small-mindedness of those who wanted to capitalize on that property and drive away the memory of Baldwin, "that black man." Middle-aged now, Pitou Roux knew "Uncle Jimmy" as a child, and she adored him throughout his life in St. Paul-de-Vence. She recalls having long conversations with him into the night when she was a young woman in her twenties, when she needed "life advice." I first spoke to her in 2000, and she was much more lively in her manner and hopeful about Chez Baldwin's prospects at that time; her mother, Yvonne, was too ill to speak to me. She remembered her first sighting of Baldwin then, at the restaurant where we were sitting: he was so striking and charismatic, ugly and beautiful at the same time, that she thought he might have been one of Joan Miró's drawings come to life.[107] She cherishes his memory and continues to receive visitors and field their many questions. At the same time, by 2014, she seemed slightly paranoid about being recorded against her will. When we were about to leave, she asked Caz to unroll a hoodie he had been holding over his arm—"What do you have in there? Show me?!" She wanted to make sure we had not been spying on her; I was both disturbed and amused by this suspicion, while my son found it mean.

Madame Pitou Roux's establishment, which in the past belonged to her parents, saw Baldwin on a regular basis and created its own set of memories and legends about him—his favorite chair at the bar, the entrance he usually took, the conversations that lasted into the wee hours of the night, the celebrities and artists who came to dine with him (Yves Montand and his wife, Simone Signoret; Miles Davis; Nina Simone; Caryl Phillips; Stevie Wonder; Bill Cosby). La Colombe d'Or has kept Baldwin's traces safe in the stories and anecdotes of those few who still recall him (besides Pitou, there is an elderly waiter who seems to remember him well), but it does not display any mementos of him anywhere prominent, at least to my knowledge.[108] This might not be a thing to do, since Baldwin frequented the place for the mere decade and a half that he lived in St. Paul-de-Vence, the period that now seems forgotten. His traces have been erased, for if you don't know of his link to La Colombe d'Or, you are not likely to discover his face peering at you from photographs on the wall; a random guest will not be prompted to ask, "Who is that black man?"

While at Baldwin's house this time, I took as many digital photographs as possible of what was left of the property. When I ran out of space on my card, I shot more, even video, with my iPhone. I found myself obsessively tracing the progress of the damage since my first visit, though it seemed a hopeless endeavor. For example, I discovered that the gorgeous frescos that once adorned the stairwell ceiling were gone, plastered over and whitewashed, most likely due to a repair of the leaky roof. The slightly damp air, occasional creaking of shutters, and swishing grasses and weeds outside amplified the melancholy nature of my labors.

CODA

> No road whatever will lead Americans back to the simplicity of this European village where white men still have the luxury of looking at me as a stranger.
> —"Stranger in the Village"

When I returned to the site of Baldwin's house in June 2017, its remnants were hard to see from the street. The developer who owned it, and had had two-thirds of the structure bulldozed in 2014, erected large, colorful billboards advertising soon-to-be-built luxury villas clustered around an expansive swimming pool. The ironic name of this new incarnation of the famous writer's house and garden was to be "Le Jardin des Arts"; the sales were held by Sotheby's and advertised nineteen "grandly" chic apartments with "a panoramic view of the sea," urging potential buyers to "reserve yours now!" Behind a new, locked, black metal gate stood the gatehouse, stripped of its hot-pink flowering vines and carelessly transformed into a real estate office for those who could afford the best views of the Mediterranean. It was segregated from the main house by a huge billboard sporting the image of the future swimming pool, with the inevitable couple of frolicking vacationers in the water. A cleverly camouflaged door inside that image led to the site; Chez Baldwin's diminished façade, only partially visible behind it, appeared blackened, as if by smoke.

We did not enter the site through that glamorous door, but via a gap in the fence we reached through an alley to the right, which was discovered by my fifteen-year-old son. Hoping that no one would see us from the gatehouse/office (this time, there *were* signs prohibiting entry and confirming surveillance), we circled the property and took many photographs of what was left of Baldwin's once lush abode. Reduced to its core central part, which now towered three stories high, the crippled building—soon to be a pool house—bore imprints of demolished rooms on both its sides, with the left one still bearing remnants of the tiled bathroom wall from Baldwin's downstairs study, and of the kitchen that had been located above it. The site was mostly stripped of its vegetation, with a lone palm tree still standing roughly where Baldwin's patio table used to be, an orange tree here and there, and a few surviving ancient olive trees that were a hundred or more years old, and which, as I had just then heard, were supposed to be under the protection of the French government.

Three years after his first visit to the site, this time Caz offered to break down a side door that was nailed shut, so that we could enter and take more photos of the interior of Baldwin's last room. I wanted to do it, but I told him otherwise, sadly aware that we could likely get away with photographing the structure for the purposes of research, but not with having caused "damage" to it. We had spent the week before documenting Baldwin's archive, then stored at the house of Leonore, Jill's daughter, in the tiny Alpine village of Guillaumes, about two hours from St. Paul-de-Vence. Having documented the riches of his library, David's many paintings, the writer's photos and posters, we found the visit to the house sad, even disturbing. The boxes whose contents I had photographed painstakingly, and some items stored at Jill's house, including the famous welcome table, were then the sole material effects of the writer's domestic life. As we were leaving, I had the feeling that this was my last pilgrimage to the site of Baldwin's domicile. I picked up as a keepsake a small shard of what might have been a brown clay flowerpot from the dirt where his study used to be.

Most of the physical topography of Baldwin's intimate house has been lost forever—there are few preserved images from the time he lived there and the site remains unmarked. Like me, many readers and scholars have visited St. Paul-de-Vence in hopes of glimpsing the structure that housed the famous writer. These trips come about because those who read and study this complex writer crave material reminders of his life, especially given that so few of them are present in the United States. We, the privileged few who have managed to travel to Chez Baldwin, have craved tangible connections with the surroundings that fed the author's imagination and framed his late years.

As Quentin Miller writes in the first issue of the *James Baldwin Review*, "I have read all of his books to the point that I've had to tape the bindings together, but I wanted something else, something that came from being where he had been."[109] Writing in the *Times Literary Supplement* about a visit to the site that involved vaulting over a fence, Doug Field expresses dismay at the state of Baldwin's study, while populating the space with imagined stuff: "photographs and personal, homely objects: a painting by his old friend Beauford Delaney; an exhausted looking typewriter; a drink . . . ; cigarette packets; and a sheaf of papers—a manuscript—but which?"[110] In 2014, the poet and critic Ed Pavlić had gone to see the house with Lynn Scott and her husband days before my journey there, and he sent me a photograph that helped me to find my way onto the grounds without serious acrobatics. Pavlić's reaction to the state of Chez Baldwin was more upbeat than mine or Doug's, as he thought the house sturdy and solid and simply needing "lots of love."[111] The house of James Baldwin, whether still standing or not, and regardless of its legal ownership, remains an important access point—literal and literary—to Baldwin's legacy.[112]

After my three visits to the site and obsessive rereading of Baldwin's house-tour narrative in *Architectural Digest*, I realized that the only way to deal with the material on hand was to attempt to excavate, if you will, what remains of Chez Baldwin despite its gradual erasure, to write into being its material and metaphorical stories as a black queer domestic space that was key to the writer's later works.[113] As Toni Morrison claims in the essay "The Site of Memory," writing is a form of "literary archeology," where memory, imagination, and language come together to create continuities in black lives past and present: "On the basis of some information and a little bit of guesswork you journey to a site to see what remains were left behind and to reconstruct the world that these remains imply. What makes it fiction is the nature of the imaginative act: my reliance on the image—on the remains—in addition to recollection, to yield up a kind of truth. By 'image,' . . . I simply mean 'picture' and the feelings that accompany the picture." Morrison emphasizes that, in contrast, the traditional task of a "trustworthy" literary critic or biographer is to trace the "events of fiction" to some "publically verifiable fact," to excavate the "credibility of the sources of the imagination, not the nature of the imagination."[114]

Given my dual tasks of writing a story of my visits to James Baldwin's house and arguing for literature and architecture as inseparable bedfellows in my reading of the house as a transnational, black queer, domestic space, my goal in this chapter's concluding lines falls somewhere in between the two approaches Morrison has delineated. Although as a critic and biographer, I appear to be merely a collector of "publically verifiable fact[s]," I insist on the right to claim access to "pictures" and "feelings" inspired by the onsite research of Baldwin's house and close readings of his works. As Trinh T. Minh-ha reminds us, "Writers of color . . . are condemned to write only autobiographical works. Living in a double exile—far from the native land and far from the mother tongue—they are thought to write by memory and to depend to a large extent on hearsay. . . . The autobiography can thus be said to be an abode in which . . . [they] take refuge."[115] While Baldwin fits this description to some degree as a writer rendered homeless by his identity,

2.29. An upstairs bedroom window with vines. Photo by author, 2014.

he also expands it by demonstrating that building one's abode in language through writing goes hand in hand with establishing domestic spaces, however temporary, that can accommodate a rare and unique subject, a black queer American who has chosen to dwell in the world.[116] It is a great loss that his house in St. Paul-de-Vence can serve as such a space only symbolically, and now only as a memory and an elusive, fragmentary reminder of things past.[117]

James Baldwin reclining on the steps of his house. Image from the documentary film *James Baldwin: The Price of the Ticket* (1989); courtesy of Karen Thorsen, Douglas Dempsey, and the James Baldwin Project. Photo by Yves Coatsaliou, Nice.

CHAPTER 3

Life Material

Haunted Houses and Welcome Tables,
or The First Teacher, the Last Play,
and Affectations of Disidentification

> I was haunted . . . by Alexandre Mannette's document, in *A Tale of Two Cities*, describing the murder of a peasant boy—who, dying, speaks: I say we were so robbed, and hunted, and were made so poor, that our father told us it was a dreadful thing to bring a child into this world. . . . Dickens has not seen it all. The wretched of the earth do not decide to become extinct, they resolve . . . to multiply: life is their only weapon . . . life is all that they have. . . . The civilized have created the wretched . . . and do not intend to change the status quo; are responsible for their slaughter and enslavement; rain down bombs on defenseless children whenever . . . their "vital interests" are menaced . . . Those people are not to be taken seriously when they speak of the "sanctity" of human life. . . . There is a "sanctity" involved with bringing a child into this world; it is better than bombing one out of it.
> —*The Devil Finds Work*

As a child growing up in a family of nine children, James Baldwin knew well the wretchedness of poverty and the sanctity of human life. As the eldest, he served as a parental figure while still very young, helping his mother, Berdis Baldwin, to keep house and raise his eight stepsiblings. By the time he published his fifth essay volume, *The Devil Finds Work* (1976), he had acquired a tribe of nieces and nephews, whom he adored and spoiled, and who, like Daniel Baldwin (the son of his brother David), Trevor Baldwin (the son of his brother Wilmer; Wilmer was also known as "Lover"), and Aisha Karefa-Smart (the daughter of his sister Gloria; Gloria is now executor of his estate), remember his love and devotion as a profoundly important part of their lives.[1] Family, home, and haven have been key tropes in Baldwin's writings, and the life-cycle narrative of black male origins, coming of age, and the search for racial and sexual identity from childhood to adulthood and old age has been central to all his works, including even the strongly political and polemical ones like *The Fire Next Time* (1963), *No Name in the Street* (1972), and *The Evidence of Things Not Seen* (1985).

In *The Devil Finds Work*, another essay volume that links life writing and cultural critique, Baldwin recalls having been "haunted" by the words of Charles Dickens in *A Tale of Two Cities* (1859) and its film version, which a teacher took him to see when he was a young child. Baldwin looks back at a time when he was a student, one of the neediest, at the Harlem elementary school known as P.S. 24. That old school still stands on 128th Street, between Fifth and Madison, and seems largely unchanged, although it has since become the Harlem Renaissance High School. (The stretch of road alongside it was renamed James Baldwin Place on the writer's ninetieth birthday on August 2, 2014.) While attending that school, with "the book in one hand, the newest baby on my hipbone," Baldwin discovered a passion for reading and a hunger for culture in virtually all of its manifestations, especially cinema and theater. His haunting by the French peasant boy's death and the last words in Dickens's novel reveals deep empathy for suffering, a budding passion for social justice, and an instinctive understanding of class and political power well beyond his years. Like the little prophet in *A Tale of Two Cities*, Baldwin was no ordinary child.

By 1936, when he was twelve, the particular book in his hand, which he read "compulsively," was Harriet Beecher Stowe's *Uncle Tom's Cabin* (1852)—that sentimental call to right the wrongs of slavery in the national house—and, as he confesses in *The Devil Finds Work*, he was "trying to find out something, sensing something in the book of an immense import for me: which, however,

3.1 and 3.2. A David Baldwin collage and close-up image with James Baldwin holding a nephew or niece. Photos by author, 2014.

I knew I did not really understand." This determination to read closely and understand the book's as-yet-incomprehensible messages deeply concerned his mother, who frequently hid the volume to break him of his obsession. To no avail, young James always found it and continued to reread it. Berdis eventually gave up and, "though in fear and trembling, began to let me go" (PT, 565).

By the time Baldwin understood the significance of this novel, written by a white abolitionist woman—that "impassioned pamphleteer," as he later describes her—he was in his twenties and ready to take on race as literary representation in both *Uncle Tom's Cabin* and Richard Wright's *Native Son* (1941). He did so in an essay, "Everybody's Protest Novel" (1949), which compared both writers' essentialist portrayals of black characters, thus criticizing and offending Wright, who was then the acclaimed African American writer. That essay, first published in the Paris journal *Zero*, soon became a metaphorical slaying of his literary black father figure, Wright, who helped the younger writer obtain the important Saxton Fellowship for his first novel, *Go Tell It on the Mountain* (1953), which paid his way to Europe.[2] The ensuing literary scandal, which confirmed the sad American reality that there could be only one significant "Negro writer" on the scene, ensured Baldwin's essay a wide readership on both sides of the Atlantic, and it later compelled him to pen two more pieces on Wright—"Many Thousands Gone" (1951) and "Alas, Poor Richard" (1961). In both, he tried to repair his relationship with the older writer, while also justifying his dismissal of what he considered to be "protest" literature, offering instead his own complex and compelling meditations on the history of the "American Negro" and the difficulty of being a black writer in the twentieth-century United States.

As he describes these dilemmas in "Alas, Poor Richard," a "real writer is always shifting and changing and searching . . . knows defeat far more intimately than he knows triumph. He can never be absolutely certain that he has achieved his intention" (PT, 269). While Baldwin admits in this passage that "Everybody's Protest Novel" brought about some unforeseen negative effects, and while he pays homage to Wright, he nevertheless reiterates his original criticism of *Native Son*. He does so by commenting on the older writer's short story, "The Man Who Killed a Shadow," which was also originally published in the same issue of *Zero*. Claiming in "Alas, Poor Richard" that alongside "most of the novels written by Negroes until today (with the exception of Chester Himes's *If He Hollers Let Him Go*), there is a great space where sex ought to be; and what usually fills that space is violence," Baldwin volunteers to be *the* American writer who successfully attaches sex to race in examinations of national identity. In making that identity whole for the first time in American history, he becomes not only a black queer prophet, but also an outcast from the two tribes divided by the color line that have come, reductively enough, to represent his homeland (PT, 273). His fourth essay volume, *No Name in the Street*, begins with an epigraph from the Book of Job that seems to echo his sense of his diminishing popularity in his birth country as the 1970s went on: "His remembrance shall perish from the earth and He shall have no name in the street. He shall be driven from light into darkness, and chased out of the world" (Job 18:17–18).

From the vantage point of the brink of the twenty-first century, José Esteban Muñoz explains prophetic literary endeavors like Baldwin's. In the process of "dissing" majoritarian identity, "minoritarian subjects" like Baldwin "need to interface with different cultural fields . . . [for] their identities are formed in response to the cultural logics of heteronormativity, white supremacy, and misogyny . . . that . . . work to undergird state power."[3] In considering his rich oeuvre, it is astoundingly clear that Baldwin—a writer who revolutionized our thinking about identity, no matter how disempowered he was at times—has brilliantly succeeded in this complex endeavor. At the same time, it is also clear that the theme of violence and its impact on identity and authorship, and its simultaneous embroilment with race and sex, remained his deep concern. Never quite at home or able to work at his craft in the United States—whose institutions not only upheld but indeed pushed "heteronormativity, white supremacy, and misogyny" as attributes of proper citizenship—he had to seek writing havens abroad. (The FBI followed him there, as we know from their copious file on him. As relayed to me by Brenda Rein, the wife of the U.S. cultural attaché in Istanbul, she suspected some of the visitors to Baldwin's various abodes in that city were there undercover.)[4]

In "Notes for a Hypothetical Novel" (1960), an essay that begins as a commentary on the role of the writer in American culture that should be read alongside the ones I mention above, Baldwin calls for embracing what could be cast as a stereotypically feminine, if not sentimental, realm akin to what he dismissed categorically in Stowe: "the *level of the private life* which is after all where we have to get in order to write about anything and also the label we have to get to in order to live" (PT, 243, emphasis added).[5] The role of the writer, thus conceived as someone who explores that *private* realm, and who in a sense is entrusted with the literary preservation of humanity's best ideas, however, involves facing a dual task whose outcomes are not meant to appeal to sentiment but to social action: first, describing "the *American experience*...this enormous incoherence...shapeless thing"; second, "to try and make *an American*," a character, person, portrait (243, emphases added). This requires making the incompatible, disjointed, and fragmented "shapeless things" fit together into a coherent composite, which in turn has all to do with freedom and personal choices of the author.[6]

As Baldwin reminds his audience at San Francisco State College, where he first read his essay as a symposium address, freedom is not anything that "can be given," but "is something people take and *people are as free as they want to be.*"[7] Using freedom not "so much in a political sense...as in a *personal* sense," he points out that writers are essential to culture for they alone can "somehow...unite these things...*find the terms of our connection*, without which we will perish" (PT, 243, emphases added). Such socially invested writers are the only ones who can "describe things which other people are too busy to describe," though their "special function" in the United States is "yet to be discovered" (244). Baldwin's own task is to become *the* American author—not just a "Negro writer" as his editors and critics wanted to peg him—who can do it all, who can save the fragmented country from itself, for "it seems to me that the situation of the writer in this country is symptomatic and reveals, says something, very terrifying" (242). The terror has to do with willful ignorance and the scripting of national identity through myths and ideologies that destroy both the individual and his or her compatriots. That "illusion about America, a myth about America...has nothing to do with the lives we lead," Baldwin writes. The national drama of identity, violently mythologized in popular culture and benumbed by consumerism—"Cadillacs, refrigerators,...all the paraphernalia of American life"—creates "a collision between one's image of oneself and what one actually is" (244).

By now, scholars like Judith Butler, E. Patrick Johnson, Diana Fuss, and José Muñoz, among others, have discussed the "fiction of identity" as a performative and socially and culturally constructed set of behaviors.[8] To Baldwin, who articulated this theoretical concept in 1960, this "very painful" problem has two solutions that echo and complicate W. E. B. Du Bois's concept of double consciousness, which I described in the introduction: "you can meet the collision head-on and try and become what you really are or you can retreat and try to remain what you thought you were, which is a fantasy, in which you will certainly perish" (PT, 244). The deployment of the biblically inflected verb "perish" in this essay on novel writing suggests an annihila-

3.3. An image from the archive of Baldwin reading, 1977. Photo by author, 2014.

tion of apocalyptic proportions that may sound overwrought today. Yet, to someone like Baldwin, living a life of Thoreau's "quiet desperation" is not an option. Instead, he embraces a kind of determinism, a black queer form of civil disobedience, if you will. If you are born black and queer and an artist, and you have managed both to conquer and leave the pulpit in your church to become a writer, you have no choice but to sing your song, no matter the consequences. In that sense, the compulsion to literary expression is as much beyond his control as his sexual identity; in that, he echoes his female inspirations, Bessie Smith and Lorraine Hansberry.

The first solution Baldwin proffers for wrestling with the fictions of identity in "Notes for a Hypothetical Novel" is "meet[ing] the collision head-on," the only option for a writer. He calls for the examination of "the person" as a building block and means of transforming the country. He also asks his young audience for more: "We made the world we're living in and we have to make it over." The social project he has in mind links the private and the political, the individual and the social, the intimate and the public; it is as if one is rewriting a bad novel into a good one by turning away from sentimental pretensions and toward embracing social activism, which always begins in the private realm of one's own tormented heart, or what we today might call one's affective realm (PT, 244).[9] And while this stance seems similar to the second-wave feminist agenda in its linking of the private and political, Baldwin's insistence on grappling with more multiply inflected social identities, or what the legal theorist Kimberlé Williams Crenshaw called "intersectionality" in 1989, suggests as complex and as dynamic an optic that arises from a skillfully deployed combination of autobiographical and intellectual experience of a black queer man.[10]

Despite this erudite theorizing of the American writer's creative problem, it took Baldwin until the later essays of his last two decades, with which this chapter opens, before he could reconcile multiple attempts to fully embrace himself as a complex composite of fragments, reflections, and, indeed, often confounding intersectional and gendered personas, whose choices and freedoms could never be taken for granted. Only in his late works does he accept himself as someone who has had to delve deeply into his own "level of the private life" to become, as he states in the introduction to *Notes of a Native Son*, "an honest man and a good writer." In racialized and gendered terms, such a trajectory defies the simple narrative of white masculine progress toward power and recognition that passes for the so-called American Dream.[11] It also complicates its flip sides, the white feminine narratives of domestic fulfillment, confinement, and marginalization, as well as the queer black/nonwhite male/female/trans one of oppression, subjugation, and deprivation that is the unspoken but necessary price of that Dream that must be paid by many so that a few can cash in on happiness.

The theme of self-discovery and acceptance, of puzzling his own self out of disparate fragments, intertwines in Baldwin's later works with the theme of violence lurking around, blurring, or obscuring interrelated key aspects of identity—race and sex—and all of this takes place at the heart of gendered performances of national identity seen as both individual and collective enactments of self at home.[12] This complex struggle comes to the fore especially clearly in another essay published thirty-six years after "Everybody's Protest Novel" and a quarter-century after "Notes for a Hypothetical Novel"—"Freaks and the American Ideal of Manhood" (1985; later retitled "Here Be Dragons"). Baldwin looks back at his teenage years and early twenties, which he spent away from his family in Harlem, working odd jobs and desperately trying to become a writer at home in the bohemian Greenwich Village. Writing from the perspective of having recently entered the seventh decade of his life, he recalls feeling "the youngest, the most visible, and the most vulnerable" there (PT, 684):

> There were very few black people in the Village in those years, and ... I was decidedly the most improbable. Perhaps, as they say in the theater, I was a hard type to cast.... I felt absolutely, irredeemably grotesque.... It wasn't only that I didn't wish to seem or sound like a woman, for it was this detail that most harshly first struck my eye and ear. I am sure that I was afraid that I already seemed and sounded too much like a woman ... a sissy. It seemed to me that many of the people I met were making fun of women, and I didn't see why. *I* certainly needed all the friends I could get, male *or* female, and women had nothing to do with whatever my trouble might prove to be. (PT, 685, emphases added)

Right before this confession, he also remembers "the queer—not yet gay—world" he then entered, and he compares his situation to finding himself in a "hall of mirrors," or an "even more intimidating area" of self-estrangement, for "the mirrors threw back only brief and distorted fragments of myself" (685).

This poetic way of conveying his youthful confusion about racialized gender and sexual identity resonates with his sense of never fitting in, of feeling homeless, lost, and conspicuous, "impossible," even "grotesque," as a young black man filled with homoerotic desire and freshly removed from Harlem, the place that was home, but where he suffered from homophobia and at the hands of his stern stepfather and racist police. He relays a similar sentiment in an interview, "Go the Way Your Blood Beats," with Richard Goldstein and published in 1984 in *The Village Voice*, a year before the essay "Freaks" appeared in *Playboy Magazine* and took those sentiments further.[13] Read together, the interview and essay record a culmination of Baldwin's thinking on identity and identification that he explored in novel ways from the 1970s until the end of his life, especially in the essay volumes *No Name in the Street*, *The Devil Finds Work*, and *The Evidence of Things Not Seen*; his last two novels, *If Beale Street Could Talk* (1974) and *Just above My Head* (1979); and his last play, *The Welcome Table* (1987).

This chapter and the one that follows look to these works as recording the writer's journey from childhood to adulthood, and vice versa, his back-and-forth narrative journey of self-making and domesticating the world of writing, and of becoming an author as a black man, which he so movingly describes in "Notes for a Hypothetical Novel." In these works and in the course of nearly three decades since "Notes," Baldwin shifts from seeing himself as an uprooted "oddball" ("Notes") to "impossible," an "odd quantity," and "freak" (NNS, "Freaks"). And while each of these designations denotes someone who does not fit in, it is clear that in his later works they become more

LIFE MATERIAL 153

emphatic, or that he sees himself less and less as a "Negro" and "American" than he professed himself to be in 1960. By the 1980s, he admits that his goal as a writer has been all along to embrace being a part of multihued humanity—a singular existence caught up in the conundrums of oppression, freedom, and self-discovery. He confesses that he often got lost in that process, as though in a hall of mirrors, for we all "are rarely what we appear to be." At the same time, he accepts otherness and difference as his lot as he ends "Freaks," admitting that we are *all* "freaks," as "human beings who cause to echo, deep within us, our most profound terrors and desires" (PT, 242, 689, 690). It is only by embracing such an identity and such an approach to self-making that one can feel at home within oneself and inhabit the world as an artist.

In examining this conundrum of "freakish" humanity that Baldwin has come to domesticate late in life at his home in St. Paul-de-Vence, this chapter also argues for the author's pioneering theorization of *disidentification* by returning to his last play, *The Welcome Table*, whose experimental characters offer the starkest illustrations of this concept and theory. I explore this work in greater detail than past studies, placing the play in the context of its transnational origins and focus on female characters, all of whom were based on Baldwin's actual friends and household members. Set against the domestic scenery of Chez Baldwin, which provides its setting, furnishings, and objects, the play blends autobiography, or life writing, with dramatic genres inspired by the writer's deep fascination with international theater. In that sense, it experiments with old and new forms, recalling, for example, the historic device of the masque (some of the main characters are transformed from the males they are in actuality into female characters) and tweaking it to accommodate improvisational African American musical and poetic forms, and the highly individualized sense of self-presentation and personal styles of the dramatis personae.

Designed to be improvisational, and a departure from his first two plays in its transnational setting and form, *The Welcome Table* must be read as well in conversation with the classic plays of the famous modern Russian playwright, Anton Chekhov (1860–1904), whom Baldwin used as an inspiration and genre model. Aptly, given its focus on women; Chekhov's plays—the acclaimed *The Three Sisters* (1901) among them—have been called "revolutionary in that they dealt primarily with the paradoxes of emotion, the contradiction of behavior, and the significance of environment."[14] Few critics note, though, that their "revolutionary" character has much to do with Chekhov's centering of his plays' messages on what could be recognized as stereotypically feminine, domestic values and locales focused on the homes and intimate interiors, behaviors, and concerns of the characters around whose complex lives his dramas revolve.

This section also looks closely at one of the core drivers of Baldwin's fascination with the stage and his search for a place he could call home, namely his lifelong relationship with Orilla "Bill" Miller, a white radical woman from Illinois who was his elementary school teacher and mentor, and who "directed my first play and endured my first theatrical tantrums and had then decided to escort me into the world" (PT, 558). Miller, who came to New York to work for the Works Progress Administration (WPA), recognized young Baldwin's genius and helped awaken and nurture his threefold passion for theater and cinema, reading, and writing, all the while bringing him cod-liver oil and clothes when, as he recalls in *The Devil Finds Work*, "I seemed destined . . . to be carried away by whooping cough" (PT, 559). She was a surrogate mother, in a way, one who helped him to find his vocation as a writer and public intellectual, during a period when his own mother was too busy with domestic work for white people and too overwhelmed with her large family to have much time for her gifted firstborn. Miller showed young Baldwin what was key to his self-discovery, namely, that he had every right to feel at home in the world of theater and cinema, and often discussed Charles Dickens's novels with him for hours. In an unpublished letter dated December 27, 1984, Baldwin wrote to his mentor what he had already expressed countless times: "You were very very important to me."

The resources for this chapter include, among others, the private correspondence between Baldwin and Miller that took place between 1955 and 1985, and two manuscripts of *The Welcome Table* that I have been able to locate.[15] Like Hilton Als, I hope that my work on Baldwin will help bring about both the long-overdue publication of his marvelous letters, and, like Walter Dallas, who collaborated with Baldwin on *The Welcome Table* in the 1980s, the publication and staging of his last play as his fascinating literary testament. This play culminates the promise and ambition of all of this writer's works by challenging American literature and national theater with its progressive racial, gender, and sexual politics, as well as by offering an impassioned appraisal of the effects of twentieth-century U.S. politics on the domestic lives and private passions of black artists.[16] Most important, perhaps, it demonstrates powerfully that we would be wise to embrace its message in our twenty-first-century moment, when previously marginalized identities may have a chance—to echo the title of a recent memoir by Janet

Mock—of "redefining realness" at the same time as the very basis of democracy and freedom in the U.S. national house has been upended by the presidential election of 2016.[17]

"I WAS NEVER AT HOME IN IT": (WHITE) GAY WORLD DISIDENTIFICATIONS

> I never understood exactly what is meant by it. I don't want to sound distant or patronizing because I don't really feel that. I simply feel it's a world that has very little to do with me, with where I did my growing up. *I was never at home in it.* Even in my early years in the Village, *what I saw of that world absolutely frightened me, bewildered me.* I didn't understand the necessity of all the *role playing.* And in a way I still don't.
>
> —"Go the Way Your Blood Beats" (emphases added)

When asked by Goldstein at the start of their 1984 interview whether he felt "like a stranger in gay America," Baldwin retorts, "Well, first of all, I feel like *a stranger in America* from almost every conceivable angle except, oddly enough, as *a black person*" (JB, 59, emphases added). That his blackness is an aspect of his identity that is *not* strange, but in fact deeply American arises from his lifelong explorations of the complex constructions, manifestations, and representations of race and racism as the ideological foundation of the U.S. national home. At the same time, Baldwin quickly explains the reasons other identity labels, especially the "the word 'gay'," which was all the rage in the 1980s, "always rubbed me the wrong way." This explanation—contained in the epigraph for this section—reflects Baldwin's focus on semantics and affect, as he claims he "never understood exactly" what was meant by the term "gay" and he still does not, as well as his insistence that he follow his feelings about the matter and remain true to his origins, for the gay world had "very little to do with me ... *where* I did my growing up" (JB, 59, emphasis added). Being unable to feel "at home" in that world caused him fear and bewilderment; it reminded him of a stage on which actors were playing their roles, but from which he was barred, indeed, as that "difficult type to cast" as he would soon define himself in "Freaks."

When Goldstein probes further, asking Baldwin incredulously, "You never thought of yourself as being gay?" Baldwin is emphatic again that he feared and was confused by the term: "No. *I didn't have a word for it.* The only one I had was 'homosexual' and that didn't quite cover whatever it

156 CHAPTER THREE

was *I was beginning to feel....* It was ... very personal, *absolutely personal. It was really a matter between me and God*" (JB, 59, emphases added). The feelings of fear and homelessness that the writer experienced when considering himself vis-à-vis the "hall of mirrors" of the post-Stonewall gay world around him are compounded by yet another instance when language and semantics fail him in the process of naming the structures of feelings around his sexuality.[18] He is exiled, yet again, and only partially voluntarily it seems, from the nomenclature that others would have him domesticate as his own.

Baldwin's affective withdrawal from the meanings created by, and required performances of, "role playing," of what he sees as the American gay world—that house he could never inhabit, as he confesses in "Freaks"—compounds his insistence that existing terms are useless to him as a black man from Harlem whose sexuality is difficult to pin down. Perhaps what he is referring to, both in the interview and in the essay "Freaks," is the American *white* gay world that enthusiastically embraced his second novel, *Giovanni's Room* (1956), as a coming-out narrative about white male characters—an American and an Italian who meet and fall in love in Paris. As I have argued elsewhere, that novel is all about race, albeit seen through the lens of whiteness as a seemingly unmarked category contingent on blackness as its reverse, as well as about the impossibility of separating sexuality from gendered performances of national identity forever embroiled with homophobia and its vile sidekick, misogyny.[19] Baldwin's refusal to embrace the term "gay" can thus be seen, at least partially, as a refusal to simplify the readings both of his works and of his person, along with the readings of his authorial persona as represented by the white-dominated media whose delegates, in a fashion, Goldstein and the *Village Voice* appear to be.

Baldwin's emphatic response to Goldstein's questions concerning his sexual identity echoes what in Sedat Pakay's 1973 film *James Baldwin: From Another Place* he calls his right to privacy: his sex life is "not to be spoken about." At the same time, he acknowledges that as a public person he must say something "to the world," so he admits not only that he has loved "a few men and a few women," but that "love" is in fact all that matters because it has "saved" his life. As Baldwin echoes this stance in the Goldstein interview, his choices of lovers and gendered personas are "a matter between me and God," or an article of absolutely private faith and observance. Another reason for his stern dissociation of his life experience from the labels used to describe American men who love other men may have something to do with his early childhood memories of having been called a "sissy."[20]

As he describes it in "Freaks," he was one in Harlem while growing up, and was afraid of being taken for one having moved to the Village; he dreaded being punished for it, for violence is what is meted out to such freakish boys and men (in an interview with Julius Lester he mentions "getting my head beaten when I was walking the streets").[21] As he explains, it has to do with being identified with feminine qualities and the performance thereof—"I already seemed and sounded too much like a woman." The sissy is a vilified incarnation to misogynists and homophobes alike, who despise the confusion of a female in a male body and who find his ability to blur gender boundaries threatening and an invitation to violence. On the other hand, bordering on a transgender character of sorts to those who embrace gender fluidity, the sissy is a subject position that has been reclaimed and embraced in the queer and trans worlds today, but at this time it was not anything that Baldwin was ready to embrace and inhabit unproblematically.[22]

The young writer's confrontation with queer-then-gay identity codes in the Village compounds his illusion of identity as a hall of mirrors, at the same time as the lack of concrete alternatives to the "brief and distorted fragments of myself" he refers to implicitly in the Goldstein interview, and explicitly in the essay "Freaks," demonstrates that he cannot find a comfortable place and name for himself as a black male writer who loved some men and some women even in his later years. Yet while he could neither see himself as a fitting subject of, nor sanction anyone applying to his person, life, and lifestyle, the adjective "gay," it is clear that in his later works he was forging an alternative identity to those based in reductive binaries, such as gay, that others wanted to pin on him.

In fact, the "hall of mirrors" quotation from "Freaks" that describes Baldwin's transition to Greenwich Village contains the seeds of the concept that the late José Muñoz, unequivocally acknowledging Baldwin's inspiration, brilliantly termed *disidentification*.[23] This important concept is worth unpacking not only to emphasize that Baldwin, whom Muñoz identifies as the "black and queer belles-lettres queen," got to its meaning and description of its function in *Devil Finds Work* long before it was embraced by scholars (artists and prophets often do so, as those who love books know well), but also to highlight once again the writer's penchant for theorizing identity in deeply sophisticated ways and by means of skillful deployments of autobiographic references.[24] As Muñoz writes about it in 1999, disidentification hits all the elements that Baldwin already highlighted in his self-analysis as an oddity and misfit that we have glimpsed above: language and meaning-making, estrangement from exclusionary groups, and the necessity of remaking one's own identity: "Disidentification is about recycling and rethinking encoded meaning. The process of disidentification scrambles and reconstructs the encoded message of a cultural text in a fashion that both exposes the encoded message's universalizing and exclusionary machinations and recircuits its workings to account for, include, and empower minority identities and identifications.... [It] is a step further than cracking open the code of the majority; it proceeds to use this code as raw material for representing a disempowered politics or positionality that has been rendered unthinkable by the dominant culture."[25] Baldwin's exclusion from the "hall of mirrors" that was the *queer* world of his youth in the Village, and which later became the *gay* world—that "false refuge" about which Goldstein asks him—is not only caused by his blackness and poverty (JB, 71). As a man who engaged in sex acts with "some women and some men," he fit neither the hetero- nor the homosexual performative script of sexual identity. As such, he needed a "survival strategy," as Muñoz labels his particular case of disidentification, amid "a false argument, a false accusation" of gayness (JB, 73). The trouble was that there were no models available, and Baldwin had to forge, and name, whatever he wanted to become as he went along; he had to create his own idiosyncratic world in which who he was and whom he loved and had sex with would be equally at home. In that sense, his quest could be called quintessentially "American" in its insistence on individualism, at the same time as its very nature calls into question the stereotypical qualifiers of that term, or white, male, and straight, by deploying and rewriting Manifest Destiny rhetoric through the black queer experience and art.

Baldwin's visual and auditory self-perception of seeming and sounding "like a woman" is thus undesirable because it makes him feel "grotesque" and "miserable" in such a one-dimensional costume. He cannot perform as "an American," that is. This sensation immediately leads in his mind to the queer fear of violence that in twentieth-century U.S. culture, and to this day, arises from the twin poisons of homophobia and misogyny. He thinks himself "improbable" and realizes that gender is not only performative, but also in fact the very stuff of the theater where as black *and* queer, he would indeed be "a hard type to cast." In the end, however, he sides with those with whom he so desperately did not want to be identified—women—by stating that he needs all the friends he can get.

This moment in the interview leads to the disclosure of his sexual involvement with "a couple of white women," as there were "virtually no black women there when I hit those streets." The contentious racial and class politics that inevitably emerge from these relationships frame the parenthetical reference to "the first black girl who dug me." His confession of having fallen in love with, lived with, and "almost married" that "black girl" is an important corrective to being perceived as a sissy, for it turns out that there were women who embraced such a black male identity (PT, 685). While we have no idea of who that "black girl" was, or how she may have identified in gender and sexual terms, she may well have inspired some of the female characters in his late novels and plays, as well as helped the writer begin to feel at home with the feminine self-identification that he embraced most fully at his home in St. Paul-de-Vence, the place filled with queers that some labeled "the house of sin."[26]

Baldwin's disidentification with the label "gay" has as much to do with his writing process in his later works and his insistence on identity and identification as performative processes, as with his embrace of freakishness and intersectionality as the only modi operandi for his complexly gendered, racialized, and sexualized self. He tells Goldstein that "the discovery of one's sexual preference doesn't have to be a trauma. It's a trauma because this is such a traumatized society." He then condemns "this... very biblical culture; [where] people believe the wages of sin is death" and where each person must confront the "terror of the flesh." He links this terror of sensuality and the erotic, of what in *Giovanni's Room* he calls the "stink of life," to the fear of affect—to choosing a sentimental semblance of sensation over a struggle with true and powerful personal feelings: "Americans are terrified of feeling anything... homophobia is simply an extreme example of the American terror that's concerned with growing up. I never met a people more infantile in my life." Then he also stresses that while "the sexual question and the racial question have always been entwined" (JB, 63–64), to most of us "the sexual question comes after the question of color" because race tints how we immediately see others and ourselves and how we perform and feel about our gender and sexual identity (67).

Almost exactly a month before his conversation with Goldstein, in an interview with Julius Lester for the *New York Times Book Review*, Baldwin speaks of the need to realize that "the world is not white." While he had made similar pronouncements in his 1953 essay "Stranger in the Village," he fully embraces this postwhite optic in the 1980s as key to forgoing the straitjacket of performing what and who others perceive us to be. As he claims, "The real terror that engulfs the white world now" is "a visceral terror... of being described by those they've been describing for so long." While Lester claims that identity politics matter, for "some black writers of my generation might say that the responsibility of black writers is to write about black people," Baldwin notes that his point about a writer being free to write about anything and anybody, including whiteness, does not contradict such a view. "If our voices are heard," he emphasizes, "it makes the concept of color obsolete." While utopian and revolutionary (not to mention light years ahead even of today, when the resurgence of whiteness results in murders of black citizens by domestic terrorists and police), this approach signals Baldwin's disidentification from both the concept of race as constructed on white terms and the racialized concepts of manhood and sexuality that rest on similarly bipolar American-made oppositions (JB, 53).

As he tells Goldstein, "The capacity for experience is what burns out fear," and it is only through experience of ourselves with others that we can learn to know ourselves (JB, 70). Cautioning his interlocutor, "don't be romantic about black people," when Goldstein wonders about the possibilities of black-gay alliances, Baldwin makes clear that racial oppression does not erase the capacity for homophobia, while insisting on the right to forge his identity and identification on his own terms as a black man whose sexuality escapes definitions (69): "one's sexual preference is a private matter" (71). A man who loves other men "is called a faggot because other males need him," he explains, and because the state and the church "care that you should be frightened of what you do. As long as you feel guilty about it, the State can rule you. It's a way of exerting control over the universe, by terrifying people" (65). Because of their "terror of being able to be touched" (70), white men who control the state and men of all hues who control the church need others to victimize.

Still holding on to his right to define himself and his world, Baldwin nevertheless concedes to Goldstein by the end of their interview in matters concerning the practicalities of survival as the other, as "the transgressor . . . [the] despised" for those who, perhaps, do not have the benefit of his mind and craft, not to mention social standing: "if the so-called gay movement can cause men and women, boys and girls, to come to some kind of terms with themselves more speedily and with less pain, then that's a very great advance" (JB, 72). But for himself as a writer, echoing his statements from "Everybody's Protest Novel" and its companion essays, he emphasizes the necessity of forging a new idiom of identity, or for disidentification from both whiteness and gayness: "My own point of view, speaking out of black America, when I had to answer that stigma, that species of social curse, it seemed a great mistake to answer in the language of the oppressor. As long as I react as a 'nigger,' as long as I protest my case on evidence or assumptions held by others, I'm simply reinforcing those assumptions. As long as I complain about being oppressed, the oppressor is in consolation of knowing that I know my place so to speak" (72). Advising Goldstein and their readers to "go the way your blood beats" and "live the only life you have," he cautions against false identities and costumes that American culture is so fond of imposing not only on its others, but also on everything and everyone within its white embrace. Baldwin's "black America," from which he speaks as a writer with a complicated gender and sexual identity, is neither ideal nor myth. It is a utopian space, a home where one is accepted and loved; it is a community of his own making, where the church and the state, bent upon control and profit, have no power.

In the next section I trace the ways in which Baldwin arrived at such a domestic vision of his national identity. I do so by examining the ways in which his later works reconstruct his childhood and the learning processes that led a budding writer to become the prophet and poet he chose to be for us, the one he can be for us today.

THE FIRST TEACHER AND THE "TERMS OF OUR CONNECTION"

> That brother was my brother, that father was my father, those dead are my dead.
> —*The Devil Finds Work*

> I was a child . . . and, therefore, unsophisticated. I don't seem ever to have had any innate need to . . . distrust people: and so I took Bill Miller as she was, or as she appeared to be to me. . . . From Miss Miller, . . . I began to suspect that white people did not as they did because they were white, but for some other reason, and I began to try to locate and understand that reason. She, too, anyway, was treated like a nigger, especially by the cops, and she had no love of landlords.
> —*The Devil Finds Work*

The Devil Finds Work, written largely in St. Paul-de-Vence, is "in one sense a fifty-year-old's evaluative reminiscence," as David Leeming explains, and it opens somewhat similarly to *No Name in the Street*, with a close-up of a memory of Baldwin as a child in the company of women, within a section entitled "Congo Square."[27] The writer recalls the very first film he saw "with my mother, or my aunt," *Dance, Fools, Dance* (1931), in which he fixated on

"Joan Crawford's straight, narrow, and lonely back" moving down a train corridor (PT, 557).[28] In a familiar Baldwinian fashion, *Devil* uses "movies as catalysts for an extensive discussion of the American psyche, his own life, and the socio-political climate in America"; it is written in a voice "of a celebrity/elder statesman who dares to carry his work as a witness into the heart of popular culture."[29] More important for my purposes, Baldwin's early delight in the movies has much to do with their depiction of the ways femininity and home are experienced, imagined, and represented, which, to his child's mind, folded into the cinematic, "that movement which is something like the heaving and swelling of the sea . . . and . . . something like the light which moves on, and especially beneath, the water" (PT, 557).

Although very young at the time, Jimmy was already an astute observer of others and a voracious consumer of culture. He was thus subtly aware of race as an undercurrent of cinematic beauty standards, for while watching Crawford on the screen, he states that "with quite another part of my mind, I was aware that [she] was a white lady." Yet he also remembers encountering, at a neighborhood store, "a colored woman, who, to me, looked exactly like Joan Crawford . . . so incredibly beautiful—she seemed to be wearing the sunlight, rearranging it around her from time to time, with a movement of one hand, with a movement of her head, and with her smile" (PT, 557–58). Mesmerized by this woman, who was flesh and blood and yet seemed to have stepped off a movie screen, the young writer-to-be discovers that her smile at him does not embarrass him—"which was rare" (558). In that brief moment, Baldwin's fascination with women and their representations marks him and informs his subsequent interest in gender and sexuality.

While the centrality of women and femininity occurs more explicitly and vividly only in his later years, there are memorable female portraits in his earlier work, too: for example, his first and third novels, *Go Tell It on the Mountain* and *Another Country* (1962), where Deborah and Florence are admirable and strong each in her own way in the former, and Ida and Cass are key to understanding the writer's message about gender and sexuality as not only racialized but also inflected by national and cultural identity in the latter. Baldwin's plays *The Amen Corner* (1954) and *Blues for Mister Charlie* (1964) also feature strong female characters, whose importance I will discuss while contextualizing *The Welcome Table* in the next section.

Baldwin's autobiographical recollections throughout his oeuvre make it clear that he questioned received notions of identity from his earliest years, and that the films he saw from his childhood onward provided him with fertile ground to do so. All along, he was also very much a "product of his time" and thus took for granted, for example, the use of the masculine pronoun—a certain machismo he thought he needed to embrace as a male himself (with rather varying degrees of success as we know). He may have even taken for granted, at least for a while, the lower social status and objectification of women in Hollywood.[30] All the while, women and their depictions intrigued him, and they were implicitly and sometimes explicitly at the center of his thinking about race and gender. For example, the many white actresses who appear in the pages of *The Devil Finds Work*—Bette Davis, Geraldine Fitzgerald, Olivia de Havilland, Blanche Yurka, Elizabeth Allan, Sylvia Sidney, Lana Turner, Margaret Sullivan, Carole Lombard—made it painfully apparent to young Baldwin that "no one resembling... [a black labor organizer in the Deep South], or anyone resembling any of the Scottsboro Boys, nor anyone resembling *my father*, has yet made an appearance on the American cinema scene" (PT, 568, emphasis added). Focusing his critique on the absence of black male bodies in Hollywood, he consoles himself with the fact that women's representations seem a bit more flexible or racially fluid to him, for "Sylvia Sidney... reminded me of a colored girl, or woman... the only American film actress who reminded me of reality" (PT, 569). Here, the sissy has been freed to imagine himself as the star.

In another, rather surprising take on race as performative and contingent on class and the experience of suffering, he and a friend agree that Henry Fonda in *The Grapes of Wrath* "had colored blood. You could tell... by the way Fonda walked down the road at the end of the film: *white men don't walk like that!*" (PT, 569, 570). (Could his despair, poverty, and desire to fight the Man/banks/capitalism despite his misery "make" Steinbeck's hero black? And could this case signal the possibility of such a racial disidentification for dispossessed white males?) The film noir classic *You Only Live Once* (1937), directed by Fritz Lang and starring both Fonda and Sidney, "was the most powerful movie I had seen until that moment," he recalls. As he stuns himself with the recollections of his precociousness while writing these memories down, "It is the top of 1937. I am not yet thirteen" (570).

Young Baldwin felt some affinity with the half-Russian and half-Romanian immigrant Sophia Kosow, who became Sylvia Sidney and starred in crime dramas in which she always played an underdog. She would be "facing a cop.... It was almost as though she and I had a secret: she seemed to know something I knew.... She was always being beaten up, victimized, weeping.... But I always believed her" (PT, 570). Sidney's emotional credibility and her second-class-citizen status in the films were remarkable to him for another crucial reason: she reminded him very much of Orilla "Bill" Miller.

He recalls meeting Miller on the second page of the "Congo Square" essay that opens *Devil*:

> I had been taken in hand by a young white schoolteacher, a beautiful woman, very important to me. I was between ten and eleven. She had directed my first play.... She gave me books to read and talked to me about the books, and about the world: about Spain ... and Ethiopia, and Italy, and the German Third Reich; and took me to see plays and films, plays and films to which no one else would dream of taking a ten-year-old boy.... Her name was Orilla, we called her Bill. (PT, 558–59)

It may be a minor phonetic leap from Orilla to "Bill," though I have often wondered how young Miller, who was only twelve years older than Jimmy when they met, took to that masculine moniker. A radical, and definitely an independent and sophisticated young woman, she probably did not mind it, perhaps even loved it, knowing that it came from affection and awe that she inspired in the children she taught. She definitely liked it in her later years, for in letters to Baldwin between 1955 and 1985, she uses that name and he also uses it when referring to her in his. He opens the first one with "Dear Bill," and then adds, "I don't know if people call you that anymore," and follows that with a plea to let him keep using that special name, for "it's still the way I think of you."[31]

I am fortunate to know Lynn Orilla Scott, Bill's niece, who has generously shared with me a videotaped interview she conducted with her aunt in August 1989, when her aunt was living in Manistee, Michigan. The interview was informal, and it clearly communicated Bill's warmth and charisma, as well as the idealism that must have captivated young Baldwin; Miller (who later took on her husband's last name, Winfield) died of cancer soon after it had been conducted. The brief biography of Bill that follows is meant to make that remarkable woman more familiar and to recognize the importance of the gifts of education and open-mindedness that she bestowed on Baldwin as his teacher. The information I include is gleaned from the videotaped interview Lynn conducted and my several conversations with Lynn, a joint presentation at an international Baldwin conference in 2014 by Lynn and Ken Winfield (Orilla's son and Lynn's cousin, respectively), and my subsequent interview with both of them, as well as Lynn's pioneering study, *James Baldwin's Later Fiction: Witness to the Journey* (2002), which was among the inspirations for my own.[32]

Born in the Midwest in 1912, to Nell and John Miller, Orilla was raised in a small farming community in Galva, Illinois, with two younger sisters,

Margaret and Henrietta; the former is Lynn Orilla Scott's mother. When Orilla Miller met Baldwin in the 1930s and became Bill, she was forced to abandon her education at Antioch College. Her father, a populist and a Farmers' Cooperative organizer, advocated for women's learning and was a mayor nicknamed "Good Roads John" for his infrastructure commitments. He lost everything during the Great Depression.[33] While the family coped as well as they could with severely reduced circumstances that included having been forced to send their daughter Margaret to live with their neighbors, Orilla sought employment as a housekeeper and governess in New York City. She later worked for room and board at the Labor Temple, entered the Columbia Teachers College, and found work with the WPA's Theater Projects Educational Division.[34] She lived with her younger sister, Henrietta Miller, nicknamed "Henri" (another masculine moniker), and the two worked together for social justice. Orilla helped her family financially after they lost their house and land, and her teaching (she explicitly requested to be assigned to Harlem, as she lived within walking distance of the school) eventually took her to P.S. 24, where James Baldwin was a student.[35]

Her work at the school opened her eyes to "the worst poverty" she ever encountered; it was a segregated school, "99 percent black, except for a couple of very blond Finns," and the children were "all hungry" but were luckily fed at the school. Young James's teacher welcomed Miller's help and let her take him out of class as much as she wanted to "because he already knew everything" they were doing. As Miller remarks in her interview with her niece, he was "a remarkable child" and became her "assistant director" on the special programs she was running. They spent a lot of time together, which she considered "a real break"; she recalled how they were both "enthusiastically reading *A Tale of Two Cities*" and would have "long conversations up in the attic of the school about Dickens," which she "enjoyed more than the conversations about Dickens [she] had with adults."[36] Orilla's sister Henrietta, who worked for the YMCA, often accompanied her to visit the Baldwins, who lived within a short walking distance of their apartment. Orilla decided to meet James's parents soon after taking an interest in him, as she wanted to show him more theater and more of the world beyond Harlem.

While working with James, Orilla married Evan Winfield, who, like her, was a member of the American Communist Party in the 1930s (they both left later on, disillusioned), and she took his last name. Their political affiliation made them familiar to the New York Police Department as targets, although as Scott recalls, her aunt did not talk about that much, even though Scott suspected that there had been more than one standoff with the police,

3.4. Bill Miller on a bed. Photo from Lynn Scott's archive. Used by permission.

3.5. The Miller family. Photo from Lynn Scott's archive. Used by permission.

given their hostility toward what Miller-Winfield euphemistically called the "idealistic people of the time."[37] Orilla and Evan lived with Henrietta in an apartment on 12th Street, and the three of them often took James along on their outings "like a little brother . . . a very sweet child . . . always a pleasure to have around."[38]

Unaware that to James's stern father, white people's "very presence in his home" was a "violation," as Baldwin wrote in "Me and My House" (1955; retitled later as "Notes of a Native Son"), Miller appeared in his life "when [he] was around nine or ten." She directed a play he wrote at that young age and, as Baldwin recalls, rather tongue-in-cheek, "decided to take me to see what she somewhat tactlessly referred to as 'real' plays."[39] He stopped seeing her at fourteen, when he entered the pulpit, having been "saved." Evan was a Merchant Marine and was stationed in Puerto Rico during World War II, and so he and Orilla left New York for good. They later moved to California; had two sons, Steve and Ken; and managed a few reunions with Baldwin. They were both active with the Women's International League for Peace and Freedom and supported the Congress of Racial Equality (CORE).

The reunions happened following a long break in their contact, after Baldwin's "Me and My House" had been published in *Harper's Magazine* in 1955, and Orilla saw her name mentioned on its first page. It was the mid-1960s when she and Evan finally met James for the first time since their fateful parting in New York, upon the occasion of Baldwin's travels with CORE in Southern California. Orilla was mesmerized hearing him speak as a grown-up for the first time. As she told Lynn, she was "utterly surprised" and recognized him as "an absolutely stunning and dramatic speaker. He had the whole audience in the palm of his hand." To everyone's regret, however, they did not manage a visit longer than a few minutes, as he was whisked away to a fundraiser soon after the speech. As they exchanged hugs, Orilla was immediately concerned about his health: he seemed to her "the most exhausted looking person I've ever seen."[40] They kept in intermittent contact—he was not easy to keep in touch with—for which he frequently apologized in his letters.

On May 15, 1963, after that brief reunion following an L.A. CORE meeting, Bill wrote James tenderly:

> I am writing this note while the impact of the L.A. CORE meeting is still fresh. It was hearing you and touching you that completed the picture. We knew much of you . . . through your books but could never create the adult from the child by this medium. James, I want to tell you that the

promise of the wonderful child has been fulfilled in the man. I am not referring alone to the development of your writing ability, the incisive use of your intelligence in social commentary. I am referring to the moral you—in that broad sense of one's individual relationship to man around him. That Evan and I had a small part in your life adds to the value of ours. I also say, thank you, that there is this James Baldwin in America in the year 1963.

Orilla and Evan's son Ken told me in an interview in 2014 that he heard a lot about Baldwin while growing up. He also remembers his mother using the serious "James" as the only name to refer to him, and that he and his brother both knew that the writer was their mother's "first son"; they did not mind that deep connection. Ken witnessed their last meeting in 1986, when Baldwin lectured at the University of Santa Barbara and came to pay a visit. He was likely already suspecting his cancer was terminal, so the meeting was intense, with James focused on Bill the whole time. "It was like sitting in a gallery . . . he went to Mom's rocker, and held her hand for two hours without letting go. . . . [They] talked about their years together in Harlem." Lynn added that Bill and James had rather "similar qualities . . . were open, interested in other people" and that "people were attracted to her like they were attracted to him." Bill had been admired for her charisma and had her "own entourage . . . mostly women" who followed her, including moving to another state to continue to be close to her. Bill was tremendously "proud of [James's] political activism."[41]

Evan's demise in 1984 was a devastating blow. Orilla later moved to Michigan, where Lynn interviewed her in 1989, and where she died in 1991, "four years after Jimmy," also from cancer. As Scott writes about her aunt, she was "a strong advocate for racial justice and an avid reader," who left their family with "a legacy of hope that we can cross barriers of race, class, and culture, that we can share a vision of the way things should be, that we can be friends, comrades, and lovers."[42] Orilla and her sister Henrietta kept in regular touch with Berdis Baldwin, James's mother. Orilla asked Lynn to read a letter from Berdis to her when they saw each other for the last time, "about a month before [Bill's] death."[43]

I do not think it an overstatement to claim that, without Bill's love and care, without her passionate investment in young James as if he were her own kin from the moment she "took him in hand," he would not have become the genius writer and intellectual that he is remembered as today. Lynn tried to persuade me in one of our conversations that such a statement might be an exaggeration. I never met her aunt, of course, but I cannot help feeling haunted by the way Baldwin writes about Bill in his works and letters to her, as someone who was absolutely key to his development. Teachers have a tremendous role to fill, and those few great ones, like Bill Miller, are literally able to change lives. It was she, after all, who initially ignited in Baldwin the passion that later made it possible for him to spread his wings and trust his abilities, no matter that he could not afford a college education. He continued to read widely, learn about the world outside of the United States, practice critical thinking and argumentation in the pulpit and beyond, and take his access to the theater and cinema for granted all because she showed him that it was not only possible, but also his *right* to participate in and comment on any aspect of culture that interested him.

Though not explicitly dedicated to her (it honors the writer's youngest sister, Paula-Maria "on her birthday," and John Latham, and "brother" David Moses), Baldwin's fifth book of essays, *The Devil Finds Work*, is a tribute to Miller as the writer's surrogate parent in the same way that *No Name in the Street* is a tribute to his mother and grandmother and to his matrilineal heritage that ushered in his artistic vocation.[44] He remembers defining Bill by the white qualities she did *not* possess even though she clearly looked "white" to him—an important early lesson about racial stereotypes: she "was *not* at all like the cops who had already beaten me up ... *not* like the landlords who called me nigger ... *not* like the storekeepers who laughed at me" (emphases added). To young Baldwin whites were "unutterably menacing, terrifying, mysterious ... wicked" (PT, 559). By the same token, his descriptions give us a sense of his already brutal scope of experience at that time, not to mention the yearning for care and attention that Bill fulfilled and that James must have needed badly as a child who was forced to grow up very fast, and whose overworked parents had little time to give to him: "Yet, the difference between Miss Miller and other white people, white people as they lived in my imagination, and also as they were in life, had to have a profound and bewildering effect on my mind" (PT, 559).

Indeed, Bill emerged to young James as an individual possessing uniqueness similar to his own, who showed him that it was not right to judge others solely on the basis of the hues of their epidermis. This revelation would become vital to his message about racial identity, especially his understanding of "whiteness" and "blackness" as being created through the complex historic, economic, social, and political processes that made the "American Republic." From the perspective of his sixth decade in *Devil*, he asks himself the "unfathomable question" about the reasons for the wickedness of white Americans (and I would love to see it printed in every American history book): "What, under heaven, or beneath the sea, or in the catacombs of hell, could cause any people to act as white people acted?" (PT, 559).

And there was Bill, as white as any of the "wicked," but armed with love, care, and attention, and on a stubborn mission to help James reach his potential. As she wrote him on May 15, 1963, she was worried about his well-being: "If the schedule you maintained in L.A. is at all representative of your present life, I am quite fearful. You will be destroyed physically and creatively.... If you ever need a hideaway and can sneak into L.A. unrecognized, we will have one for you—quiet-peaceful-green ... you would never be discovered." Baldwin recalls his early feelings about her:

> I loved her, of course, and absolutely, with a child's love; didn't understand half of what she said, but remembered it; and it stood me in good stead later. It is certainly partly because of her, who arrived *in my terrifying life* so soon, that I never really managed to hate white people—though, God knows, I have often *wished to murder more than one or two*. Bill Miller ... *was not white for me* in the way ... that Joan Crawford was white, in the way that the landlords and the storekeepers and the cops and most of my teachers were white. She didn't baffle me that way and she never frightened me.... I never felt her pity, either. (PT, 558–59, emphases added)

Baldwin appreciated Bill's dedication as a teacher, and he perhaps gleaned how to be a great one from her, which would serve him well in the years he taught creative writing at several U.S. colleges and universities. Her tact and reserve in matters of race and class were important, too, for she "could instruct me as to how poverty came about and what it meant and what it did, and, also, what it was meant to do: but she could not instruct me as to blackness, except obliquely, feeling that she had neither the right nor the authority, and also knowing that I was certain to find out." Bill wrote him in the letter from May 15, 1963, that she recalled with delight how they met, started discussing Dickens, and how "you were the gifted, outstanding child of P.S. 24.... Then my sense of wonderment-kinship-love whatever it was that developed to where I could not bear that your life should be so confined. I probably thought of something that wonderful child should do.... Then the relationship expanded to include your family as a part of you."

She helped him understand crucial notions about identity early on, suggesting "the extent to which the world's social and economic arrangements are responsible for (and to) the world's victims." He soon realized, having seen the 1936 Metro-Goldwyn-Mayer production of *A Tale of Two Cities* with Bill, that "a victim may or may not have a color, just as he may or may not have virtue: a difficult, not to say unpopular notion, for nearly everyone prefers to be defined by his status, which, unlike his virtue, is ready to wear" (PT, 562). This sentiment in particular resounds powerfully in the context of the sometimes viciously homophobic critiques of Baldwin's work and person in the United States of the 1970s and 1980s, and especially in the context of his vilification by the members of the Black Power movement, who could not stand his openness about black queer sexuality, not to mention his involvement with male lovers of all hues. (Take that, Eldridge Cleaver of the "prêt-a-porter" penis pants.)[45]

Bill Miller would not let the kids in her care be victimized by the hostile white world; she may have risked her own safety and reputation while standing up for them; she may also not have believed that other whites would dare do anything against her charges in her presence. No matter, James recounts an incident when she had to make cynical use of her whiteness while staring down hostile law enforcers who did not want to entertain the poor kids from Harlem whom she was chaperoning on a picnic downtown: "There was supposed to be ice cream waiting for us at a police station. The cops didn't like Bill, didn't like the fact that we were colored kids, and didn't want to give up the ice cream. I don't remember anything Bill said. I just remember her face as she stared at the cop, clearly intending to stand there until the ice cream all over the world melted or until the earth's surface froze, and she got us our ice cream, saying *Thank you,* I remember, as we left" (PT, 570). Baldwin adds, while discussing the film *Dead End,* "In my own experience . . . and not only because I was watching Bill, I had observed that those who really wished to save the children became themselves, immediately, the targets of the police" (573–74). How salient, and terribly so, this comment sounds today, during the new Trump presidency that has vowed to demolish what children need most: education, healthcare, access to clean water, housing, and culture.

Tellingly, Baldwin ends the police and ice cream story with references to two films: *You Only Live Once* and *The Childhood of Maxim Gorky* (1938). Lang's *You Only Live Once* was concerned with "the fact and the effect of human loneliness" but also human monstrosity, and Mark Donskoy's *The Childhood of Maxim Gorky* provided another important lesson on race from a very unexpected place, for that film "for me," Baldwin writes, "had not been about white people" (PT, 570). The latter film was about the wretched life of a twelve-year-old boy, just like Baldwin, who lived a century earlier and in faraway Russia, but whose lot James could relate to better than to that of many of his white American peers (571). Baldwin opens *Devil* as well with a remark that shows how clearly he remembers, or is able to reimagine, his childhood and the experience of learning from the American and foreign movies he saw with Miller: "A child is far too self-centered to relate to any dilemma which does not, somehow, relate to him—to his own evolving dilemma. The child escapes into what he would like his situation to be" (557). The films served this dual purpose and gave Baldwin access to visual representations of his particular dilemma; they were vehicles that enabled him to inhabit various characters and identify with lives either disturbingly similar to, or dramatically different from, his own. Along with the books and the plays Bill made sure he encountered, these films opened his young imagination to stimuli it needed—stimuli that, sadly, were not readily available to him then in the richest country in the world.

I remember watching the same film based on Gorky's autobiography—of which we had to read fragments in Russian, too—some decades later, as I was growing up in communist Poland. I also remember being unable to keep myself from crying over the tragic lives of the children and serfs it portrayed, no matter that I and the other kids at the time all knew well that we were *made* to see it, and cry over it, too, so as to fall for Soviet propaganda. The story was always the same: the poor had it really bad under feudalism, but the Great October Revolution and communism/socialism changed all that, so no one had to starve again, ever. We all knew from our own experience that this was not true, not for everybody, not everywhere. What we did not know was the power of representation and truth of human experience that the film conveyed, too, and that Baldwin understood, so far away in the United States.

As much as we resisted liking that 1938 film as kids, so as not to be taken for the supporters of the "regime," young Baldwin read the dire lot of Russian children portrayed in *The Childhood of Maxim Gorky* as another lesson on how race is always entangled with class. He saw in it children whose poverty seemed to have marked their Slavic bodies with a nonwhite racialized identity in his eyes; perhaps he also realized that the black/white American racial lens was as inadequate in assessing the lives of people elsewhere as it was in assessing the lives of the racialized poor within the United States. This realization runs through many of his works, and especially powerfully throughout the essays "Encounter on the Seine: Black Meets Brown," "Stranger in the Village," and "Princes and Powers" and in *The Fire Next Time*, which all mention the Cold War as the great geopolitical context for the events they describe, and caution against simplistic generalizations and reductive conflations of peoples with the regimes or regions in which they live. Instead of seeing them as the foreign other, Baldwin implies, we ought to recognize them as kin—another lesson badly needed as the refugee crisis unfolds worldwide.

Baldwin's nuanced approach to otherness—individual, social, national, cultural, ethnic, ideological, or political—came, again, from the influences of his mother, who taught him to respect all people, and of his remarkable teacher, who was a communist and idealist, and to whom he wrote, in a beautiful letter dated December 27, 1984, that love "does not exist in the past tense." In telling her, again, "you were very very important to me," he assures her that these sentiments, about which he is writing as a grown man, could not exist in the past tense either.[46] This letter, which he explains he has been "trying to write" for "a very long time, now," begins with "My dear Bill" and mentions his having been "unforgivably busy" and "grimly unhappy," to the point where sometimes the "water seems to close over one's head."

Drowning in his own sorrows, he adds immediately that he is aware of the recent death of her husband—"none of that," his trouble, means anything "compared to your loss of Evan"—and recalls his childhood memory of seeing her in love, and how "very happy I was for you." His recollection of Bill with Evan—"in the way of the child I was then"—elicits a memory of her in her 12th Street apartment "at dusk, silhouetted against the window." As if watching a screen with a love scene projected onto it, he describes Evan and Bill "talking to each other, face to face, and the light in his face, and in yours." Baldwin writes with disarming honesty about how he "felt very shy about being there," but also was "enormously privileged" to witness her good fortune. He thanks Bill for allowing him to witness that scene, as if it, too, had been part of his learning process: "You hid nothing from me." Her happiness was "very beautiful" and helped him, later on, to appreciate true love with a partner, "when such a moment came, for the first time, for me."[47] (See plate 20.)

Now that he is an adult, it is Baldwin's turn to console Bill. He does so by sharing a memory of Evan, who released him "from a recurrent nightmare," which involved, as he thought, *A Tale of Two Cities* and himself being "about to be trampled by a horse" like the anonymous peasant boy who dies in the novel and the film. A true student of Beauford Delaney, Baldwin shows this scene rather than describing it: "the horse's head is in the air, against the sky" and then "the hooves are above my face, coming down." As the hooves begin to descend, he wakes up. Evan told him that that scene was no dream, and it actually took place as they marched together in a May Day parade, "when [James] was thirteen," when, around 15th Street and Eighth Avenue, "the cops charged us." Evan saved James from being trampled by a mounted policeman—"I was about to go beneath it," Baldwin writes. Later, Evan also told James that "he [Evan] was scared shitless." Afterward, James was dispatched home with subway fare.

Baldwin ends this story with a classic comment on childhood trauma: "it's funny," because he could clearly remember "Evan's face at the top of the subway stairs," but could not remember that Evan dragged him "from under the shadow of death." He recalled the kind face of the adult who helped him, but repressed the traumatizing memory of the terrifying event itself. Later, the event became conflated in his imagination with images from Dickens's novel and its screen version, which kept returning in nightmares and flashbacks. The act of Evan "releasing" him from that nightmare, which happened during a brief meeting the three of them had in California, helped him to exorcise that terrifying memory and strip it of its debilitating power. Baldwin's letter forcefully emphasizes Bill and Evan's importance to his development—they were "models of courage and integrity and love."

"You do not know, my friend," he writes, how much "that example meant to me" later on, when "my time for choices came." The letter becomes even more profoundly a love letter when he lays this tribute at her feet: "you helped me to get beyond the trap of color," and then, "once beyond that trap, so many others!" He explains how he wanted to come and be with her, to "see you and kiss your eyes" and "take you to dinner and a movie" and also to "spoil you with champagne," adding, "which I can still do." He writes her the addresses and telephone numbers of his brother David, his mother "(who has never forgotten you)" and with whom Bill corresponded until Berdis's death, and his own number at Chez Baldwin, "in my home away from home," with a directive to call him collect. He signs off with a quotation from Henry James: "Sorrow wears us and uses us . . . but we wear and use it, too, and it is blind, whereas we, after a manner, see." The sentiment is a "colder comfort than I thought," Baldwin writes, because there is "much much more than that to see."[48] (The letter is signed with a flourish, "Jimmy B," with the "B" ballooning at the bottom of the long downward line of the last "y" in his name.)[49]

The love and affection in this epistle were long overdue, as the last meeting between Bill and fourteen-year-old James in New York was not a pleasant one. Bill brings up its memory in a marvelous and deeply felt handwritten letter from Los Angeles, dated May 12, 1976, in which she mentions having read and been moved by his recently published *Devil Finds Work*: "And James,

LIFE MATERIAL 175

in a remarkable way, forty years later, you are writing so beautifully what we would like to say. It is through individual influence that 'good' goes on.... I am still shocked at my insensitivity that I would say to you those final words on religion—I was very immature, I think. And I never knew that your father 'disliked' me—I assumed he didn't approve of our taking you with us but I was fierce in my determination that you should see or know other worlds and I always sensed your mother's approval." Baldwin recalls their parting in *Devil*, the very words that she must have read in his book before writing her letter to him: "I had never forgotten Bill's quiet statement, when I went down to her house on 12th Street to tell her that I had been 'saved' and would not be going to the movies, or the theater anymore—which meant that I would not be seeing her anymore: *I've lost a lot of respect for you.* Perhaps, in the intervening time I had lost a lot of respect for myself" (PT, 577). The words Bill uttered are repeated in *Devil* in italics, and nearly a decade later Baldwin recalls them in his December 27, 1984, epistle, reassuring her that she should not "fault" herself for having said them. Having written in *Devil* about discovering that she was right—"When I entered the church, I ceased going to the theater. It took me awhile to realize that I was working in one" (575)—he explains in the letter that she did him a great favor: "Thank God you said it." He adds, "I loved you so deeply" and also "trusted you so much" that the words "rang in my head." Later, Bill's words continued to help him, he writes, when his "hour came and my faith pulverized," and he knew he "had to move" and leave the church to become a writer.

In the letter from 1976, Bill tells Baldwin how much she cherishes the memories of their time together, closing with a recollection of their early theatrical collaboration that involved other children: "Remember when we were practicing for a program and our cast insisted on clinking the steam pipes in the auditorium? Wouldn't practice or go home—just clink and slide! Finally, I started crying—I didn't know what else to do. Half the cast joined me—the rest looked on in amazement and we all quietly went home? We were a team after that—With great affection Orilla (Bill M)." It took communal tears and violent noise to bring the children of the cast and their young teacher/director together. Was the discord taking place because she was white? Was it because she was young and not authoritarian and they were not sure she was serious or seriously enough invested in them and their endeavor? Real team spirit emerged only after the emotional release, after the sole adult realized this collective cathartic experience was necessary before they could begin working together in earnest. Baldwin would deploy the lessons of their early theatrical work in his directorial debut of *Düşenin Dostu* in Turkey in 1969–70, when instead of rehearsing he sat with his actors around a table for weeks to discuss the play's characters and message, to make the players realize and feel fully the meaning of the lives they were entering as they stepped into their roles, as they internalized the detailed literary "treatments" of the characters Baldwin created for them.

THE STAGE, NOT THE SCREEN: "RESPONDING TO ONE'S FLESH AND BLOOD"

> For the tension in the theater is a very different, and very particular tension: this tension between the real and the imagined *is* the theater, and this is why the theater will always remain a necessity. One is not in the presence of shadows, but responding to one's flesh and blood.
> —*The Devil Finds Work*

When Baldwin writes about the "very particular tension" of the theater in *The Devil Finds Work*, he highlights the differences between staged and cinematic productions in terms of their audiences' responses—differences he first encountered as an elementary school student under Bill's tutelage. He writes, "I am still about twelve or thirteen," when Bill takes him to see young Orson Welles's production of *Macbeth*, "my first play," with an all-black cast and its action transposed to Haiti and involving voodoo rituals. That performance "both terrified and exhilarated me," he recalls, and these early impressions inflected his subsequent theatrical endeavors (PT, 578). As he remembers, too, that was the last play he saw for a while, for his "conversion" and preaching period came "hard upon the heels of *Macbeth*" (577). He was convinced, he writes in *Devil*, that "I was carrying around the plot of a play in my head, and looking, with a new wonder (and a new terror) at everyone around me, when I suddenly found myself on the floor of the church, one Sunday, crying holy unto the Lord" (578).

Bill brings up her memory of taking him to Welles's production, staged at the Harlem Theater, in the letter to Baldwin from April 12, 1985, in which she also reports about "a leg operation," in the wake of "a rare cancer of the bone" that she has "developed." She then admonishes him again for his hectic schedule and poor health, adding, however, "Of course, there is so much you want to *write* and *do* that it is very understandable! Please take care of yourself." Bill's worry about James's health is reasonable, for he seemed often to be physically affected by what he witnessed as a spectator, and later by his work, speeches, and travel—a way to take on intensity and excitement into his body that she had already seen in him as a child. Theater, especially, made Baldwin acutely aware of the power of the human form, of life performed on stage, "in flesh and blood."

About that performance of *Macbeth* he writes, "I knew enough to know that the actress (the colored lady!) who played Lady Macbeth might very well be a janitor, or a janitor's wife when the play closed.... Macbeth was a nigger just like me, and I saw the witches in church, every Sunday, and all up and down the block." By the time he found himself on the floor of that church—the experience of conversion that is dramatically and beautifully depicted through John Grimes's body in *Go Tell It*—he realized something about the church/theater, that "flesh and blood had proved to be too much for flesh and blood" (PT, 578). The lesson about embodied spirituality and the centrality of the visceral experience involved in theatrical audience participation convinced him of the theater's superiority over the cinema, for the actors in the *Macbeth* performance "were those people and that torment was a torment I recognized.... They could *be* Macbeth only because they were themselves; my first apprehension of the mortal challenge." The theater does not "corroborate ... fantasies," while the cinema is based on a subjective pointing of the camera—it "sees what you want it to see. The language of the camera is the language of our dreams."

When he sees Canada Lee performing Bigger Thomas at a Sunday matinee at the St. James Theatre, he is "hit so hard" by the actor's authenticity and the power of his embodied presence that he almost falls from the balcony to the pit: "I will not forget ... [his] performance as long as I live ... [for] *his physical presence gave me a right to live.* He was not at the mercy of my imagination, as he would have been on the screen: he was on stage in flesh and blood, and I was, therefore, at the mercy of *his* imagination" (PT, 578, 579, emphases added). The foundational experiences for James Baldwin the playwright were laid with the best directors, actors, and plays. No wonder he was hooked for life.

Bill realized that matters of the flesh and spirit came in between them when, not long after that *Macbeth* performance, James came to tell her he was saved and would not see her anymore. To her, an atheist, it likely felt that James was choosing safety and the pretense of power he had as a boy-wonder preacher, instead of the hard work of an artist that both scared him and seemed a long way away in his uncertain future. She was obviously deeply hurt, as that visit could not be read as anything other than an implicit rejection of her, her feelings for him, and her (secular) plan to "save" him.

In a card written to Baldwin on December 8, 1981, Bill felt the need to explain how much he really meant to her then, and how she considered hers somewhat of a parental role: "James, did I ever tell you what a solemn, delightful boy you were? Apparently, I felt as strongly towards you as I did my own children later on."[50] Too young to understand those feelings at the time, she finally confessed them when they were both much older. In a lovely short letter to Bill on July 5, 1982, Baldwin hopes to see her and Evan around Labor Day, and he mentions the "hard trials" and "great tribulations" of trying to finish *The Evidence of Things Not Seen*. Falling smoothly and sweetly into a recollection of having once been Bill's pupil, he adds that he hopes "to become a great writer" when "I grow up" and mentions his mother's response ("as my Mama said, . . . 'boy, that's more than a notion!'"), which, he concludes, should tell them all they need to know about his "stubborn morale."[51]

In the years in between his parting from Bill and his leaving the church, that morale must have been working hard. In *Devil*, he remembers a moment "around the time that I was seventeen," when "my best friend, Emile . . . an American Jew, of Spanish descent . . . one of the most honest and honorable people I have ever known" took him to see "a Russian movie . . . because he was trying to help me leave the church" (PT, 576, 577). The three or four years between that memorable performance of *Macbeth* Bill took him to and that unnamed Russian film that he saw with Emile contain Baldwin's turning away from the secular world and becoming a preacher: "my life changed so violently when I entered the church . . . I ceased going to the theater." They also contain his eventual discovery that his new life as a saved member of the congregation was not what he had been looking for (575). He recalls that his friend's challenge—"Emile was the only friend who knew to what extent my ministry tormented me"—to forgo the Sunday in church for a movie with a friend who was *not* a Christian brought back memories of his sad, final confrontation with Bill Miller. "I could not stay in the pulpit," he realized. "I could not make my peace with that particular lie—a lie, in any case, for me. I did not want to become Baby-Face Martin—I could see that coming . . . since I found myself surrounded by what I was certain to become" (577).[52]

In this context, his fear of becoming a false prophet in the pulpit, equal to becoming a cinematic character that is not of flesh and blood—or Baby-Face Martin from the film *Dead End*—revealed to him that "I had no right to preach [the gospel] if I no longer believed it." The Kierkegaardian "leap" he faces in the wake of his decision to skip Sunday at church and meet Emile at the movies instead "demanded that I commit myself to the clear impossibility of becoming a writer, and attempting to save my family that way" (PT, 578). *Devil* reveals Baldwin's realization that his choice to become a writer is the choice of the theater over cinema; it is the choice of flesh and blood over "the language of our dreams." It is also a choice of his family, even though he physically has to abandon them in order to pursue his vocation, over the fear the "impossibility of becoming a writer" brought up for him.

This book of essays is thus only superficially about cinema, as it is, primarily, yet another exercise in life writing through theater and film criticism; it is an attempt to write into life both himself as a child and his teacher-surrogate-mother, Bill. (Perhaps it also contains the seeds of a play that he never got to write.) His early life teaches him that safe/"saved" occupations are not for him, for they are akin to watching films, in which the "distance between oneself—the audience—and a screen performer [is]...an absolute." He chooses the "impossibility" of becoming a writer, the only pursuit in which he finally has faith, the only one worth the leap that true faith requires: "For, the church and the theater are carried within us and it is we who create them, out of our need and out of an impulse more mysterious than our desire" (PT, 576). He chooses to become a flesh-and-blood writer, who will be at the mercy of his desires and who will have to reinvent himself through each and every new work he produces on the stage of his own life. This is what he has been truly called for.

At the end of *Devil* he sums up his reading of the 1973 film *The Exorcist*, as much as this calling, while reflecting on the national house: "The Americans should certainly know more about evil than that; if they pretend otherwise, they are lying, and any black man, and not only blacks—many, many others, including white children—can call them on this lie; he who has been treated *as* the devil recognizes the devil when they meet" (PT, 635). The final sentence is long and jeremiad-like, describing the painful legacy of American history, or "the grapes of wrath" that are "stored in the cotton fields and migrant shacks and ghettoes of this nation, and in the schools and prisons, and in the eyes and hearts and perceptions of the wretched everywhere," including the "ruined earth of Vietnam, and in the orphans and the widows, and in the old men...and in the young men," who demand from him, the haunted artist, that he be their witness and write it all down, for, just like in *A Tale of Two Cities*, they "have forgotten nothing" (635).

ALL THOSE STRANGERS AT THE WELCOME TABLE

> All I had, in a word, was me, and I was forced to insist on this *me* with all the energy I had. Naturally, I got my head broken, naturally people laughed when I said I was going to be a writer, and naturally, since I wanted to live, I finally split the scene. But when I came back to sell my first novel, I realized that I was being corralled into another trap: now I was . . . a Negro writer, and I was expected to write diminishing versions of *Go Tell It on the Mountain* forever.
> —"Notes for *The Amen Corner*"

When Baldwin wrote "Notes for *The Amen Corner*" (1968), the play itself, the writing of which he says was "a desperate and even rather irresponsible act" (*The Amen Corner*, xi), had been finished for nearly a decade and a half.[53] As he recalls, his agent at the time, a woman, was adamantly against that project, telling him that "the American theater was not exactly clamoring for plays on obscure aspects of Negro life, especially one written by a virtually unknown author whose principal effort until that time had been one novel" (xi). As Baldwin contemplated those remarks, his relative penury at the moment, and his need to become known in "the *magazine* world," as the agent recommended, he realized that "I couldn't explain to her or to myself why I wasted so much time on a play" (xi).

And yet, while admitting this, Baldwin felt "very cunning, with myself concerning the extent of my ambition." Deep down he knew he wielded a weapon for which American theater was quite unprepared, namely, "I was armed . . . by the fact that I was born in the church. I knew that out of the ritual of the church, historically speaking, comes the act of the theater, the *communion* which is the theater" (xi, xvi). This conviction served Baldwin well in writing and envisaging his last play, especially given his desire to undertake something new and experimental with its characters and message. Unlike those in his first play, the strong female leads in *The Welcome Table* have moved far away from worshipping in Christian churches like Sister Margaret in *The Amen Corner*. As with Sister Margaret, however, the stories of their lives demonstrate (in ways still strikingly relevant) that we need Baldwin's idea of theater as a gender-bending "communion" just as badly today as he did in his own time.

His two earlier dramas were firmly rooted in African American culture, with the aforementioned *Amen Corner* portraying a Harlem storefront church community with a female pastor at the helm, and *Blues for Mister Charlie*

3.6. The welcome table on the veranda of Chez Baldwin, showing Bernard Hassell and Baldwin with friends. Image from the documentary film *James Baldwin: The Price of the Ticket* (1989); courtesy of Karen Thorsen, Douglas Dempsey, and the James Baldwin Project.

depicting a segregated town in the American South and a racist murder inspired by Emmett Till's tragic death in Money, Mississippi, in 1955.[54] In contrast, *The Welcome Table* is located far away from the United States; it embraces African Americans as part of a larger, transnational community of expatriates, émigrés, and transient artists.[55] Set amid a rural French southern landscape and inside a Provençal house very much like Baldwin's, it features a host of international characters who surround the three female leads—Edith, Laverne, and Regina—including a Muslim gardener, Mohammed, and a "pied noir," or expatriated French Algerian woman, the elderly Mlle. LaFarge, whose birthday party is the play's culminating event.

All of the white and African American characters who appear in the play as guests or residents of the household have been traveling and living away from the United States for various reasons, performing diverse incarnations of Baldwin's persona of the "transatlantic commuter." As explained by the character Daniel, an aspiring writer who has come to stay with Edith for a few weeks (in the version of the play currently at the Harvard University library), being abroad allowed him to "breathe"; as he tells Edith, his host and mentor, only in France does he realize that he "could breathe . . . no need to look around you."[56] He is awed by this realization of "how simple" and "how forbidden" this is, to which Edith responds that she understands him perfectly well, especially the forbidden part, for when she was young, she was certain that breathing—by now a metaphor for being free to be oneself—was made impossible by "those other wicked people . . . who weren't me."[57]

The transnational context and content of *The Welcome Table* are amplified not only by Baldwin's having been influenced by his Turkish experience and his subsequent residence in the South of France while writing it, but also by his love for Russian literature, especially his study of Anton Chekhov's early twentieth-century plays and the extensive guides to them written by the English theatrical director Tyrone Guthrie. Baldwin greatly admired Chekhov's *The Cherry Orchard* (1904) and used it as an inspiration in his directorial debut in Turkey; he kept it in mind while he wrote *The Welcome Table*. His last play is also clearly inflected by the characters, setting, and class and gender conflicts that propel another of Chekhov's famous plays, *The Three Sisters*.

Masha, Olga, and Irina, Chekhov's leads, seem to have inflected Baldwin's late twentieth-century black and white women characters in complex ways, especially in their preoccupation with the affective fallout of losing their family's fortune, which has resulted in the women being stuck in the countryside, with their profligate brother reducing their already strained circumstances every day. Because they are women, their agency is drastically limited, and in order to survive they must either marry (as Masha does, unhappily, to a country-bumpkin schoolteacher she soon despises and cheats on) or hold jobs they do not like (as both Olga and Irina do to support themselves). Without political agency or financial means, the women are unable to return to their beloved Moscow, where they believe their lives would be free and whole again; with time, the city becomes a lost paradise and unfulfilled promise of a better life.

Eager to experiment with form and location, but in ways that rewrote what by then could have been seen as a traditional Chekhovian dramatic form, Baldwin rooted his play in the identity-obsessed late twentieth century and placed what is understated or absent in Chekhov's play—erotic attraction, sexual desire, and racial and gendered performance as well as show business between the United States and western Europe—at the center of *The Welcome Table*.[58] The drawing-room-drama genre that had been inspired by Chekhov's classics received a deeply Baldwinian twist, for while he preserved some of the original aesthetics of his model—its nuanced, understated vignette-dialogues, subtle shading of characterization, and ultimately unresolvable message about "history happening"—he meant for the final product to appeal to the younger generation, or the "children of our era" who must learn that "love is where you find it."[59] Baldwin thus not only wrote against what Joseph Beam termed the "nationalistic heterosexism" embraced by some black writers of his time, but also advocated in his play for nonbinary, or queer/quare, approaches to sexuality and gender vis-à-vis national identity long before the emergence of feminist theory, not to mention gender, queer, or black queer studies and the queer of color critique.

Throughout the play, as Leeming notes, the "literal point of view was very much Baldwin's Saint-Paul-de-Vence 'scene,' the biracial, bisexual, confessional milieu that had been so important to his personal life and his prophecy," and "all of the main characters are female."[60] *The Welcome Table* was originally begun in Istanbul, Turkey, around 1967.[61] Baldwin drafted some of its early parts soon after the staging of *Fortune and Men's Eyes* (1964), a play about prison homosexuality by the Canadian playwright John Herbert that he directed in Istanbul in 1969–70.[62] Early work on *The Welcome Table* coincided as well with the completion of *No Name in the Street*, a two-essay volume about Baldwin's female ancestry, the Civil Rights Movement, black masculinity, and Baldwin's visits to the American South and Germany, which he also largely wrote in Turkey. In the Turkish play and the essay volume, as well as his last novel *Just above My Head*, he rehearsed ideas and phrases that were later echoed in the characters and dialogues of *The Welcome Table*. As with his other works, many of the published passages first appeared in letters to friends and family, especially in those to Engin Cezzar, the Turkish actor and director who was Baldwin's close friend and who had first invited him to Turkey.[63]

Baldwin's last play dramatized the bold message of his 1985 essay on androgyny and failures of national masculinity, "Freaks and the American Ideal of Manhood." Beam's appraisal of Baldwin's legacy as the forefather figure of black men who loved other men, or even more specifically black men who are queer, summarizes the meaning of this message aptly: "Because he could envision us as lovers, our possibilities were endless. We could be warriors, artists, and astronauts; we could be severe, sensitive, and philosophical. . . . Not a bad legacy for someone whom the Republic wished deaf and dumb by age fourteen."[64] From an overawed student who discovered theater at an early age, Baldwin became the author of three groundbreaking plays, while his novels, especially *Tell Me How Long the Train's Been Gone* (1968), which he finished in Turkey shortly before his directorial debut there, explored how black bodies were barred from and only reluctantly admitted onto the American stage.

That novel's protagonist and first-person narrator, a black actor named Leo Proudhammer, is an important figure who provides a link between the two earlier plays and *The Welcome Table*. Unlike the characters in *The Amen Corner* and *Blues for Mister Charlie*, Leo is a second-generation transplant from another country, whose parents are immigrants from "the islands," specifically Barbados in the Caribbean. (This might be a nod to Sidney Poitier and Harry Belafonte, both of whom the writer knew well and deeply admired.) Proudhammer has made it to stardom, but the cost of his ascent has been enormous, and the novel opens with his heart attack—"brought about by nervous exhaustion and overwork"—as he is performing onstage and struggling to stay conscious and fulfill his role until the curtain falls (TMHL 70; also 215). When the doctor asks him about the reasons for his exhaustion and collapse, Proudhammer, who is thirty-nine and "not a boy" anymore, offers an explanation that directly mirrors Baldwin's situation as a black queer playwright on the white American scene: "In my own case . . . it's been both easier and harder. When I say easier I guess I mean that I'm not at all—*likely*—so when I *get* on a stage, people notice me. But I'm what's known as a hard type to cast—and a hard type to cast has got to be better, about thirty seven thousand times better, than anybody else around—just to *get* on a stage. And, then, when you start getting jobs—when they start *casting* you— . . . well, you've got a certain kind of advantage. But you can't afford to lose it" (TMHL, 71). The doctor concludes that Proudhammer is "an obsessional type," which makes Leo feel rather unmanly, "on the brink of tears," though the doctor comforts him, saying that "most artists . . . are obsessional types. There is nothing to be done about that. . . . But you must think about what I have said" (72). After the doctor leaves, Proudhammer reads a telegram from his young black lover, Christopher, who has sent him a basket of fruit: "*Stop jiving the people and get yourself back here. You know you can't get sick*" (72). While this missive is proof that he is loved, or at least appreciated and needed, it also makes him question "if I would ever feel anything again, for anyone." He then recalls the words of his past lover, lifelong friend, and current costar, Barbara, a white woman who escaped from her family in Kentucky: "*Leo . . . you also have the right to live. You have the right. You haven't got to prove it*" (73). Barbara brings back memories of their "grimy, untidy, frightening years" on the East Side trying to enter the theater world as young, idealistic people with nothing to lose. Caught between his love for Barbara and for Christopher, bisexual Proudhammer recognizes in the past, and in that youth and vulnerability, "a blasphemed beauty, a beauty which I never recognized and which I had, myself, destroyed" (73).

This recollection of beauty destroyed, of self-destruction brought about by the desire to be loved and fulfilled as an artist, echoes the rhetorical question

Baldwin first asks at the end of *The Fire Next Time*—"What will happen to all that beauty?" This question returns in *The Welcome Table*, whose three central women characters' stories reflect and refract it away from its earlier, stereotypically masculine context of politics, activism, and professional success. In the play, beauty emerges in fleeting moments of human communion, music and art, language and song, the tenderness that can be shared by men as much as women, the tenderness that is possible once the traditional boundaries of gender roles and sexual conduct have been breached. In that sense, *The Welcome Table* links the writer's exilic locations in Turkey and France, where he learned to think of race, gender, sexuality, and religious and national identity in new ways, and it offers an important glimpse into his thinking about the twin issues of Americanness and drama as vehicles for representing androgynous, or even transgender, identity as the 1980s came to a close.

The play's formal composition, which to some degree echoes the similarly improvisational arrangement of *Just above My Head*, mixes African American and European art forms by blending a jazzlike flow of intermittent dialogues with scenes whose hushed tone and careful wording recall Chekhov's *Cherry Orchard* and *Three Sisters*. It consists of riffs and solos by specific characters that circle around multiple, sometimes contiguous, sometimes opposite, topics. It is also filled with music and singing—the words and sounds of black spirituals resounding within the rural architectures of a Provençal landscape. Framed by the classic drawing-room-drama format, inspired by Chekhov, and staged against a setting that is indisputably Chez Baldwin, these literary-musical exchanges invite readers and audiences to glimpse the complex social, historical, and political forces that underwrite them, while gleaning the autobiographical flashes that are Baldwin's trademark.

Given that all the dramatis personae have been based on people from within Baldwin's entourage and circle of friends, and that he himself was enamored of a fantasy of becoming a woman, the play might also toy with the conventions of a masque. *The Welcome Table* reworks this sixteenth- and seventeenth-century European genre—which used mask-covered actors, elaborate stage sets, and music, movement, and song—into a modern play located in between the omnipresent United States and western Europe locked in the Cold War against the Soviet East, via a detour to Chekhov's Russia, and with African Americans and women at its center.[65] The device of the masque is also significant, as it throws shade on Baldwin's life writing in the play, given that the lead character of Edith is his porte-parole, and that all the others reflect him and his relationships in complex ways. This can then be read as a form of authorial transgender masquerade, an attempt to take further the ideas on identity and disidentification through both the openness of the dramatic form and the plasticity of his play's characters.

This last play also reflects and amplifies the strong, albeit only partially fleshed-out, female characters from *The Amen Corner* and *Blues for Mister Charlie*, in which Sister Margaret, Mother Henry, and Juanita appear as strong, unconventional, and dynamic African American women. Baldwin may have been somewhat ambivalent about portraying such women at the time, so they do not seem to command as much space or have as much dialogue as the men do.[66] As I discussed this issue with Roberta Uno, who directed a groundbreaking performance of *Blues for Mister Charlie* at the New World Theater at the Fine Arts Center at the University of Massachusetts in Amherst in 1984, however, she convinced me that a nuanced reading of *Blues* compels a rather different interpretation. As Uno emphasizes, Baldwin's play leads us to a realization that Richard, although a victim of a racist murder, is not at all a sympathetic character. His lover Juanita, on the other hand, fulfills this role. A student, activist, and marcher, she is "a woman who exists in all of us . . . who loves somebody who is flawed."[67]

Viewed through such a lens, Baldwin's earlier dramas signal his growing preoccupation with women characters and the domesticity that is always framing them, and they serve as fertile terrain from which to examine the evolution of his ideas. Thus, even though Sister Margaret loses her congregation in *The Amen Corner* in the end, she gains an understanding of herself and of the humanity of others that allows her to change her life, to let go of the straitjacket of religious dogma that she has used like a mask to hide from her need for love and affection. Deprived of her power over her church by a scheming competitor, she learns to see herself in a new light and embraces spirituality and love while renouncing the falseness and petty politicking of organized religion. Before, she created herself into a powerful and often-unforgiving pastor—a patriarch in a woman's body and hence a performative gendered persona modeled on male preachers in black churches—to forget a lover and husband, Luke, who had left her and their son, David, for the unholy world of jazz music in the city. After Luke has come back home to die, and with David following in his father's footsteps as a budding jazz musician, she finally lets herself understand her husband's love and her son's desire to embrace music beyond the confines of the holy sound allowed in the church. Most important, she also finally gives in to her own need to find and love herself for who she is.

The themes of self-acceptance and self-love, with which women seem to have an easier time than men in Baldwin's plays, continue with the character of the elderly Mother Henry, the protagonist Richard's paternal grandmother, who is the only character in *Blues for Mister Charlie* not consumed by the hatred and anger that propels the men, and who sees through the machismo of both black and white men in the segregated southern town around her. Although acutely aware of the dangers they are all facing, she embraces a humanism and openness that seem to reflect the qualities of Baldwin's own mother, who instilled in her son a conviction that hatred and anger destroy not only their object but also those who harbor and act on them. Representing the younger generation of student protesters and marchers, Juanita, Richard's childhood friend who has become his lover, sees herself as his equal in the struggle against racism. After his murder by Lyle, Juanita wills herself to "be pregnant" with a black warrior who will foment a national revolution.

Juanita's resistance and charisma stand in stark contrast to Richard's manic and virtually suicidal insistence on confronting and provoking the white supremacist Lyle, who murders him in cold blood. Richard seems to choose death so as not to appear cowardly before Lyle, in order to protect his honor and manhood. Not an entirely sympathetic character, he does not treat Juanita well, and his boasting of sexual exploits with white women when he lived in the North is often in poor taste. The clash between black and white men in *Blues*, in characteristic Baldwinian fashion, is also represented through a psychosexual lens on the nation and nationhood. As a synecdoche for the country, Plague Town USA, where the play takes place, is further reduced to a favorite American confrontation—a "walk down" between two men representing opposing racialized forces. This tension/trope is thus reminiscent of, or grimly satirizes, another American popular genre: the western with its white- and dark-hatted characters. The Lyle vs. Richard walk down plays out as a contest between racialized heterosexist machismos, with Richard taunting Lyle with references to black sexual prowess and homoerotic innuendos. This is absolutely unacceptable to Juanita, who has tried dissuading Richard from meeting Lyle. As Uno explains Juanita's fiery declaration of wanting to be pregnant with Richard's child after she finds out about his death, she "chooses to be a mother" and is thus an "incredible figure" who is not afraid of being an unwed black mother, who defies convention in her desire to rear a new generation of black people.

Though young, Juanita is already, much like Mother Henry, an astute reader of the complex relationships between the play's male characters, black and white alike. In that vein, while she does not let the town's white liberal, the journalist Parnell, off the hook after the trial that acquits Lyle, she lets him join the black marchers: "You can walk with us." I agree with Uno that this is a moment of "humanity and generosity" of which no other character in the play is capable; it is Juanita, that seemingly marginal female character, who in fact delivers Baldwin's key message at the end of the play—the marches must go on, and the whites who want to walk in the same direction are welcome to join. That women were given agency and space to that extent in *Blues* is in fact "subversive," as Uno emphasized. Like Baldwin's admiration and love for women, these characters have always been there, gathering strength and exerting influence, and it is up to today's readers and audiences to realize their important roles and power in his works.

The women characters of Baldwin's earlier plays were harbingers of an increased focus on gender, the feminine, and the domestic themes to come in Baldwin's later writing, especially in the novels *If Beale Street Could Talk* and *Just above My Head*. By the time he wrote *The Welcome Table*, Baldwin had begun to see his craft in increasingly feminine terms, which often took the form of a childbirth metaphor in his correspondence. In letters dated July 1982 and March 1983, he wrote to his friend, the African American actor David Moses, about his hopes to finish the draft of the play, and he expressed some of his ambivalence about being entrapped in feminine creative, indeed procreative, processes. He directly compared writing *The Welcome Table* to giving birth, in rather troubled gendered terms: there was something "unspeakably feminine" about being a writer—"labor pains," the book "kicking," and then the author having to "shit it out."[68] The play, initially titled *Inventory or Investments*, proved difficult to write because he was determined to try something very different in it; part of its demand was witnessing and narrating his own transformation from a masculine- to feminine-identified man, which he may have found rather challenging, but which he could not resist.[69]

Staging Queer Domesticity

> Americans are always lying to themselves about that kinsman they call the Negro, and they are always lying to him, and I had grown accustomed to the tone that sought your complicity in the unadmitted crime. The directors I had talked to had to suspect,

> though they couldn't admit, that the roles I was expected to play were an insult to my manhood, as well as to my craft. I might have a judgment on the clown or porter I was playing. They could not risk hearing it.... I could not risk stating it, though there were also times when I couldn't resist stating it... the common knowledge of an unspeakable and unspoken lie.
>
> —*Tell Me How Long the Train's Been Gone*

Leo Proudhammer's musings on his place in the American theater as a black actor who was "difficult to cast"—playing bit parts of a "clown" or a "porter"—put at the center of his identity a manhood that he feels to be under constant assault from the "unspeakable and unspoken lie" of race that is at the heart of American culture. These thoughts materialize as Proudhammer speaks to a European immigrant director—clearly based on the actual Greek expatriate artist, Elia Kazan, with whom Baldwin developed a close friendship—who wants to hire Leo to play the lead in a Welsh play by Emlyn Williams, *The Corn Is Green*, which premiered in London in 1938 and came to Broadway in 1940.[70] The focus of that play on a woman who inherits a house that becomes the site of the plot and character development is significant, for it places female characters and the domestic sphere at the center of the drama in which Proudhammer is to test his acting abilities. In Baldwin's novel, the Welsh context of that play is transformed to portray African Americans' struggle for education in a remote mining town. That the main characters are a schoolteacher and her gifted male teenage student certainly enhances the deep autobiographical context of that intertextual reference in *Train*. As Leeming writes, this was "a book [Baldwin] *had* to write, not one he wanted to write; it was the therapy he needed to break through the psychological crisis... his psychosomatic illness"; "Leo Proudhammer *is* James Baldwin, complete with large eyes, 'pigeon toes,' and 'jiggling behind.'"[71]

As Leo realizes, having been offered the role, "It was the first time in my life... that I was handled as an actor. Perhaps only actors can know what this means, but what it meant for me was that the track was cleared at last for work, I could concentrate on learning and working and finding out what was in me" (TMHL, 417). Soon, he realizes that the director "worked me like a horse," but treats him with "that demanding respect which is due every artist," and that this is what he has been searching for: something infinitely better than his previous experience of "simply hanging around, like part of the scenery" (417). But while Proudhammer's career takes him

3.7. A view of the house on the side from the garden. Image from the documentary film *James Baldwin: The Price of the Ticket* (1989); courtesy of Karen Thorsen, Douglas Dempsey, and the James Baldwin Project.

a long way from these beginnings to fame and security, he pays for the hard work with the loss of his health, for the novel opens with his heart attack from self-destructive exhaustion and overwork.

Unlike Proudhammer, Edith Hemings of *The Welcome Table* has no doubt about her abilities and charisma; as she tells her young protégé, Daniel, "I am a pro, bambino."[72] She is the diva and queen, or as the dramatis personae page introduces her, "actress-singer/star" who has transcended her origins—"Creole from New Orleans." In the twilight years of her rich career, but still at the height of her powers, she is presiding over a veritable court of household dwellers, assistants, visitors, hangers-on, and admirers. Like Baldwin, she commands the scene and her entourage at her southern French estate. Edith's strong femininity is a counterweight to the male characters who have dominated Baldwin's earlier works, at the same time as she also becomes part of the masque the writer creates to deploy a new, postbinary transnational American identity. Another way of approaching this play's focus on gender is to see it as remapping the U.S. national identity from without the United States. As he got older, Baldwin took for granted the transatlantic perspective that often perplexed his critics and readers at home. He used it to develop his late style; he anticipated the growth of identity studies across cultures and borders. The play's turning inward, toward home and family—however alternative to the nuclear heterosexist model such arrangements might be—to love for children, and to close human connections signaled as well s realization that the world was changing and expanding rapidly. What he ιuld not have known, given his passing in 1987, but what his play seems to signal, is what he may have certainly sensed upon his 1986 visit to the Soviet Union at Mikhail Gorbachev's invitation: that the Cold War was drawing to a close, and that with it not only certain political and militaristic models but also certain gendered identities needed to go, too.[73]

Because none of the manuscripts of *The Welcome Table* are widely available yet, I introduce the story below in some detail, while also examining it as Baldwin's attempt to put traditional notions of dramatized Americanness in conversation with black and queer sexualities that he advocated in that play, and as his engagement in a transcultural dialogue with Chekhov's plays that he admired. The action of *The Welcome Table* takes place at a house exactly like Baldwin's during a single day, from early morning until "round around midnight," just like the first two acts of *The Cherry Orchard* and all of *The Three Sisters*. Echoing Chekhov's descriptions of the old estate, which was surrounded by cherry trees, Baldwin's detailed stage directions describe "an ancient, rambling stone house" in Provence, a room that is a combination of "dining room and office," "an arch," "le salon," and a "spiral stair-case," all of which mirror the actual interiors and architectural features of Chez Baldwin.[74] (See plate 13 as an example.)

While the Russian plays both focus on the decline of families, and, in the case of *The Cherry Orchard*, on the inevitable loss of the estate and ancient trees that define it, in Baldwin's play, there is no danger of such a loss, but rather a sense of peace, safety, and permanence emanating from the house, whose all-embracing presence is taken for granted. Chekhov's famous main character in *The Cherry Orchard*, Madame Ranyevskaya, the widowed, aging female owner of the estate, has been duped into squandering her fortune by a ruthless French lover, and thus she may have ruined many lives around her, given that her family and servants depend on her financial solvency. Somewhat similarly, Baldwin's protagonist is an aging but still beautiful and glamorous woman who has had many lovers, but never married, and who is not of aristocratic origins yet has lived internationally and built a worldwide career. Edith is black, and while she is melancholy about her past, she nevertheless knows that she has been tremendously successful as an artist; a self-made aristocrat, if not royalty of the stage by now, she expects to be celebrated and graciously accepts her role as both a glamorous diva surrounded by a loving household and a wise woman whom people travel the world to meet and listen to as a musician and dispenser of life advice.[75]

As the play's homeowner and protagonist, Edith Hemings is James Baldwin's porte-parole.[76] She is an intriguing, turban-wearing, aging star who can be read as a transgender figuration of James Baldwin / Josephine Baker / Nina Simone, for she was once "a skinny bow-legged child" like Baldwin, but now has become, again, what he terms an "actress-singer/star" of mixed origins, a veritable Black Atlantic character, "Creole, from New Orleans."[77] Her cousin Laverne (possibly inspired by Bernard Hassell, the choreographer friend and manager of Baldwin's house) runs the household with an iron hand and employs Angelina, the maid (possibly modeled on Valerie Sordello, Baldwin's cook), and Mohammed, the Algerian gardener (who was to be the hero of Baldwin's unrealized novel *No Papers for Mohammed*, and who was based on an actual person once in his employ). Another character, Regina, is Edith's old friend, a white woman who has recently been widowed and who drinks heavily (possibly modeled on Mary Painter, whose copious 1950s correspondence with Baldwin is now available).[78] These three women are central to the play's action; everyone else revolves in their orbits.

Of the others, Rob is Edith's rather younger "protégé and lover." Mark, a Jewish man, is also Rob's lover and may be similar in age to him, although we don't know it precisely. Elderly Mlle. LaFarge (inspired by Jeanne Faure) is a "pied noir," a French woman exiled from Algeria. There are also Daniel, a former Black Panther and "clumsy arsonist" who is trying to become a playwright (modeled on the writer Cecil Brown, who often spent time at Chez Baldwin, and on a Panther emissary sent by Eldridge Cleaver to ask Baldwin for money); Terry, a photographer; and Peter Davis, a black American journalist from Detroit (modeled on Henry Louis Gates Jr.).[79] The dramatis personae section ends with a note that sorts out the characters' epidermal hues, specifying that Regina, Mark, and Rob are "in appearance" and "legally" white, as is, with "something of a difference," Mlle. LaFarge. Terry's character is supposed to be completely open to interpretation: male or female, black or white. Baldwin's idea of his/her gendered, sexual, or racialized identity is never revealed or defined through dialogue or stage directions, so we are free to imagine that Terry could be identified as anyone, including a queer figure, whose definition I would like to expand to someone who could also, possibly, be transgender, given Baldwin's interest in androgyny at the time and his mixed feelings when he heard of a friend who had considered transitioning from male to female.[80]

It is worthwhile to pause over Terry, for his/her appearance in the play not only embodies the principles of androgyny that Baldwin set out in "Freaks," but also confirms a decisive turn in his later work toward more ambivalent and nonbinary identities.[81] Baldwin's oeuvre is filled with characters who possess that which could be called "unfulfilled queer potential"—from Florence and Deborah in *Go Tell It on the Mountain*, through Vivaldo and Rufus in *Another Country*, Ernestine in *If Beale Street Could Talk*, to Blinky in *Little Man, Little Man* (1976). It is quite problematic to many of his readers, including this one, that Baldwin never directly wrote about or imagined women who loved other women, or were lesbians or bisexual or queer, in any of his works. Were she to be construed as female and sexually involved with women, Terry's presence could be seen as, finally, opening a possibility for casting such a character in a production of *The Welcome Table*.

At the same time, s/he is someone who invites a broader (dis)identification from normative identities; hence we may want to imagine her as queer or trans, which would be my inclination. In fact, such an approach seems in order, given the variety of gendered and sexual identities represented by the other characters in the play. Not incidentally, Terry's craft of photography signifies the emphasis on different and multiple modes of seeing (and literally recording) people and their surroundings, her lens and flashing light an indication of a focus on identity as performative, staged, mutable, or forever taking shape in the eye of the beholder. With the aid of technology, the camera can be used to either blur or sharpen contours. As Baldwin explains his stance on the visual arts in his introduction to *Perspectives: Angles on African Art*:

> The artist's work is his intention.... The form *is* the content. I think the work of artists is to be useful.... It's very different to me, and not all real to the people who may be looking at these objects. They will not know, in short, what they are looking at. One way or another they don't want to see it.... But they know it contains their lives too. And I have other things to do than to try to translate anything for people who don't want to hear it. The mathematics of their lives, the algebra of their lives is built on not knowing it.[82]

Captured in photographs, the bodies of Terry's subjects become immobilized; they can be repeated, or frozen into haunting images that always hide or reveal something happening "at the edge of sight," as Shawn Michelle Smith explains: "the dynamics of seeing and not seeing, of seeing the unseen,

3.8. A view through a balcony window from the interior of the Gatehouse, where Bernard Hassell lived. Photo by Lynn Scott.

and of seeing that we don't see that photography sets forth.... Photographs capture more than their intended subjects."[83] Both Terry's presence as a free-floating subject whose identity is fluid and mutable and Terry's craft signify that, despite its formal aesthetics, Baldwin's play is firmly rooted in the late twentieth century; and in its bold take on identity and the technologies of its reproduction and representation, it is clearly looking into the next one.

In this context, *The Welcome Table* thus can be seen as toying with the drawing-room-drama conventions rather self-consciously, as if inviting us to appreciate its improvisational character through random conversations that reverberate with the rhythms of the jazz records playing in the background and the songs that Edith sings and plays throughout; it updates the genre from Chekhov's realm to the scene at Chez Baldwin with gusto. Its action revolves around Peter Davis's interview with Edith on the day the household celebrates Mlle. LaFarge's ninety-third birthday, echoing an actual party for Mlle. Jeanne Faure that took place in Baldwin's house in 1985. As we progress toward the party—another echo of a similar event in Chekhov's *The Cherry Orchard*—and a late-night interview following it, we glimpse complex erotic entanglements between the characters, with the main emphasis on the females' life stories and their views on the social and political roles of men and women. While Peter and Edith talk, at first haltingly and later with familiarity and pleasure, the focus shifts from one group of interlocutors to another, allowing for a mixing of main and marginal characters' stories and inviting the reader to glimpse the complex forces of love, desire, fear, and need for acceptance that underlie their dialogues.

Baldwin's house serves as both location and active participant in the play, and the way it engenders and frames the stories of its inhabitants and visitors is akin to how his women friends in St. Paul-de-Vence embraced him and helped him to settle into late-life domesticity. The expanding scene of human interactions in *The Welcome Table* places women and their concerns at its center, while their views on gender, race, and sexuality appear to be more open, liberated, and inclusive than those of the men. Such a shift of gendered emphasis from men to women also involves the power to make meaning: the female characters are good listeners but also have the most important, Baldwinian lines to deliver.

By far the longest and thickest in terms of dialogue, Act 1 begins with Peter Davis, a journalist from a Detroit paper, *The Sentinel*, a hardworking man with no time "to piss and moan," who arrives in a Paris hotel and prepares for an interview with Edith Hemings later that day.[84] He takes a phone call from Serena, who seems to be his ex-wife and mother of his son who is "in trouble." While hinting that both father and son favor recreational drugs, from alcohol to harder stuff, Peter insists that the young man get himself out of this trouble on his own. We then see the "home" of Hemings, where Daniel King, the "genuine born-again" Black Panther, as he describes himself, is writing and studying, and where Edith's cousin Laverne picks up the call Peter has placed to inquire about his interview. We witness Laverne "holding" Edith's hand, or managing her household and affairs: she receives calls about the birthday party for Mlle. LaFarge that Edith is hosting that night, haggles with vendors, and directs the Muslim gardener, Mohammed, to prepare the garden for the party; she also comments on the help and having to pay them. She is the quintessential multitasking manager and is not altogether happy with her role.

Daniel briefly joins Edith—our first apprehension of her on the stage is by means of her voice and accompaniment heard in the background—or "insinuates himself into the beat" at the piano where they sing a few tunes together and discuss the progress of his work as a budding writer (and "genuine born-again Black Panther").[85] Echoing Baldwin's vision of the "artist as lover," she advises him to get his hands on "a codpiece" and "a Bible," no matter that he is "shy of both the Word and the Word 'made flesh.'"[86] Daniel has been at Edith's house for three weeks and is grateful for the haven she has provided; much like young Baldwin when he first came to France, but also like some of Baldwin's younger black lovers, Daniel can now "breathe" and try to learn how to write so he might channel his anger and politics into art. Emboldened by his position as a protégé of the famous artist, he dares to tell Edith that she drinks too much, echoing perhaps a somewhat similar exchange that Baldwin once had with Leeming about his "anarchic" life while living at Pasha's Library in Istanbul in 1966–67.[87] Unlike Baldwin, who chastised Leeming for questioning his ways of living his life and doing his work, Edith refrains from promising any improvement and speaks to him with a semiparental authority, referring to both him and her own lover, Rob, as the "children."

Regina, Edith's friend who has just lost her diplomat husband—a big fish in South America—arrives at the house. She is trying to "drink herself to death" and is dressed all in white, contrasting dramatically with Edith's somber black, which they both comment on. (Their color-coordinated garments reflect those of two of Chekhov's three sisters, the youngest Irina, usually clad in white, and the eldest Masha, in black.) While waiting for the other guests, Edith and Rob, who appears soon after, discuss Mark, who is also Rob's lover; their exchange sketches the central love triangle of the play with Edith as its center.

In his defense of what may be read as Baldwin's take on male androgyny, or male femininity, or bisexuality, if not simply queerness, Rob argues that as long as the situation is clear to all involved—Mark knows about Rob and Edith as lovers, and Edith knows about Mark and Rob as lovers—all should be fine. We learn that Rob and Mark, who had been a couple for a while, were taking a break after a lovers' quarrel, and that Edith and Rob met while rehearsing a play together. She was so "nice" to him, valuing him and helping him with his craft, that he fell in love with her despite their age difference. In that sense, he is the "typical Baldwin lover," as Leeming notes, for whom "the risk of love had to take precedence over the safety of orderly relationships."[88] Edith, whom Leeming sees as expressing "Baldwin's other feelings on the matter . . . in Edith's desire for . . . domestic stability," reminds Rob she is old enough to be his mother, to which Rob replies that love defies convention and is not anything one could take back to the "store for a refund."[89] Echoing "Freaks," Rob pronounces that nobody "makes" himself or herself, and that a man who "digs" both men and women can in fact be "trusted" more than others, thus offering the first celebratory pronouncement on bisexuality in the writer's works. Here the play seems to model Rob partially on Lucien Happersberger, who confessed to Jill Hutchinson several years after Jimmy's death that he truly fell in love with Baldwin when they had first met in Paris and then lived together in Löeche-les-Bains.

Unlike Rob in the play, however, Lucien was not comfortable remaining bisexual or gay for that matter, having discovered later on that he preferred sex with women and wanted children. Importantly, he nevertheless affirmed and embraced his relationship with Baldwin, claiming that he was aware that very few people allowed themselves to fall in love with a person of the same sex. He truly loved Baldwin and their connection was serious for a while, but he realized with time that he "was not a homosexual." As he emphasized, again as if his words have come from Rob, it is only having experienced loving sexual relationships with both men and women that one could decide one's true sexual preference.[90]

If sexual preference or a choice of lovers is what one needs in Lucien's mind, then Baldwin's play rewrites his stance in favor of freedom to choose both sexes if one so desires, again affirming bisexuality as a desirable identity. As Rob fervently states, one's lovers are "key" to one's identity; they open one up as a person, and being wide open about one's desires makes honest erotic and emotional attachments possible. As the Baldwinian creed goes, love is "where you find it." Edith responds with what may be read as the first female pronouncement hinting at homoeroticism in Baldwin's works—what, again, I would term an instance of an unfulfilled queer potential—when she mentions "some of the [unexpected] places" where she has found, and lost, love.

Curiously, Baldwin does not follow this opening that might have led to our discovery of Edith's bisexual or lesbian, or indeed queer, past, though he based Edith largely on Josephine Baker, who famously embraced queer love. At the end of scene 3, however, it is Regina who surprises us with a glimpse of female homoeroticism by proclaiming to Edith, who has "style . . . to spare," half-jokingly, half-seriously, "I really should have married *you*!"[91] This remark hints at a possible past relationship between the two women, at the same time as it reads as Regina's oblique confession concerning her own sexuality.

When Regina and Edith reunite and chat in the next scene, Mark appears fresh from a shower and exchanges a passionate kiss with Rob. The men comment on Regina, who is by now visibly drunk, in a rather misogynistic manner (so much for feminist men in the play!), calling her a "lush." Meanwhile, the women talk about having lived apart for fifteen years—Regina as a wife, having been "Mrs. Paul Burke," endowed with lovely stationery, and Edith as an artist, having become the "twisted and possessed" star and diva who feels fully alive only when impersonating someone else. Mlle. LaFarge, who is bitter as a result of having been driven away from Algeria after the revolutionary war for independence there, joins the members of the household. She talks about the long-lost, idealized Algeria of her childhood, where everyone knew his or her place in the colonial order of things. This was the only order she knew and learned; she cycles through nostalgia and regret as the evening progresses.

Being the guest of honor at her formal birthday party, which culminates the play, Mlle. LaFarge has to be indulged. She describes her aristocratic roots, her father (a military general), and the loss of her family's riches and status, "a mansion, servants, everything!" She also proclaims France to be free of racism, which provokes disagreement from Rob, Daniel, and Mark. But they are Americans, she accuses them, with no comment on their skin color, for in her eyes national identity and culture override everything else. Echoing Giovanni's discussions with David on the differences between France and the United States in *Giovanni's Room*, she claims that "Americans" know nothing about "suffering." When Mark's Jewishness is revealed and he and Rob wonder if Jews are better off in "America" or "France," the old lady reconfirms her idea of the superiority of her country and boasts of having helped Jews hide inside her house throughout the Nazi occupation.

From this discussion of race and ethnicity in the context of World War II and French imperialism, the conversation veers back to sexuality and gender. While Rob toasts free love—"Vive la difference!"—drunken Regina proclaims that physiological features and sexual equipment do not make gender. A woman is not a woman only because she can bear a baby and a man is not a man only because he can "pump" one into her. Again, while promising, this train of thought is not carried far enough, as no one seems to pay much mind to Regina the lush (not to mention Regina the closeted queer who is pining for Edith). This character provides a masque for Baldwin's close friend, and possibly onetime lover, Mary Painter, who, as Leeming notes, "in the 1980s had lost her own husband and been defeated by alcoholism . . . [and was] a frequent visitor in the house and a source of certain irritation, in spite of the many years of close friendship."[92]

Daniel takes center stage at this point and explains the historical underpinnings of the American psychosexual landscape by using a metaphor of the "mint julep," a sweet, alcoholic herbal drink from Louisiana. In his story, whose core is definitely straight, a "delicate, transplanted" French lady is sitting on a verandah, waiting for her husband's return. She is bored and "*untouched*" and takes a little "refreshment" of mint with her bourbon to stave off the "heat." She has a male "darky" slave fan her—and perhaps help her pass the time in other ways as well. The result is the great "civilizing arrangement," with the white husband being "fucked *out*" and the mixed "darkies" being born, presumably, both to the French lady and to the master's slave women. Laverne, scandalized by this miscegenation parable of national origins, chastises Daniel for bringing up the horrid subject. As she vehemently asserts, her mother and grandmother were never the "play-things" of white men; in her Louisiana parish, she insists, women were respected, "*everywhere*." Daniel apologizes, explaining that he was merely trying to "clue-in" the "old lady," Mlle. LaFarge, about her beloved country's former colony in North America.

Echoing Baldwin's essay "Princes and Powers," the ensuing discussion links the transatlantic history of slavery to European colonial empires and contemporaneous political events in the Americas. Regina confesses that her late husband was a supporter of the Augusto Pinochet regime in Chile (his diplomatic status meant, of course, that he had operated with the tacit blessing of the U.S. government). As if picking up where Daniel's story ended, she raves drunkenly about young men being beaten, hanged, castrated, and tortured in Chile, admitting to feeling that, as his spouse, she had been her husband's "accomplice." A passive wife who sat on her porch drinking mint juleps, she knew well "what he was doing," but like the French lady in Daniel's story, she never did anything about it.

In Act 2, Peter Davis arrives for his interview with Edith, and we see Terry photographing the star with much flash activity. The guests scatter around the room as the maid, Angelina, clears the space after dinner. For a moment, Peter and Regina talk and flirt, and he resists her efforts to get him a drink, indicating that he has been sober. As Peter's interview with Edith begins at her piano, the lights dim and focus on them. Talking more like friends than a star and a journalist, she tells him about a surgery and fateful health prognosis she has hidden from Laverne; he speculates about her religious beliefs.

All the while, in snippets of dialogue and stage directions, we keep track of the conversations involving the other guests and household members: Mlle. LaFarge is still raving about the bygone Algeria of her childhood, Rob and Mark are teasing each other about love (Rob argues that they can share a good life as a male couple with all of his female lovers in the wings), Regina is drinking and talking with Laverne about their respective marriages (of which Laverne has had three), Terry and Daniel are getting to know each other (while we wonder whether there is an erotic spark between them, and if so, of what kind, given Terry's polyracial androgynous persona), and Daniel is introduced, in passing, to Peter, who takes an interest in interviewing him.

When Peter—who comes from Natchez, Mississippi—tells Edith about his stint in the U.S. Army in Germany following World War II, he admits that he was haunted by the smell of the "burning flesh." Edith explains that he should not be surprised at this sensation, that as a black man from the American South he had already carried this smell with him across the Atlantic to Europe. Peter also tells Edith about having met, interviewed, and befriended a young German army soldier who had served in Poland during the war, and that he was surprised to actually like the former Nazi. Linking American and European histories of racism and genocide in a way that echoes the message of *No Name in the Street*, this moment in *The Welcome Table* sums up Baldwin's view of the West's shared responsibility for the "civilizing experiments" of the twentieth century.

When they discuss Edith's birthplace in a Louisiana bayou and her ancestry as "entangled as the weeds," she tells Peter about having been seduced by music for the first time. As a child, she sneaked out to a local brothel to listen to the piano player. At that house of ill repute, which was also her first concert hall, she discovered unexpected connections between sexuality and race. The madam, Lady Jones, who was a "*nice*, nice" woman, was very dark, while Edith, a Creole, was lighter-skinned, which was supposed to "make" Edith "better." Edith confesses that she did not understand colorism or what was "wrong" with that epidermally charged situation. She thought the "wrongness" had to do either with Lady Jones's "color" or her "job," and she ended up with her mind "fucked" or, as we might read it, convinced that Lady Jones's skin color and job, as much as her gender, sexuality, and class, were inseparable. Edith also mentions her envy of Laverne's beauty and prestigious marriages, and recalls her own thwarted college love—a track star, Romeo, with skin the color of "gingerbread," who could have been the love of her life had he not "moved away."

Romeo's possible fate is symbolic of American black men of Edith's generation: he could have died on the needle or in prison, or become a black entrepreneur, if not someone like Peter. An exchange between Laverne, Regina, and Mlle. LaFarge adds another layer to that discussion, as Laverne reveals her own envy of Edith, the "star . . . but the shy one." Laverne compares Edith to Bette Davis and calls her "bull-headed," a "maverick," and a "black sheep" of their family who, as Louisiana Creoles, lived as if in an "echo of France." Laverne resents having had to leave Ireland to follow Edith to France when she had to "save" her cousin from a "devastating" love affair, as Edith did not know how to "protect herself."

As Rob assures Mark of his love in Spanglish (and here we begin to imagine that Rob might be Latino), Daniel and Terry talk about "Uncle Sam," whom they love but with whom they do not "get along," as he once placed Daniel in prison. While they contemplate which European city Daniel may visit next in his trek from one friend's place to another, the French-speaking Mohammed, whom Daniel calls "mon frère," or his Algerian brother, enters and they invite him to have a drink with them in a clear violation of Laverne's rules regarding the help. They comment on how those living in France perceive Americans and their country. Mohammed finds all things American "strange" and is surprised when Daniel tells him that all the people in Edith's house, no matter their differences of status, appearance, and gender, are all equally American. He also complains of the racist treatment his people receive in France, wishes he could invite Daniel to Algeria, and hopes he can one day accept Daniel's invitation to the United States.

At that point, Edith tells Peter that her secret surgery was a result of a long-ago abortion that followed her teenage pregnancy with Romeo, as if incorporating into the action Baldwin's own illness and surgery earlier in 1987. Romeo was forced to leave town because her family disapproved of him; too dark-skinned, he could not pass the proverbial "paper-bag test" confirming a light-enough epidermal shade that was de rigueur in her social caste, based in class as much as in colorism.[93] Dutiful Laverne told on them, so Edith's youthful love story ended tragically, like Juliet's, only to be followed by other abortions later on.

Peter reciprocates with a story about his son, "little Pete," who is his "soul's salvation," but who lost respect for his father's work as an ad writer for beauty products for Blacks. Like Daniel, little Pete has been in jail and is now "kicking his habit" in a "clinic." Edith and Peter, a barren bride facing a serious medical procedure that may be her last, and a failed father, can exchange sorrows and confess to things journalists usually do not hear about, but they cannot comfort each other. At the same time, their symmetrical confessions and exchange of regrets make them very much autobiographical masques for Baldwin. Like Edith, he always wanted but never had children; like Peter, he often played a father figure to younger men, kin, friends, and lovers.

The brief third act begins with the presentation of the lit-up birthday cake for the guest of honor. The three candles Mlle. LaFarge blows for good luck have been set up by Edith: one for Algeria, another for France, and the third one for Mlle. LaFarge as the daughter of both countries. The old lady is photographed with Edith by Terry, and soon Peter and Terry are invited to spend the night at the house, while Mohammed will drive the ancient heroine of the evening home. Peter and Edith briefly resume their interview at the piano but decide to continue the next morning. As Laverne and Regina return to gossiping about Edith's excesses, we learn that Edith's "French" lover, Xavier, from whom Laverne "saved" her, was a black man from Haiti who had arrived via Marseilles and "by way of North Africa." Certainly an echo of Baldwin's own stormy love affair with a man of similar origins, as Happersberger mentioned in our interview and Leeming confirms, he supposedly ran away from "her love for him."[94] While some guests move into the garden, Daniel and Peter begin talking at the bar, and Daniel reveals that he has an older sister who lives in Copenhagen and is married to a Dane. He also confesses to having been a Black Panther, and someone who was ready to commit murder for his convictions. He received an indeterminate prison sentence but was released after five years, due, he thinks, to his sister having married a white European. Soon Daniel is crying and confesses to missing "his people" and being able to talk about this with "nobody." He is especially stricken by the separation from his parents.

Like the characters from Baldwin's novels *If Beale Street Could Talk* and *Just above My Head*, Daniel's parents are simple people: a cook and a porter from Birmingham, who followed their son to Oakland, California, when he went to jail. They sold all they owned to help him get to Europe, where he sought refuge with Edith, the trustworthy "black singer," who seemed to be a savior to so many black Americans drifting throughout Europe. As Peter ministers to Daniel, he joins him in drinking, finally abandoning his teetotaling, and takes on the paternal role in which he could not succeed with his own son. Everyone else is either going to bed or having a nightcap. Regina, quite sauced by now, invites Laverne to share one with her upstairs in her bedroom.

As the party slowly disbands, Peter promises to give Daniel addresses of friends who could help him. The day has ended with love and hope, no matter its bittersweet edges in conversations on contentious topics and Mlle. LaFarge's statement foreseeing that this has most likely been her last birthday party. Peter rejoins Edith at the piano, next to a wall where "a full length mirror" hangs; the mirror "must be felt," Baldwin insists, although it "need not be seen," as if confronting their reflections in it is something the characters may choose to act upon. Tender and easy with each other now, they listen to Edith sing while Laverne, who had seen the old lady to the car, pauses on the threshold between the garden and the house. Laverne's hesitation before she mounts the two steps from the garden into the house may signify not only her desire to change her life, but also her resigned acquiescence to playing second fiddle to the universally adored Edith. At this liminal moment, the curtain falls.

Unlike in Chekhov's play, where the ending brings about the destruction of beauty and young love, represented by the cherry orchard being felled by axes, and by an ominous sound of a broken string that accompanies an old manservant left behind who is dying alone in the empty house, in *The Welcome Table* the resolution is left to the imaginations of the audience and readers. (In that sense, the ending of Baldwin's play echoes that of *The Three Sisters*, in which nothing is resolved, and the women remain in limbo, with Masha saying what Juanita would have certainly agreed with: "We are left alone to pick up our lives again.... We must go on living... we must go on.")[95]

Contexts Revisited

Begun in 1967 in Turkey, where Baldwin studied Chekhov and Guthrie's productions of Chekhov closely while directing the play *Düşenin Dostu* for Engin Cezzar's and Gürliz Sururi's theater, *The Welcome Table* was a project that Baldwin would work on for a while, then shelve for some time. It was later resurrected and finished in collaboration with the African American theater director Walter Dallas, who headed Freedom Repertory Theater in Philadelphia. Dallas dates the beginning of his working relationship with Baldwin to 1983, when they attended a party at Coretta Scott King's house in Atlanta, after which Baldwin read to him from the first act of the play. Dallas attended the Yale Drama School, some years after Baldwin's Turkish friend Engin Cezzar, and staged a powerful performance of *The Amen Corner* at the Center Stage in Baltimore in 1981. Baldwin saw that performance and it so inspired him that he asked Dallas to become his collaborator, wanting him to direct his new play once it was ready. *The Welcome Table* was staged at the University of the Arts in Philadelphia during the 1990–91 season, following a videotaped reading with Baldwin and student actors in 1986, and a studio reading in 1989 for Ruby Dee, David Baldwin, and other friends.[96] On May 27, 1995, the play had a reading at Lincoln Center directed by Dallas;

the Lincoln Center project did not materialize into a public performance, however, as the Baldwin Estate did not allow it.[97]

As Dallas told me in an interview held at the Freedom Theater, during which we looked at Baldwin's letters to him and watched a VHS-format videotaped reading of the play by University of the Arts students, Baldwin was "terrified" of what he was trying to do in *The Welcome Table*. He explained in unpublished letters to Dallas, written between August 18, 1983, and July 27, 1987, that he was trying "new things" in it as a playwright and intellectual.[98] In the letters, Baldwin would reveal his busy and overextended writing schedule by apologizing for a long silence and reporting that he was living under "unmentionable" stress and struggling in a "sea of troubles" so vast he feared drowning. He would ask Dallas to take over the revisions, as he had been too exhausted and had "nothing to say about it." By 1987, he felt he was done with it and again wanted Dallas to "take it over"; the barely legible handwritten revision notes containing alternative dialogue fragments (included with the Harvard manuscript) confirm his increasingly frail state.[99] Just months before his death, he reported that he was putting the finishing touches on *The Welcome Table* and cutting it by "about twenty pages." He called its characters "my people," and he wanted "coherence" and "precision" in their final portrayals. Daniel, originally modeled on "a couple of Black Panthers," possibly Huey Newton and Bobby Seale, was a tough one to get done. In Dallas's copy of the play, there is a pencil note in his handwriting asking whether Baldwin meant "Huey?" or "Cleaver" as Daniel talks about having followed after that "born again sex pants freak!"[100] As *No Name in the Street* in 1972 revealed Baldwin's revising of his views on masculinity, it was no surprise that by the late 1980s, he concluded that the masculine dilemmas in his play—what in the letters he calls "our troubles"—"didn't begin" and "haven't ended" with the Panthers' model. Dallas, who had his own Black Panther period, complete with the wardrobe and stance, as he told me jokingly, understood well that the dilemma of the play's black male characters existed "outside politics," and he welcomed the opportunity to refine the characters of Daniel and Peter in his own way, although he never managed to bring his attempts at directing it to full fruition.

The last letter from Baldwin to Dallas is the most moving, as it not only mentions the "blow" of "losing [his friend, the actress] Gerry Page," who was the same age as he by the time she passed, but also hints at thoughts of his own mortality; by then Baldwin was rather ill with cancer and may have suspected that he might not recover. Ever circumspect about serious matters having to do with his health, he does not mention the cancer but confesses that he is "convalescing," and that in that state "everything is new," but also "old" and "frightening" because one's body "refuses to be taken for granted." In light of this, it can be surmised that his last work performed on two levels: as marking his farewell to authorship, and as celebrating his sociability and circles of friends whose meetings he reimagined around the welcome tables in his last dwelling place and dramatized as a play, while approaching what would be his last birthday party in August 1987.

As his friend from the Turkish 1960s, Florence Ladd, who would later be a frequent visitor in his house in St. Paul-de-Vence, recalls, Baldwin was weak and in low spirits during their last meeting in June 1987, just weeks before he wrote his last letter to Dallas. He posed for a color photograph she took, in which he appears solemn, but his usual, impeccably dressed and groomed self. He also welcomed her insistence that, no matter what, he should host his birthday party on August second. "He knew he had a terminal illness . . . he knew there was a finality to [t]his birthday." The idea perked him up, she told me, and he was truly looking forward to that gathering. It seems that his mood may have found its way into the descriptions of Mlle. LaFarge's party in the last draft of *The Welcome Table*, at the same time as the house emerged throughout the text as a character on par with its guests and inhabitants.

As Leeming notes, Baldwin indeed saw his last home as the place that reflected and embraced him, so in the play the "house itself is a metaphor for his mind, for his many selves."[101] Not only do Baldwin's stage directions link the outdoor and indoor spaces, but they also involve the reader in actively imagining the set by stating that the rooms in Edith's abode exist "by suggestion," with the main one appearing as a "combination" of a dining room and office by virtue of a "prominent," large wooden table that holds the tools of the trade of the author: a typewriter, paper, and books. I was fortunate to see that very table the writer had in mind and was able to photograph it during my visits to St. Paul-de-Vence in 2000 and 2014. Salvaged from the house by Jill Hutchinson, who had barely a day to empty the structure of the Baldwin brothers' possessions after it had been lost in the final court case, at which the family let it go without a fight, it now stands in her apartment in Vence. "I love this table," she told me. She and David spent many happy moments sitting at it; it was his favorite piece of furniture in the whole house because Jimmy loved it very much and immortalized that seemingly mundane object in his last work.[102]

3.9 and 3.10. The indoor welcome table. Baldwin's tambourine and clock sit upon it. These items are now at Jill Hutchinson's in Vence. Photos by author, 2014.

As Leeming comments, the table was also "rooted metaphorically in the welcome table of the other world, where the weary traveler would find 'milk and honey' and in the welcome table/altar of the church that had once been Baldwin's"; it was also a secular place for a gathering of "his communion congregated," and a place "of witness, where exiles could come and lay down their souls."[103] Now it stands in Jill's living room, and if I did not know that it was *the* table from Chez Baldwin, I would have missed it.

Published in January 1985 in *Playboy* magazine, with a subtitle hinting at the writer's sexual orientation—"the shortest distance to sexual identity isn't always a straight line"—Baldwin's "last major essay... an autobiographical article," "Freaks and the Ideal of American Manhood," was most likely written in St. Paul-de-Vence, possibly at the welcome table, at the time when he was also working on his last play. The essay focuses on the idea of androgyny, but also on what could be called the theatrics of love and erotics that so animate *The Welcome Table*, for "love between any two human beings would not be possible without the spiritual resources of both sexes" (PT, 677) and provides yet another key "metaphor to contain [Baldwin's] gospel."[104] Under a new title, "Here Be Dragons," included in the last volume published during his lifetime, *The Price of the Ticket: Collected Nonfiction, 1948–1985* (1985), the piece confirms Baldwin's late-life preoccupation with what Leeming termed the "idea of gender identity," the topic whose domestic contexts, as I show in more detail in the chapter that follows, he found fascinating since first engaging it in his early writing in the 1940s and 1950s, and then with varying success throughout his prolific career.

The *Playboy* piece also explains how, throughout American history, sexuality and gender have intersected with, and been used to pathologize, those whose race, class, nationality, or religion were deemed other or nonnormative and often violently persecuted inside the national house: "the idea of one's sexuality can only with great violence be divorced... from the idea of the self. Yet something resembling this rupture has certainly occurred... and violence has been the American daily bread... [and] appears to be admired and lusted after, and the key to American imagination" (PT, 678). Mixing social and cultural commentary with confessional passages and glimpses of the writer's childhood, the essay reaffirms Baldwin's abhorrence of violence and machismo. It also doubts that the "present sexual revolution is either sexual or a revolution," identifying it as "a reaction to the spiritual famine of American life."[105] More forceful than ever before on the subject of alternative identities, Baldwin embraces gender-bending pop singers like Michael Jackson and rejects hetero-patriarchy, or the "keepers of the keys and seals" (688–89). He recalls his youthful recognition that a combination of homophobia and misogyny drove those who called him "faggot" or "pussy"; he admits that for a long time he was terrified to appear effeminate and emasculated (681, 685).

Baldwin's late-life impulse to transform his terror of appearing effeminate into a productive female disidentification in and through his late works, to recall again Muñoz's concept with which this chapter begins, was both an act of self-defense for a black queer man vilified by younger, homophobic black critics like Eldridge Cleaver, and a result of fruitful transgender imaginaries, or prophetic visions if you will, that he developed throughout his global travels, but especially at home and among friends, while writing the last pages of his life story in St. Paul-de-Vence.[106] These themes propel his last play, and remain salient today, as we are witnessing a transgender revolution in the media and, more important, in life writing, with, among others, Janet Mock's *Redefining Realness* (2014) not only quoting Baldwin but also helping, to a provocative degree, to translate the conundrum of his predicament in the past through the experience of hers in the present.[107] As Mock describes her rare success, and guilt, as a black trans woman, author, and media darling, "Being exceptional isn't revolutionary, it's lonely. It separates you from your community. Who are you, really, without community?"[108]

On the last pages of *The Evidence of Things Not Seen*, Baldwin writes about having been produced by his community: "I had been told to *love everybody*. Whoever else did not believe this, *I* did" (122). Then he describes being a transgressor, anticipating, and in fact making possible, Mock's statement: "The way of the transgressor is hard . . . because the community produces the transgressor in order to renew itself. . . . [C]ommunity . . . as I have understood it, simply means our endless connection with, and responsibility for, each other" (122). While in Chekhov's play the orchard stands as a symbol of lost family ties, love, and trust that to Baldwin might signify his early understanding of community, in *The Welcome Table*, within the walls of Edith Hemings's unique abode, racialized gender and androgyny become a unifying symbol for the alternative beloved community she has gathered.

On the two title pages of the original *Playboy* publication, a drawing depicts a stack of multihued female and male faces that fit into each other from top to bottom like ceramic cups or bowls. The first is the largest and depicts the chin and mouth of a white female face wearing red lipstick; the last belongs to a black female with partially obscured eyes that peer over the rim of a white male face with green eyes; in between there are four more partially visible male and female faces of varied hues that compose a complete human face. Next to the drawing Baldwin's text reads, "The last time you had a drink, whether you were alone or with another, you were having a drink with an androgynous human being."[109] Here's to the welcome table of identities freed from the straitjacket of Hegelian binarisms.

Baldwin's essay also explains that like race, gender, and sex binaries, love and sexual desire must not be taken literally, at the same time as they provide indispensable fuel for creativity: "love and sexual activity are not synonymous: Only by becoming inhuman can the human being pretend that they are.... But this by no means sums up the state or the possibilities of the human being in whom the awakening of desire fuels imagination and in whom imagination fuels desire."[110] And while it is imagination that makes humans unique among animals, it is its glaring lack that is to blame for what Baldwin deems the uniquely American "panic" regarding gendered, racialized, and sexual identity. He recalls his childhood awakening to this problem: "all of the American categories of male and female, straight or not, black or white, were shattered, thank heaven, very early in my life" (PT, 681).

Like his late essays, the last play and literary testament of *The Welcome Table* signal that Baldwin had big plans for thinking and writing about domesticity and its impact on the making of the self beyond 1987, plans cut short by his untimely passing. The very fact that *The Welcome Table* remains largely inaccessible and unrealized is a sad but fitting representation of these unfulfilled authorial plans, for the very categories that Baldwin challenges in this play—home, gender, race, domesticity, nation, identity—are always also in-process and unfinished. That his actual house in St. Paul-de-Vence, and especially his study and living quarters, no longer stands is sad and fitting, given the lack of attention and reverence given to black writers' homes and physical archives.

Yet, as a home in which alternative, often marginalized and vilified, nonbinary, revolutionary identities could not only find shelter but also flourish, Baldwin's late writing demonstrates the power of place to form and liberate the self from social and cultural constraints through story. As the next chapter shows, the matter of his domestic location, the material of his life story, and the metaphorical embrace of them both in his late novels resulted in a dramatic rewriting of his vision of the national American house and of the most intimate recesses of domestic life that take place as much in the bedroom as in the human heart. By turning his eye and pen to the ways in which national politics and urban life bred violence and racism and to how black nationalism excluded women from culture-rebuilding projects in *If Beale Street Could Talk*, as well as to the ways in which black queer artists and black women were rendered homeless in their very homeland of Harlem in *Just above My Head*, Baldwin highlights the centrality of spatially contingent gender and sexuality to discussions of race and citizenship as much as to those of love, desire, and privacy.

Baldwin and Hassell in front of Chez Baldwin. Photo by David Baldwin.

CHAPTER 4

Building Metaphors

"Sitting in the Strangest House I Have Ever Known," or Black Heterotopias from Harlem to San Juan, to Paris, London, and Yonkers

> Now that I am getting older I . . . feel . . . bewildered. . . . Looking back you see some things so clearly . . . that you couldn't see then. And you say to yourself, "I wish I could have seen it then." But you couldn't see it then. *You have to get to where you are before you can see where you've been*. . . . I feel, actually, as a writer, that I may have gotten rid of a whole lot of shit, really. And as a writer I'm not old. *As a writer, I'm still fairly young*. So there's a great deal that I might hope to be able to do which I couldn't have hoped to do when I was forty-two. . . . I'd like to use the time that is left. Time is fast but the time ahead of you doesn't go as fast as the time behind you. . . . I'm just thinking about something I used to say to my mother when I was a little boy, which was, "I'm going to be a great writer when I grow up." And that's what I mean, you know? That I'm going to be a great writer when I grow up.
>
> —Baldwin, in Bonetti, "Interview with James Baldwin" (emphases added)

> A room is still a room
> Even when there's nothing there but gloom
> But a room is not a house
> And a house is not a home
> When the two of us are far apart
> And one of us has a broken heart
> —From "The House Is Not a Home"
> (B. Bacharach and H. David, 1964), sung by Dionne Warwick

Among the few surviving images of Baldwin at work in his St. Paul-de-Vence house, one used by Karen Thorsen and Douglas Dempsey shows him in his study, leaning over a sheaf of papers, a pen in his left hand, electric Adler typewriter pushed off to the side.[1] Shot in black and white, it depicts Baldwin seated in a wicker armchair and framed against a darkened fireplace, wearing heavy-rimmed glasses, a light batik T-shirt with crisscrossing arabesque patterns, a dark-faced watch on his right wrist, and rings on both hands. There is the inevitable cigarette in his right hand and a drink to his left that seems barely touched. Behind him, on the partially visible mantelpiece, lie stacks of books that include three hardcover copies of *No Name in the Street*, a rolled-up poster, and two photographs—close-ups of the faces of David Baldwin and Nikki Giovanni—facing away from each other and bracketing the ends of the mantelpiece. Given the publication of *No Name in the Street* in 1972, and Giovanni's photograph, perhaps taken around the time she and Baldwin met to talk and were featured on Ellis Haizlip's TV show *Soul!*, this image likely dates to the early to mid-1970s.[2] When David Frost asked Baldwin around that time where home was for him, he replied, "To the artist, home is where he can work."[3]

The only other visual depictions of the writer's studio at Chez Baldwin that I have recovered also come from Dempsey and Thorsen, and they seem to have been taken after the writer's death; they were included in the documentary *James Baldwin: The Price of the Ticket* (1989). The four stills, originally shot in color, which both artists generously shared with me, show sunlight streaming through arched windows, animating the rich wood grain in the furniture, softening the edges and corners. These views of Baldwin's uninhabited workspace seem frozen in time, as if painted by a Renaissance master. A sequence of four images, suggesting a semicircular sweep of the camera, moves from left to right, from a gleaming wooden wardrobe and floor-to-ceiling bookshelves filled with volumes on the wall opposite the window, to the fireplace with a tambourine hanging over a large photo of

4.1. Baldwin at work in his St. Paul-de-Vence study. Image from the documentary film *James Baldwin: The Price of the Ticket* (1989); courtesy of Karen Thorsen, Douglas Dempsey, and the James Baldwin Project. Photo by Jacques Gomot, St. Paul de Vence.

Baldwin's face, to a vaguely African figurine and a skinny cross adorning the wall and mantelpiece above it. The writing table remains at the center of each image. In the second, a low, dark bookstand next to it comes into focus, along with a board above it filled with photographs, clippings, and postcards, with Jeanne Faure's black-and-white face in the middle. The third and fourth images show a wide-open window that partially frames the garden outside, branches and leaves spilling inside along with the sunlight.

With its back to the window and resting in front of the typewriter that sits in the middle of the table, the empty writer's chair is present in three of the images, though most prominent in the last one. A rather ordinary armchair, better suited, perhaps, for a patio rather than a writing table, it is made of bent brown wicker and cushioned with a squished and wrinkled reddish pillow. The space gives the impression of having been recently abandoned: a stack of stationery and letters in a dark stand bears the writer's name in white capital font; folders and files lean against the left side of the typewriter that still holds a half-typed sheet of paper; and to its right is a plastic rotary telephone. Jimmy might be back any minute now, it seems, and the typewriter will come back to life, while the music filling the room will continue playing one of his favorite songs, Dionne Warwick's "The House Is Not a Home" (1964). (See plates 9–12.)

A closer look at the sheet of paper inside the typewriter reveals the following text, which seems to echo Warwick's message of a broken heart and search for home—a message that also interweaves Bessie Smith's homeless

BUILDING METAPHORS 215

4.2. Close-up of the typewriter, with the last text Baldwin was working on. Image from the documentary film *James Baldwin: The Price of the Ticket* (1989); courtesy of Karen Thorsen, Douglas Dempsey, and the James Baldwin Project.

"Backwater Blues," which once so impressed the young writer, into the rich, mysterious texture of this last piece of writing:

> ONE
> Sitting in the strangest house I have ever known—because I am in the process of moving into it—like a squirrel, I rummage, not without panic, through drawers and boxes, trunks, old suit-cases, books, checking to see if my hoard will carry me through what remains of the winter of my life, and I am stopped by a fragment, scribbled on a piece of paper, in my hand, God knows when:
>
> It is better to be born with the thunder of a vanished civilization beating in one's veins, crying for resurrection—but with nothing left of . . . [*the typewriter covers this next line*] . . . than to be born into what seems to be something, this something which . . . [*obscured*] the eye and crumbles under the hand, this something which like a land- . . . [*obscured*].

It is unclear what project Baldwin was drafting—perhaps *Remember This House*, which was to take on the lives and assassinations of "Medgar, Malcolm, and Martin," or *No Papers for Mohammed*, in which the Algerian gardener from *The Welcome Table*, based on the writer's onetime employee, was to become the central character.[4] That this mysterious sheet of typewritten paper is, indeed, the last one Baldwin touched is apparent when one notices a slightly wilted, bright red flower on top of a tray on the other side of the table and a tall reddish votive candle next to it. The room becomes a still life, a sanctuary, a space of mourning and absence compounded by the fact that the wing of the house where it was once located—with all that vibrant creativity and passion that must have filled it—was permanently demolished in November 2014.

It was in this room and at this table that Baldwin labored over his last two novels, different yet interlinked tales about black domesticity, published within five years of each other: *If Beale Street Could Talk* (1974) and *Just above My Head* (1979). He also worked there on his last volume of essays, which discussed the Atlanta children murders, *The Evidence of Things Not Seen* (1985), whose last page names the locations where Baldwin took its manuscript as he traveled and taught in the 1980s—Atlanta, New York, Amherst, St. Paul-de-Vence. *Evidence*, about which the late Amiri Baraka says, "That's some high-speed, elegant speech, but the activism in that... the actual popping of these people up the side of the head is remarkable," exerted a heavy emotional and physical toll on the writer, which manifested in the volume's breathless, staccato, and at times raging tone, as well as in the thick files of documentation and Xeroxed pages Baldwin amassed while researching it.[5] While the majority of Baldwin's contemporaries misread that intensity and passion, attributing their discomfort with reading it to the writer's waning powers, new scholarship offers astute analyses of that complex coda to his published nonfiction, as well as to his last two important, complex novels, which I read closely in this chapter.[6]

In what follows, I examine Baldwin's meditations on the national house in *Evidence*, and trace the utopian and dystopian black and queer domestic spaces he crafts with his collage-like late style in *Beale* and *Just Above*, the spaces where, away from traditional African American families, nonnormative identities find shelter, albeit temporary, or are rendered terrorized and homeless within and without the United States. Given its concern with *story*, this chapter triangulates with the concerns that animate chapters 2 and 3—*space* and *self*—and explores the ways that Baldwin's later work helps us understand his sense of being "home free," at his full authorial powers, as he tells Nikki Giovanni in their *Dialogue* in 1970, and of dwelling in his late style, nourished and enabled by his home spaces in France. This later work embraces the interpenetration of literary and autobiographical/life-writing domestications

4.3. *The Black Collegian* on top of folders and surviving materials related to *Evidence*. Photo by author, 2014.

that evidences his rethinking of how racialized and class-inflected gender and sexuality could be represented in fiction, as he arrived at perhaps the most complete acceptance of himself as the aforementioned "aging, lonely, sexually dubious, politically outrageous, unspeakably erratic freak" embraced and beloved in St. Paul-de-Vence (NNS, 18). This chapter moves sometimes retrospectively, sometimes chronologically, much like Baldwin's narratives do, from a discussion of racist terror in *Evidence*, through the Baldwin-Giovanni *Dialogue* and its focus on black feminist rewritings of African American male-female relationships and authorship, to examinations of how Baldwin implements his revised perspective on black masculinity and femininity in the experimental narration and characterization of *Beale Street* and *Just Above*.

Beginning with *No Name*, as Baldwin moves away from a focus on black masculinity toward black femininity in his subsequent works, reading him against chronology reveals his authorial development as a cyclical rather than linear spatial-temporal process. For example, changing representations of Harlem in early essays like "The Harlem Ghetto" (1948), which depict it as a synecdoche for the whole country, blend metaphorical and material representations of American urban space to engender a novel concept of mid-twentieth-century national identity that resonates in his 1970s works, especially *If Beale Street Could Talk*. That short novel is a fertile site for reconsidering representations of the national house that bridge Baldwin's earlier and later works and that anticipate the disidentification from whiteness and heteronormativity at the core of *Just Above*, where he constructs a heterotopian vision of black queer domesticity as an alternative to the unrealized homes and homelessness that pervade *Beale*.

In this context, my reading of *Beale*'s pivotal role in Baldwin's literary journey out of Harlem and into the international worlds that he later occupied focuses on its portrayals of the writer's native ground as a space of oppression and liberation that frames his black characters' affective relationships with other Americans, particularly Jews and European immigrants. The first-person narrator and main character of *Beale*, Tish Rivers, offers valuable gendered insights into the late twentieth-century national identity of the United States as spatially contingent, multidimensional, and inflected in powerful ways by race, ethnicity, and sexuality. By so doing, her narrative also begins to question black nationalist models of gender and sexuality that are based in hegemonic, patriarchal, heterosexist machismo, which end up being not so different, structurally and in their relationship to women, from the system those professing black nationalism originally set out to oppose. Baldwin's representations of Harlem and the United States as a "house of bondage" put a new spin on what Raymond Williams famously termed the "structures of feeling" by both revealing and challenging the constructedness and spatial underpinnings of the black-white divide at the heart of the twentieth-century American literary imagination, which has by then become powerfully imprinted with images of incarcerated black bodies.[7]

Though seemingly a very different novel, *Just above My Head* reads well in dialogue with, or as a response to and continuation of, *Beale*, with its bold suggestion that U.S. national identity, which has excluded Blacks and other nonnormative and queer bodies, must be reconstituted with black queer identity and alternative models of domesticity at its center. The utopian space that Arthur and Jimmy occupy at the end of *Just Above* offers a momentary, transitory shelter that brings about the love, safety, and joy that one longs to find at home. While such shelters are high-priced and often short-lived, they glimpse a better world, such as that attained by Julia, for example, in which multiple identities, seen as "others" from both the black and white sides of the color line, can flourish and affect positive transformation around them. While reading *Just above My Head*, I also pay attention to Baldwin's mining of his memories of his childhood home in his nonfiction, especially those connected to his difficult relationship with his stepfather, which can be read as casting a shadow of trauma over the novel's representations of heteropatriarchal domesticity. Baldwin's two models of black queer heterotopias in *Just Above* are posed as risky alternatives to segregated spaces where neither his black queer characters nor Baldwin as their author could fit: exclusionary spaces dictated by the whiteness of the national house on the one hand, and equally exclusionary spaces hostile to queers, feminists, and trans people dictated by black nationalism on the other.

Thinking back to the metafictional passage on that last half-written page in Baldwin's typewriter that inspired the title of this chapter, we can read the expressions in it—"the strangest house," "in the process of moving into it," "rummage, not without panic," "my hoard will carry me," "what remains of the winter of my life," and "stopped by a fragment scribbled on a piece of paper"—as compounding, black-on-white as it were, the importance of the writer's domicile and its objects to the process of his late-life creativity. The rhythm and repetitions in this mysterious draft echo those from the interview that provides this chapter's epigraph, indicating a more improvisational and self-reflexive prose style. The images of his study and empty chair also help, again, to pull together the conceptual triad that drives my project by showing how the relationships between matter, material, and metaphor, or between Baldwin's domicile, life story, and fictional and life-writing apparatuses, interact organically. They seep into the words on the page and alchemize into his complex, bewildering, often challenging, yet marvelous works that cannot leave their readers unchanged.

THE AMERICAN DILEMMA IS . . . A SPACE OF RACIST TERROR

Coming after his last two novels, *The Evidence of Things Not Seen* is a fascinating coda to Baldwin's meditations on the national house. It elaborates on "Notes on the House of Bondage" and provides a retrospective commentary on the issues of identity, social space, and storytelling that are central to this project and to rereading his works today. In terms of scope, *Evidence* takes place in Atlanta, where Baldwin investigates the case of the African American Wayne Williams as the main suspect in the Atlanta children murders, and in a wider transnational context, in which history is cyclical—"What goes around, comes around" (82)—and in which the United States as part of the West has immobilized itself in that history's mythic distortions ("a hymn to White people" [80]), "somewhere between the Statue of Liberty and the pillar of salt" (82). At the center of the resulting historical and geopolitical "horror" stands "their religion," the "Christian church" that historically has brought Blacks "devastation and death" (83). Its incarnation in black communities Baldwin repudiates, though he values some of its cultural and social contributions, such as its "warrior" preachers who "told us that *trouble don't last always*" (82).[8] *Evidence* also illuminates the spatial aspects of key tenets of Americanness against the background of the approaching fin de siècle: "The paradox of what we react to as the *American Dream* and as the American dilemma is that it *is a space*—it is certainly not yet a nation . . . ruled by Whites and dominated by Blacks" (84, emphases added).

The "domination" of that prenational space is apparent in the novels, too, and has nothing to do with actual power, of which those labeled "black" have little, but everything to do with the power of the racist imagination that spreads over the minds and hearts of all citizens. For those who think themselves "white," that imagination, or what Henri Lefebvre would call "representational spaces," creates a paranoid interpretation of the national house as under constant threat by various "others." Inside that mind-set, which tragically continues to precipitate murders of black citizens by the police and domestic terrorists, the imagined, paranoid, and guilt-driven threat of blackness is seen to pervade public national spaces as well as the privacy of the home and bedroom. Baldwin shows the brutal workings of this misguided perspective already in the portrait of the damaged, white supremacist protagonist of the short story "Going to Meet the Man" (1965). By 1974, in *Beale*, it not only dominates the urban landscape of Harlem and New York City that his black characters inhabit, but also has spread to the nation's "unincorporated territories," filled with brown and black bodies, such as Puerto Rico. While present in *Just Above*, where Arthur Montana's international roaming echoes that transnational perspective, and the accounts of his travels in the South and life in New York always reverberate with an awareness of the racist mind-set's madness, the narrative focus shifts to Arthur's older brother, Hall Montana, and his recounting of Arthur's life and death. Here the emphasis is on the characters' quest to achieve privacy and intimate domesticity with families and lovers, thereby eliciting the power of those fleeting shelters created and inhabited by queer black male artists and women.

Given Baldwin's use of essays to probe issues central to his novels, as he explains to Kay Bonetti in a 1984 interview at Amherst College, where he was then teaching, it is crucial to read his diverse works in conversation with one another.[9] As I show in the introduction and chapters preceding this one, dialogic readings *across* his oeuvre need not adhere to chronology. Baldwin's rethinking of key themes like whiteness, blackness, domesticity, the psychosexual underpinnings of national identity, or his life story as both unique and representative of the history of twentieth-century Americanness proceeds cyclically, evoking and reevoking past experiences and events through new temporal lenses, locations, contexts, analytics, and geopolitical circumstances. Tracing such cycles enables provocative connections and analyses, such as Quentin Miller's, whose *Criminal Power* (2012) deftly reevaluates Baldwin's contribution to rethinking the apparatuses of the law and the racialized and regionally contingent U.S. judicial system. Miller shows that *Evidence* cycles back to Baldwin's early experience with the law in France and that Baldwin's argument "has to do with power . . . and largely to do with a perception" that "operates prior to rationality and impedes impartial judgment."[10] Baldwin's association of the word "guilt" with "'privacy,' one of America's most cherished ideals, and yet one that is routinely threatened in [his] works," is a key insight of *Evidence*, which demonstrates how, "under the magnifying glass of courtroom scrutiny, the truth can somehow be distorted rather than illuminated."[11]

Evidence helps elucidate the association of both privacy *and* guilt with the home, or lack thereof, in the two 1970s novels that precede it—*Beale Street* and *Just above My Head*—and is Baldwin's essayistic elaboration on their fictional and life-writing representations of alternative black domestic spaces. Along with affect and imagination as forces that propel desire, the racist terror central to this text underpins the black queer heterotopic spaces Baldwin constructs in *Just Above*. It is also in *Evidence* that he discusses most openly the ways this terror informs, shapes, and distorts embodied childhood memories of home, adding yet another dimension to the analysis of the two novels:

> What I remembered—or imagined myself to remember—of my life in America (before I left home!) was terror. And what I am trying to suggest by what *one imagines oneself to be able to remember* is that terror cannot be remembered. One blots it out. The organism—the human being—blots it out. One invents, or creates, a personality or a *persona*. Beneath this accumulation . . . sleeps or hopes to sleep, that terror which the memory repudiates. . . . Yet, it never sleeps—that terror, which is not the terror of death (which cannot be imagined) but the terror of being destroyed. (ETNS, xiii–xiv)

The racism-driven "terror of being destroyed"—and of becoming a destroyer of others, as he admits on multiple occasions—is what drove Baldwin from the United States. Usually reticent about his physicality, in this passage he uncharacteristically reveals his careful performance of memory, the acting "persona" whose creation has been necessary to the "organism—the human being" (Baldwin housed in a material, vulnerable body)—to survive that terror.

We can trace this covering of the material body with an act and costume, with the performative "persona" that resembles to some extent his device of the masque from *The Welcome Table* (discussed in chapter 3), throughout many of his works, and even back to his profound childhood fear of his abusive stepfather, which erupts through the narrative fabrics of "Freaks and the American Ideal of Manhood" and *The Devil Finds Work*. This device is necessary, too, to bear the memories of the dangers he had to confront wherever he turned as a black queer child and young man in Harlem, New York City, and the United States. As *Evidence* makes clear, he sees this performance as crucial to his survival; perhaps that is why he discloses its workings most directly only in this last, underappreciated and likely least widely read work, not featured in the popular volumes of his collected essays, *The Price of the Ticket*, or the Library of America's *Collected Essays*.

Baldwin locates the roots of that terror, the perception of the larger "horror" that is the West housing persecuted black bodies like his own, not only in the national house or childhood home, and within the writer himself, but also in the very sanctum of his religious community. Recalling a story of a friend, Buddy, in his family's church, which he also mentions in "To Crush the Serpent" (1987), he is bewildered as to why his community, where he "had been told to *love everybody*," rejects that friend:

> I was about fourteen. He was seventeen.... He had been a friend of the "older" boys in church, but they no longer spoke to him.
>
> I remember seeing him, for the last time, on the avenue.... I remember the cigarette because the cigarette signaled, proved, his sinful state. He had... "backslid," had "gone back into the world," and we were forbidden to speak to him.... Yet I spoke to him.... I still remember his face, lightless and lonely, unbelievably lonely.... I remember watching him walk away.... I never saw him again. Very shortly afterward, he died, I was told, of TB: tuberculosis. (ETNS, 121–22)

Communal complicity ensues in the demise of Buddy, who, with neither option offering freedom nor fulfillment, chose the sinful "avenue" instead of the shelter of the church. Baldwin takes it gradually: "I had the feeling, dimly, then, but very vividly later, that he died because he had been rejected by the only community he knew, *that we had had it in our power to bring the light back to his eyes.*" As he matures, this realization transforms into a compulsion to say what, at first, in the sanctified community that rejected all nonconforming "others," he thought unspeakable: that "we are all sinners." As Baldwin says, when "I found myself unable *not* to say it . . . I, too, left the church—the community" (122, first emphasis added).

Baldwin was also seventeen when he "backslid" himself—going to the movies with his friend Emile Capouya instead of to the church one Sunday, as he describes in *Devil*—and decided to live by and through writing. In time, another paradox emerged, which has driven the life-writing thread of his oeuvre: "That the community that had formed me had also brought about that hour and that rapture," thus enabling him to leave the pulpit while holding on to some of its lessons. Though he realizes that the terror of one's origins remains written on the body like the beatings his stepfather gave him, he learns to put his memories to good use, for "our identities, with every breath we take, are being altered" and "one is always doing one's first works over" (ETNS, 122–23). Buddy's story and his own, then, teach the writer that there is always hope. His idiosyncratic form of humanism emerges in reaction to this story, for "while there is no guarantee that the community could have . . . 'kissed the hurt away,' [Buddy's] sense of being valued might have made the split-second difference between choosing life and choosing death" because the only truth one can be certain of is that "our lives really hang on some such tiny thread and it is very dangerous not to know this" (123). Baldwin, who attempted suicide several times, knew this well.

His youthful lessons concerning communities, as well as his experience investigating black children's murders in Atlanta, also teach him that the protective persona/masque is necessary for artists, for "a writer is never listening to what is being said ... never listening to what he is being told. He is listening to what is *not* being said ... listening to what he is *not* being told, which means that he is trying to discover the purpose of the communication" (ETNS, 95). This revelation may be read in the context of Paul Laurence Dunbar's famous poem "We Wear the Mask" (1896), and it signals the depth of hidden pain under the mask that covers not only someone's face but also their speech. It appears before Baldwin's narrator recalls Buddy's story, though it is clearly a result of Buddy's story, thus illustrating the cyclical, diachronic, and improvisational approach to time and location he adopts in his later nonfiction. This approach, more present in the narrative fabric of his novels, including the early *Go Tell It on the Mountain* (1953) and *Giovanni's Room* (1956), in which the narrative often loops through the past into the present, also pervades his essays, beginning with *No Name*, and confirms that his fiction and nonfiction work more in tandem than his critics may realize. This is key to reading *Beale* and *Just Above*, for both novels, no matter how different at first sight, deploy Baldwin's method of mining the terror of memory on the one hand, and his lesson concerning "what is *not* being said" and "what he is *not* being told" as revealing "the purpose of the communication" on the other.

Another lesson from *Evidence* is Baldwin's reworking of the idea of community, which "as I have understood it, simply means our endless connection with, and responsibility for, each other" (122). Yet though "we are all born into communities" as human beings, Baldwin cautions, "in the modern State, the idea—the sense—of community has been submerged for a very long time." From that statement, seemingly dealing with semantics, Baldwin moves to the identity-in-social-space interpretation, or an association of this submergence with class that evokes race, ethnicity, colonialism, and imperialism—for "the submerged" in this national, exclusionary context means "the 'lowly': the Native American, the Mexican, the Puerto Rican, the Black" (123). This list of racialized icons "can be called communities because they are informed by their knowledge that only they of the community can sustain and re-create each other. The great, vast, shining Republic knows nothing about them and cares nothing about them." While useful at times, "during a military adventure ... or an election year, or when their dangerous situation erupts into what the Republic generally calls a 'riot' ... these communities, incipient, wounded, or functioning, are between the carrot and the stick of the American Dream" (123–24).

The impossible, in-between space these communities of color occupy, then, is not recognized as the space of the nation, nor even that utopian construct called the American Dream, but as that of the Other. Michel Foucault's 1967 definition of "heterotopia," with heavy Baldwinian modification, can help explain that minority space as "a sort of counter-arrangement... in which... all the other real arrangements that can be found within society, are at one and the same time represented, challenged, and overturned: a sort of place that lies outside all places and yet is actually localizable."[12] Here is what could be Baldwin's response in *Evidence*, which follows Foucault's abstract definition by more than a decade and a half, depicting the West as isolated and lost in its imperialist dream: "There are no more oceans to cross, no savage territories to be conquered, no more natives to be converted. (And those for sale have been bought.) In a world made tedious by man-made poverty and obscenely senseless war, it is hard to predict the future of money: when the South African miner leaves the mines, what happens to the price of gold?" (124). At the end of *Evidence*, Baldwin puts together local, regional, national, economic, and international spatial-geopolitical perspectives, claiming, "The present social and political imperatives cannot serve human need." In light of not only recent, but ongoing murders of black Americans by the state and domestic terrorists, and in light of the revenge killings of police officers, family members, and peers by distraught and irreparably damaged war veterans, Baldwin's question about the South African miners, posed when that tortured country was still struggling to overthrow apartheid, gains terrifying timelessness: "It is this apprehension that ferments in multitudes today, looking at the bodies of their menaced and uselessly slaughtered children, all over this world" (124).

Baldwin's version of the heterotopic alternative to the American Dream, and to the national identity so conceived, rests on his refusal to give up on his country and its people's unfulfilled potential.[13] His conclusion to *Evidence* is another jeremiad, echoing the one from *The Fire Next Time* (1963), more clearly urging a rebuilding of the national house and consciousness. In this prophetic vision, the peoples inhabiting that house, in all their diversity and challenge, must become examples—*not* of a shining city on a hill, but of hard work carving out spaces for truth and liberation from national myths and the denial of history. Baldwin embraces the fiery rhetoric of the pulpit, while distancing himself from posturing as a savior by cautioning that he not be misunderstood. He recalls Emile Zola's "Letter to the President of the Republic" from April 1898—"I do not have the European (or provincial) liberty to write *J'Accuse*. (Think about it)"—as he explains his vision of American democracy:[14]

> This is the only nation under heaven that contains the universe—east and west, north and south, black and white.... The only nation... that can hope to liberate—to begin to liberate—mankind from the strangling

idea of the national identity and the tyranny of the territorial dispute. I know this sounds remote, now, and that I will not live to see anything resembling this hope come to pass. Yet, I know that I *have* seen it—in fire and blood and anguish, true, but I have seen it. I speak with the authority of the issue of the slave born in the country once believed to be: *the last best hope of earth.* (ETNS, 124–25)

The authority Baldwin claims in this invocation is anonymous and collective, historically contingent, racialized, and autobiographical all at the same time, that of "the issue of the slave." The place his country occupies in the present is not yet claimed, for its only identity lies in a past long gone, in the space of the "once believed." His last words in *Evidence* distinguish between the "author of the crime" and "he who collaborates," making it clear that the latter is "doomed, bound forever in that unimaginable and yet very common condition which we weakly suggest as *Hell.* In that condition, and every American walking should know it, one can never again summon breath to cry *let my people go!*" (125). Evoking the comparison between the United States and the "house of bondage," or the history of slavery and the rising prison-industrial complex, Baldwin reiterates and expands his vision of national/domestic crisis against the soundtrack of "Go Down Moses" and the images of the Old Testament Exodus. And however resigned he might feel about the future of his country—he reveals a pessimistic attitude in many late interviews—he refuses to give up on others and the power of humanistic imagination to change minds and hearts and to affect actions.

PUTTING ONE'S SOUL ON THE LINE, OR "IT'S ALL RIGHT, BECAUSE WE'RE HOME FREE"

> I've changed precisely because America has not. . . . I had a certain expectation for my country years ago, which . . . I don't have now. . . . I think that it is a spiritual disaster to pretend that one doesn't love one's country. You might disapprove of it, you may be forced to leave it, you may live your whole life as a battle, yet I don't think you can escape it. . . . You don't pull up your roots and put them down someplace else. At least not in a single lifetime, or, if you do, you'll be aware of precisely what it means, knowing that your real roots are always elsewhere. If you try to pretend you don't see the immediate reality that formed you I think you'll go blind.
>
> —Baldwin, in Standley and Pratt, *Conversations*

On November 4, 1971, in London, England, Nikki Giovanni, a young feminist Black Arts Movement poet, and James Baldwin, the older and established writer living abroad, met to record an interview that appeared during two episodes of Ellis Haizlip's popular and beloved show *Soul!*[15] Debonair Haizlip introduced Baldwin and Giovanni as "two brilliant and eloquent members of the black family." A frequent guest, and "old friend of *Soul!*" and for some time its coproducer, Giovanni appears in a resplendent Afro and a purplish dress adorned with silver jewelry. All in black, sporting a silver necklace, Baldwin holds a cigarette in one hand, while on the other a silver ring gleams. Theirs is an enormously entertaining and intellectually stimulating exchange, with close-ups and intimate camera angles that frame Giovanni's sparkling gaze, wit, and smile and that convey Baldwin's hand gestures, physiognomy, and passionate delivery; the joy in their faces when they hit a point they agree on is another bonus. (It is unfortunate these recordings are not available these days, as the issues they engage remain current and would provide valuable teaching material.)[16]

At the beginning of their conversation, Giovanni asks Baldwin why he left the United States. His answer links the concept of U.S. authorship with race, identity, and great European writers of African descent whose blackness he discovered only outside of his homeland's borders: "I moved to Europe in 1948 because I was trying to become a writer and couldn't find in my surroundings, in my country, a certain stamina, a certain corroboration that I needed.... No one ever told me that Alexandre Dumas was a mulatto ... that Pushkin was black. As far as I knew when I was very, very young there'd never been anything.... As far as my father knew, which is more important, there'd never been anything ... called a black writer."[17] The missing "stamina" and "corroboration" meant that the authors he was reading as a child, and later as a young man in Harlem in the 1930s, and the literary world that he dreamed of entering in the 1940s were coded in exclusionary racialized terms. No matter the national or geographic origin, or even actual phenotypes as was the case with French Dumas and Russian Pushkin, the term "writer" then presumed "white." U.S. imperial power and a cultural coding of authorship fostered such representations by structuring the always racialized meanings at home and abroad, by dictating what and who was visible (that a writer envisioned so was male went without saying). Hence Dumas and Pushkin appeared "white" to aspiring-writer Baldwin as their racial difference was covered with nationality, something in which equally racist France and Russia were complicit.

4.4 and 4.5. Screen shots of Baldwin and Giovanni from the show *Soul!* (1971).

Giovanni replies to this complex statement poignantly: "I can dig it—those feelings."[18] By the time she started writing and imagining her career, though, she had Baldwin and many other black writers to read and consider as antecedents, while Baldwin had to travel widely outside of the confines of the American literary imagination and authorial identity politics to discover the fallacy of the presumed whiteness that marked and masked the identities of (inter)national authors he admired. Along with his enormous erudition, however, travel and exile were not the only reasons Baldwin came to know better. Even before leaving for Europe, he had met Richard Wright and later had a famous literary quarrel with this mentor and literary father figure; he also came to know Langston Hughes and Countee Cullen; he read Ralph Ellison, Ann Petry, and Gwendolyn Brooks. Yet none of these writers, nor scores of others whose names began to feature on college course syllabi in the 1970s and 1980s—Olaudah Equiano, Phyllis Wheatley, Jupiter Hammond, Harriet

Jacobs, Frances Harper, Frederick Douglass, Zora Neale Hurston, Nella Larsen, Alice Walker, Maya Angelou, Toni Morrison, and others—were represented as "American" writers, the adjective that Baldwin preferred to the marginalizing "Negro."

Baldwin's insistence on the lack of literary antecedents in their conversation with Giovanni has everything to do with American history and its impact on his home life and exile, as well as his memory—his stepfather's madness and death and his difficult childhood in his stepfather's shadow. It also has to do with generational dynamics—he is the elder to the young black writers represented by Giovanni—and with gender as an increasingly important aspect of identity that cannot be divorced from race. The presence of numerous books by Maya Angelou, Alice Walker, Toni Morrison, even Ruby Berkley Goodwin, whose *It's Good to Be Black* was published the same year as Baldwin's *Go Tell It*, in his library confirms this connection.

While immensely entertaining, the Baldwin-Giovanni dialogue on *Soul!* is not always harmonious. Visibly aware of their considerable difference in age and ideological approaches to how gender, race, and class exert influence on black lives, Giovanni often speaks vehemently against the nationalism and sexism of Black Power, trying to make the elder writer see her feminist vantage point, while Baldwin stubbornly tries to defend black men at first, but slowly begins leaning toward her position as their exchange develops. In an interview, Giovanni told me that their main difference lay in the fact that, as she put it, to Baldwin, the important thing was "learning *to* love," while to her it was all about "choosing... deciding *who* to love," as well as being responsible for "who we let love us." Her desire as an artist was exactly the same as Baldwin's, though, for what she "always wanted to be [was] me, Nikki."[19]

In her account of Black Power television, Gayle Wald parses out the "complex dynamics of misfittedness and celebrity in both writers," reading their exchange closely for such clues as body language and tone, and concluding that "the critique of nationalism's recuperation of patriarchal gender relations hovers over it as a point of simultaneous agreement and contention."[20] Wald also recognizes the erasure of Baldwin's homosexuality from the interview, and the fact that both writers perform something they are not, "a black couple who try to work out private differences that stand in for larger, public debates," noting poignantly that some of the most interesting, if not contentious, parts were edited out of the published version of the interview.[21]

While I agree with Wald that it is important to note how carefully the Giovanni-Baldwin conversation was later packaged into a book that reads much more fluidly and indeed "straight," I emphasize Baldwin's growing recognition and acceptance of Giovanni's feminist perspective that is clear in both. It is almost as if, in defending the perils of black masculinity faced by his stepfather's generation, and in trying to explain his thinking about Giovanni's contemporaries, he is inadvertently covering and precluding any discussion of his own. For while, as Giovanni says, they may be "the weirdest looking people on earth," that weirdness is rendered safe, as Wald notes, by association with the "heterosexual intimacy" that the two writers inadvertently perform on the show.[22] As I see it, however, Baldwin demonstrates his willingness to learn from others and change his views, as he does with Giovanni's feminism. Despite that, he is left without a space where someone like him could exist as a queer male in black communities, or anywhere else for that matter.[23] When Giovanni complains about "homosexual hype" close to the end of the program, it only compounds that exclusion.[24] As a result, although Baldwin warmly thanks Giovanni for having asked him the "loaded question," for making him think in new ways about contemporary vicissitudes of survival and love between black women and men in a racist society—what she calls "a tremendous responsibility," within what he describes as the American reality in which "most people ... accept without very much question the assumptions they're given"—he is, yet again, left alone in a no-man's-land of identity and terminology.[25]

Hence, his concluding "It's all right, because we're home free" suggests that he and Giovanni may have become allies who can collaborate on refurbishing the national literary house. As writers, they are "forced to look behind the word into the meaning of the word" (Baldwin) and "into the actions produced by the words" (Giovanni). It also implies, though, that in the home so envisioned by the younger generation represented by Giovanni, men like Baldwin do not belong any more than they did in that of his father's generation or of his own.[26] This loneliness, being left out of the communities they are discussing in the interview, provides yet another layer of context for Baldwin's late-life shift in his views on racialized gender and sexuality as contingent on social space. It could be argued that his later turn toward androgyny in "Freaks" is a result of his having realized that there would be no space for him, or for his ideas about identity, family, and domesticity, unless he created his own, both materially and metaphorically in his life and works.

The de facto rejection of "misfitting" black men like Baldwin by Giovanni is especially vivid early on, when he comments to her as a representative of the new generation of black writers, doing so almost beseechingly: "You have no idea, and I can never express to you, to what extent I depend on you. . . . I mean you, Nikki Giovanni, and I also mean your generation. . . .

I am very proud of you."[27] This statement is important not only for its singling out of a female poet as the spokesperson for the writers Baldwin sees as his successors, but also because it sounds almost desperate, as if the older writer were hoping for acceptance and recognition, indeed, for "being home free" with that younger generation, despite the evidence that it is not possible. On the other hand, his embrace of Giovanni also contextualizes his later literary use of her—a single black mother who refused to marry the father of her child—as an inspiration for the protagonist-narrator Tish in *Beale*.[28] His discussion with Giovanni, along with an earlier exchange with the anthropologist Margaret Mead that was published as *Rap on Race* in 1971, echoes in the female characters of *Just Above*, too, especially Julia and the minor characters Florence, Martha, and Ruth.

As Giovanni told me, her conversation with Baldwin fulfilled her dream of meeting the famous writer and asking him some serious questions. Transcribed and edited, it was later published as *A Dialogue* (1973).[29] Bracketed by a foreword by a renowned African American journalist, Ida Lewis, and an afterword by the Caribbean American writer Orde Coombs, who immigrated to the United States from St. Vincent, the book also contains another dialogue. That one takes place between the authors of the foreword and afterword, or Lewis and Coombs, whose autobiographical stories about relationships between black men and women introduce and conclude the volume and, in a fashion, mediate it for its readers. Such packaging and presentation mean that the publisher and perhaps Baldwin and Giovanni, too, were interested in providing a wider context for their conversation on gender roles, especially the male-female conflict brought to light by the black feminist activism whose viewpoints Giovanni represented. Such packaging renders Baldwin's queerness safe, and it projects an exclusionary heteronormative vision of African American and Caribbean communities. As Baldwin's direct and indirect interlocutors, Giovanni, Lewis, and Coombs appear as the next generation of black writers whom his works and thinking influenced, inspired, and provoked in their own, idiosyncratic ways. They are some of the "children" or literary successors he had been concerned about nurturing since the 1960s. In 1986, less than a year before his death, he repeats: "The most important task [in front of us] is to attempt to liberate the children . . . [whom their elders] betrayed . . . by throwing Jaguars at them and TV sets . . . instead of trying to raise them . . . instead of loving them . . . the children are not easily fooled."[30]

In her foreword to *A Dialogue*, Lewis—a pioneering black journalist who established *Essence* magazine—compares Baldwin and Giovanni to builders of a new national literary house: "Sharing this dialogue will perhaps cause the reader some sad moments. But buildings are demolished to put new buildings up, to start new blocks. *Jimmy and Nikki are a cornerstone.*" She admonishes, "*The next brick is yours.* You can hurl it or you can put it in place.... *Love, the most vital tool the workman possesses*, must not become another relic in our community chest. The journey of a thousand miles, we are told, begins with a single step.... I believe that together we can."[31] Lewis's foreword also recalls her favorite childhood friend, Danny, and his wasted potential, for he ended up a broken man and a drunk.[32] Similarly, Coombs's afterword remembers a buddy of his from St. Vincent, Clive, who was brilliant, but whose economic status and lack of access to education curtailed his development and social mobility. Both black men in these stories were victims of their circumstances, were counterexamples to Lewis and Coombs and Baldwin, who represent those few from their neighborhoods who "made it." As Baldwin puts it in an interview with David Frost in 1970, "For every Sammy Davis, for every Jimmy Baldwin, for every black cat you have heard of in the history of this country, there are a hundred of us dead."[33]

The *Dialogue* accomplishes three things that are important for this chapter of *Me and My House*. First, it is a still largely underappreciated building block—a cornerstone indeed—in discussions on race, gender, black feminism, and nationalism for the 1970s.[34] Lewis's and Coombs's texts bracketing the volume drive that point even further with their diasporic, autobiographical interrogations of black masculinity and femininity in the United States and the Caribbean, and they amplify the transcript's striving for a heteronormativity that excludes both men like Baldwin and black lesbians and female queers. Second, Baldwin's conversation and encounter with Giovanni and his fascination with her story mark a pivotal moment in his late twentieth-century ideas on black domesticity, gender, and queer authorship, with his last two novels interrogating black gender roles against the binaries established by Black Power and national whiteness. Third, Baldwin's last two novels' attention to women and queers anticipates and embraces the position of the Combahee River Collective (1974) on identity as inclusive of nonnormative sexualities.[35] As the next sections show, *Beale Street* employs feminist intersectionality in its portrayals of female characters, especially of Tish; her mother, Sharon; and Fonny's mother, Mrs. Hunt. It also returns to the domestic and neighborhood spaces of the street and church in Harlem where Baldwin came of age and where he first realized the workings of spatially contingent identity.

FROM HARLEM TO SAN JUAN: DISORDERLY AFFECTS, ETHNIC ENCOUNTERS, AND FEMININITY UNINCORPORATED IN *IF BEALE STREET COULD TALK*

> History, I contend, is the present—*we*, with every breath we take, every move we make, *are* History—and what goes around, comes around.
> —*The Evidence of Things Not Seen*

> The order I am talking about is *a very private order*. When I am writing a novel, I *am writing about me and all of you*, and the great difficulty is to discover what connects us. Something does connect us, and what it is is hidden. It is not science or prosperity; it is not to be found in any church, so far as I know. . . . What one needs is a way of making one's life really endurable. This calls for testimony by people who have witnessed life, who put it on canvas or write it or put it in sound. What you see then is something that tells the truth about you.
> —Baldwin, in Standley and Pratt, *Conversations* (emphases added)

Written when its author was just twenty-four years old and published in the February 1948 issue of *Commentary*, the essay "The Harlem Ghetto" provides a useful introduction to Baldwin's early works, and it is a surprising yet necessary introduction to the Harlem landscape depicted in *If Beale Street Could Talk*, which Baldwin published more than two decades later.[36] The essay crafts a series of detailed representations of the African American's Other in black Harlem—the Jew—and locates the discussion of the conflicted relationship between New York's Jews and Blacks within the sometimes overlapping, and sometimes discrete, realms of religious, popular, and news-media discourses. Baldwin writes here about his home ground, the place he came from and had to abandon to become a writer.

In a brilliant move that anticipates what interdisciplinary scholarship in literary and cultural studies would theorize only decades later, Baldwin saw these discourses as key sites for articulating the conundrums of gendered, racialized, and sexualized American identity as a process.[37] In mapping the ways in which polarized representations of Jewishness and whiteness are useful to creating a uniform model of blackness, his essay moves between the local and the national, between his native ground and the larger landscapes of American imaginary that were profoundly affected by the racist fallout of World War II at home and abroad, and thus provides his vision of his native ground at two key moments of his life: first, when he left Harlem for Greenwich Village and, second, when he left New York for Paris. This vision is important to his changing views on the role of gender and social space in his later works, and especially to the portrayals of Harlem, to which he returns in his last two novels.

As he explains it in a 1961 interview with Malcolm Preston,

> If we can deal with the conundrums that face us now, people later may think of us as having begun a Renaissance or even a golden age. Because I believe there is something sleeping beneath the chaos that is of extraordinary value, if only we have the courage to go down and bring it up. To destroy, for example . . . the myth of the founding fathers and discover who they really were, why they came here and what they did. Because we are the issue of those beginnings, and until we excavate our history, we will never know who we are. . . . The foundations of society are shifting and have been broken. . . . Some other basis will have to be established if we are all going to remain alive, human, free.[38]

"The Harlem Ghetto" reflects what first prompted this kind of thinking in the young writer, who was assigned this essay by Robert Warshow, his beloved editor at *Commentary*. Baldwin recalls the process of having to rewrite the piece several times decades later, in a conversation with David C. Estes for *New Orleans Review* in 1986: "When he saw me come close to what I was afraid of, he circled it and said, 'tell me more about that.'" Baldwin's fear concerned "the relationship between Negroes and Jews in Harlem," the topic he never "consciously thought about . . . before," which soon "began to hit me on a profound and private level because many of my friends were Jews, although they had nothing to do with the Jewish landlords and pawnbrokers in the ghetto." His realization that "I had been blocking it out" because he discovered his own propensity for prejudice "was a kind of liberation for me. . . . I suddenly realized that perhaps I had been afraid to talk about it because I was a closet anti-Semite myself. One always has that terror. And then I realized that I wasn't. So something else was opened."[39]

"The Harlem Ghetto" proceeds from a gripping opening that locates the writer's family in Harlem's architecture—"the buildings are old and in desperate need of repair, the streets are crowded and dirty, and there are too many human beings per square block"—through sections criticizing its "perpetually embattled" black leadership whose "dramatic and publicized battles are battles with the wind." Then comes a hard look at the "Negro press," which "supports any man, provided he is sufficiently dark and well-known—with the exception of certain Negro novelists accused of drawing portraits unflattering to the race," with that last comment being clearly self-referential. Next, "The Harlem Ghetto" offers a glimpse of its black churches, which Baldwin sees as dishing out religion that operates "as a complete and exquisite fantasy revenge: white people own the earth and commit all manner of abomination and injustice on it; the bad will be punished and the good rewarded" (PT, 165–68).

This indictment of black religious institutions for their role in maintaining and perpetuating rather than fighting poverty and ignorance of the area, which will echo in *The Fire Next Time*, dovetails into a frank examination of what Baldwin calls the "Negro's ambivalent relation to the Jew." That he brings up this divisive issue at all at the time when American culture is struggling to combat anti-Semitism in the wake of the Holocaust is a confirmation of his disorderly conduct as a self-described "[aspiring] Negro novelist."[40] By pointing an accusing finger at his fellow African Americans, he draws a portrait that is "unflattering to the race" and thus risks the hostility of some of his readers and critics.[41] The "Jew" in Harlem, Baldwin explains, is but a discursive concept whose roots are both religious and secular and whose uses illustrate the irreconcilable political purposes, multivalence, and omnipresence of American homegrown racism. Paradoxically, on the one hand, the term "Jew" is meant to "include all infidels of white skin who have failed to accept the Savior," while on the other, it is a powerful symbol of black unity and resilience, as "the wandering, exiled Jew . . . [is] a fairly obvious reminder of the trials of the Negro." In the latter approach, the Jew is someone to identify with, as "the more devout Negro considers that he *is* a Jew, in bondage to a hard taskmaster and waiting for a Moses to lead him out of Egypt" (PT, 166–69).

Ambivalent and powerful, the concept of the "Jew" thus perceived serves Harlem preachers as a handy rhetorical and emotive device to shape the ways their flock sees themselves and their neighbors, if not the whole country, in exclusionary and always racialized terms. Like the casual mask worn by Harlem for the sake of a white passerby, the mask worn by the "Jew" imagined and discursively circulated throughout Harlem's black churches conceals and obscures a painful paradox. For while a devout churchgoer knows that "the image of the suffering Christ and the suffering Jew are wedded with the image of the suffering slave, and they are one: the people that walked in darkness have seen a great light," the same churchgoer will also "wear anti-Semitism as a defiant proof of [his/her] citizenship" outside of the church because he or she needs to hate the "infidels" and "taskmasters" and because the darkness of "hatred must have a symbol." Caught in the "American crossfire," or the economics and politics of ethnicity, race, and class, the relationship between Jews and Blacks in cross-ethnic Harlem reflects and refracts the racialized national scene: "the Negro, facing a Jew hates ... the color of his skin" and enacts a fantasy revenge inspired by what he or she has heard in church. Black anti-Semitism is yet another symptom of the national house rules and illustrates how national attitudes affect local practices, the all-American way of positing an identity of a majority by means of scapegoating a minority: "Georgia has the Negro and Harlem has the Jew." Moving in the opposite direction at the end of the essay, from the local to the national, Baldwin's sweeping panorama of his neighborhood and its main players becomes an indictment of "the American white Gentile ... [whose] structure of the American commonwealth has trapped both these minorities into attitudes of perpetual hostility" (PT, 169–70).

Speaking against "the social and political optimists," or those whom in his later works Baldwin will brand simply as "white liberals," "The Harlem Ghetto" mocks a naïve belief that suffering makes anyone a better human being: "Oppression ... does not imbue a people with wisdom or insight or sweet charity: it breeds in them instead a constant, blinding rage.... There seems no hope for better Negro-Jewish relations without a change in the American pattern" (170). Baldwin's depiction of the American nation in "The Harlem Ghetto" hinges on a triangle of symbolic personae—a white American, an African American, and a Jew—locked in a perpetual struggle to claim a place in the national house, which is key to understanding both his earlier and later works, especially his late essay volumes like *No Name* and *Evidence*, and the novels *Tell Me How Long the Train's Been Gone* (1968), *Beale*, and *Just Above*.[42] And while it can be said that his essays make this point clearer and in some cases sooner than his novels, Baldwin's creed that no one, not even its victims, is immune from the virus of exclusionary and ethnocentric identity politics is at the heart of all his works, regardless of genre.[43] In the world depicted in Baldwin's novels, no one is exempt from the seductions of power, envy, greed, and rage. Harlem is one of the locations where the consequences of these potent emotions on the lives of literal and literary characters play out most poignantly, as the author knows from painful, personal experience.[44]

Filled with the rage of the oppressed, the 1943 Harlem riots took place just days before Baldwin's father's funeral, and they had a large impact on his essay "Me and My House" (1955; later retitled "Notes of a Native Son"), in which Baldwin depicts his neighborhood both as a wasteland of destruction and as his primary, and primal, literary inspiration (PT, 127). Like in "The Harlem Ghetto," the place he describes in "Me and My House" is stunted in temporal terms—"infected by waiting" and "violently still"—and reflects "racial tensions throughout the country." Everywhere there is reinforced police presence, "on foot, on horseback, on corners everywhere, always two by two." The violence of the riots is destructive but also serves a social purpose because in its aftermath the least likely people band together in ways that defy stereotypes of class, gender, and status that had ruled the area until World War II. United by a "common vision" and fear, they appear in the "strangest combinations" that disorient even the keenest of observers: "Large, respectable churchly matrons... with their hair tied up, together with a girl in sleazy satin whose face bore the marks of gin and the razor,... heavy-set, abrupt, no-nonsense older men, in company with the most disreputable and fanatical 'race' men, or these same 'race' men with the sharpies, or these sharpies with the churchly women" (PT, 136–37).

This topsy-turvy vision of Harlem's population is already present in Baldwin's first novel, where John Grimes's choices are narrowed down to an impossible juxtaposition: either the "church" or the "street," either the company of those who follow a religious calling and become "saved" or the company of those who follow a secular calling and embrace crime, drugs, sex, and violence.[45] John's identity conundrum is sketched in ways that echo the rhetoric of the conflicted, discursive figure of the "Jew" from "The Harlem Ghetto" and that echo later in Baldwin's first play, *The Amen Corner* (1954), where David Alexander is a preacher's and jazz musician's son who must choose between the stifling religious framework preferred by his "saved" mother or the scary and sinister outside world that has both inspired and ruined his estranged bohemian father.[46] David's embrace of the messy life of an artist, an outcast in the eyes of respectable Harlemites, signals that to early Baldwin "the street" and not the church is the place where Blacks must embrace their creativity. In these early works, Baldwin portrayed Harlem as "a place where people still clung to the possibility of a normal life. It was dilapidated, but it had not yet given up."[47]

His later publications offer gloomier visions, though not without glimmers of hard-won hope. Like John and David, the jazz-musician siblings Rufus and Ida Scott of *Another Country* (1962) struggle to get away from the powerful influence of their social and cultural roots in Harlem, yet unlike them, cannot shake it off, torn by erotic desire, cross-racial unions, betrayal of the younger generation by the state, wars abroad, racial and gender discrimination, homophobia, sexism, and the class and racial segregation of mid-twentieth-century New York City. Their lives resonate with the plight of Peter and Ruth from the short stories "Previous Condition" and "Come

Out the Wilderness" that Baldwin collected in the volume *Going to Meet the Man* (1965).[48] In all of these texts the neighborhood is pitched against the rest of the city as a location where conventional middle-class and religious life, or poverty, crime, or untimely death are the only options for young black people. At the same time, love and resilience and especially ties within black families that are not bound by religiosity provide hope and saving grace, no matter that these families' values often fly in the face of the politics of respectability that Baldwin rejected so clearly in "The Harlem Ghetto."

As Baldwin wrote about his own coming of age in Harlem in *The Fire Next Time*, local and individual dramas have national dimensions: "this innocent country set you down in a ghetto in which ... it intended that you should perish" (PT, 335). As all of his Harlemite characters realize, any attempt at survival is an escape artist's feat; the trick is to get out by means of a "'thing,' a gimmick to lift [one] out, to start [one] on [one's] way" (341).[49] Baldwin's gimmick was writing and a prodigious intellect. As his works published in the wake of *Fire* demonstrate, women and alternative representations of home become more and more central to his literary visions of Harlem, African America, and the nation, and nowhere else is it presented more clearly than in *If Beale Street Could Talk*.

"The Poor Are Always Crossing the Sahara": Tish Rivers's Blues

> The other places in Harlem are even worse than the projects. You'd never be able to start your new life in those places, you remember them too well, and you'd never want to bring up your baby there. But it's something, when you think about it, how many babies were brought into those places, with rats as big as cats, roaches the size of mice, splinters the size of a man's finger, and somehow survived it. You don't want to think of those who didn't; and, to tell the truth, there's always something very sad in those who did, or do.
> —*If Beale Street Could Talk*

Thinking about her birthplace and its inhabitants, Tish recognizes that in Harlem there are only two kinds of people: those who do not make it and leave scary memories in their wake, and those who do and offer tales of survival and sorrow. Tish's first-person narrative, much like David's in Baldwin's acclaimed second novel, *Giovanni's Room*, is a retrospective that loops back and forth between past and current events. It consists of two books whose titles, in ways familiar from Baldwin's other works and especially the one that proceeds it, *No Name in the Street*, evoke black spirituals and biblical references: "Troubled about My Soul" and "Zion." Interestingly, these titles evoke two unlikely bedfellows, or African American and Judeo-Christian female figures Baldwin might have had in mind as providing symbolic contexts for his portrayal of Tish: the performer Lillie Knox, whose gospel song may have inspired the title of the first book of the novel, and the New Testament's "Daughter of Zion," a symbolic incarnation of his Church and bride of Christ, who may have inspired the title of the second. Tish sings her Harlem sorrow song against a background thick with references to the Bible, black music, the blues, gospel, and spirituals. As a pregnant woman and her lover Fonny's savior, she also embodies hope, faith, and possibilities for new life; she is a survivor whose gender, Baldwin seems to indicate, has something to do both with her power to get out of Harlem and her ability to survive calamity and engage with other people.

Dedicated to his friend, collaborator, and unrequited lover, the illustrator Yoran Cazac, and published when Baldwin's star was waning in the eyes of his critics, *Beale* marked his return to Harlem and intensified focus on the dynamics of urban, mid-twentieth-century black families that continued in his last novel, *Just above My Head*.[50] At the same time, and to a degree that has not been sufficiently explored, it offered a mix of realistic and allegorical ways to read Americanness through representations of national domesticity, as complexly spatial, gendered, and racialized. Its epigraph, "Mary, Mary, / What you going to name / That pretty little baby?" echoes a line from a spiritual, but also the story of Mary giving multiple names to her divine son: Jesus, Emmanuel, Savior. When Tish begins her narrative, the analogy with the spiritual is clear: she is a symbolic, black, Harlem-born mother who names herself and her lover, while leaving their yet-to-be-born child nameless. Having been given the name Clementine, she comments, "People call me Tish," whereas Fonny was "christened Alonzo . . . but, no, we've always called him Fonny" (1B, 3). The naming process reflects Tish's role as a storyteller and nurturer of her community, who is also a Harlem ambassador shuttling between her neighborhood and the prison world, where her lover awaits trial for a crime he did not commit.[51]

Received with mixed responses by reviewers, some of whom rejected its narrator as "improbable" for reasons of her age, race, and class, and a few of whom received it enthusiastically, like Joyce Carol Oates, who proclaimed it "economically, almost poetically constructed," "quietly powerful, never straining or exaggerating for effect," and "timeless," this novel has become a beloved text of adolescent readers and is garnering attention from a new host of scholars.[52] In his biography of Baldwin, Leeming defines it as a "prison parable," a

4.6. Chez Baldwin archive: Foreign editions of *Beale*, *Devil*, *Giovanni's Room*, and *No Name*. Photo by author, 2014.

"fictionalization of [Baldwin's] prison concerns" during 1968–73, a result of the writer's "long meditation on psychological, emotional, and intellectual imprisonment."[53] Quentin Miller sees it as "a pinnacle of the incarceration motif in all of [Baldwin's] fiction," while Trudier Harris notes that it marked "Baldwin's progression away from the church" and a conscious move on his part to shift "positive black women characters . . . beyond active participation in the church," to a realm where "questions of morality are no longer simplistically two-sided" and where they "no longer believe themselves guilty beyond redemption."[54] The rich history of the reception of this novel signals not only that this book warrants a fresh reading by literary scholars, but also that it may have been underestimated as a pivotal text in Baldwin's later career.[55]

This pivotal nature of *Beale* has foremost to do with its depictions of Harlem and with Tish's narrative voice and specific vantage point on her native ground. At first, her comments echo young Baldwin's voice from "The Harlem Ghetto," as she, too, thinks of her birthplace as a dead-end space: "You'd never be able to start your new life in those places . . . never want to bring up your baby there" (38). She considers New York City the "ugliest and the dirtiest city in the world," with the "nastiest people" and "worst cops." It is

BUILDING METAPHORS   241

"so close to hell that you can smell people frying" (10–11). While she is on the subway, the crowd around her reminds her of the "drawings . . . of slave ships" (141).[56] When she recalls her first and only visit to the church with Fonny and his family, the moment that echoes later on in *Evidence* and its associations of memory with terror, she is struck by the fact that they both realize their exclusion from the sanctified Harlem at the precise moment when the spirit possesses other people: "Whoever loved us was not here. It's funny what you hold on to get through terror when terror surrounds you." When she visits Fonny in jail, the memory of the church, "that awful place," and of prison blend together in a radical juxtaposition: "When I first had to go and see him in the Tombs, and walked up those steps and into those halls, it was just like walking into church" (32). Tish is a rebel driven away from the church, and she makes no secret of her loathing for both the institution and its hypocritical members.

The penitentiary spaces not only remind her of that sense of imprisonment she and her lover felt inside the church, but also seem to represent the bowels of the U.S. justice system, which is based in the western Christian values that Baldwin lambasts even more vehemently a decade later in *Evidence*. Tish is a weary traveler by the time the story opens. Her every trip to visit Fonny in the Tombs entails a crossing of a deathly expanse whose description mocks the happy stories of American settlers' westward progress. A literary and literal urban space, it represents her misery and loss; it is the representative space of her journeys, crossings, and rites of passage as a daughter of her people: "these big, wide corridors I've come to hate, corridors wider than all the Sahara desert. The Sahara is never empty. . . . If . . . you fall, by and by vultures circle around you, smelling, sensing, your death. . . . The poor are always crossing the Sahara" (7). Tish's thoughts also reverberate with unequivocal references to the Book of Exodus and align, once again, the African American and Jewish stories of exile and passage through the American urban wilderness.

These stark visions, however, do not doom Tish, for the novel also embraces her and Fonny's love story, resulting from their having grown up together in Harlem. Nineteen and twenty-two years old, they represent the hopeful, and hopelessly betrayed, generation of African Americans who came of age after the Civil Rights Movement. Surrounded by ideological and visual inspirations of the Black Arts Movement, Tish and Fonny dream of a carefree life in Greenwich Village, though the visions of their future domesticity are dictated by Fonny, who is an artist and a man. They rent a loft where Fonny plans to pursue his sculpture and where he imagines Tish tending the hearth and mothering his children in ways that exclude her agency or need for creative fulfillments. Paradoxically, it is only with Fonny in jail that Tish begins to discover the possibilities of inhabiting an independent self.

She learns to accept herself as a young woman entering full bloom: she is happily in love with Fonny and is carrying his child; she has the support of her family and of Fonny's father; she embraces her out-of-wedlock pregnancy without shame. She is coping with her situation and growing as a person because, like her mother, father, and sister, she does not fall prey to the "fantasy revenge" offered by the church—the view embraced, unfortunately and destructively, by Fonny's "sanctified" light-skinned mother and sisters, Mrs. Hunt and Adrienne and Sheila, who deny their dark-skinned son and brother once he has been imprisoned. Like Eric in *Another Country*, Tish chooses to live by her own and Fonny's set of recognizably, though not always unproblematic, Baldwinian morals. Among them, being loyal to one's kin is at the top of the list; hence, "lifting from the Jew" to provide money for Fonny's bail is fine, along with celebrating erotic love for its spiritual and transformative properties—it is referred to as "some strange anointing" (212, 101). If the Hunt women are all about the church, Tish's family, the Riverses, are all about the street, but seen through a new lens, as street-smart and savvy about the world in which they live, rather than being corrupted, trapped, or victimized by either organized religion or racist society.

As Tish's journey progresses, she engenders a new way of seeing herself and her fellow Americans. She becomes a sharp observer and commentator on her reality, having found out that her trouble has taught her to "see people like . . . [she] never saw them before. They shine as bright as a razor. . . . This makes them very strange to you" (9). A female reworking of John Grimes if you will, that first teenage protagonist in Baldwin's fiction, Tish comes to terms with her body and her family, and she embraces her ability to feel the "strangeness" in others. She is the "despised black mother" and carrier of the new world, who is "kicking in the belly of its mother . . . ready to be born," amid the "global, historical crisis" that Baldwin identified in the epilogue to *No Name in the Street* (196–97). Serving as Baldwin's porte-parole, as a character/narrator Tish is a lens through which we can reconsider other key figures from his earlier and later works. Immersed in her emotions, often contradictory and confusing, features compounded by Baldwin's mixing his omniscient and third-person, limited narrative perspective with hers, Tish offers a powerful optic on American race relations through youth, gender, and affect. This optic helps explain why she is fascinating to today's young readers, why Baldwin's early critics saw her characterization and narrative as unreliable, and why her disorderly characterization was both deliberate and necessary in the development of his oeuvre.

That Tish's narrative resembles David's in *Giovanni's Room* and opens in exactly the same way as his is no coincidence: "I look at myself in the mirror.... I'm tired, and I'm beginning to think that maybe everything that happens makes sense.... But that's really a terrible thought. It can only come out of trouble—trouble that doesn't make sense" (IB, 3). Baldwin uses her to offer a powerful rewriting of David's white male American vantage point from an African American female perspective. Unlike David, who hopes to escape his troubled sexuality and family by going to France, Tish is stuck in Harlem, in the midst of the segregated heart of the American house of bondage, her only escape Greenwich Village, where the likes of blue-eyed policeman Bell roam the streets. Her coming-of-age story can thus be understood to be as much an allegorical retelling of the nation's story as David's is; it is also a clear statement on the racialized male and female possibilities of mobility.[57] Published at a time when Blacks were becoming disillusioned with the results of the Civil Rights Movement, when Black Power postulated misogynist and heterosexist machismo, and when many of the Black Arts Movement proponents advocated ethnocentric and Afrocentric identity politics, Baldwin's novel offered glimpses of a different world. That new world appears in Tish's narrative and interior monologues, which combine sorrow songs about hard reality with glimpses of a utopian, multicultural, egalitarian society of the righteous who do not go to church. It is also the world Fonny hopes to join, but in his version of it Tish would be following him and be relegated to the domestic sphere as a helpmeet, rather than an equal partner.[58] In contrast, Baldwin shows through Tish's eyes a vision of a world in which women are as important as, if not more important than, men. And that is where Tish's song must be recast within yet another, earlier context of Baldwin's location, life, and work.

Tish's changing vision in *Beale* recasts Baldwin's earlier approach to artistic homelessness, which he first saw and heard in Bessie Smith's songs, offering in its place a mature, though not unconflicted, gendered perspective that begins to favor women. In a 1961 interview with Studs Terkel, Baldwin is introduced as having been oppressed by his blackness, but he also can be seen as passing on the burden of race and its damaging stereotypes to black women. This is evident in the language Baldwin uses to reference the power of Smith's music in his essay "The Discovery of What It Means to Be an American," from which Terkel quotes in their interview. In it, Baldwin expresses the possibility that out of the tragedy and sorrow of Smith's blues syntax, he was able to forge his complex creative expression in *Go Tell It*. Of this process, whereby he learned both to access his past and move beyond it as a solitary endeavor, he writes, "I began to re-create the life that I had first known as a child and from which I had spent so many years in flight" (PT, 172).[59] This unlocking of repressed childhood memories goes hand in hand with the recollection of sensory, visceral experience that stamped his memory of growing up in Harlem in the 1920s and 1930s. "Bessie Smith," the writer explains, "helped me to dig back to the way I myself must have spoken when I was a pickaninny, to remember the things I had heard and seen and felt. I had buried them very deep" (NKMN, 5).

Baldwin finds a key to his own story and childhood self in the art of Bessie Smith, for her music enables him to recover his "buried" past for the sake of his first novel, and to come to terms with his adult identity as a black American writer in Europe, thus anticipating Ann duCille's argument concerning the blues as a "metonym for authentic blackness."[60] More important, Smith's blues, that home idiom from which he has been trying to flee, allows the writer to breach a gap within his own identity. He implicitly identifies that gap by referring to class—between his humble origins in Harlem and his present situation as a rising literary star on national radio—while describing how Smith's music helped him to "dig back" to his childhood and to remember *who* and *what* he was, then. Baldwin further intensifies the meaning of this literal and literary excavation by using the past perfect tense within his description, which gives it an air of both wistful speculation on the one hand and deep certainty on the other: "I... must have spoken," "had heard and seen and felt." The blueswoman's power thus enables the writer's sensory power that translates into the power over language. He can now access his past with all of its complexities, repressions, and paradoxes, even pain and anguish, regardless of the unlikely location in which this triangulation of identity between past and present takes place.

Even more important, Baldwin admits that until he left his homeland, Smith's music was in fact a *forbidden* racial territory/signifier/auditory experience: "I had never listened to Bessie Smith in America (in the same way that, for years, I would not touch watermelon), but in Europe she helped to reconcile me to being a 'nigger'" (NKNM, 5). Then, in the oft-quoted following sentence, Baldwin admits that it was impossible for him to make that ambivalent reconciliation at home in the United States, that he *needed* the remoteness and strangeness of western Europe to "be able to accept my role—as distinguished... from my 'place'—in the extraordinary drama which is America." It was only from within the context of this self-imposed psychic and geographic distance between himself and his native country that the writer could be "released," he writes, "from the illusion that I hated America," and that he could be released into black artistic manhood (NKMN, 5).

The combination of the brutal racist imagery conjured by the terms he deploys—"pickaninny" and "nigger"—and the coming-of-age authorial narrative (one must leave home and go abroad to become an American writer) is signature Baldwin.[61] The paradox of becoming American, but away from one's country of birth, and of reconciling with one's racialized national identity, but by means of embracing and reappropriating the racist stereotype subsumed under the n-word, has been his modus operandi as a thinker throughout his works. What has not been as frequently noted, however, is the deeper implication of the fact that it was Smith's music, or female creativity and women's expressive influence more broadly, that was key to the development of Baldwin's authorship, and that this was so not only regarding his early career, but throughout his entire trajectory.

At the end of the interview Terkel tells the listeners that the young writer has "confessed in a very beautiful way," and then he asks Baldwin, "Who are you, now?" Baldwin's hesitant answer echoes a sense of impermanence attached to the black male identity he has to embrace—"you do discover that you are a writer and then you haven't got any choice"—and amplifies his complex perspective as an African American artist and intellectual: "[long pause] I may be able to tell you who I am, but I am also discovering *who I am not*. I want to be an honest man. And I want to be a good writer. I don't know if one ever gets to be *what one wants to be*."[62] That last statement remains a potent reminder, considering his examinations of masculinity and femininity in his later works. That he saw black women like Smith not only as enablers of his talent as a black male writer, but also as carriers of American blackness, *and* as embodiments of its racist stereotypes adds another important and ambivalent dimension to his views on race, gender, and national identity that we must consider as we reread his works today.[63] In this context, *Beale*'s female-centered narrative and imagery offer a badly needed corrective to his youthful, and perhaps naïve, vision of black women.

Indeed, Tish's Harlem is a space populated by African American women and children; it is the new world of growing gender equality, African Diaspora immigrants, and political activism advocated by Angela Davis, Audre Lorde, and Nikki Giovanni, all of whom Baldwin knew and admired.[64] As Tish assesses the situation in the scene when she reveals her pregnancy to her family (her father, Joseph; mother, Sharon; and sister Ernestine) and to Fonny's family, who came to listen to her (his father, Frank; mother, Mrs. Hunt; and sisters Adrienne and Sheila) she realizes that "these six women [in the room] ... had to deal with each other" (85). Although the fathers are there, she realizes that it is their story as a group of women who are either supporters (Sharon, Ernestine, and Tish) or enemies of her and Fonny (Mrs. Hunt, Sheila, and Adrienne). Baldwin's female characters in this novel reflect the changes in gender and race relations and in their literary representation that he not only witnessed but also, in ways perhaps more implicit than explicit, helped to bring about. They are both victims of and agents struggling against social forces beyond their control.

Such an approach to gender and race was novel, especially coming from a male writer who was included in the trinity of twentieth-century greats like Ellison and Wright. As Harris notes, "Baldwin has made a much more consistent attempt to portray black women than either of the other two."[65] His representations of his hometown and its dwellers highlight the roots and consequences of gendered rifts as much on the American literary scene as in the black communities in the late 1940s and 1950s—rifts that cast a long shadow over the Civil Rights Movement and its aftermath. Writing about gendered strife, not to mention colorism, whose destructive effects are blatantly evident in the Hunt family, was nevertheless a risky proposition.

By emphasizing confusion, anger, and frustration in his characterization of Tish, and her belligerent sister Ernestine, Baldwin shows that they are only beginning to realize their feminist possibilities and embrace the burdens of political agency. When she learns that it will not be easy, or even possible, to get Fonny out of jail, Tish understands that "time could not be bought" because "the only coin time accepted was life" (IB, 117). It is by embracing and trusting her feelings and by accepting who she is, by opening up to other people despite color lines and racial stereotypes and by appreciating her origins and community, that she is able to forge new relationships that help her cope with her situation. Tish learns to cross black-and-white racial lines, and to do so she ventures outside of Harlem and beyond the bipolarity of the church-vs.-street spaces that have so far delineated her possibilities as a black woman. Her story records a growing self-reflexivity and awareness of her body, and in that sense makes it possible, again, to trace the ways in which Baldwin wrestled with the racialized, gendered, and geographically located deployments of affect.[66] In several instances, Tish learns to step back from and course-correct her negative feelings, which enables her to form important affective relationships not only within her own community, but also with nonblacks.

For example, when Hayward, the white leftist lawyer her family has hired, tries to console her, she initially resists his kindness, having appraised his elegant office and family photos as a white space: "There was no connection between this room, and me" (115). Yet she soon recognizes Hayward's dedication as a civil rights lawyer, and she learns to look beyond the whiteness of his face, thinking that "something really human happened between us, for the first time" (120).[67] On another occasion, when she remembers her and Fonny's search for a loft in Greenwich Village, she recalls "this cat, whose name was Levy," a young Jewish landlord with a wife and two small children, who "dug us ... [who] dug people who loved each other." Levy, who, in Tish's parlance, "wasn't full of shit," and whom she saw as not exactly white, "was an olive-skinned, curly-haired, merry-faced boy from the Bronx, about thirty-three ... with big, kind of electrical black eyes" and had agreed to rent them a loft that was ideal for their needs (163). Tish and Fonny's suspicion about Jewish landlords, voiced earlier by their friend Daniel, was that "this country really do not like niggers ... so bad ... they will rent to a leper first" (123). Baldwin remarks on the same phenomenon in an essay written in 1967: "When we were growing up in Harlem our demoralizing series of landlords were Jewish, and we hated them ... because they were terrible landlords, and didn't take care of the building" (PT, 423).[68] However, this stereotype crumbles in the case of Levy, as Tish experiences a moment of strong connection with him, one that anticipates her later contact with Hayward: "[Levy] didn't make either of us feel self-conscious."[69] He is not only egalitarian but also supportive of their love and, sensing their sexual passion, gives them what amounts to a brotherly blessing by urging them to make "some beautiful babies ... the world damn sure needs them." But Levy is not naïve about living in America, as he tells them to watch out for the cops in the Village because "they're murder" (164–66). Later, debunking yet another anti-Semitic stereotype, he keeps the place reserved for them, no matter that Fonny has been sent to jail.[70]

Another moment of contact and understanding that defies color lines and expands Tish's affective possibilities takes place after she has been attacked by an Italian "greaser" while shopping at a vegetable stand in the Village. An elder immigrant, "the Italian lady" who runs the establishment, defends Tish against the "miserable urchin" who attacked her, and when Fonny comes to Tish's aid and knocks down the attacker, the older woman defends the couple in front of a white police officer who is about to take Fonny in for assaulting a white man (166–71). Informed by an immigrant story about whose contents we can only wonder, the Italian lady's reaction includes an aside meant only for Tish that suggests her sense of gendered kinship with the young black woman: "You have a good man.... Take him home. Away from these diseased pigs.... I have been in America a long time.... I hope I do not die here" (171). While this comment links the women across generations, ethnic groups, neighborhoods, and nationalities, it does not erase the fact that it was the Italian's whiteness that allowed her to talk back to the cop and thus postpone his retaliation against Fonny.

Taking place in the Village, this encounter also suggests that, beyond Harlem, the world of New York City is teeming with ethnics and newcomers, as well as dangers to black bodies. Fonny's friends include Spanish and Mexican immigrants, among them vivacious Pedrocito, who runs a restaurant and feeds the couple on numerous occasions. When Fonny is in jail, Pedrocito continues to take care of Tish and drives her home on the day she goes into labor. When Tish's mother, Sharon, travels to Puerto Rico to seek out a woman who has accused Fonny of rape and beg her to change her testimony, she relies on the kindness of a young man there, Jaime, who becomes her chauffeur and chaperone.[71] Ernestine, Tish's feisty sister who might be the only character in the novel who is semi-queer-identified, takes advantage of her friendship—and possible romance—with a liberal white actress, who helps the family raise the money for Fonny's bail.[72]

Solidarities Unincorporated: "We on the Same Garbage Dump"

> The blue sky above, in the bright sun: the blue sea, here, the garbage dump, there. It takes a moment to realize that the garbage dump is the *favella* [sic]. Houses are built on it—dwellings; some on stilts, as though attempting to rise above the dung heap. Some have corrugated metal roofs. Some have windows. All have children. . . . The smell is fantastic—but the children, sliding up and down their mountain, making the air ring, dark, half naked, with their brilliant eyes, their laughter, splashing into and out of the sea, do not seem to care.
> —*If Beale Street Could Talk*

Some encounters with others in this novel, however, turn lethal in their brutal application of the illogic of racialization and discrimination that Baldwin signaled already in "The Harlem Ghetto." Following the run-in with the white police officer, Bell, who intervened at the vegetable stand, Fonny and Tish realize that they have acquired a mortal enemy. Seeing in their blackness the cause of his perceived slighting by the Italian woman, Bell vows to destroy Fonny. His threat to the couple that he would "see" them later materializes when Fonny is taken in for a police lineup as a suspect in a rape case and, as the sole black man there, is pointed out as the perpetrator by a traumatized Puerto Rican victim, Mrs. Victoria Rogers. As with the ambivalent vision of the "Jew" in his early essay, Baldwin makes it clear that he does not want his readers to think of the national house in simple black-and-white terms. The part of the novel that drives this point home takes place outside of the country and links the plight of American women of color to those beyond its boundaries, also demonstrating deep divides between them caused by the police and judicial systems, class, and location of the United States.

Sharon Rivers's trip to Puerto Rico in search of Mrs. Rogers, who has disappeared from New York following Fonny's imprisonment, takes place over three-quarters of the way into *Beale*'s action. Baldwin uses it to relocate the plot that centers on a black American family in Harlem to Puerto Rico and San Juan, or what has been known as the "unincorporated territory of the United States." Although a seemingly minor part of the book takes place in a San Juan slum—or "favella," as Baldwin misnames and misspells it—I argue that an encounter between an African American and a Puerto Rican woman in that part of the novel helps us to reread Baldwin's text through a multilayered lens containing not only gender, race, and national identity, but also a transnational space created in the wake of U.S. imperialism.[73] Such a reading is important to a larger project of reevaluating Baldwin's later, post-1963 works as signaling his growing concern with the U.S. military and neocolonial presence outside of its borders and, as scholars have demonstrated, with the law and burgeoning prison-industrial complex. This rarely discussed moment in *Beale* brings focused attention as well to the feminine and feminist perspectives, to sexism, and to violence against women within and outside communities of color, within and outside the United States.[74]

It also shows Baldwin grappling with what could be called a version of a womanist narrative voice, for Sharon's journey is told by enmeshing a Henry Jamesian third-person, limited perspective with the observations of Tish and Sharon. Even though Tish could not have been there, readers have insights into Sharon's and Tish's minds (as if in response to her mother's telling), but are excluded from accessing that of the former Nuyorican, Victoria Rogers. As Brian Norman argues, while Baldwin has addressed women's issues in his writings broadly, beginning with his early essays and their appeal to white women—who could see in them reflections of a "women's liberation project of sisterhood"—and later does address black and brown women in *Beale*, this text enters a murkier territory, or "literary conversations about

US imperialism, the placement of African Americans in imperialism, and the possibilities and limits of black-brown solidarity."[75]

As Fonny's accusation rests on the victim's testimony that identified him as the alleged rapist, the only hope is to put Mrs. Rogers on the witness stand and have her recant. The lawyer Hayward suggests that she might be hiding in San Juan and, given that the family cannot afford a private investigator, Sharon Rivers agrees to travel to Puerto Rico carrying Fonny and Tish's photo. Sharon's journey thus links the island of Manhattan, or its uptown (above 59th Street) filled with black and brown bodies, to the multihued archipelago of the northeastern Caribbean, the unincorporated U.S. territory of Puerto Rico. Although she might pass for an inhabitant of San Juan, Sharon finds herself in a completely foreign land as an American, and her clothes and mannerisms immediately brand her as an outsider. And while she recognizes marks of the African Diaspora on the bodies and buildings around her—a friendly taxi driver who could be her son, an archway "abandoned by the Moors" (204)— she quickly learns from her conversation with Victoria Rogers, now Sanchez, that "people always know the outside better than they know the inside" (226). It seems that all the women of color portrayed in Baldwin's novel learn this the hard way.

At first, Sharon has a difficult time tracking down the woman who holds the key to Fonny's salvation, and once she finds her, she is ready to extract it by any means necessary. Middle-aged, kind, compassionate, and a mother, Sharon can sense Victoria Rogers-Sanchez's pain and hurt, yet admonishes her like a child with appeals to racial and gender solidarity: "Daughter . . . you pay for the lies you tell. . . . You've put a man in jail, daughter, a man you've never *seen*. . . . He's black . . . like us" (208). On the inside, "very close to tears," the black American woman from Harlem realizes her advantage as she confronts her desire to use Victoria, the optically "whitened" brown woman whose bleached hair's "dark roots" are showing, to use her for a noble cause, but to use her nonetheless. Once Sharon has shown Victoria a photograph of Fonny and Tish, the "thin girl, with immense dark eyes in a dark face," the unincorporated woman from Puerto Rico tells her: "One thing I can tell, lady—you ain't never been raped. . . . It *looks* like him. But he wasn't laughing" (205, emphasis added).

The verbs *look* and *see* appear many times throughout the scene and emphasize the worldwide racist optics that have divided and conquered the globe in the wake of multiple slave trades and colonialisms. In the heart of the Black Atlantic in the 1970s, black bodies still appear interchangeable, not only in the eyes of the warped U.S. justice system, but also, ironically, in the eyes of victims themselves. Victoria knows her own invisibility and powerlessness all too painfully: "They didn't see him when—when *I* saw him—when he came to *me*! They *never* see that. Respectable *women*—like you!—they never see that" (208). Coerced or not, Victoria's accusation against Fonny guarantees her importance and visibility as a witness, albeit tragically; it makes her somewhat "respectable" because she is victimized, a status she clearly does not want to give up, no matter Sharon's attempts to elicit her sympathy and understanding.[76] "Señora... I am not a North American lady," Victoria reminds Sharon, who responds, "I am not a lady. I am Mrs. Rivers" (203). Sharon may appear to be an elegant American in Puerto Rico, but she knows that back home she would be called what she calls Victoria here, a "girl." Their tortured attempts at communication underscore that the women can truly see neither the other, nor, for that matter, themselves outside of American and international politics of race and gender. Surrounded by a slum much worse than Sharon could have imagined despite having seen the worst of Harlem—likely based on the notorious San Juan barrio of La Perla—the two women are nevertheless excluded, unincorporated together as subjects of the superpower, or, as Sharon puts it later on, "We on the same garbage dump.... Who*ever* discovered America *deserved* to be dragged home, in chains, to die" (227).

At the end of their conversation Victoria is completely defeated and so is Sharon, but for different reasons. The Puerto Rican "girl" has refused to take back her testimony and thus save the black American family man. Sharon does not want to dwell on the fact that Victoria most likely cannot recant her statement. She witnesses the younger woman's emotional and physical reaction to the stress of her visit, her breaking down and yelling for help. A crowd of women comes to Victoria's rescue and silently watches Sharon leave: "There is nothing she can say to them.... She gets past them slowly, and, slowly, gets down the staring stairs. There are people on every landing" (210). The familial connection Sharon has tried to forge has failed miserably, on the one hand, while, on the other, it has been reaffirmed in its alienating and divisive results on that family's dark-skinned members in Harlem and San Juan.

Baldwin's world in this novel defies a simple black-and-white perspective of any kind, as Sharon's experience of La Perla in San Juan and her miscommunication and lack of connection with Victoria reveal that there is no solidarity based solely in skin color, just as there is no gender solidarity based solely in social roles and assumptions about familial, national, and ethnic identities. Further, though Tish was herself under sexual threat from predatory policemen like Bell, in whose eyes one day she sees "rape which promised debasement and revenge" (IB, 173), or other men like the youth who groped her in the Village, she has no kind feelings for Victoria. When she learns of Victoria's refusal to recant her testimony, she can only see her as an extension of Bell: "That filthy bitch ... that filthy bitch" (113), she rages in the lawyer's office. Hayward responds with a generalization perhaps more charitable, but still assuming Victoria's passivity and lack of insight: "She is a distraught, ignorant, Puerto Rican woman, suffering from aftereffects of rape. Her behavior is not incomprehensible" (114). Nineteen-year-old Tish cannot imagine Hayward's reasoning, nor that Victoria's action must have been a result of psychological abuse, threats, and coercion; she has lied, perhaps, but she is still a traumatized victim. In the world governed by the U.S. judicial system, in which, as Hayward explains to Tish, "The truth of a case doesn't matter. What matters is—who wins," the rape victim has no chance of winning at all (115). Hayward knows that Bell is a "racist and a liar" but he also knows that "the D.A. in charge of this case ... is worse" (115–16). While astute in these observations that are steeped in, and the result of, the racist field of vision that is an American national and geopolitical sense of reality, neither Hayward nor Tish can see the Puerto Rican woman as entirely human.

Victoria's insistence on having her suffering acknowledged casts a shadow on the novel's romance. She has been raped, and by a black man. She has been multiply violated: by the rapist, the police, the United States, even by Sharon and her family whose needs, directly or not, lead to her nervous breakdown and miscarriage. Sharon describes that part of the story to her family back in Harlem: "they carried the chick away. She was screaming. She was having a miscarriage.... She had already started to bleed.... She was carried to the mountains ... she will never be seen again" (227). Tish, observing the scene, can only think in response, "There goes the trial, the prosecution having fucked itself out of its principal witness" (227). Indeed, Victoria Rogers-Sanchez has disappeared for good.[77]

Victoria's seemingly marginal story raises serious questions about trust between black men and women, questions that no one dares to ask and that make the ending of *Beale* disorderly and ambivalent, with the vision of the black family closing the book deeply fraught. Was Fonny capable of hurting another woman if he loved Tish so much? After all, as Tish realizes during the altercation that brought them in contact with Bell for the first time, Fonny *is* capable of violence and he values his manly honor more than her feelings or even their safety. Much like Richard from *The Blues* tells Juanita, Fonny tells Tish, "with a dreadful quietness ... 'Don't ever try to protect me again. Don't do that.'" When she responds that she realized he was protecting *her*, that she also wanted to protect them, he tells her, "It's not . . . the same thing," and then smashes the bag of tomatoes she has just bought against "the nearest wall," an act whose rage and violence frighten her and bring her to tears, for they reflect his feelings about her having taken a stand, in what he considers to be the man's, his, place (140).

In the context of this rage, was Sharon right to assume Fonny incapable of rape only because she knew him "all his life"? Doubt and fear and, yes, rage at constant uncertainties never leave the women characters in this novel. They also affect some of the men, as Frank, Fonny's father, buckles under pressure and kills himself after he is exposed for having stolen at his job to cover the costs of the trial. Daniel, a friend of Fonny's, comes to him to be comforted after his time in prison, where he had seen "nine men rape one boy: and he had been raped," but cannot ever recover his old self (174). In such a context, even the love and happiness that Tish and Fonny share is overshadowed.[78] Nobody is safe anywhere, and there are no havens.

Like her mother, who returns home to Harlem weary but not defeated, Tish learns to live with her troubling feelings and perceptions, even though they teach her that things are often, if not always, not what they seem. Her maturing perspective and growth as a character mark the end of the novel: Fonny is back, out on bail, and the baby has been born happily. Still, it is clear that the kind of hope such a conclusion offers is at best tentative, for Tish is the one taking care of the baby, who keeps crying "like it's trying to wake up the dead," while Fonny is working on his art. As Amiri Baraka writes poignantly in his manifesto on gender roles and the black nation, "Black Woman" (1970), the female role is to be "a divine complement . . . for her man," a relationship that cannot be equal, given that "nature has not provided thus."[79] He clarifies that the whole notion of gender equality comes from those who are "devils and devilishly influenced," and the black woman's role is to be a man's "house . . . because there is no house without a man and his wife."[80] Putting her forever in her place as both matter/architecture and body/geography to be inhabited, used, and taken for granted, Baraka explains, "You are essential, to the development of any life in the house, because you are the house's completion. . . . By being the nation, as the house, the smallest example of how a nation should be . . . you're my 'house,' I live in you, and together we have a house, and that must be the microcosm, by example, of the entire Black nation."[81] Baldwin's risky, feminine-centered narrative in *Beale* challenges Baraka's views and develops his earlier approaches to social space, race, ethnicity, gender, and national identity, as well as making his later, complex, even experimental, works possible. That is why he lets Tish tell her story in ways that reflect the preponderance of what Kathleen Stewart defines as "ordinary affects," or "an animate circuit that conducts force and maps connections, routes, and disjunctures . . . a kind of contact zone where the overdeterminations of circulations, events, conditions, . . . and flows of power . . . take place."[82] Literary applications of broadly understood "affects" are familiar to readers versed not only in Raymond Williams and the third-person, limited perspective of Henry James, but especially to those familiar with the works centering on female voices, perspectives, and imaginaries by such writers as Zora Neale Hurston, Nella Larsen, Gwendolyn Brooks, and Ann Petry, all of whom Baldwin would have read. And while Tish may not feel entirely liberated at the end of the novel, she has gained a sense of self that is rare in male literary portrayals of women. Hence, what in these black women writers' works seemed natural, in Baldwin's seemed, to many of his critics and reviewers, unnatural and, indeed, unincorporated.[83]

Baldwin's novel offered glimpses of a different world, glimpses that today reverberate with memoirs such as Itabari Njeri's *Every Good-Bye Ain't Gone* (1982) or Margo Jefferson's *Negroland* (2015), and genre-redefining novels such as Alice Walker's *The Color Purple* (1982), or Maya Angelou's *I Know Why the Caged Bird Sings* (1969). That new world of women and their wisdom, voices, and ways of seeing appears in Tish's narrative and interior monologues; it is glimpsed in the sad encounter between Sharon and Victoria, and in the bitter confrontation between the Riverses and the Hunts, when Mrs. Hunt's colorism and religious fundamentalism are apparent, as she abandons her son and curses his child in Tish's womb as a product of sin. It is a world in which women are rather more important than men, where they band together as the Rivers women do against the likes of Mrs. Hunt and her daughters. In short, *Beale* might be seen as Baldwin's stab, perhaps only partially successful, but a stab nevertheless, at a feminist or, better yet, a womanist novel.

"A CURSE ON BOTH YOUR HOUSES": FROM *BEALE STREET* AND *LITTLE MAN* TO ENGENDERING TRAUMA AND BLACK QUEER HETEROTOPIAS IN *JUST ABOVE MY HEAD*

> I was a maverick . . . in the sense that I depended on neither the white world nor the black world. . . . That was the only way I could've played it. I would've been broken otherwise. I had to say, "A curse on both your houses." The fact that I went to Europe so early is probably what saved me. It gave me another touchstone—myself.
> —Julius Lester, "James Baldwin: Reflections of a Maverick"

> Because the responsibility of a writer is to excavate the experience of the people who produced him, the act of writing is the intention of it; the root of it is liberation. Look, this is why no tyrant in history was able to read but every single one of them burned the books.
> —Baldwin and Giovanni, *Dialogue*

Although by the end of *Beale* Harlem remains largely unchanged as a physical location, much as the national house and the state do in "The Harlem Ghetto," its inhabitants' dynamism and disorderly conduct beyond its boundaries, and especially the affective relationships they forge beyond and against its color and class lines, begin to challenge that fixedness.[84] If, as Baldwin claims in "A Fly in Buttermilk," "I found myself . . . alchemized into an American the moment I touched French soil," *Beale* helps us see that his Harlem roots, the influence of people he met there, and the power his native ground held over his literary imagination made this alchemization both possible and necessary (PT, 161).

When Baldwin published his last two novels in the 1970s, genre and gender were still delineated rather neatly, in mutually exclusive terms that reflected cultural, social, and political mores: men wrote "muscular" works and women wrote autobiographically; action and analyses of social processes, such as seen in the works of Baldwin's presumed literary compatriots, were the domain of male writers, while affect and psychological nuance belonged to females. In such a context, Joyce Carol Oates's review of *Beale Street* is not only astute, but also ahead of its time in its perceptive reading of Baldwin's deliberate gendered and affective transgressions: Baldwin "certainly risked a great deal by putting his complex narrative, which involves a number of important characters, into the mouth of a young girl." Oates praises Tish's voice as "absolutely natural" and her "flights of poetic fancy" and "her articulation of what it feels like to be pregnant" as "convincing," and credits this to Baldwin's insistence on the primacy of feeling and affect as key forces driving the story.[85]

With the exception of Oates, both the white/downtown and black/uptown critics were puzzled by the vision Baldwin articulated. Like a congregation imprisoned by its own dualistic rhetoric, they saw in him the "two-headed monstrosity," a gender and genre transgressor, a new incarnation, perhaps, of that other, who, like the proverbial "Jew" sketched in "The Harlem Ghetto" decades earlier, was a product of both affective religious rhetoric and the nationalist racist imaginaries. Likewise, Baldwin's turn to female characters and insistence on articulating the nuances of sexuality and gender in what many condemned as an "integrationist" work such as *Beale* turned many younger African Americans away from him. At the same time, he became an inspiration and friend, sometimes an elder brother-teacher, to Audre Lorde, Nikki Giovanni, Toni Morrison, Maya Angelou, Paule Marshall, Alice Walker, and many others.

Baldwin spoke about the role of black women writers in a National Press Club address in 1986, claiming, worried that he might "exclude someone," that "the arrival of Toni, Maya and Paule Marshall, Alice Walker, Louise Meriwether was in many ways inevitable, because of the role that black women have played in this country . . . and in the lives of black men." He stressed that theirs "has always been a troubled and dangerous role," as they had to "respect their fathers and protect their sons and lovers without emasculating them." Most important, he admits that women need to tell their stories and truth about their experience, implying that black men may have had something to do with their necessary writing being also "a ventilation . . . of a family quarrel." He concludes that "what they have to say is somewhat terrifying but true," and that they are here "to clarify the role of black people. . . . So Toni and Maya are excavating us all from a very dangerous myth."[86] The very words he uses here—with *excavation* anticipating Morrison's idea of writing as archaeology in her 1995 essay "The Site of Memory," and *myth* being one of the key words in his own national house vocabulary—underscore my argument about the importance of reading his works in dialogue with these women writers.

In a *Xavier Review* interview, when asked who he considers worthy descendants of Ralph Ellison, he mentions John Wideman and James McPherson, but emphasizes, "I think too of young people such as Toni Morrison and Maya Angelou, Paule Marshall. . . . Many levels of consciousness have arrived in the last thirty years. People don't know quite what to make of it."[87] When the interviewer asks him to address the "war between the sexes" on the 1980s literary scene—"There seems to be a kind of renaissance among black women writers now. Some people have gone so far as to say such writers . . . have stolen the spotlight away from black male writers. What's your comment?"—Baldwin responds, "I don't think that is true. I think it was an inevitable phenomenon and probably a very good phenomenon." He qualifies this answer with a telling comment on masculine pride: "Although black men may find it a little difficult to be described by black women, men assume that they can describe everybody," an assumption in which he himself has been complicit.[88] The merit of "the ladies" having taken "upon themselves to explicate that . . . [family problem] . . . can only make things clearer

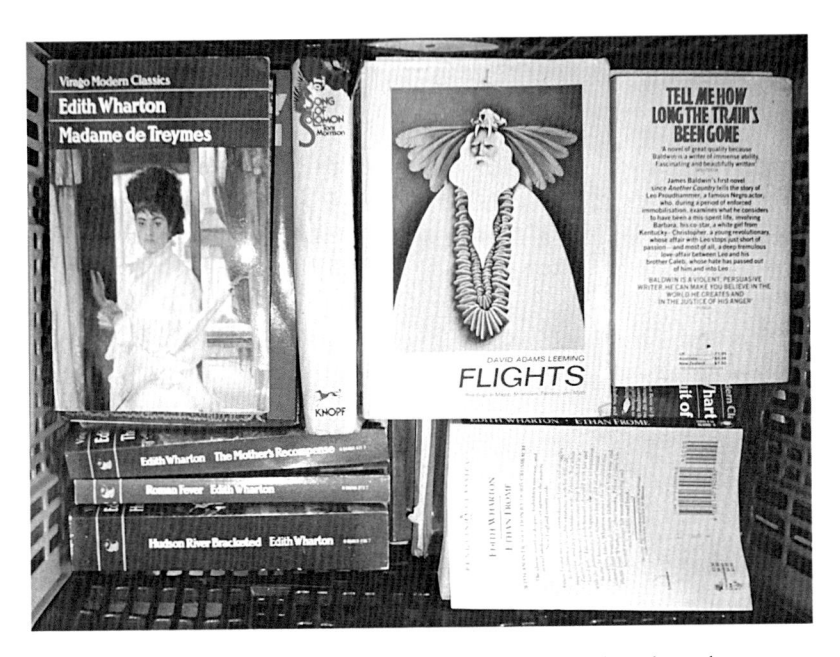

4.7. Edith Wharton's books from the Chez Baldwin library. Photo by author, 2014.

and healthier. . . . Some of the work that is being done now is very important for tomorrow."[89] These thoughts, clearly influenced by his reading of black women writers, as well as by his admiration for such classic American or English authors as Edith Wharton or Jane Austen, reveal a mature writer, comfortable with what he does and says, who welcomes challenges posed by the younger generation, including their demand that gender be recognized as inflecting economic, social, and cultural realities in ways that may be as important as race.

Baldwin's little-known children's book, *Little Man, Little Man: A Story of Childhood* (1976), written with Yoran Cazac, a Yugoslavian-French illustrator, and dedicated to Beauford Delaney, continues the theme of young Harlemites dreaming of a better future. Like in *Beale*, children wise beyond their age live both in the streets and at home. Using Black English, Baldwin offers a unique view of Harlem's everydayness through the eyes of the five-year-old narrator/character TJ (based on his own nephew), whose imaginative, vivid descriptions of the neighborhood blend musical references, film snippets, and books like *Muhammad Speaks*.[90] When TJ's father says about that book, "Don't believe everything you read," his mother adds, "But read everything son, son, everything you can get your hands on. It all come handy one day" (LM, 70). Reading and telling stories is a tricky business, for, some-

258 CHAPTER FOUR

what similar to Tish's, TJ's occasional lapses in reliability call the reader's attention to the gravitas of the events he relates as a black child of Harlem.[91]

Though considered a singular text in Baldwin's oeuvre, *Little Man* can be read as a bridge between representations of the black home in *Beale* and *Just Above*. TJ starts his story on a joyful note, while bouncing his ball against the sidewalk and hearing "music all up and down this street," but he soon seems to echo perceptions of the area that Baldwin signaled in "The Harlem Ghetto" nearly three decades earlier (LM, 4, 14–19). He knows about the dangers lurking in Harlem's streets: drugs (the boys who "shoot that dope in their veins" will not survive long) and omnipresent violence (he is scared even of his best friend, WT, who "beat on his brother, he slap him all over his face with both hands hard as he can" [27]). Amid violence, danger, and fear—"This block always seems real sad and strange . . . silent. . . . Nobody play no music" (70)—there are moments of kindness among the kids, and between them and adults, which give the young narrator hope and enable his resilience, possible future survival, and creative expression: "TJ . . . start doing his African strut and WT just crack up" (95).

There is a kind Puerto Rican storeowner with whom the children exchange smiles and greetings in Spanish. There are moments of tough love between the children and adults, and pauses in which one can marvel at the beauty and pain of various dwellers of the neighborhood, some of whom migrated from the American South, the Caribbean, Central and South America, and various places in Europe, and whose sad stories the young narrator hopes to understand one day. Illustrated with Cazac's lovely watercolors, which Margo Crawford reads as a complex graphic-literary contribution to the Black Arts Movement, while Nicholas Boggs approaches the book as "a child's story for adults," *Little Man* shows that the boundary between home and street is more porous for children than for adults, and that their approach to family and domesticity is also more flexible and expansive.[92] I see Baldwin reaching back in this experimental book to his childhood memories of reading Dickens's novels such as *Bleak House* and *Oliver Twist* with Bill Miller, for, like Dickens's characters, his children in *Little Man* are complex and sharp observers of reality.

While TJ is one of those characters, another is Blinky, an eight-year-old girl who wears "eye-glasses blinking just like the sun was hitting you in the eye. . . . She say she can't see without them." Blinky is singled out negatively at first—"but she a girl"—and on another occasion has the power of vision others do not, due to her glasses (10). Boggs sees in her "blinking" eyeglasses "the imprint of Delaney's lesson on Baldwin and Cazac's collaborative vision for the book," a lesson not only about the ocular power of the eye, but also, as I see it, about social space as a field of vision that can be either naturalized or challenged.[93] Baldwin comments on this element of his writing style in a 1984 interview, "The Art of Fiction," claiming he knows nothing about "technique," only that "you have to make the reader *see* it," having learned this from "Dostoyevsky, from Balzac."[94] Like an echo of a complex nineteenth-century character from a thousand-page Russian novel, Blinky is quick, smart, tomboyish, and more knowledgeable about the adult world than the younger boys are. When they end up at Mr. Man's and Miss Lee's place after WT's foot is injured by a broken bottle likely left there by Miss Lee, Blinky explains, knowingly though mysteriously to the boys' ears, about their hostess, "She real sick." To which Mr. Man, "real low and evil, between his teeth says to his wife, . . . 'One of these days I'm going to have to put you away again'" (90). This moment confirms the children's astute perceptions of the adult world, as they all, beginning with Blinky, then TJ and WT, try to diffuse its ugliness by dancing and clowning, in the closing scene of the story.

Harlem seen and represented in such complex and playful ways is also one of the main settings in Baldwin's last novel, *Just above My Head*. Published five years after *Beale*, this last novel takes what was largely absent in the earlier one as its central theme, namely homoerotic possibilities and attachments between black men, and glimpses the possibility of queer households and even queer parenting.[95] The narrator of *Just Above*, middle-aged Hall Montana, both tries to escape and cannot live without Harlem and its memories. With the passing of time he realizes he has been as inextricably rooted in his native ground as in his actual or imaginary flights from it, first as a hip young man frequenting clubs in the Village, then as a soldier shipped overseas to fight his country's imperial wars, and finally as a middle-aged family and business man who loves his wife and children and their house in the New York City suburb of Yonkers. Harlem is where Hall has met diverse people, like the child evangelist Julia Miller, who used to preach in a church on 129th Street and Park Avenue, the church where Hall's younger gay brother, Arthur, began his musical career (JAMH, 9).[96] Arthur is the primary trigger for Hall's memories, and in Hall's mind Arthur remains "a nappy headed mother [who] did not know how to protect himself." Arthur grew up to become an internationally famous gospel and soul singer, thus linking his native ground to places as remote as Paris or Istanbul. When the boys are still young, Hall, Arthur, and their parents live at 135th Street, between Fifth and Lenox, and worry that the powers that be "were going to tear down our building to make room for a housing project" (72).

As Baldwin paints its picture in retrospective vignettes throughout the expansive, epic text of his last work of fiction, Harlem comes into focus as a place whose history and social and cultural tensions reflect and refract the crises of his characters' singular lives. It is where they first learn about safety and love, but also where they experience danger and trauma that affect the course of their lives. Although there are many other places to which the characters in *Just Above*, especially Arthur, Jimmy, and Julia, travel, their childhood neighborhood and its immediate vicinity remain the location and lens that focus Baldwin's most extensive, Dickensian, examination of African American life as the twentieth century crests into its last two decades.[97] Taking its characters from childhood, to adulthood, to middle age, from the North to the South in the United States, and from Europe to Africa, against panoramic views of several decades of black American history, *Just Above* succeeds in conveying the state of crisis enveloping the whole country. It also refocuses the ways in which this crisis registers on local, individual, and especially black domestic levels at the height and subsequent waning of the Civil Rights Movement. As critics like Pekka Kilpeläinen and Lynn Orilla Scott have noted, it also places local and national issues against an expansive international canvas, where "encounters between people of different national, ethnic, racial, and cultural backgrounds...epitomize both the problems and the redemptive potential of transculturation."[98]

Evoking Eleanor Traylor's vision of Baldwin as residing at the center of an African American literary "House of Tales," Scott sees *Just Above* as "an extraordinarily self-reflective and self-reflexive novel" that achieves several crucial goals: "By reintroducing the figure of the homosexual black artist as the [African American cultural] medium," she claims, "Baldwin complicates the cultural project he formulated in *Beale Street* and reflects on his own challenge as a black artist...writ[ing] himself into the American and African American literary traditions." Its autobiographical and "autotherapeutic" functions are key pillars of its thematic structure, because, as Baldwin admits after its publication, it freed him to take on new challenges.[99] As we have seen, this last novel becomes a bridge/rite of passage that leads him to new genres and characters that, via *Evidence*, ultimately lead him to *The Welcome Table* in the late 1980s.

My reading traces the ways Arthur, Julia, Jimmy, and Hall search for domestic havens—along with the friends and families who form their changing and evolving communities—throughout the narrative of *Just Above*. As Harris notes, one of the main achievements of this novel is the acceptance of the extended family model "across oceans, across nations and nationalities, across sexes—as a viable alternative to the restrictions of the nuclear family."[100] Hence Julia's tragically shattered home and the horrific trauma she has experienced at the hands of her father are a dystopian take on black, nuclear, churchgoing domesticity in Harlem. On the other end of the spectrum is the happy, black queer abode of artists created by Arthur and Jimmy, described in book 5 of the novel, which enacts a radical *heterotopian* alternative to Julia's story. In both cases, the extended family model helps the characters to find a home that anchors, supports, and nourishes their identities, no matter how nonnormative. For Julia this means she has to accept her original family's destruction and dispersal as necessary to her individual survival in the world outside of Harlem, New York, and even the United States. Her travels in Africa, and especially her two-year residence in Ivory Coast and love affair with an older man, and a chief, in Abidjan, connect her to a wider and more inclusive diasporic culture and identity that, as Kilpeläinen also notes, has utopian potential.[101]

As a survivor who later uses her trauma and pain as building blocks for a new self—again, much in the tradition of Smith's blueswoman, but also going beyond it—Julia manages to create yet another alternative version of domesticity, one that, as the novel resolves, encompasses and gathers them all. Echoing Craig Wilkins's architectural revisionism of western philosophy based in the concept of "black space" that is infused with music, I show how both the aforementioned extreme examples of black domesticity in *Just Above*—the tragic Millers' house versus Arthur and Jimmy's black queer, utopian loft—work to rewrite through the form of the novel heterotopic "elements fossilized by Foucault."[102] I argue that Julia's version of home genders the concept of heterotopia beyond both Foucault's and Wilkins's visions, providing shelter for queers, artists, and (childless, independent) women who fit no normative social mold. The fictional-autobiographical-intertextual-musical black space of *Just Above* is where Baldwin theorizes such a recasting of Foucault's 1960s model by means of alternative representations of domesticity.[103] Baldwin's literary model accounts for the conundrums of identity (e.g., race, class, gender, sexuality, nationality, and religion) missing from Foucault's abstract philosophical one and for those (e.g., gender and sexuality) missing in Wilkins's architectural-aural one.

Let us look at Foucault's definition, a useful jumping-off point as an important mid-twentieth-century approach to spatial workings of power, albeit limited to western European contexts. Six elements define the Foucauldian concept of heterotopia, which reflect the larger workings of power with which it is primarily concerned (such as institutions, states, governments, traditions, etc.): first, a utopia or "arrangement which has no real space"; second, an existing space made to function in a different way; third, a space that juxtaposes in "a single real place different spaces and locations that are incompatible with each other"; fourth, a "heterochronism," or temporally contingent space, linked to "bits and pieces of time . . . [that exist in] total breach of . . . traditional time"; fifth, spaces that "always presuppose a system of opening and closing that isolates them and makes them penetrable at one and the same time" (e.g., prisons); and, sixth, those with "a function that takes place between two opposite poles . . . not one of illusion but of compensation."[104] I find Wilkins's description of black space helpful to reading Baldwin's deployment of idiosyncratic black heterotopias in *Just Above*, as it accounts for "their liberating potential . . . for Black identity formation" by means of a hybrid conception of social space. Wilkins's notion of social space blends western European materialist philosophy and African American cultural studies models, or "Lefebvre's spatial production, bell hooks's notion of marginality as a space of power, the legacy of Black town spatial politics . . . [and] the notion of sound," which to him signifies hip-hop aurally and culturally.[105]

My close reading of black heterotopias in *Just Above* adapts and recasts Wilkins and Foucault with the following modifications. First, in Baldwin's representations of black domesticity, not hip-hop but earlier black musical forms—the Trumpets of Zion (Arthur's gospel singing troupe) and later Arthur's gospel and then soul musical expressions—account for the notion of "sound" modifying and pervading social space with blackness that goes beyond the aural and its manifestations. Second, the visions of home and national house that Baldwin sketches are based on what is absent in both Foucault's and Wilkins's models, or *intersectional identities* of his characters that take for granted that gender and sexuality are always inextricably intertwined with race, class, social space, and narrative (and musical) representations. Thus while Wilkins recasts his scholarly exposition in a section entitled "Remix," which uses Black English and hip-hop metaphors to throw shade on the meaning of his social space and architectural theory from Locke to Foucault, to Lefebvre and hooks, I show how Baldwin is "makin' do in [multidimensional and -sensory] space" with revolutionary literary notions of domesticity of which neither black nationalist nor white mainstream cultures would approve. Against a rich musical and lyrical soundtrack, Baldwin's representations of domesticity in *Just Above* triangulate the notions of space, self, and story to build revolutionary shelters for nonnormative black bodies. Such visions, to borrow Wilkins's final expression, "got folks runnin' scared," and, as Baldwin puts it in the last line of his novel, make us realize there "ain't nothing up the road but us, man" (584), for both the national house and the intimate homes that shelter us from it are the results of human actions, of our own individual and collective makings and unmakings of ourselves and places where we live.[106]

"Throw Me off a Tower, but You Cannot Tell Me What to Write," or "Makin' Do in Space"

> Black pride, baby, is what got my father through. Drove him mad, too, and finally killed him. There's nothing new about it, and people who think it's new are making a mistake.... After all, I've been treated as badly by black people as I have by white people. And I am not about to accept another kind of cultural dictatorship.... You can shoot me and throw me off a tower, but you cannot tell me what to write or how to write it.
>
> —Baldwin, in Standley and Pratt, *Conversations*

In an interview with Baldwin published in *Essence* in October 1970, near the end of his Istanbul period, as he is about to relocate to France, Ida Lewis mentions "the new black pride."[107] Baldwin retorts, "It's not new," adding, diva-style, after the passage quoted above, "Most people talking about black pride and black power don't know what they are talking about. I've lived long enough to know people who were at one time so white they wouldn't talk to me. And now they are so black they won't talk to me. I kid you not."[108] Having dispensed with what he sees as superficial masquerades of identity, Baldwin explains that he has at long last begun to accept his own, to "trust myself more than ever before," and that he has understood "something about the role I play, which I didn't want to accept." This mature rearticulation of the tentative self-assessment he first attempted in 1955 in "Me and My House" reveals what he has learned in Harlem and the United States, as well as in France and Turkey: "I am a witness. That's my responsibility. I write it all down."[109]

In 1978, while still working on *Just Above*, he tells Yvonne Everson that he also sees himself as immersed in a global literary effort, and that the artistic output of the African Diaspora "excite[s] ... me. There are no rules about it." Speaking about grounding his own work process, he explains, "You are driven to *where you should really come from*, what you really feel apart from all the things which you think you have learned and forgotten. But when all the chips are down and you are really trying to work *out of the soil that you've been given*, there is no place else to go.... The passion that creates a work of art is really not cerebral."[110] This definition of the writer's work as signifying a point of no return ("no place else to go") and arising out "of the soil that you've been given" affirms Baldwin's connection to the material circumstances of his artistic process. It involves toiling with what we might call the major elements that the human clay comprises (experience, memory, senses, and affect), all of which imprint themselves on the artist's body (tissues, organs, bones, joints, and the topography of the face) as one lives one's life. Baldwin's writing involves the material *and* spiritual creative realms without an organized religious framework—the sweat and blood of the body, and the "passion . . . [that is] really not cerebral," that, perhaps, as *Just Above* puts it through the brief narration in Jimmy's voice close to its end, "jumps . . . on [you] just exactly like you jump on a piano or a sax or a violin or a drum and you make it sing the song you hear: and you love it, and you take care of it, better than you take care of yourself . . . but you have no mercy on it" (576). Writing is a little bit like being possessed by the spirit in the church or on the stage like a musician, and it could also be seen as reaching back, implicitly or explicitly, into deep, often incomprehensible, uncontrollable, and ultimately unknowable ancestral realms.

It is in that joining of the "not cerebral passion" and the "soil" he has been given that Baldwin can be considered a diasporic writer. Like the song that "does not belong to the singer," for "the singer is found by the song," his stories and the people populating them are results of scatterings and migrations—they find him and demand to be brought to life and taken care of until they are done, until their lives and worlds have made sense as a book; indeed, until they have been domesticated inside Baldwin's complex narrative worlds (JAMH, 576). Evoking critics who link the body and the literary—Judith Butler, Elaine Scarry, and Peter Brooks—Robert Reid-Pharr explains Arthur's artistic gift in *Just Above* much in the terms in which, I think, Baldwin wants us to see his authorial prerogative: as a form of aesthetics in which "the body is always involved, bathed in light . . . the spiritual is dependent upon the carnal . . . the traditional is dependent upon the contemporary."[111]

As an artist singing his own song, and one who risks his body for the sake of his work and activism, in *Just Above* Baldwin reveals and disidentifies from the powers that have always occupied the racialized, sexualized, and gendered social space of the national house: the street and the church, the state and its repressive institutions, the haves and have-nots, the cleaved North and South, and the historical, social, cultural, and economic markers of whiteness and blackness. The domestic spaces of the novel where this disidentification occurs represent alternative, unsanctioned, sometimes revolutionary options to his characters. As such they can be seen as reflective of Foucault's third and fourth elements of heterotopia, or as juxtaposing incompatible spaces and locations in a single real place (as in Arthur and Jimmy's loft) and as opening breaches in the traditional notions of time (as in Julia's African Diasporic house) keeping in mind the role sound plays in infusing these spaces with blackness and creativity. Like in *Beale*, Baldwin's representations of domesticity in *Just Above* offer alternatives to the national house, throwing into sharp relief the second Foucauldian element of heterotopia: its ability to take an existing space and make it function in a different way by placing black bodies and their spatial desires at its center.

Just Above is divided into five books—"Have Mercy," "Twelve Gates to the City," "The Gospel Singer," "Stepchild," "The Gates of Hell"—that reflect the aforementioned centrality of Julia and her domestic tragedy to all the other characters and their stories, with Hall narrating his own and Arthur's story in the first, Julia's in the second, and Arthur's, Julia's, and Jimmy's in the third, fourth, and fifth. The "structure of *Just Above* . . . is both repetitious and additive, not unlike the musical forms that inspire the novel," as Scott explains, with book 1 functioning "like the 'head' in a jazz performance . . . [setting] out the tune without embellishment."[112] Its main storyline seems to be all about Arthur, yet it is also about Hall and his attempts to overcome the grief and trauma of his brother's death, and his striving to find a woman who can become his home and refuge—which he eventually finds in his wife, Ruth. It is also about Julia's tragic story, her travels in West Africa, and her return to New York as a mature woman who remains the social and familial center for her younger brother Jimmy as well as Hall and his family: Ruth, and their teenage children, Odessa and Tony. Julia is linked to all the characters through her body, for both she and Arthur were once lovers of Crunch, who was part of the Trumpets of Zion; she also had had an affair with Hall before leaving for Africa, and before he met Ruth.

The narrative arc of *Just Above* spans two versions of the story of Arthur Montana's death in a London pub, both performed by Hall. While Hall provides the main consciousness through which all the stories are told, Baldwin injects a healthy dose of his favorite third-person, limited perspective from time to time, and in book 5, Hall briefly hands the narrative over to Jimmy, Arthur's lover, to "play" his part in it on his piano. In doing so, Hall finally recognizes Jimmy as a voice that cannot be absent from his brother's story; he comes against the limits of his access to his brother's life, acknowledging, "I didn't live with him." Importantly, the narrative begins and ends with Hall's dreams, in which all main characters are present, dreams that have to do with homes and families. These take place while Hall sleeps in his bed at home, under a ceiling that is also Baldwin's ceiling in St. Paul-de-

Vence, where the novel was, indeed, first dreamed up and written, as I noted in chapter 2. Such a mixing up of the authorial, fictional, literal, and literary dreamscapes of domestic spaces provides a complex metacommentary on several versions of black domesticity in the novel.

Just Above challenges the reader with its length, its historical and social complexity, and its thick references to music and other black cultural forms. Constructing its fictitious world with great care, Baldwin weaves lifewriting strands in and out of it, for, as Scott notes, and I agree, given Baldwin's many statements on the subject, Baldwin also "refigures his troubled relationship with his father and his early church experience" in its pages.[113] He uses actual locations in Harlem, New York, Paris, and London, thus linking the material and metaphorical spaces within and without the novel.[114] While its plentiful musical references may seem the most obvious structure for reading *Just Above*, I approach it not as a sprawling improvisation, but as a carefully and deliberately designed composition of heterotopic and dystopian domestic spaces.[115]

Briefly, we enter the narrative through Hall and Ruth's single-family home on the edge of Yonkers, then move to Julia's, located further out in that same neighborhood that, as Hall notes, "[is] good for the children" (JAMH, 15). As Hall's story unfolds, its retrospective vignettes—a "thousand piece puzzle" as Harris aptly describes its fragmented composition—take us back to the houses in Harlem occupied by the two key families: the Montanas (Paul, Florence, Hall, and Arthur) and the Millers (Amy, Joel, Julia, and Jimmy).[116] The former family lives in an unremarkable place on 135th Street between Fifth and Lenox, and they "worried because we heard that they were going to tear down our building to make room for a housing project" (70). The latter family occupies a showy two-story brownstone apartment on Edgecombe Avenue—a gaudy, "buried . . . secret house" that was "taken over by the Holy Ghost," for which they pay with the "pretty penny" Julia earns in the pulpit (111, 113, 154).

There are also transitory spaces and semidomestic shelters like the hotels in the "pastoral apocalyptic" South and Washington, D.C., where Arthur and Crunch travel with the Trumpets of Zion gospel group, the spaces in which they first have sex and discover their love for each other (51). Later there is Crunch's barren rental room on 14th Street, where Julia and Arthur often spend time after Crunch's departure for Korea, as well as Julia and Jimmy's top-floor loft on East 18th Street, which she obtains during her modeling career, and Hall's apartment on West End Avenue, which then was fast becoming the Park Avenue of the West Side (346, 370). Hall recalls as well his girlfriend Martha's Caribbean aunt's place on 139th and Seventh Avenue, where he liked to spend time before his stint in the army. After Arthur's death, Jimmy revisits international locations where they traveled together, like Istanbul (which Arthur loved so much he once wanted to buy a house there), London, Berlin, Geneva, Venice, and Barcelona—"we'd been very happy in Barcelona" (48). Jimmy's return to New York, to the party at Julia's house where the whole extended family gather that Sunday afternoon when Hall's story begins, is marked by his announcement, "I believe I've started my book," thus linking his travels and Hall's story to Baldwin's own authorial occupation and international movements (including the idea of buying a house in Istanbul, which Baldwin once entertained). Jimmy also mentions an aborted film project that, like his book, it is implied, would have had Arthur's life and stardom as its subject (48–49).[117]

All the traditional black domestic spaces in Harlem seem imperiled to a lesser or greater degree, with the Montanas' place facing demolition and the Millers' first overshadowed by fundamentalist religiosity, then destroyed by Joel's abuse and near-killing of the teenage Julia after her mother's death. Even Crunch's decrepit rental room is policed by shady downstairs neighbors, who suspect Julia and Arthur of turning tricks there. If some of these spaces seem fairly safe and stable, like that of the Montanas, they are not filled with what the novel communicates are the necessary ingredients of home: sexual and spiritual love, passion, acceptance, and creativity. In Baldwin's larger spatial design, these domestic examples all fit around, as if in concentric circles, the recasting of a New York City loft as the black queer, domestic haven of Arthur and Jimmy that I first mentioned in chapter 2.

Today, a Manhattan loft signifies an architectural and cinematic cliché of bohemian dwelling, yet Hall describes the one where Arthur and Jimmy's life together began as a run-down space:

> It was on the top floor over a three- or four-story building. The inferior stories were occupied by various small businesses, visibly and swiftly entering bankruptcy.... All day long, throughout the building, motors whined and rumbled.... After five or six o'clock... the building, and the entire neighborhood, became silent and empty. Virtually no one lived down here.... Arthur... could experiment as loudly as he wished all night....
>
> It was marvelously retired and peaceful on Saturday afternoons; and this is a Saturday.

*Oh,
the world is hungry
for the living bread.*

Arthur sings this in a low voice, standing at the window, watching the shuttered windows of the luncheonette across the street. . . . Jimmy, wearing an old green jumpsuit, is sitting at the piano, fooling around, but also, listening to Arthur. Arthur is in blue jeans . . . , a sweater, and sandals, and is walking up and down, combing his hair.

*Trust him,
and do not doubt
the words that He said:
I'll draw all men
unto Me!*

And Arthur goes behind the sheet, to the bathroom, to check on his hair, and to get rid of the comb.

Jimmy continues his investigations, very peacefully, with Arthur's tempo ringing in his head. . . . Sometimes Jimmy responds to Arthur's line—he's called—by repeating it precisely, sometimes he questions or laments, sometimes he responds from close by, and, sometimes, from far away.

Sometimes they both feel imprisoned by the song, leaping to go further than the song, or Arthur's tempo, allow: then they sweat hardest, learn most. There is always a beat beneath the beat, another music beneath the music, and beyond. (564–66)

Baldwin writes the Day Street loft and the call-and-response scene taking place there as if they were part of a play. It is the space where Arthur and Jimmy sleep, make love, cook, and make music, and where they thus defy and upend not only white heterosexist but also black notions of straight respectability and a nuclear family. The hymn they are working on is the nineteenth-century "Lift Him Up," whose refrain "I'll draw all men unto Me!" provides a playful commentary on the homoerotic undertones of the scene and is part of a number they are preparing for an upcoming performance on Christmas, that quintessential American family holiday.

As a black queer heterotopia, the loft is a familiar space made unfamiliar by the alternative family of two black queer musicians. In the space of one room it contains several others—kitchen, bedroom, bathroom, living room, and studio, with bedsheet curtains as pretend walls. Time also works differently inside it than on the outside, as the images of the loft, music, dialogue, and even the clothes on Arthur's and Jimmy's bodies are all recollected or imagined by Hall, and are in that way timeless, plucked from snippets of remembrance at different moments, or simply invented. Of course, Hall knows the physical location and features of the loft, as he was there often while Arthur was alive, and then again, "putting things in crates and boxes, closing Arthur's eyes" after his death. His revisiting of that space is a crucial part of his mourning process (563–64). Hall's memories in the extended loft sequence are entwined with imagined scenes between Arthur and Jimmy that he could not have witnessed, which Baldwin narrates through his third-person, limited perspective: moments of intimacy between the couple, their sexual passion, and ordinary moments they shared only with each other. In that sense, Hall is inventing a vision of domesticity that has been largely inaccessible to him, leaving him on the outside looking in.[118]

Given the sheer number of pages the loft scenes occupy, Hall treats it as the most important domestic space of all, and he not only appears to want to enter Arthur and Jimmy's domestic bliss, but also invests it with details of his own making. This vision is held up as the most important of all the representations of home in his story because of his need to overcome grief and depression, to eventually accept himself, and to come home, as it were, to his wife and children, from whom Arthur's death and mourning process have distanced him. That is why, when Hall imagines Jimmy professing his love for Arthur in the loft, it is in terms of leaving a home behind: "Oh, come on, baby, you left home a long time ago, you ain't nothing but a gypsy—you made *me* leave my happy home" (567). Jimmy's line is ironic, for his home was not at all happy, but was dominated by his older sister Julia, who bullied him, and his father, who beat him. After their mother's death, implicitly caused by Julia, who forbade Amy to see a doctor and promised to cure her by prayer and the laying on of hands, Jimmy is removed to stay with family in New Orleans. Guilt-ridden teenage Julia remains with her father, Joel, who abuses and rapes her, after she declines to go back to the lucrative pulpit. While we do not know whether Jimmy realizes the full extent of the violent sexual abuse his sister has suffered, we know his home with Arthur is indeed his first happy and loving one.

In another moment, soon after their teasing leads them to contemplate performing "Since I Fell for You," which begins with the exact line Jimmy has already played on—"you made me leave my happy home"—Arthur weeps in Jimmy's arms. "He is astounded by the force of his tears, astounded that he cannot stop, amazed that he can weep at all, and in the arms of a boy: for Arthur, too, is the elder brother" (569). They are lovers, but also brothers and friends, buddies, musical companions; they play for each other all the roles, Baldwin seems to suggest, that need fulfilling when one is truly accepted and loved, truly at home. Significantly, such a moment of deep connection and comfort has never taken place between Hall and Arthur.

In a moment, tears gone and tenderness administered in ways most men are ashamed to admit needing from other men, they "keep laughing." And that is when Hall loses it, and the vision of his brother's domestic bliss vanishes, for Hall's next words are "Yes. But what is Arthur doing, lying on his back, on the floor of the basement of that London pub?" (569). This rapid shift in perspective to Arthur's lonely death scene, one that takes place not in a lighted, elevated space like the loft, but below street level in a dark basement, signals the plunging of Hall's story into desperate speculation that "Jimmy came too late." But Hall also realizes his confusion, both that "I'm left with what I don't know" and that "I could, equally, be saying, with tears in my eyes, I *knew*!" (570). At this difficult moment, he commands the play inside his head to return to the happy domesticity where his brother was alive and safe: "Well. Let us go back to the loft."

In the next scene the lovers are even happier, teasing, horsing around, and discussing dinner plans. Jimmy goes into the kitchen to prepare a meal, leaving Arthur to "just lie easy, till I call you, baby" (571–73). Arthur thinks about his love and happiness with Jimmy and its cost. To dispel his rising (homosexual) panic, he imagines that

> he will go behind the halfhearted partition, grab Jimmy by those two dimples just above his ass, growl, and bite, into the nape of his neck, sniffing the hair there, just like a cat, cup both his hands under Jimmy's prick, and grind Jimmy's behind against his own prick, playfully, while Jimmy protests—playfully—and lets the onions burn while he turns and takes Arthur in his arms: too late.... Jimmy laughs and Arthur laughs: *bewildered by his happiness, and, quiet as he hopes to keep it, terrified. He cannot believe that Jimmy loves him, cannot imagine what there is in him to love.* (574, emphasis added)

In this scene, Arthur's terror and insecurity, as well as his sexual arousal concerning Jimmy's ass, continue to be imagined and narrated by Hall. By envisaging what his brother could have been thinking, feeling, and fearing, the elder brother tries to find both a definitive reason for Arthur's death and a way of accepting his homosexuality (and perhaps his own enjoyment of same-sex escapades in Korea), which gave him quite a bit of trouble as we learn in bits and pieces throughout his story.

Now we are back again in the pub basement of "that historical city" of London, the space of the loft having been penetrated by other spaces and memories that Hall crams into it (all puns intended). By no accident does this shifting back to the death scene come as the lovers in Hall's mind's eye are about to engage in sex, something that mostly straight men like Hall simply must not contemplate—with the exception of homo-sex romps with soldier buddies that were better than jerking off, as he admits. The only sexually explicit escapades that find their way into his sexual history are with women, Julia and Ruth. The former (a lengthy stream-of-consciousness steamy lovemaking scene) illustrates the nearly incestuous lover/sister relationship Hall had with Julia, while the latter (brief and not very raunchy) takes place in his marital bed and illustrates the kind of safety and happiness to which he thinks he is entitled and can handle.

The next spatial-temporal narrative shift also takes place in the loft, and since it is more low-key and only takes a couple of lines to describe, it might easily be missed. In terms of the narrative voice, however, it is the most abrupt one in the entire novel, for Hall realizes, "I must do now *what I have most feared to do*: surrender my brother to Jimmy, give Jimmy's piano the ultimate solo: which must also now, be taken as the bridge" (574, emphasis added). The term "bridge" has a double meaning here: first, referring to yet another space of passage and impermanence that can be read as heterotopic, and, second, signaling a musical bridge, or the sonic transition from one melodic structure to another.[119] At that moment, Jimmy takes over in the first-person singular just as Hall has done so far, so the shift to his voice seems less significant, though it is clear that Baldwin intends the careful reader to pay close attention to it.

Jimmy returns to the scene in the loft exactly at the point where Hall left off: "So: Arthur walks through the halfhearted partition, *and, man, he bites me on the neck*. He starts fooling around with me. I don't mind that, in fact, I dig that, but my hands are slippery with grease and onions, and I can't move for a minute" (574). They begin kissing and suddenly Jimmy is feeling what Hall and Arthur have been feeling in Hall's telling of the scene—Jimmy is suddenly "scared, too." "I don't know why. Well. I do know why, in a way . . . your brother's eyes, are asking *something of me which no one has ever asked before*. . . . You hope you can answer the question, you see. You hope you can give what is asked of you. It's the most important thing in the world, the only thing in the world, to be able to do that. What you *can* do hardly matters, if you can't do that" (574–75, emphases added). What Arthur's eyes are asking for is never named, but we can speculate that it is related to Baldwin's ideal and challenge of embodied and spiritual love. Again, the narrative does not lead to sex, as Jimmy is suddenly away from the loft. It is after Arthur's death, and only now, alone and bereft, is he tormented by the "moral shit" that the external world attached to their relationship. He sounds as if he may be talking to Hall, as he describes pacing his own room—whose location is unclear—walking the streets, driving, trying to make peace with the death of his lover whose "every inch . . . was sacred to me. And I mean sacred" (575–76). Jimmy's love for Arthur is described in sentimental and religious terms by Hall, as a holy offering and a sacrament; their love is a church in which holy sexual rites take place . . . out of sight.

That Hall's narrative perspective cannot be trusted becomes clear when the sweet Jimmy of his memories becomes a different person while talking to him. Jimmy meets Hall at his house and lets him know he is angry about Hall's apparent refusal to accept his brother and be truthful about his life and legacy following his death. Jimmy lets him have it: "So, now, *you* have become a liar, and everybody returns the favor you did them . . . and tells you only what *you* want to hear." Hall's lack of acceptance seems to have had something to do with a breakdown that may have led to Arthur's death, and with his fear and terror that came up earlier, for "Arthur got hurt, trapped, lost, somewhere in there" (577). Jimmy lets Hall know that Hall did not do his job either as an older brother or as his younger brother's manager. It was Jimmy, Arthur's lover and piano player, who "had to deal with some of his old friends, lovers, leeches, from Paris to London, to Amsterdam to Copenhagen" (577).

Hall could not deal with the messy sexual and promiscuous part of his brother's life, no matter his sentimental recalling of Arthur and Jimmy's love nest. This is a revelation Hall must accept, as he must also accept Jimmy's final words: "That wasn't no easy scene, our love, but we *did* hang in there, baby, for almost fourteen years" (577). With these words, Jimmy's brief interlude is over, and the reader is back with Arthur in the lonely spaces of the English pub, now seeing it all through his eyes for the first and last time. It is only natural that Jimmy's song be followed by Arthur's, but then the perspective begins to shift back and forth between Jimmy and Arthur and Hall, to finish with Arthur's "journey across the [pub] room . . . the longest journey he has ever forced himself to make" (582). It is on that journey that the space and architectural matter rise up to meet him, for he "starts down the steps, and the steps rise up, striking him in the chest again, and pounding between his shoulder blades, throwing him down on his back, staring down at him from the ceiling, just above his head" (582).

This moment of death and its last glimpse of the ceiling metaphorically crashing down at Arthur, killing him, loops back to the moment of Hall's nightmare featuring his own death that opens his story, to the images of the ceiling in his family's house, "whitewashed . . . with the heavy, exposed, unpainted beams . . . dropped to crush me" (15). Hall escapes the nightmare that visually links his future death to the one that has already taken Arthur by joining his family at Julia's spacious house. His ceiling having returned to its place, "fixed there, forever, like the sky outside, fixed forever, just above my head," suggests the permanence of his loss and sorrow (15). As mentioned before, the image of the ceiling in Hall's house is that of the ceiling in Baldwin's study and throughout his house. This unorthodox interpenetration of the actual authorial and fictional domestic spaces in the novel—even the ceiling at the pub Arthur watches while dying is part of the mix—is yet another reminder of Baldwin's deliberate infusion of life-writing elements within his fiction. The ceiling, a trivial-enough architectural feature, links Hall's inability to have done for him what Arthur has asked of Jimmy, to have loved his brother fully and unconditionally, "old friends, lovers and leeches" included. It links them all—Jimmy, Arthur, and Hall—in an uneasy homosocial and homoerotic triangle to James Arthur Baldwin's own life story, in which an unfulfilled dream of making a lasting home and family with a lover became material for this last novel.

The trauma of Arthur's death overshadows all the home spaces in the novel, yet the care and detail with which his and Jimmy's black queer space is represented makes it clear, again, that their loft once held something as close as possible to an ideal of domestic love and happiness. Hall is fixated on that space not only because he needs to convince himself that his late brother was once happy, but also because of his guilt at having failed him at a key moment when they were younger. Hall is the only one who ever heard about Arthur's traumatizing encounter with a pedophile at the age of thirteen, when Hall was twenty. Though Hall first learns about this event when they are both adults, he still fails to reassure his brother, who naturally expects a reaction to his confession. Instead, Hall relates, "I watched Arthur, and held my breath. . . . I try to see the scene as a minor, adolescent misadventure, as common as dirt. But this is not what Arthur's eyes are saying, nor his voice" (52–53).

The shift between past and present tense in this passage indicates that the issue dividing the brothers persists, and that Hall's guilt follows him after

4.8. Baldwin sitting on top of his patio table in front of the study. Image from the documentary film *James Baldwin: The Price of the Ticket* (1989); courtesy of Karen Thorsen, Douglas Dempsey, and the James Baldwin Project. Photo by David Baldwin.

his brother's death. At the end of Arthur's story, which describes an act of sexual molestation by an older man that took place without much violence, but, significantly, on the way to the man's house, where he wanted to fetch money to send Arthur to the store for him, Hall feels "a shyness I might not have felt with a friend, or a stranger, [that] refused to release my tongue." He immediately reassures himself, "Nothing so terrible had happened, after all; much worse might have happened," as if Arthur's having been fellated by a sexual predator was not an act of violation only because he did not get penetrated: the "much worse" that Hall has in mind but cannot articulate (54).[120] Moreover, he cannot see, or does not let himself see, any relationship between Julia's rape—she a young teen at the time of her calamity, too—and what Arthur describes as his sexual violation.

A biographical detour may be helpful here: Baldwin lived through a somewhat similar sexual molestation incident, which, as he describes it sparingly in 1985 in "Freaks," happened when "the idea of myself as a sexual possibility, or target . . . had never entered my mind." The idea did enter his mind, but only "by means of the rent made in my short boy-scout pants by a man who had lured me into a hallway, saying that he wanted to send me to the store" (PT, 681). The essay's narrator does not elaborate, concluding, "That was the very last time I agreed to run an errand for any stranger" (681). In *Just Above*, in Arthur's telling of his sexual violation, there is much more detail, as if unpacking in fiction what may have been inspired by an allegedly barely remembered event in the author's own life. In the novel, Arthur confesses that, having heard a slamming door, the predator released him finally, so Arthur, who was crying, "ran home . . . all the way . . . [and] locked [himself] in the bathroom" (53). Having at first dismissed the scene, Hall then realizes that he is ashamed of his response, for "Arthur never thought to tell his older brother of this violation: he could certainly have told no one else." Why could not Arthur have talked to his parents? Paul and Florence are caring and open-minded people who help Amy and Julia, and they seem tender and loving as they notice young Jimmy's distress. They teach their children to pay attention to other people's emotions. Thus it seems strange that Arthur is alone with his trauma, suggesting that perhaps it somehow taints him. Perhaps, mindful of the politics of respectability, his parents can identify distress in others close to them, but not in their own child, who has clearly never been told that he would be accepted and loved regardless of his sexuality.

Again, Hall is the key to this conundrum, as he concludes his remarks on Arthur's confession while letting himself off the hook by using the conditional mood: "It would probably never have occurred to him to look for me, to talk to me. He would have been too frightened, too ashamed" (54). It is Hall who is ashamed that he cannot do more for his brother even in the moment of Arthur's telling of his story, when they are both grown men and should be able to discuss it in mature ways. When Arthur says, "I wouldn't be able to live, man, if I thought you were ashamed of me," Hall "makes a sound like a laugh, a thin, demented sound," and cannot shake off the feeling, while trying to reassure Arthur lamely, that "my voice sounded hollow, and, yes, I was afraid" (55). As Hall recalls his feelings later on, having agreed to be Arthur's manager, he begins to feel oppressed by his responsibility for his brother, whom he cannot help but see as damaged in some way: "My life was really controlled by some profound and wordless sense of the role I was to play in Arthur's life. . . . I wasn't free" (127).

Arthur's childhood trauma may have been later released in his domestic life with Jimmy, the life in whose blissful and healing qualities Hall so desperately needs to believe. Yet Jimmy, Arthur's consoler in the crying scene between them described earlier, which Hall so specifically imagines perhaps because he has never been able to console his brother like that himself, holds on to memories of violence and damage, too, having to do with his own family home. Jimmy was not only bullied by his sister and slapped in the face by his mother—an event the Montanas witness one day while having the Millers over at their house—but also beaten by his father, usually out of sight of the others. And here the events in the novel and in Baldwin's own life, at least as narrated in "Freaks," come together in the larger context of the intertwined autobiographical and domestic stories that populate his works: "Once, my father gave me a dime . . . to go to the store for kerosene for the stove, and I fell on the icy streets and dropped the dime and lost it. My father beat me with an iron cord from the kitchen to the back room and back again, until I lay, half-conscious, on my belly on the floor" (PT, 680). It is instructive that this recollection from the writer's childhood appears in an essay that indicts American masculinity, machismo, and patriarchal oppression in the national house. Published as the concluding piece in *The Price of the Ticket* (1985), it seems to echo the introduction to this volume that gave it its title, whose first page informs us that, at fifteen, the writer "was getting on so badly at home that [he] dreaded going home" (PT, ix). In literary terms, this eruption of a memory of violent abuse at the hands of his preacher stepfather, David Baldwin, is an instance of a life-writing flashback in the essay that refers to childhood trauma and possible lasting damage that the writer suffered in the aftermath of one instance among many involving severe corporal punishment.[121]

Baldwin, who wrote about his stepfather extensively in many works, explains his view of him in an interview given in 1969: "He was righteous in the pulpit and a monster in the house. Maybe he saved all kinds of souls, but he lost all his children, every single one of them. And it wasn't so much a matter of punishment with him: he was trying to kill us. I've hated a few people, but actually I've hated only one person, and that was my father. . . . He didn't like me. . . . I was not his son. I was a bastard. What he wanted for his children was what in fact I became." In the same interview, Baldwin mentions that his mother "was the only person in the world we could turn to, yet she couldn't protect us."[122] Memories of beatings, verbal abuse, and rage against a cruel stepfather found their way, in various incarnations, into many of his works, from John Grimes's tribulations at home and church in *Go Tell It*, through Rufus Scott's suicidal harangue against God the Father in *Another Country*, Richard's conflict with his minister father in *Blues for*

Mister Charlie (1964), the short stories about white and black fathers and sons in *Going to Meet the Man*, Leo Proudhammer in *Tell Me*, and Julia in *Just Above*, as well as essays that deploy various retellings of his troubled childhood in Harlem.

All these characters' stories echo what Baldwin confesses in "Freaks"—that as a child he was "unbelievably unhappy and pathologically shy." In the soundtrack to the documentary Karen Thorsen made about him in 1989, he mentions that his father "frightened me so badly" that nothing much seemed scarier in his later life. He also writes that his stepfather "kept me in short pants longer than he should have, and I had been told, and I believed, that I was ugly" (PT, 681). David Leeming's biography mentions that Baldwin remembered another instance of having his body subjected to the demands of his stepfather, or the "terrifying event" he mentions in the opening of *No Name*, when David Baldwin had him circumcised at the age of five in order to somehow erase the sin of his illegitimacy. As Baldwin explains to Kay Bonetti in 1984, he found out about his illegitimacy "by accident . . . when I was thirteen," having overheard his mother and stepfather having a fight. "I couldn't tell anybody," he adds, asking rhetorically, "who would you tell?" As a kid James could do "nothing right" in the eyes of his increasingly paranoid stepparent, and "it all exploded, finally," as he left the pulpit and his home to become a writer at seventeen.

Reverend Baldwin also despised and denigrated as ungodly all that his young stepson loved and that provided him with an escape from the reality of poverty and abuse at home: books, writing, theater, film, and nonreligious music. He put down James's white friends, many of them Jews, by the time he attended the DeWitt Clinton High School, but he did allow his elementary school teacher from P.S. 24, the midwestern communist Orilla "Bill" Miller, to take him to plays and movies because he did not dare refuse a white woman in a position of authority. In an interview with her niece, Lynn Orilla Scott, Bill Miller recalls visiting the Baldwins in Harlem in the 1930s, the extreme poverty in which they lived, the "dignified father and mother," and their "railroad" apartment on Harlem's Park Avenue, which consisted of four rooms linked like train cars, with windows at the beginning and end. This layout explains why that beating that Baldwin received from his stepfather for having lost a dime had that linear, back-and-forth quality.

I realize I am treading on shaky ground here in my readings of Baldwin's essays and fiction *together* with his autobiography and biography as their indispensable context. I feel compelled to do so, however, given his many references to his life story as seeping into his writing, which can be seen in his letters, and in his embrace of the permeability of the boundaries between literary genres, fictitious and actual people, and the places where he lived and those he imagined. In light of this, and given Julia's horrific rape and abuse at its center, and the several tellings her story requires throughout the narrative of *Just Above*—by women, by men, by the community—this last novel can be read as narrating trauma as a tragic, but unavoidable part of domestic life. And while Julia has suffered the worst apparent damage of all the characters, Arthur's, Jimmy's, even Hall's (unacknowledged, repressed perhaps, war memories) traumatic stories erupt throughout the narrative, thus reiterating their important role both in Baldwin's fiction and in his life story, a literary resource he often mined.

The ways masculinity and femininity are constructed and proscribed in domestic spaces in the black communities where Baldwin's characters belong in *Just Above* can be seen as gauging how much can be told, or must be concealed, thus anticipating Baldwin's statement on writers mining what is not being told and what is hidden in *Evidence*—a book about the communal and individual trauma of the Atlanta children murders. As Kalí Tal reminds us, "Literature of trauma is written from the need to tell and retell the story of the traumatic experience, to make it real both to the victim and to the community. Such writing serves both as validation and cathartic vehicle for the traumatized writer."[123] In the next section, I continue my discussion of heterotopic domestic spaces in *Just Above*, but with the added analytical categories of trauma and gender that help illuminate why Baldwin saw his late writing moving in new directions.

"All the Characters Are Some Facet of You . . . Take You on a Journey, and You Have to Trust Them"

> From my house to Julia's house takes about half an hour, through a placid and terrifying landscape. It's terrifying because it isn't true. It's here, but it's not; it's present, but it's gone. Some people, some faces, make you feel this, like the face of a woman who knows that she is beautiful. . . . The streets I am driving through . . . frighten me like that, because nothing I am seeing is true. These houses, these penny-pinched lawns, the angular streets . . . it was never intended that *we* should live here. This is not yet forgotten. The trees and the houses and the grass remember; the stoplights remember, the fire station, the churches, and the courthouse. The people do not seem to remember.
> —*Just above My Head*

In his depictions of Julia's house as the communal, extended family's domestic space that is key to the conclusion of his last novel, Baldwin provides what can be read as the third heterotopic element from Foucault's definition, the space that juxtaposes in "a single real place different spaces and locations that are incompatible with each other."[124] Julia's house in Yonkers becomes a generative and commemorative space for all the main characters, a location that, like a magnet, attracts memories of other places, people, and events, as well as one that contains multiple versions of domesticity. Like Arthur and Jimmy's loft, it is open and flexible, but unlike the loft, it does not seem so at first sight. On the one hand, Julia's is a middle-class African American home, where she hosts Hall and his family, including his children, thus affirming it as a space for the display of normative sexual and gender roles. They barbeque meat in the backyard and dance to Tony Preston—Ruth with their son, Tony; Hall with their daughter, Odessa—affirming the centrality of familial rituals to what keeps them all together, something "strange and beautiful . . . one of the few real reasons for remaining alive," Hall muses (JAMH, 26). On the other hand, Julia's house also contains upstairs living quarters for the black queer artists, Jimmy and Arthur, into which they moved after their early days in the Day Street loft, following her return from Abidjan.

Julia's house is thus a domestic space open to all sexual, and possibly also gendered, possibilities, though we are never quite sure of that, as the hostess's "secret lover," who is mentioned a few times, is never revealed. She may be straight, queer, or celibate. Her house is a sanctuary for her as a single and self-sufficient black woman, "dominated by cushions and pallets and low tables and African sculpture: genuine" (27). Her sexuality may be muted and implied only, but she is a powerful female and projects her reign over her space, which is protected by an "African deity" and also contains a piano, as her brother cannot live in a house without one (29–30). The mixed elements of decor, rich food, music, and photographs of her loved ones complete the picture. Those who come to her house do so because it is a home for all of them; here they can bask in Julia's wisdom, cheer, humor, strength, and inner peace.

Julia's house is comfortable and welcoming to such diverse characters because it is a site of communal and individual memory, too, where temporal planes mix and jostle, and finally begin falling into place as Hall regains his voice so he can recount Arthur's life. If Arthur and Jimmy's idealized, black queer love space in the loft stands as the ideal for all the domestic spaces in the novel, Julia's is the one enabling and framing the stories of all the others. In that sense, her house echoes the fourth heterotopic principle, heterochronism, for it not only incites but also nourishes and keeps alive Hall's and other characters' memories and stories of home, and it memorializes the absent Arthur. It is a timeless, free-for-all home and house, affirming again the importance of women's perspectives both to Baldwin's later works and to his own late-life self-acceptance as an effeminate black queer man and artist/witness. When Ida Lewis interviewed him in 1970 for *Essence* magazine, and asked about "the new James Baldwin" for the 1970s, he responded that he could no longer live in the United States and that his mission was to be a witness through written accounts, both fictional and not, thus blurring the line between the two—"I write it all down.... It doesn't mean I saw it. It means that I was there. I don't have to observe the life and death of Martin Luther King. I am a witness to it. Follow me?"[125]

By 1984, in an important interview, later published as "The Art of Fiction" in *The Paris Review* (which should be required reading for every MFA student), he elaborates that with time "you learn how little you know" and that "the hardest thing in the world is simplicity. And the most fearful thing, too." Most important, his late style requires self-knowledge and nakedness of the self, for "you have to strip yourself of all your disguises, some of which you didn't know you had." The ultimate goal is to "write a sentence as clean as a bone."[126] Coming five years after the publication of *Just Above*, these comments clearly derive from the lessons learned through its composition, one of which also concerns the theme of mortality that enters Baldwin's writing about the time *No Name* was published in 1972. In 1984, from the vantage point of sixty years of age, he explains, "a person is in sight of his or her death around the age of forty. You see it coming. You are not in sight of your death at thirty, less so at twenty-five. You are struck by the fact of your mortality, that it is unlikely you'll live another forty years. So time alters you, actually becoming either an enemy or a friend."[127]

Baldwin's approach to time and mortality links *Just Above* and *Beale*. Although very different in length and focus, they engage in an important literary dialogue that has to do with how Baldwin's last novel deploys gender as a category of analysis and how this in turn affects the narrative structure and politics of home and mourning. While in *Beale*, in addition to race and class, gender is the lens through which Tish increasingly begins to see herself and others, in *Just Above*, Baldwin's steady attention to masculinity and femininity helps us see how specific characters relate to the intricacies of grief both within and outside of black communities.[128] In this context, we can say that the disorderly characterization of, and narration by, Tish in the former novel has in fact made Hall Montana's complex and Harlem-rooted story of a middle-aged man and war veteran possible in the latter.[129] This way of reading Hall's voice in *Just Above* as at least an echo, if not a direct descendant, of Tish's narrative can be seen, for example, in Hall's observations about spaces around him, how he sees other people and himself. After his return from Korea, for example, he notices a new way of apprehending his whereabouts:

> I had not seen these streets in so long, and I had seen *so many other things, that they hit me like a hammer*. People adjust to the scale of things around them—cottages, streams, bridges, wells, narrow winding roads—and *now I was in a howling wilderness, where everything was out of scale*. . . . I had not heard this noise in so long—incessant, meaningless, reducing everyone to a reflex, just as the towering walls of the buildings forced everyone to look down, into the dog shit at their feet. *No one ever looked up . . . except to watch some maddened creature leap from the walls, or to calculate their own leap*—yet people lived here, and so had I . . . *I was repelled*, but fascinated: embittered, but home. (288–89, emphases added)

In this scene, Hall looks at his home city through the eyes of a returned soldier and glimpses memories of the Korean landscape that overlay that of New York before his eyes. He has witnessed unspeakable, violent things, yet his answer to his brother's loaded question, "How was it over there?," is macho, cocky, and racist: "Just a small police action, son. Had to put them gooks in their places. They worse than the niggers, thinking they got a right to a whole country. . . . We put them in their place—six feet under" (288).

Hall cannot talk about, or even admit, his war memories, because as a black man he had to hold on to his performance of strength as the straight, older brother. His answer does not fool Arthur, however, for he "had been watching my face." Perhaps due to his queer masculinity, not as bound by the gender proscriptions to which Hall submits, Arthur can sense that his brother's answer is bravado not substance, that his war memories might intrude through the wall of his masculine pride; in short, that he is putting on a show for his, Arthur's, sake. Hall answers Arthur in riddles, treating his younger brother as if he were someone delicate and in need of protection, like a woman, for when Arthur probes further—"It was bad?"—Hall says, "Oh, yeah, baby, it was filthy. Thought I was going crazy, don't know if I ever get clean" (288). By referencing dirt and madness, Hall reassures his brother that he has survived both by putting them in the past tense, with the exception of "don't know if I ever get clean," hinting at action to take place in the present. Like the men in Tish's story, especially her father, Joe, and Fonny's father, Frank, who must engage in illegal activities to raise money for Fonny's bail, Hall is supposed to be the backbone of the community, to be tough and impervious to excessive emotion, no matter the circumstances. And if there is some cleaning up left to do as a consequence, it will be done proudly and out of sight.

That Hall is repressing trauma while playing the role of the strong older brother is clear after Arthur's death, as his story begins, when he projects his grief on all the places around him, which appear filled with dread and danger. His telling must take place, for it is a form of narrative healing, just as the songs Arthur sings have soothing properties. But Hall must first be able to find his voice, as the trauma of his brother's death has rendered him virtually mute; he can still speak, but he cannot process his loss and mourning verbally. Orpheus-like, he is trying to return to light from the depths of depression and grief. Yet his descent into the hell of mourning, where he dwells until he can recover both his brother and himself, does not end up with a happy emergence into the light. The opening and closing scenes, in which the images of the ceiling "just above my head" appear first over Hall then over Arthur, lead to the final one in which Hall wakes up from a dream of home and family with his brother still alive, "and [his] pillow is wet with tears" (584). Hall's tears closing the novel, closing the story of his beloved brother's life and death, may be also falling in response to, and as a lesson of, the tears he imagined in the tender scene between Arthur and Jimmy in the loft. In that scene, filled with Arthur's grief and tears, it is Jimmy, the "younger brother" in that relationship, who is holding Arthur, "the older brother," in his arms, supporting him and "kissing the sadness" away. That role reversal is what Hall needs from his brother. Finally, Hall is ready to cry like a man and be held and consoled by a man. But there is no one to hold him.

The change in Hall, however subtle it may seem, takes place in a series of domestic spaces he inhabits and visits. At the beginning of his story, "I sat ... in the kitchen, staring through the ... windows at the exiled trees which lined the sad streets of the despairing void ... one of the blood-soaked outposts of hell. The day is coming, swiftly, when we would be forced to pack our things, and go. Nothing can live here, life has abandoned this place" (17). The dystopian vision outside Hall's window is a projection of his feelings; the wasteland he apprehends outside is linked to an architectural element inside his house—that ceiling, again—which descends upon him in a nightmare to crush him or imprison him as if in a coffin: "A thunder rolled inside my head . . . and I woke up. My whitewashed ceiling, with heavy, exposed, unpainted beams, had dropped to crush me—was not more than two inches, just above my head. This weight crushed, stifled, the howl in my chest. I closed my eyes: a reflex." But then the sensation is gone: "I opened my eyes. The ceiling had lifted itself, and was where it had always been. I blinked. The ceiling did not move" (16). Hall is badly shaken by this nightmare that reminds him of his own mortality, of how one day, "The darker sky, the earth, will scour me to bone, then powder: powder in the bowels of the earth" (16). This reminder forces him to realize that death is always a lonely, tragic, inevitable business. This is the moment he begins to realize that in order for him to live, to fulfill the days still ahead of him, he must overcome his silence and tell his brother's story, thus revisiting his own as the child, youth, and young man he once was.

Like Tish's in its retrospective narrative looping between the past and present that contains her story and Fonny's and their families' in *Beale*, Hall's story also contains his coming of age in the background of Arthur's. Like Tish, he faces a calamity—his brother's death—while Tish has Fonny's imprisonment, her harassment by Bell, and her child's future on her mind. Like Tish, too, Hall follows the learning curve concerning his own place and identity in the communities he inhabits while telling the story of his brother; he must mature in order to begin telling it in the first place. Unlike Tish, however, who occupies a somewhat liminal space between girlhood and womanhood at the beginning of her story, Hall is a much older, middle-aged black man, a war veteran and a father of teens at the beginning of his. He is steeped in life experience that is alien to Tish, and he is contemplating his own mortality in ways that anticipate Baldwin's comments in "The Art of Fiction" five years later. There may be room to read him as undergoing a rapid maturation of self, finally, the maturation that his female counterpart in *Beale*, like Julia Miller in his own story, was forced to deal with much earlier in life precisely because she was female and black.

Black women, Baldwin thus implies, have no choice but to mature sooner than men in their communities; this is both a sweeping stereotype and an undeniable truth of American reality that Harris describes as "the serving position in which most Baldwin women find themselves."[130] That is why Hall needs his wife, Ruth, to cradle him like a baby when he needs protection from the world run by men. She must play the role of both lover and mother for him, even when they have sex, when, as he does in the opening pages of *Just Above*, "he shot it all into her, shot the grief and the terror and the journey into her, and lay on her breast, held like a man and cradled like a child, released" (9). This unfair but apparent disparity between men and women is clear in Hall's observation about Julia, at that Sunday party at her house that frames his narrative: she is thirty-nine years old, but "if she looked her real age, whatever it is, she'd turn to dust" (26). Julia, who had been once pregnant by her rapist father as a teen, had a miscarriage as a result of his violent beating that nearly killed her. Now, years later, having returned from Abidjan, she reveals to Hall that she is barren. He calls her "old obeah woman," and she tells him, echoing Baldwin's pronouncements on his work and place in the world, that she has learned to "trust what I don't know," having realized that she is part of "something other, older, vaster," and that "childbirth takes many forms, that regret is a kind of abortion, that sorrow is the only key to joy" (556). Despite her inability to have children, she is a complete, fulfilled woman, indeed, a matriarch/goddess figure in her community.

In 1984, speaking with Bonetti, Baldwin echoes the Flaubertian authorial confession, when speaking about *Just Above*, that "all the characters are some facet of you . . . the people arrive and they take you on a journey, and you have to trust them." In the same interview, he seems to echo the title of a Pirandello play, claiming that the characters always find him whenever they need him to write them into existence. Speaking of his last novel, he emphasizes, "The people take over, Hall and Arthur, Julia and Jimmy. Especially Julia . . . right?"[131] The power of seemingly minor characters in Baldwin's last novel is indeed key to understanding its composition. As Trudier Harris succinctly sums up Julia's character, "In . . . nearly six hundred pages, marked by extraneousness, . . . [she] is provocative, engaging, and disgusting," for she not only transgresses with the sin of pride by seeing herself as the Lord's "anointed," but also, as a child and later teenager who has lacked proper parenting, "she is trying to play God"—her unruly behavior encouraged by her superstitious mother and money-grubbing father.[132] As an astute observer of others, Hall learns from this negative example, for when he becomes a father himself, it is clear that he has gained the experience to do a good job.

What is even more important for my argument on domesticity, however, is that the domination of the Millers' domestic space by a female child spoiled by lack of parental discipline and phony pride instilled in her by organized religion is what ruins her family and home: she forbids her mother to seek medical attention, so the mother dies. Left with the father she adores, she finds out, too late, that he is a shallow, vain, and violent man suffering from alcoholism, whose only way of relating to her is through sexual and physical abuse. The trauma that ensues could have killed her, but Julia, again, like the blues singer's persona in "Backwater Blues," climbs her "lonesome hill" and achieves her identity by any means necessary, which includes prostitution, modeling, raising her brother, and international travel. It is in her house that Hall's story begins and ends, again, framed by a Sunday afternoon during which Julia's extended family gather around her—that mythic presence in her bright African dress, hair rag, and talisman earring. As Scott explains, Julia's house "provides not so much a frame for the novel as a *doorway* or introduction to the people and events that will take up Hall's narrative."[133]

In that single, black, "barren" woman's domestic space is born a narrative catalyst for Hall's story about characters forming an extended family through both blood and experience. Julia's home becomes a literal and literary womb through which the other characters' lives are ushered; it is a representational space where black femininity is used, yet again, for the purpose of representing black male stories entangled with hers. As Harris notes, Julia begins her role "in a serving position . . . [but] in some ways, . . . finally becomes the freest of all Baldwin's female characters."[134] In that sense, we can think of Julia as a precursor to Edith Hemings in *The Welcome Table*, and if we do so, the gendered domestic picture in *Just Above* becomes more complicated. Baldwin's autothematic remark that he is all the characters about whom he writes must be taken seriously, and Leeming's biography corroborates that with examples of dreams that James and his brother David had in St. Paul-de-Vence—dreams that in fact made it into the novel's beginning and end.[135] Leeming also claims, like Harris and Scott, that "Julia's childhood preaching and her abuse at the hands of her father are directly and metaphorically related to Baldwin's own childhood. . . . As in dreams . . . the characters and situations simultaneously reflect the world around the dreamer and the world within him."[136] Echoing Baldwin's message about literary interpenetrations of blackness and whiteness, Toni Morrison corroborates this by reading the subject of the dream as the dreamer in *Playing in the Dark*.

In the context of Julia's influential presence, dreams, and powerful emotions filling *Just Above*, it could be perhaps said, riskily again, that Baldwin may be grappling with his own femininity, or the woman he has been trying to "become" or create through his fictional characters and narrators. Given that all the while he was also working out his ideas on gender and homosexuality in his later essays, which led him to embrace the idea of androgyny by 1985, this approach seems plausible. His house in St. Paul-de-Vence—a potent presence inflecting the interiors, moods, and characterizations of his last novel—corroborates it, being the material setting where he dreamed up this novel, where its characters found and claimed him, and where he took the journey they invited him on by laboring over *Just Above* in his "torture chamber."

> "All Those Strangers Called Jimmy Baldwin . . . [and] a Woman, Too"
>
> My father did one thing for me. He said, "You can't do it." And I said, "Listen m_____ don't tell me what I can't do." . . . [Interviewer: *Why couldn't you do it, according to him?*] . . . Because I was black, because I was little, because I was ugly. He made me ugly. I used to put pennies on my eyes to make them go back. [*But out of that an identity emerged.*] Yes, all those strangers called Jimmy Baldwin. . . . There's the older brother with all the egotism and rigidity that implies. . . . I grew up telling people what to do and spanking them, so that in some ways I always will be doing that. Then there is the self-pitying little boy. You know: "I can't do it because I'm so ugly." He's still there some place. [*Who else?*] Lots of people. Some of them are unmentionable. There is a man. There is a woman, too.
>
> —Baldwin, in Standley and Pratt, *Conversations*

In an interview with Eve Auchincloss and Nancy Lynch, recorded in 1969, Baldwin speaks candidly about his difficult childhood, emphasizing how his stepfather's negative reinforcement is also what paradoxically enabled his identity as a writer. To David Baldwin Sr., James was an illegitimate, petite, black sissy kid who stood no chance of redemption. Instead of yielding to the doomsday scenario his father drew, Baldwin made his origins, especially his illegitimacy, the central force of his works, in which we can follow multiple trajectories of the composite life story of all those strangers called Jimmy Baldwin: the "older brother," "self-pitying little boy," "a man," and "a woman, too."

While the masculine-gendered "brother," "boy," and "man" require little explanation, the "woman" at the end of Baldwin's list of his intrinsic identities could be seen as a rather startling addition in 1969, given how much his works until then were concerned with male homosocial relationships: between fathers and sons, brothers, friends, collaborators, artists, and gay lovers. Perhaps not surprisingly, then, although that sole feminine-gendered noun "woman" appears as clearly as the full stop at the end of Baldwin's sentence, Auchincloss and Lynch take no interest in it. Their next question—about the writer's "two obsessions: color and homosexuality"—seems to fold the "woman" part of him in a rather homophobic manner into his sexual preference, with that familiar whack of misogyny that often underlies that form of discrimination.

At the time of Auchincloss and Lynch's interview, homosexuality was still on the books of the American Psychiatric Association as a "disease," so the question was perhaps not as startling and inane to Baldwin as it may be to us today. Baldwin's elegant and poised answer acknowledges the backwardness and shame of the question implicitly, as he patiently describes this vile approach as "one of the American myths." To him, homophobia is a peculiar form of national myopia, a delusion his countrymen embrace as a kind of proud pigheaded exceptionalism: "People in other parts of the world have never had this peculiar kind of conflict. If you fall in love with a boy, you fall in love with a boy. The fact that Americans consider it a disease says more about them than it says about homosexuality."[137]

It would have been wonderful if Baldwin addressed misogyny as the flip side of homophobia here, but it did not happen for over a decade and a half, until the publication of "Freaks and the American Ideal of Manhood" in the January 1985 issue of *Playboy*. That piece brilliantly unpacks this American myth with a no-holds-barred lashing out against racist, sexist, and homophobic violence. While disidentifying from the domestic models of masculinity, the essay also delineates "intersectionality," which Baldwin, without naming it so, sees as a fundamental, though unacknowledged, component of Americanness. That essay also proclaims androgyny the only viable model of national identity for all those who claim citizenship in, as Baldwin used to say, those not-so-United States: "We are all androgynous, not only because we are all born of a woman impregnated by the seed of a man but because each of us, helplessly and forever, contains the other—male in female, female in male, white in black and black in white" (PT, 690).[138] A powerful, gendered rewriting of the national jeremiad Baldwin so gloriously executes at the end of *The Fire Next Time*, where the "relatively conscious whites and the relatively conscious blacks ... must, like lovers, insist on, or create, the consciousness of the others" is juxtaposed in "Freaks" with a simple statement addressing what could be imagined as a collectivity of blended hues, genders, and sexualities, each of Baldwin's readers in his or her private complexity: "We are a part of each other. Many of my countrymen appear to find this fact exceedingly inconvenient and even unfair, and so, very often, do I. But none of us can do anything about it" (PT, 379, 689–90). In the late years of his short life, Baldwin offers an androgynous and interracial determinism, a model of a somewhat utopian, yet liberating, black queer space where cultural identity can dwell, no matter how far from embracing it we still are today.

By 1985, having lived in his Provençal house in St. Paul-de-Vence for nearly a decade and a half, Baldwin is far from desiring to lead the charge to integrate whole countries and societies. When "Freaks" came out, he saw that task as having been turned inward. Like in *Just Above*, it is relegated to the individual's mind, body, and spirit; it is thrust to the singular man or woman—or however else they may want to define themselves outside of cis categories— to reconcile the dichotomous racialized, gendered, and sexualized identities within themselves. Having been affixed with the epithet "Martin Luther Queen," Baldwin had to struggle his whole life with misogyny as the flip side of homophobia. Even to Wole Soyinka, who, in his foreword to Troupe's volume *James Baldwin: The Legacy*, dubs Baldwin "the diminutive prose stylist" upon their first meeting in 1960s London, his effeminacy seems taken for granted. Soyinka describes his initial perception of Baldwin's contribution as consisting of "the paradox of the *intensity* of his beliefs in the racial question, and the suppression of its inherent subjectivity for him as a black man." To him, Baldwin "spoke as a convinced universalist... perhaps cosmopolite... who... did not... see culture as an instrument of combat."[139]

But Soyinka modifies this opinion, if not outright misreading, of Baldwin's early works, having registered his surprise at the fierceness of *The Fire Next Time*. He concludes that although Baldwin responds passionately "to a specific phase in American social struggle" in that work, he has also honed "a different cast of intellect and creative sensibility from a Ralph Ellison's, a Sonia Sanchez's, a Richard Wright's, an Amiri Baraka's, or an Ed Bullins." Indeed, in thus emphasizing Baldwin's singularity of perspective as a "black writer," and his difference from his similarly hued compatriots, Soyinka describes him in terms that call to mind sentiment, affect, and affective and thus feminine-inflected erotic power: "Few writers are capable of this largeness of compassion; few can write with a grace.... Baldwin's legacy embraces this liaison of art and the mission of compassion, a unique quality that first seduces then poses its subtle challenge to the reader's moral complacency."[140]

These qualities, along with Baldwin's fascination with "the ambiguities of moral choices in human relations" and close attention to the many aspects of individual, private identity, along with his continued reliance on autobiography and confession as key rhetorical forms, align his later works with those of the second wave of feminist writers, thinkers, activists, and scholars.[141] Beginning in the 1970s, and even more so by the 1980s, Audre Lorde, Maya Angelou, Gloria Anzaldúa, bell hooks, Cherríe Moraga, Betty Friedan, Germaine Greer, Gloria Steinem, Barbara Christian, Alice Walker, and many others spoke of the consequences to individual bodies and groups of sexual, racial, and gender difference and their social and political underpinnings. They urged their readers and male intellectuals to recognize the foundational importance of women's lives and work and "feminine" values, and called for their recovery, study, and celebration. While not always agreeing, and often in open conflict driven by generational, class, ethnic, or racial perceptions of difference, these women's ideological messages nevertheless shared three larger, and by no means exhaustive, common threads: (1) the vitality of maternal and domestic preoccupations and spaces to communities and nations, as well as across national boundaries; (2) the importance of women's manual and domestic labor as part of historically invisible economies and their growing presence in public spheres and workplaces; and (3) the centrality of women's feelings and emotions, life cycles, and creative individual, collective, and family concerns as central to the project of the humanities within and without academe.[142] Most important, the various feminist movements' creeds gave permission to readers and scholars alike to attend to the realities, sentiments, feelings, activities, and communities of women previously deemed at best insignificant or decorative, and at worst silly and unworthy of public and scholarly attention.[143]

The unease with which some critics approached *Just Above*, then, has much to do with the fact that this novel embraces all three feminist principles mentioned above. Significantly, it not only describes but also celebrates a black queer, domestic space that Arthur and Jimmy create as a couple, and this celebration is performed, for the most part, by a black man who identifies as straight. What is more important, *Just Above* celebrates sexual intercourse, especially male homosexual eroticism and passion, as part of domestic space, and it does so particularly movingly in the passages that describe Arthur and Jimmy's lovemaking, and Jimmy's and Crunch's youthful eroticism and sexual worship of each other's bodies. In that sense, the novel becomes a home space for young queer readers, especially those of color like Melvin Dixon, Richard Rodriquez, Randall Kenan, Justin Torres, or Darieck Scott, who came of age seeking images reflecting who they were in American literature.

In such a context, acknowledging the existence of his inner "woman" in the interview with Auchincloss and Lynch already in 1969 was bold of Baldwin. He may have been one of the first male writers in the twentieth-century United States who not only validated feminine concerns in his personal and public life, but also embraced them openly in his later works. Matters of literary taste aside, it is interesting to ponder the dismissive reviews of those late works in the 1970s and 1980s in the context of their "feminine," if not "feminist" or "womanist," concerns, which, compounded with their strong homoerotic and queer sexual content, would have inflected how black and white critics and scholars read them and, in many cases, how they continue to read them today.

Baldwin's attention to the intertwining of class, gender, race and sexual identity in his works was inspired by, and helped to pave the way for, further discussion of various forms of oppression to which feminists of color were beginning to draw attention then, and continue to do so now: mass incarceration, police brutality, inadequate health care and education for the poor, and the hypocrisy of Christian and state institutions that exclude everyone who is not of that persuasion, straight, married, or of heteronormative or cis gender identity. In the wake of legislative support for marriage equality, with hopes that similar support will soon be extended to transgender people, and with the painful awareness of the rise in hate crimes against queer and trans people, Baldwin's words from 1984, spoken to Richard Goldstein of the *Village Voice*, seem not only prophetic but also indicative of a larger problem that still ails American culture: "The discovery of one's sexual preference doesn't have to be a trauma. It's a trauma because it's such a traumatized society" (JB, 63).

Twentieth-century African Diaspora women writers whom Baldwin must have read, given the presence of their books in his library, took on in their texts not only that national trauma, but also others, showing the roots of American malaise in the interlocking systems of oppression and persecution of difference that extended from seventeenth-century New England and slavery, as in Ann Petry's *Tituba of Salem Village* (1955), through post-Reconstruction migrations and urban industrialization in Gwendolyn Brooks's *Maud Martha* (1953) and Petry's *The Street* (1946) and *The Narrows* (1953), to Paule Marshall's *Brown Girl, Brownstones* (1959), Alice Walker's *The Color Purple* (1982), and Toni Morrison's *The Bluest Eye* (1970), *Sula* (1973), and *Beloved* (1987). That last one was on Baldwin's reading list in 1987 (most likely, it was not finished before his passing). While Baldwin saw these writers, especially the ones who came of age under the influence of his own works, as important new voices tapping into new realms of imagination, by now, he has been embraced by writers as diverse as Janet Mock, Alexa Birdsong, Alain Mabanckou, Suzan-Lori Parks, Shay Youngblood, Ta-Nehisi Coates, Claudia Rankine, Randall Kenan, and Teju Cole, to name just a few.

His oeuvre and revolutionary depictions of domesticity inspired and gave legitimacy to the black gay and queer movements. As Matt Brim explains in *James Baldwin and the Queer Imagination* (2014), what writers and artists such as Essex Hemphill, Marlon Riggs, and Joseph Beam sought in,

4.9 and 4.10. Books from the Chez Baldwin library. Photos by author, 2014.

after, and because of Baldwin was "a lineage, literary and historical, raced and queer."[144] In the context of this black queer desire for a forebear, these writers indeed found themselves at home in Baldwin's writing. As Baldwin describes being a writer in an interview in 1986, he pays attention to his maturation and to what writing *Just Above* has taught him: "One's relationship to the past changes. Yet that boy, the boy I was, still controls the man I am. If I didn't know as much as I think I do know about the boy, I would still be his prisoner. Perhaps what I'm saying is that all the action is to understand enough to be liberated from first of all one's terror and then one's self image, to keep moving into a larger space."[145] Baldwin's "larger space" refers to his life story, his domestic and work routines, and, of course, his writing, in which the past plays a tremendous role. The experience of writing *Just Above* made him realize a certain gendered determinism at the heart of this work: "I'd never been more frightened in my life either as a man or as a writer. *Yet I knew it had to be done.* That book is not directly autobiographical at all, but *it is autobiographical on the much deeper level.* . . . It truly is *a composite.* A novel or anything I write begins with an incoherent disturbance, and you can't run away from it. You have to sit and wait and see what it is. It may be the things I've forgotten or think I've forgotten that suddenly begin to stir."[146] Maybe when that happened, he was looking through the window of his study into his peaceful garden in the back of the house where a gorgeous palm tree used to grow, while Warwick's "The House Is Not a Home" played softly in the background. Maybe he was walking upstairs, admiring the view of the Mediterranean gleaming in the distance. Maybe he was in bed, in the arms of a lover, happy, and at peace. What is certain is that he was *at home* when he felt that creative "stirring." For as much as his house in St. Paul-de-Vence, his work was his dwelling, his passion, and his song, and when he got himself ready to be taken on a journey by all those strangers that were all new and all familiar, he knew that they were all himself, and that they were all of us, his readers, too.

The front of Chez Baldwin. Photo by author, 2014.

CHAPTER 5

Black Life Matters of Value

Erasure, Overlay, Manipulation, or Archiving the Invisible House

> There are many witnesses to my past, people who've disappeared, people who are dead, whom I loved. But I don't feel there are any ghosts, any regrets. I don't feel that kind of melancholy and all. No nostalgia. Everything is always around and before you. Novels that haven't worked, loves, struggles. And yet it all gives you something of immeasurable power. . . .
>
> [I am not troubled] at all by death. I'm troubled over getting my work done and over all the things I've not learned. It's useless to be troubled by death, because then, of course, you can't live at all.
>
> —Baldwin, in Standley and Pratt, *Conversations*

> —Say it, no ideas but in things—
> nothing but the blank faces of the houses
> and cylindrical trees
> bent, forked by preconception and accident—
> split, furrowed, creased, mottled, stained—
> secret—into the body of the light!
> —William Carlos Williams, "Paterson," book I

A master at juggling contradictions and explicating conundrums of a humanity that is always intersectional and paradoxical, Baldwin recast the ways Americans of all hues viewed themselves and others, how they loved, had sex, and dwelled in their homes, countries, and the world decades before scholars could fully comprehend his message. In his complex vision, memory and self are always spatially contingent, time works cyclically, and identity, like desire, is an unpredictable vortex of complex processes happening as much on material as immaterial planes.[1] Fierce creativity ensues from all of that, and some mysterious, uncontrollable nooks and crannies of the always expansive and wondrous imagination fill with music, pictures, and sensations of the ever-present body that writes down what it feels. Baldwin's black queer humanism, for that is what his prolific career has bequeathed us, profoundly transformed that foundational western humanism of Petrarch's or Dante's for the modern and postmodern worlds through the lens of the African Diaspora, and specifically black experience within and without the United States. He did it through hard work and excruciating self-scrutiny, always learning new things and dreaming up new projects, and demanding that, if we are to be worthy of his legacy, we would better do the same.

In 1984, in an interview excerpt that has provided the first epigraph to this concluding chapter, he distances himself from nostalgia—"I don't feel there are any ghosts, any regrets"—seemingly dismissing the past.[2] Two years later, he affirms the necessity of life writing and recycling the past creatively in his art: "I don't know whether you can hunt more and more of your own life or if more and more of your own life will hunt you, but it comes back to you during points in your life in another light."[3] As Adrienne Rich inimitably sums up his legacy in "The Baldwin Stamp": He "could be viewed as apocalyptic preacher, as instigator to black rebellion, as provoker of 'white guilt' (a concept he in fact devastatingly dissected)." She praises his staunch insistence on remaining "a real writer and not a mere celebrity or appointed spokesperson," admitting that such a stand did not win him an easy place in the literary pantheon, as "he was hailed (and attacked) as an early writer

5.1 and 5.2. Garden green passage and his wall mirror at Chez Baldwin. Photos by author, 2000.

of fiction on homosexual experience; criticized harshly for living in Europe while writing on America, for being too much the 'aesthete' or too much the engaged writer." Most important, he showed us that "the artist needs to dwell 'within the experience and outside of it at the same time,'" turning his "own awareness of this difficult positioning" into "a supreme artistic strength." Rich's words echo especially true today, for while "his country has put his face on the first-class postage stamp ... [it] has yet to face its own confusion in his art's unsparing mirror."[4] We do need Baldwin now.

The complex, exciting cluster of paradoxes that is James Baldwin has inspired *Me and My House*, while my experience, memories, and impressions of what used to be his dwelling at Chez Baldwin inflected my eclectic tools of the trade. In this concluding chapter, I retrace some of the stages in conceptualizing this project and map my literary critical approach and how it has been compelled by my shifting, often confounding archive. What Baldwin and the remnants and refuse of his life have taught me is that, like writers, critics, too, must dwell "within the experience and outside of it at the same time," *overlaying* what can be known with honest, careful, and hard-won interpretation and analysis. This approach has also mandated my reliance on what to some of my readers may seem an unorthodox archive in this project, as well as my weaving of biographical material and, indeed, matter, occasionally even autoethnography, into my literary analyses throughout *Me and My House*.[5] Prompted by Baldwin's own reliance on life writing, by the embrace of pivotal works by black women writers like Maya Angelou, Audre Lorde, Alice Walker, and Paule Marshall, and inspired by some of the tenets of New Materialism, I combine Baldwin's autoscrutiny and self-reflectivity with the value of "ideas ... in things," just as the lines from William Carlos Williams's poem do in my second epigraph.[6]

RACING MATTERS OF VALUE

The subtitle of this chapter, "Erasure, Overlay, Manipulation, or Archiving the Invisible House," reflects the sequence of domesticating Chez Baldwin as a space of creativity and sociability that also yielded to Baldwin's black queer "*manipulations*," as he refers to them in his 1987 *Architectural Digest* piece. It also signals what I see as an urgent task of the humanities and literary studies today: rethinking how we preserve the material legacy of literary black lives against their systematic and systemic *erasure*—a queerly raced matter, indeed. I want us to think hard about what we understand as the *matter* of black writers' lives, and how that materiality, its traces, remnants, even refuse, may and

5.3. The gatehouse with vines. Photo by author, 2014.

must be read and preserved in light of the ways we have approached the matter and preservation of (usually unacknowledged in racial terms) "white" lives in the national house. How is it, one may ask, that Baldwin's house library has been abandoned as worthless, while the Beinecke Library at Yale University cherishes Walt Whitman's reading glasses as a precious artifact?

I found myself confronting this question in October 2016, while visiting Yale University for a talk related to this book. I was thrilled that two young archivists from the Beinecke not only attended my lecture, but also wanted to meet with me to discuss the remaining archive from Chez Baldwin. To my astonishment, however, it seemed we were not speaking the same language in that meeting. Unless there were provable traces of Baldwin's "hand" on the books and other materials, these two women did not see *any* value in preserving them because they were not "unique." Weaving enthusiastic visions of seminar rooms furnished with *his* books as both one-of-a-kind scholarly resources and museum-worthy exhibits did not sway them. The problem was an insurmountable difference in vision and imagination: I saw the books, files, magazines, and clippings as possessing great, unprecedented value in the simple fact that they once *belonged to Baldwin*; the archivists, however they were trained, saw no value whatsoever in that. Even more strangely, the very fact that they were hearing all this from a respected Baldwin scholar, and that the chair of Yale's Department of African American Studies sitting next to me supported my words enthusiastically, made no difference. Most glaringly, they neither comprehended the racial underpinnings of the cruel paradox in it nor saw the point of asking that weighted question about Whitman's reading glasses versus Baldwin's personal library.

A few months after that meeting, the *New York Times* reported that the Beinecke Rare Book and Manuscript Library at Yale University had bought Jonathan Lethem's *entire* archive, including "dead-tree artifacts" that are "charmingly weird," comic books, multiple electronics including iPods and iPads, and a copious trove of drunken drawings of "vomiting cats" that Lethem and his friends executed during parties at his house.[7] As the author of the piece, Jennifer Schuessler begins her story, "Writers are different from the rest of us. Their castoff scraps can be worth money, not to mention the obsessive attentions of future scholars." She then goes on to describe all kinds of ephemera, including many from "a grocery-supply store called Samuel J. Underberg," "tawdry used signage," and in addition to the aforementioned "largest cache of drawings of vomiting cats in any university collection," "hand-drawn comic books Mr. Lethem made as a child." In his early fifties, Lethem is carefully curating his literary legacy, aided by a wealthy ivy-league academic institution, and boasting, "I wrote three novels on an electric typewriter.... If I live long enough, I could end up being one of the last living humans who can say that." That typewriter is obviously included in the archive that is referred to as an "oddball trove." As an archivist quoted in the article comments, "For an author who is so much fun as a novelist, it's interesting to see there is so much fun in his archival documents as well." Literary tastes aside, why else would this archive of a writer whose achievement and importance are clearly nowhere near Baldwin's be so carefully preserved and celebrated? Or, is Baldwin's material legacy simply not as much "fun" and not "weird" enough?

About to enter the third decade of the twenty-first century, we must make up for the lack of vision and imagination that still dwells in many more places than that one library in order to approach the preservation and representation of materiality, traces, and objects left by black lives like Baldwin's in new ways. Given the systemic historical erasure of such lives and legacies in the United States and beyond, and the ways in which the very concepts *archive*, *artifact*, *price*, and *preservation* have been imbued with racialized values and judgments, it is time to retool both how we articulate the importance of objects that furnish, contextualize, and reference black writers' creative spaces and how we preserve and evaluate them. In the American national house, filled with Islamophobic, racist, misogynist, homophobic, and transphobic discourses and acts, and immersed in nativist myths, lies, and "fake news," black people and other nonwhites, noncitizens, refugees, queers, immigrants, and migrant workers are still not made to feel at home. Even national heroes whose epidermal hues mark them as nonwhite remain homeless here, like Rosa Parks, whose Detroit house was recently slated for demolition. After Parks's niece Rhea MacCauley had exhausted her appeals to local authorities, she purchased the structure for $500 and caught the attention of an American artist living in Germany, Ryan Mendoza. He painstakingly took the house apart and paid much for its transport to Berlin, where it has become a popular museum. Why did this house have to be taken across the Atlantic to be saved? Why did the largest black city in the nation not have sufficient interest and resources to save it?[8]

As *Me and My House* has shown, the aesthetics and politics of Baldwin's private life are inextricably entwined with—and offer great insights into—the aesthetics and politics of his art. This approach draws on Baldwin's own and Audre Lorde's masterful blending of fiction and life writing, as well as on rich and diverse scholarship that explores how life writing and autobiography interact with material culture, objects, place, history, archives, and affect by Saidiya Hartman, Jane Bennett, Katherine McKittrick, Lisa Lowe, Brent Hays Edwards, Sidonie Smith, E. Patrick Johnson, Francesca Royster, Christina Sharpe, Kim Gallon, Angel David Nieves, Marisa Parham, and Christopher Reed, among others.[9] Originally trained in feminist literary theory, I am committed to interdisciplinary scholarship that values *both* the personal and the political, both the work and the person who has created it as fascinating literary and literal, narrative and material, awesome human/inhuman creations. Aware that some of my readers may remain skeptical, I accept that and welcome productive discussion and challenges to my perspective, keeping in mind Addison Gayle's defense of Baldwin and how I have adapted his prescription for literary critics to my purposes in these pages, devoting my work "not to spurious theories of art for art's sake, but to art for the sake of Black people everywhere."[10]

While it is clear that the Beinecke Library will never house the surviving Chez Baldwin archive, I am currently discussing such a possibility with the terrific curators at the National Museum of African American History and Culture (NMAAHC). I visited there in September 2016 for a soft opening and was immediately heartened by the creative and bold vision it embraces in retelling the story of American national identity with blackness and the objects pertaining to it, and in fact defining it, at the center. Baldwin's words matter to that space devoted to black history and culture; they adorn the walls in huge gold font, while his typewriter is on permanent display, and the collection of papers, artifacts, and ephemera related to this key twentieth-century figure is growing.

Baldwin's embrace and application of history in his works throw the fact of his house's demolition and erasure into stark relief.[11] As a companion project to this book, I thus plan to build a digital humanities–based Writer's House and Museum for James Baldwin in collaboration with the NMAAHC and the University of Michigan. Offering rich visual documentation of the milieu that enabled the writing of his late works, this project will resist the material erasure of Baldwin's life in the United States and France, and elucidate the unequal valuation of black and white literary legacies.

Methodologically, I situate this companion project between the imperatives of Baldwin's literary apparatus—biography, life writing, autoethnography, and genre experimentation—and material and visual culture narratives arising from his home site, which inflected his late authorship. My goal is to invite audiences to follow the enduring traces of his writing life by means of a virtual tour of his last abode that will lead to two levels of narrative/scholarly commentary. Interweaving digital pictorial and video-recorded documentation of the house, its interiors, and grounds, the visual tour highlights architectural detail, garden, and salvaged objects, and it frames Baldwin's transformation from a nomad—or "transatlantic commuter," as he called himself—into a homeowner. Two more narrative levels, accessible through several portals within the visual tour, will provide deeper contextualization and analysis of the site. The first level will offer vignettes of literary and biographical commentary that relates specific spaces and architectural elements of the house to Baldwin's works. The second narrative level, accessible from within the visual and literary tours, will offer a life-writing-inflected account detailing the chronologies, methods, processes, and approaches to documenting and discovering the house's history via onsite research, interviews with the author's friends and family members, and correspondence with various actors in his life. Reflecting on the complex processes of digital research, this level links Baldwin's autobiographical approach to authorship to African American studies scholarship, and it will guide undergraduate and graduate students toward digitally based humanities scholarship by elucidating how social space and literature exist in symbiotic, complex material and metaphorical relationships within and without the books, buildings, and

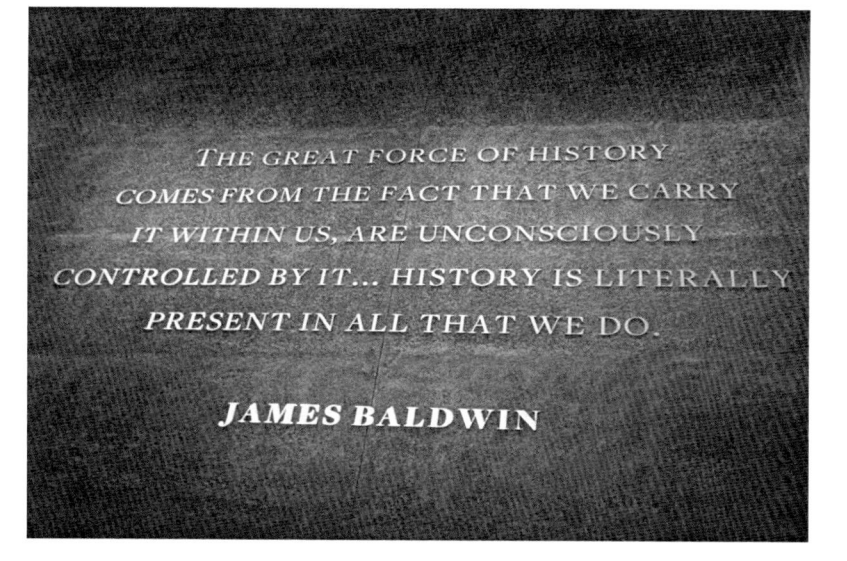

5.4. Plaque at the National Museum of African American History and Culture. Photo by author, 2016.

5.5. The interior of the National Museum of African American History and Culture. Photo by author, 2016.

bodies that create and inhabit them.¹² I show a few examples of how this works in the coda to this chapter.

HOUSE HAUNTING

Entering any physical authorial terrain where collaborations between a writer and his/her/their domestic spaces once took place—a house, studio, or garden—a visitor may be overwhelmed by the traces, imagined and experienced, that the writer's presence and texts have imprinted on it. That visitor may approach the house as theater, as Diana Fuss suggests, or as a space to be manipulated, as Baldwin does in his *Architectural Digest* farewell piece. While taking it all in, and compelled by the singularity of his/her/their experience, the visitor may also feel the need to script their own performance, imagined or desired, to create overlays that express a personal, even intimate version of the writer's imagined habitation. This happens especially in places like Baldwin's that have faced erosion, decline, destruction, and literal erasure.

Visitors to any writer's house might also struggle, knowingly or not, with the effects of what I term an "affective haunting." This term arises from my own interactions with Chez Baldwin in 2000 and 2014, and in the aftermath of my last trip there, in June 2017. In the course of that last trip, I was finally able to complete the painstaking documentation of its archive of leftover objects for my digital house-museum project in progress, and for the NMAAHC, to facilitate their possible acquisition. The term "affective haunting" has also something to do with my long-ago visit to "Kuncewiczówka"—the house of the famous Polish American writer Maria Kuncewicz—in Kazimierz nad Wisłą in Poland in the early 1990s, where I was then researching a dissertation that later became my first book.

The "affective haunting" that I experienced in both these locations can be described as a process of becoming fixated on images, memories, impressions, sensory input, and a recall of objects that contact with the place imprints on the senses, or in the so-called mind's eye, during and long after the visit, and oftentimes in its anticipation, too.¹³ This embodied emotional connection must reflect our primal memories of home in some ways, and thus influence, overlay, and color our recall of the writer's abode to a degree, and on levels that are hard to account for. Consider dreams, which Baldwin places as bookends of Hall's narrative in *Just above My Head*, and which Leeming's biography confirms as an important component in his artistic process. Dreams are something that I have experienced vividly after seeing Kuncewiczówka and then Chez Baldwin, dreams that came the night after each visit and that featured the writers I had never met in the flesh, but who appeared in impressionistic sequences inspired and framed by the interiors of their houses, and communicated powerful emotions to me. Does it matter whether the emotions were mine or imagined as theirs? Not so much, I think; what is significant is that even as researchers and literary scholars we cannot disconnect from the complex creative and imaginative processes that propel our work. These processes are often personal, at times painful, and often reach *further* than, or even *away from*, the extent of our "research"; they always demand and arise from rigorous labor.[14] The trouble one finds while researching Baldwin is precisely that "further" and "away" space, for he forces one not only to pay attention to it, but also to dwell in that uncertain space, however uncomfortably, as a condition of coming closer to his complex message. To some of us, that sense of dwelling in Baldwin, as it were, has a lasting, haunting quality, and it helps to understand the physical confrontation with the spaces he once inhabited.

The kind of affective haunting involving a writer's house that I have in mind, then, takes place in addition to, and perhaps in no small measure due to, preconceptions that visitors bring with them and that also arise from the assumptions, expectations, and knowledge of the works created in that particular authorial home space. As we read, we become imprinted with the structure of the text, its syntax, cadence, style, and the so-called feel of the work that commingles with the imaginaries we have already gleaned from our reading (and dreaming) of other works.[15] In the case of Chez Baldwin, one would arrive in St. Paul-de-Vence full of impressions of the books penned by the author of *The Evidence of Things Not Seen* (1985) that would certainly color, or throw shade on, the house and its environs in *Just above My Head* (1979) and *Beale Street* (1974), among others, as well as facts and photographs gleaned from the available biographies and documentary film footage. Along with all the layers of personal experience and foreknowledge, including those obtained in electronic formats, one also brings hopes and desires regarding one's confrontation with the space, those private and, yes, always political, feelings that are never far from the passionately beheld object of one's inquiry, no matter how "objective" (hopelessly enough, as Baldwin might add) one strives to be.

Finally, following the visit, there is stuff one has collected: documentation, or images and video footage uploaded from the digital camera or smartphone, impressions written in a journal or typed into a file on a computer screen. Then there are souvenirs recorded on and in the body—a scratched knee and bruised elbow from a fall, a smudge of soot from a fireplace one

5.6. Side view of an entrance at Chez Baldwin. Photo by author, 2014.

inspected too closely, auditory memory of the sound of creaking shutters upstairs, little noises under the kitchen sink that reminded one how ridiculously scared one was of rats, fatigue mixed with joy—in short, all the mixed-up material and metaphorical effects as well as affective and sensory recall of the space. Such impressions, memories, and artifacts that remain with us after the visit are not easy, or even entirely possible, to sort out and articulate without resorting to imaginaries, vocabulary, and images that invite the esoteric and the uncanny, and that complement Darell Fields's and Gaston Bachelard's complex phenomenology of interpenetrating literature and architecture with which I started this project.[16]

Approaching visual or photographic records, as well as visual arts in general, from the perspective of interdisciplinary geography, Elisabeth Roberts defines images as "operat[ing] at different and changing affective, representational, material and ideological registers." Taking an approach she calls "hauntological," she argues that it allows us to view images as clusters of opposites, or "as both representation *and* presentation, still *and* animate, dead *and* alive like the ghost," for the reason that images have the ability to haunt "between the visible and invisible, real and virtual, as material objects and abstract cognitive ... processes."[17] After all, we live in a world that has long accepted the interpenetration of the real and haunted, of matter and metaphor, the physical and metaphysical, or as the editors of the volume *Popular Ghosts* remark, "It seems that ghosts are everywhere these days.... [They have] entered, and are indeed part of, the popular realm.... The everyday ... [is] fundamentally intertwined with the ghostly."[18]

Most important for my purposes and clearly echoing Bachelard's much earlier take on imaginings and representations of domestic spaces, Roberts sees images as "embodied, subjective processes" that have an impact well beyond superficial sensory perception.[19] Such an approach resonates productively with Avery Gordon's claim that "scholars too are subject to these same

5.7. Material layering: Newspaper clipping about Baldwin on top of my notes, on top of David Baldwin's memorial service program, at Jill Hutchinson's. Photo by author, 2014.

BLACK LIFE MATTERS OF VALUE 307

dynamics of haunting: ghosts get in our matters as well.... Ghostly matters are part of social life."[20] Writing from within the field of sociology, she subverts received approaches and methodologies in favor of "conjuring [as a process that] merges the analytical, the procedural, the imaginative, and the effervescent," again somewhat like Bachelard's aforementioned phenomenological house poetics; a "counterpart to reification, the conjuring trick, might be better captured by Walter Benjamin's profane illumination or Marx's sensuous knowledge."[21] As Marina Warner's *Phantasmagoria* describes, "Artists, performers, and writers who are grasping the imaginary fabric that swathes and freights our consciousness today" must face the influence of technologies as "the prime shaper of human identity now and recognize their effects, engage with social issues, and revision the seductiveness of illusions as a first step to dreaming them differently."[22] As critics, scholars, and teachers, we are part of this picture, too.

In quite a different context, Sharon Holland speaks of "re-memory" and witnessing the "power" of an event and location, of people and ideas encountered as containing a complex and complete experience, "the good, the bad, and at times, the ugly."[23] She also notes that to multiply marginalized people, black queers especially, "the bittersweet tonic that many of us refer to as 'home'" is more often than not, as Harlem was to Baldwin, both a "place of refuge and escape"; it "is a four-letter word and the practice of black queer/quare studies embodies all of its double meanings."[24] Alain de Botton's rather practical approach speaks of love of home as "an acknowledgment of the degree to which our identity is not self-determined," our need for it as psychological and physical, given that in the largely hostile world we "need a refuge to shore up our states of mind ... [and] our rooms to align us to desirable versions of ourselves."[25] Their ideas help explain, among other things, how my dreams affected my understanding not only of my immediate experience of the writer's house, but also my imagined writer on a plane that was quite removed from, and yet necessary to, the intellectual.

As Baldwin explains multiple times, much of his work process is not cerebral at all, involving dreams, fleeting emotions, "stirrings," and other mysterious workings of imagination, instinct, and gut that are all housed in the ever-changing material-metaphysical-mindful human body. Most important, all these components, physiological and cerebral pieces, and material and metaphorical ephemera of person, place, and performance attending the creative process are part and parcel of what he means by the "work." Baldwin requires and demands from us what he has always delivered himself: serious labor, sometimes in unbelievably large quantities. Those who approach his writings and vision with the seriousness they deserve must be prepared that the work will not be easy. And that is exactly how he would have wanted it.

The archive that has assembled and disassembled itself throughout this book, the haunting, fragmented portrait of the writer, requires a suspension of disbelief that every good reader of literature is eager to embrace on the one hand, and an open mind toward digital documentation that has become an inextricable part of our world, and of humanities research, on the other.[26] My visits to Baldwin's house brought about its material documentation, consisting of mostly digital images and video clips (of his books, art, typewriter, records, and clippings, files, photos, and abandoned objects), and of some material artifacts like chrome slides and prints, impressions, notes, recorded interviews, the novels *Another Country* and *Tell Me* in their Polish translations, an issue of *The Nation* magazine with his essay "Notes on the House of Bondage" listed on the front page, two yellowed sheets of stationery with his name and address on it, and one brass button found on the floor of what was once his study. Along with imagined reminders and remnants, these material items form part of an eclectic vitrine arrangement—an assemblage-like portrait of fragments of Baldwin's domesticity that I have excavated and preserved, that I have also, in part, arranged in these pages. These images, objects, and memories have moved me, inspired me, haunted me even, and would not leave me alone until the idea of this book, *Me and My House*, came about and began, with all the usual vicissitudes of writing and rewriting, to take shape.

This project has also been a leap of faith into new terrains where human identity dwells and is imagined these days. These go beyond dichotomies that describe them; they are both esoteric and vibrant; they contain human and animal bodies, as much as material objects and technologies; they are haunted by easy access to images of and objects from the past and seductive fantasies of the future; they can overwhelm and overpower our senses or diminish them, as much as they enhance or strip us of our humanity. As Jane Bennett explains this new form of materialism, while "it is important to follow the trail of human power to expose social hegemonies . . . there is also public value in following the scent of a nonhuman, thingly power, the material agency of natural bodies and technological artifacts." In such a landscape, "organic and inorganic bodies, natural and cultural objects . . . *all* are affective" and we are faced with "a conception of self . . . as itself an impure, human-non-human assemblage."[27] The photographs and leftover objects from Baldwin's house thus conjure up another stage, too, one on which the writer and the reader can play along together. Counterbalancing the materialist approach, this one entails the reader's, the critic's, and even the scholar's willingness to embrace the elusive realms where literature and the literary take place, the mysterious spaces between the real and phantasmagoric, between the seen and imagined, between the material and metaphorical, between word and thought, sensation and feeling.[28] My descriptions of Baldwin's domestic space are sensitive to such literary hauntings and affects, at the same time as they also deliberately echo the author's own in *Architectural Digest*, approaching Chez Baldwin as a character, much like the writer who occupied it, for such a pairing and collaboration dominate his own narrative.

Baldwin's writerly domestication in St. Paul-de-Vence involves processes of manipulation and imaginative transformation, of dreaming and staging, and, yes, haunting and being haunted, too, to which he gives voice in his works, and whose traces and ghostly presence we can imagine by sifting through the elusive, deteriorating archive of whatever remains of his life in St. Paul-de-Vence. Such an approach brings together, in its final recall, my conceptual triad of space-self-story with the always racialized, gendered, and sexualized politics of and discourses on poetics of social space and vision. The resulting narratives of identity, of Baldwin's many lives and personas, resonate with the larger project of twenty-first-century rereadings of the African Diaspora, or a "disordered" and "difficult" diaspora, literary forms that Samantha Pinto claims we ought to mine for the "'aesthetics of identity,' not just a politics to be narrated."[29] As a writer concerned with gender, place, and national identity, Baldwin lends himself to readings beyond "the lines of nationalist comparativism" that Pinto has in mind and that, as I hope I have shown in this book, can be read as part of a community of writers who "reformulate . . . diaspora through formal innovation," who "constitutively challenge how we conceive and read for signs of race, gender, and transnational geographies, in literature, and beyond its imaginative borders."[30]

And what does this aesthetic have to do with where we are today? When Michelle Obama spoke the following words at the Democratic National Convention in Philadelphia on July 26, 2016, she irrevocably turned a new page in U.S. history: "Today, I wake up every morning in the house that was built by slaves. And I watch my daughters, two beautiful, intelligent young black women, playing with their dogs on the White House lawn." The White House still wears a coat of paint proving its name, but its inhabitants—descendants of the triangular slave trade and of African and European immigrations—finally reflected the true identity of the people this most representative of national houses should bring together in one family. This is

5.8. My son at the side entry to the kitchen in 2014.

the America that Baldwin dreamed up decades ago, where my son, Cazmir Thomas-Jordan Zaborowska, now sixteen years old, and imprinted by African American, Native American, Ashkenazi, Slavic, Asian, and Middle Eastern ancestry, fits in easily. It is the place where he feels at home almost as much as he does in my native Poland, thanks to his bilingualism and frequent visits. I say "almost" for I detest Poland's current right-wing government and its openly racist policies; its God-and-country nationalism, misogyny, and homophobia, repel and frighten me. What has been happening there has, alas, prepared me for what has come here, in my adopted U.S. home, in the wake of the 2016 presidential election.

Whenever we visit Poland, my home for roughly the first half of my life, I tremble for my child's safety almost like I do in the United States. The "almost" is both ironic and tragic, for, truth be told, I do not tremble for my son's safety as badly in Poland as I do in the United States, in Michigan, where he was born and where we still live, for I know, and it breaks my heart that Caz now knows, too, that nowhere else in the western world are black people more menaced than they are here, in the "home of the brave and the land of the free."[31] Baldwin's words come to mind, as they often do, this time from a 1985 interview at his house in St. Paul-de-Vence with Henry Louis Gates Jr.: "The truth of American history was not and had never been in the White House. The truth is what had happened to black people, since slavery."[32] Now that the White House is no longer the family home of the Obamas, Baldwin makes us realize that we must demand not just some new pages, but whole new volumes of American history that disclose its white nationalist and racist underpinnings without covering and sentimentalism. Recent Charlottesville, VA, white supremacist and Nazi marchers spring from the very core, rather than a shameful margin, of that fact-based history.[33]

Since Baldwin's passing in 1987, the Cold War ended; we have had the first two-term African American president in the White House; Poland joined the European Union in 2004; and marriage equality became federal law in the United States. His words in the epigraph for this chapter refer to "witnesses . . . [and] people who've disappeared" and to the vitality of his vision as someone who saw not only his writing but also day-to-day life as an art demanding passionate commitment and hard work. He has been our witness and will never disappear from our memory as one of our most needed ancestors, forbears, and prophets in this still-divided and contentious national house. As I write this, his words—"Everything is always around and before you. Novels that haven't worked, loves, struggles. And yet it all gives you something of immeasurable power"—strike me with their stubborn optimism and faith in human resilience.[34] He was able to say these words and to have a sense of that "immeasurable power" because he not only was a great, unique human being, but also was supported and nurtured at the home he forged at Chez Baldwin.

We are all minds enclosed in bodies that experience pain, illness, discomfort—bodies that give us joy and pleasure, and enable our work, passion, birthing, and care of others. To think of it in Baldwinian terms, as a badly needed script for the humanities today, we must live and teach, write and speak, while fully aware of embodiment in a common human home, while remaining present as material beings that recognize their own joy and suffering as the reflection of the joy and suffering of others. Writers like Baldwin, who suffered the markings of difference, yet insisted that our unique origins and selves were something that made all people kin, show us why our job in the humanities is both never-ending and necessary. Baldwin spoke often about the need for a metaphorical, spiritual even, vital touching and being touched by others, as much as the need for its material implementation in terms of genuine human contact that acknowledges and celebrates connection, commonality of suffering, and understanding despite difference, politics, and the ravages of history.

At Chez Baldwin, his idea encompassed the passionate embraces of lovers and the nurturing "laying on of hands" to comfort friends and family members, a daily routine of tender attention. As Leeming recalls, Baldwin required all those living under his roof, men especially, to greet others with a look in the eye and kisses on both cheeks. His insistence on men being close with each other and embracing what were seen as "feminine," if not sissy, gestures stands in stark contrast to the brutal experience he underwent during his first trip to the South, in 1957, when he was groped by a powerful white politician. That incident frightened him as much for its baseness as for its "assumption of a swift and grim complicity," whose historical underpinnings could, indeed, be traced back to the times of slavery. As he concludes that story in *No Name in the Street*, he saw it as indicative of a larger problem: "The despair among the loveless is that they must narcotize themselves before they can touch any human being at all.... They no longer have any way of knowing that any loveless touch is a violation, whether one is touching a man or a woman" (63).

When asked, yet again, why he deployed his life story so much in his works, Baldwin explains in a late interview, "Every writer has only one tale to tell, and he has to find a way of telling it until the meaning becomes clearer and clearer, until the story becomes at once more narrow and larger, more and more precise and more and more reverberating." That is why it took him fifteen years to even mention the groping incident in *No Name*, for the process of writing is also one of reinhabiting the past: "You begin to see more than you did before in the same event. It reveals itself—more ... you become less frightened because there is less to be frightened of—quite unconsciously."[35] Fear and terror were an inherent part of Baldwin's American national house, and they also invaded the private spaces of his childhood home, the streets of Harlem where he grew up, and the churches where he preached as a child evangelist. That is why it took him until his last novel, *Just above My Head*, to deal with certain memories, to domesticate certain traumas and their meanings.

As he muses on his work in 1984, it is simply something he must do, and for this we owe him a tremendous debt for showing us what we look like now: "I don't try to be prophetic, as *I don't sit down to write literature*. It is simply this: a writer has to take all the risks of putting down what he sees....

5.9. An upstairs window opening onto the garden in the back.
Photo by author, 2014.

It reminds me of something Pablo Picasso was supposed to have said to Gertrude Stein while he was painting her portrait. Gertrude said, 'I don't look like that.' And Picasso replied, 'You will.' And he was right."[36]

His house, of which no more than a shell remains, still nestles inside the remaining ruin, that last room, in which Baldwin's life ended surrounded by the care and love of his friends, family, and lovers. Its frescoes melting into moldy stains on the walls, it has kept an imprint of the events, the people, and their words and dreams that we must continue to read and strive to remember and preserve by any means necessary.

NOTES

INTRODUCTION

1. Leeming, *James Baldwin*, 376. *No Papers for Mohammed* was "based on Baldwin's own recent scare with the French immigration authorities and on the case of an Arab friend whom he had hired as a gardener and who had been deported to Algeria" (314).

2. I presented this project at the "'A Language to Dwell In': James Baldwin, Paris, and International Visions" conference at the American University of Paris in May, and during the meeting of the Digital Humanities Caucus at the American Studies Association meeting in November 2016.

3. See McKittrick, "Plantation Futures."

4. See Downs, "Not a Dream Deferred." See also Royal, "Kali-Ma Nazarene"; Royal, "Interview with Kali-Ma Nazarene."

5. Ghansah, "Weight of James Arthur Baldwin" (contains factual errors); T. C. Williams, "Breaking into James Baldwin's House"; Field, "On Breaking into James Baldwin's House."

6. Hodder, *Entangled*, 14.

7. Hodder, *Entangled*, 38–39. See also Lowe, *Intimacies of Four Continents*, on the historical underpinnings of "intimacies across continents in relation to the more dominant concept of intimacy as the property of the individual, often configured as conjugal and familial relations in the bourgeois home distinguished from the public realm of work, society, and politics" (28).

8. D. Miller, *Stuff*, 52–54.

9. See also Homi K. Bhabha, "The World and the Home," in Briganti and Mezei, *Domestic Space Reader*, 358–62, on the "unhomely" and being "unhomed"; these concepts, contextualized with Henry James's works in mind, fit Baldwin's situation as well. De Waal's *Hare with Amber Eyes* provides another interesting context as a memoir with a focus on material objects.

10. Troupe, "Last Interview (1987)," 189. See also "Introduction: What Is Domestic Space?," in Briganti and Mezei, *Domestic Space Reader*, on the changing meaning of the term, given that "the immense reach and influence of global and transnational economies have provoked a contrary desire for the local and the domestic quote which has increased the scrutiny of the home" (4).

11. Troupe, "Last Interview (1987)," 190–91. See also Standley and Pratt, *Conversations*, 79, 64–82.

12. Standley and Pratt, *Conversations*, 242.

13. Baldwin was accompanied by his brother David. See Clemens, *Can Russia Change?*, 204n41, 286n61; Clines, "Peter Ustinov Talks of Gorbachev's Chat."

14. This interview, conducted by an unidentified woman, is available on YouTube, posted July 31, 2009, by Afrikanliberation. I've been unable to locate its source. Baldwin identifies his age as fifty-six years old; hence it must have been made in 1980: "James Baldwin—Interview—Pt. 1."

15. See M. Elam, "Review," and her assessment of his complex legacies on 203–4.

16. See photos of the Horatio Street event, sponsored by the Greenwich Village Society for Historic Preservation and the Two Boots Foundation: "James Baldwin Plaque, 81 Horacio Street," October 7, 2015, https://www.flickr.com/photos/gvshp/sets/72157657300335823.

17. Created in 1993 by the actor and director Samuel Légitimus, "Collectif James Baldwin de Paris" operates a website and a Facebook page; Karen Thorsen, the director of *James Baldwin: The Price of the Ticket*, has initiated a complex public humanities database called "The James Project," whose website links events and venues that include "Conversations with Jimmy" at colleges, universities, and town halls in conjunction with showings of her documentary. I am among the scholar-advisors for http://jamesbaldwinproject.org/.

18. I peg Peck's production as an "art film" because its narrative design, visual composition, and overall effect echo much more Sedat Pakay's endeavor than Karen Thorsen's, these two masterworks from 1973 and 1989, respectively, being the eminent genre placeholders for an art film and a documentary in the Baldwin cinematic canon.

19. Hélène Roux Jeandheur, interview with the author, August 28, 2017.

20. See also Dayson, "Another Country."

21. See Zaborowska, *Other Americans, Other Americas*.

22. Cass Adair, a Ph.D. candidate at the University of Michigan, drew my attention to the *New York Times* accounting of that event: Frank S. Adams, "Columbia Student Kills Friend and Sinks Body in Hudson River," August 17, 1944. See also Zaborowska, *Other Americans, Other Americas* and "From Baldwin's Paris to Benjamin's." See also Baym, "Melodramas of Beset Manhood," and Brown and Clark, "Melodramas of Beset Black Manhood?"

23. See Gleason, *Sites Unseen*, 26–27.

24. Tate, *Domestic Allegories of Political Desire*, 8.

25. Nicholson, Interview with James Baldwin.

26. See Zaborowska, *James Baldwin's Turkish Decade*.

27. Said, *Culture and Imperialism*, xvii.

28. Said, *Culture and Imperialism*, xviii.

29. See Homans, *Women Writers and Poetic Identity*; Ostriker, *Stealing the Language*; Gilbert and Gubar, *Norton Anthology of Literature by Women*; Showalter, *Sister's Choice*; DuPlessis, *Writing beyond the Ending*; Yaeger, *Honey-Mad Women*; Benstock, *Private Self*. For examples of early scholarship on black womanhood, see Christian, *Black Feminist Criticism*; Nfah-Abbenyi, *Gender in African Women's*

Writing; Boyce-Davies, *Black Women, Writing, and Identity*; Pryse and Spillers, *Conjuring*; McDowell, *"The Changing Same"*; B. Smith, "Toward a Black Feminist Criticism"; Wall, *Changing Our Own Words*; Combahee River Collective, *Combahee River Collective Statement*.

30. See also Zaborowska, "'In the Same Boat.'"

31. The deep imprint of this history on the minds of those who consider themselves and their country "white" was clear during the U.S. 2016 presidential election.

32. Spillers, "Mama's Baby," 67, 72. "Domesticity appears to gain its power by way of a common origin of cultural fictions that are grounded in the specificity of proper names, more exactly, a patronymic, which, in turn, situates those persons it 'covers' in a particular place. Contrarily, the cargo of a ship might not be regarded as elements of the domestic, even though the vessel that carries it is sometimes romantically (ironically?) personified as 'she'" (72).

33. Engels and Untermann, *Origin of the Family*. See Matthews, *"Just a Housewife"*; Hansen, *African Encounters with Domesticity*; Briganti and Mezei, *Domestic Space Reader*.

34. See also Spillers, "Mama's Baby," which sketches a broad picture of the foundational "grammar" of American social space patterns since the times of slavery: "The point remains that captive persons were forced into patterns of dispersal, beginning with the Trade itself, into the horizontal relatedness of language groups, discourse formations, bloodlines, names, and properties by the legal arrangements of enslavement" (75). See also Green-Barteet, "Loophole of Retreat"; Ellis and Ginsburg, *Cabin, Quarter, Plantation*; Vlach, *Back of the Big House*. I continue this thread in subsequent chapters.

35. The few exceptions are Dixon, *Ride Out the Wilderness*, which has a brilliant chapter on Baldwin that traces how John Grimes's evolution in *Go Tell It* interrogates spatial concepts of the "mountain" and "threshing floor" (123–33) and Baldwin's "underlying theme that exposes the claustrophobia inherent in the limited space claimed by religious, sexual, or racial exclusivity" (133); Reddinger, "'Just Enough for the City'"; Mills, "Cleaver/Baldwin Revisited." See also Doug Field's rich essays "Looking for Jimmy Baldwin" and especially "On Breaking into James Baldwin's House."

36. See also Harris, *Black Women*, 206; Wall, *Worrying the Line*, 15.

37. See Reed, "Imminent Domain"; McKinney, "Leibovitz and Sontag"; Gorman-Murray, "Queering Home or Domesticating Deviance?" All three concern white queerness. Reid-Pharr's *Conjugal Union* is a brilliant exception, as is Johnson's *Sweet Tea*. Other studies include Tongson, *Relocations*; Shah, "Perversity, Contamination, and the Dangers of Queer Domesticity"; D. Morton, *Material Queer*; Retter et al., *Queers in Space*; Bell and Valentine, *Mapping Desire*; and Johnston and Longhurst, *Space, Place, and Sex*.

38. Yet another reason is the reluctance, if not outright refusal, of mainstream American culture and political discourses to embrace all the diverse inhabitants of the national house, and thus change how we imagine domesticity, especially given the passage of marriage equality in June 2015.

39. See Bachelard, *Poetics of Space*; Foucault and Miskowiec, "Of Other Spaces"; Benjamin, *Illuminations* and *Arcades Project*; and de Certeau, *Practice of Everyday Life*.

40. Publications on home and domesticity often elide race, taking whiteness as a universal and unmarked category, for example, Cieraad, *At Home*; the best approach the concept from an interdisciplinary black studies perspective that links urban and rural locations, literature and architecture, like Gleason's *Sites Unseen*, Hayden's *Power of Place*, or Vlach's *Back of the Big House*.

41. Du Bois et al., *Souls of Black Folk*, 11.

42. See Gilroy, *Black Atlantic*; Morrison, *Playing in the Dark*; West, *Race Matters*; as well as Muñoz, *Disidentifications*, and Lowe's recent take on transnational material culture, *Intimacies of Four Continents*.

43. McKittrick, "Plantation Futures," 2.

44. Kristeva, *Strangers to Ourselves*, 1, emphases added. Kristeva's model reflects the etymology of the word *foreigner* as having a feminine gendered dimension in original Greek.

45. See Appiah, *Ethics of Identity*, on cosmopolitanism as contingent on "a world of cultural and social variety as a precondition for the self-creation that is at the heart of a meaningful human life" (268).

46. See Clark, *Black Manhood in James Baldwin*, 34, 48.

47. Rogoff, *Terra Infirma*, 34. See McBride's "Can the Queen Speak?" on "the critical hazards of privileging the category of race in any discussion of black people. When we give 'race,' with its retinue of historical and discursive investments, primacy over other signifiers of difference, the result is a network of critical blindnesses which prevent us from perceiving the ways in which the conventions of race discourse get naturalized and normativized" (371).

48. Rogoff, *Terra Infirma*, 35. See Kennedy, *Race and Urban Space*, 8–10.

49. Weisman, *Discrimination by Design*, 2.

50. McKittrick and Woods, *Black Geographies*, 3, 4.

51. See Eva Hoffman's notion of "triangulation" in *Lost in Translation*; also Zaborowska, *How We Found America*; and Wilkins, *Aesthetics of Equity*, 107–8. I return to this theme in chapter 4.

52. See http://americanwritersmuseum.org/ (accessed December 11, 2016). Of more than fifty houses and museums featured on the site, only two belong to African Americans (Douglass's and Haley's).

53. Kaplan and Schwarz, *James Baldwin*, 127.

54. See, for example, Bloom, *James Baldwin*; Crouch, *Notes of a Hanging Judge*. See also these rigorous earlier volumes: Kinnamon, "Native Son"; O'Daniel, *James Baldwin*; Standley and Burt, *Critical Essays on James Baldwin*. The latter two offer essays that may seem controversial or even shocking today.

55. See also Chametzky, *A Tribute to James Baldwin*; Standley and Pratt, *Conversations*.

56. Lovalerie King, introduction to King and Scott, *James Baldwin and Toni Morrison*, 1.

57. Als, "Snaps: 1955–1965," 26.

58. The very same photograph opens Henry Louis Gates Jr.'s essay, dated June 1, 1992, "From the Stacks: 'The Fire Last Time,'" published in the *New Republic* on August 2, 2013.

59. Als, "Snaps: 1955–1965." See Ross, "Some Glances at the Black Fag," especially his comments on race and segregation on page 169. See also Ross, "Baldwin's Sissy Heroics"; this piece uses my reading of the groping incident in NNS without acknowledging it.

60. Leo can be seen as rewriting western modern characters like Joyce's Bloom or Stephen Dedalus, or even Ellison's in *Invisible Man*.

61. Dixon, *Ride Out the Wilderness*, 7.

62. Rankine, *Citizen*, 11. See also Terrie M. Williams, *Black Pain*, which, in the guise of a self-help book, engages some of these issues.

63. Coates, *Between the World and Me*, 22. I admire this book but disagree with Morrison that Coates fills the vacuum left by Baldwin. He borrows very heavily from *Fire*, and the very phrase he uses for his title comes from Baldwin's preface to the 1984 edition of *Notes of a Native Son* in which the writer interrogates his search for identity as an artist ("between that self and me, the accumulated rock of ages," ix). More borrowings can be traced to the opening pages of ETNS.

64. Standley and Pratt, *Conversations*, 171; Gayle, "Defense of James Baldwin," 206; Gayle, "Function of Black Criticism," 40.

65. Standley and Pratt, *Conversations*, 171; Ross, "Beyond the Closet as Raceless Paradigm"; Ross, "Camping the Dirty Dozens."

66. Some writers use Baldwin as an inspiration for their characters. See Jonathan Lethem, *The Fortress of Solitude* (New York: Vintage, 2004); and Sarah Shulman, *The Cosmopolitans* (New York: Feminist Press, 2016), which quotes from several of Baldwin's books.

67. See also Ken Warren on Baldwin as straddling a literary historical divide in *What Was African American Literature?*, 74–75.

68. See Avilez, "Housing the Black Body."

69. See the "Emotions" special issue of *PMLA* (October 2015). See also Grosz, *Volatile Bodies*, on the origins of perspectival access to space (47–48).

70. Hansberry, *To Be Young*, xiv.

71. Black Lives Matter Organization, http://blacklivesmatter.com/.

72. See Elam and Alexander, *The Fire This Time*; Kenan, *The Fire This Time*; Alexander's concluding chapter, "The Fire This Time," in *The New Jim Crow*; Ward, *The Fire This Time*.

73. See also Boggs, "'James Baldwin: The Last Interview and Other Conversations' by James Baldwin."

74. See chapter 5 on the recent sale of the Baldwin papers by his estate to the Schomburg Center for Research on Black Culture in New York in April 2017; New York Public Library, "Schomburg Center for Research in Black Culture Acquires Papers."

75. See also Weheliye, *Habeas Viscus*.

76. See Truszczyńska, "Widoczki znane też jako sekrety": "Ta zabawa to jak widać również trafny opis stosunków mających miejsce w 'dorosłym' życiu—mnóstwo emocji i napięć stworzonych wokół czegoś wymyślonego" (my translation: "That child's play . . . was an accurate description of relationships that took place in grown-up life—lots of emotions and tensions that were created around something that was made up").

77. Zaborowska, *James Baldwin's Turkish Decade*, 41.

78. Dixon's *Ride Out the Wilderness* is among my early inspirations, along with Ralph Ellison's *Shadow and Act* passage that Dixon includes in his introduction: "If we don't know where we are, we have little chance of knowing who we are, that if we confuse the time, we confuse the place; and that when we confuse these we endanger our humanity, both physically and morally" (Ellison, 74; Dixon, 2).

79. Schuessler, "Inside an Author's Oddball Trove of Artifacts."

80. This passage opens *James Baldwin: The Price of the Ticket*, directed by Karen Thorsen.

1. FOUNDATIONS, FAÇADES, AND FACES

1. Thorsen, *James Baldwin: The Price of the Ticket*.

2. He also talks about his birthplace in Thorsen's documentary.

3. Undated interview with Mavis Mainwaring Nicholson on *Mavis on Four* on UK's TV4. The interview was re-aired to commemorate Baldwin's death in December 1987: Nicholson, Interview with James Baldwin.

4. See Cornel West's foreword to Michelle Alexander's *The New Jim Crow*, where he describes her book as "the secular bible for the new social movement" and praises Alexander's uses of "(the great James Baldwin!)" and his *The Fire Next Time* in her searing concluding chapter (ix, x).

5. Transcript, in Standley and Pratt, *Conversations*, 3; interview on WFMT Chicago, broadcast on December 29, 1961. Terkel's *Giants of Jazz* affirms Smith as the Empress of the Blues.

6. See also Pavlić, *Who Can Afford to Improvise?*, especially 6–7, on the "importance of listening, of hearing, and of music," and on how a "song is discourse as experience." Also, on page 232, Pavlić refers to the same quotation from the Terkel interview.

7. Standley and Pratt, *Conversations*, 3, emphasis added. There are slight discrepancies between its published transcript and the interview soundtrack as it currently appears on the Internet: Tony Macaluso, "Studs's Interview with James Baldwin Published," republished on *Neo-Griot* (blog), December 8, 2014, http://kalamu.com/neogriot/2015/07/05/history-audio-james-baldwin-interview-by-studs-terkel/; "James Baldwin Interview: Black Man in America (1961) with Studs Terkel." When I quote from the interview, I usually rely on the transcript included in *Conversations*, but at times I also note the soundtrack's more spontaneous flow, marking it with words in brackets that have been edited out of the printed version. I do so, for

the sounds a body makes while speaking cannot be transcribed: sighs, the noise of a match lighting a cigarette, of Baldwin inhaling and exhaling the smoke—all these are lost in the transcript but can be enjoyed while listening to the recording.

8. Reid-Pharr, in *Once You Go Black*, calls Julia "one of the most finely wrought female characters of Baldwin's career" (115).

9. In *Blues Legacies and Black Feminism*, Angela Davis sees Smith's music as creating "a musical caricature of domesticity" and marking "the beginnings of an oppositional attitude toward patriarchal ideology" (18).

10. See also Pavlić, *Who Can Afford to Improvise?*, on the "notion of the *lyric* as a generally disruptive propensity of language, a metaphorically or literally musical interruption of the report-function usually assigned to what is called prose" (7).

11. Wall, *Worrying the Line*, 16. Wall also notes, echoing Houston Baker, another feature of black women's writing important to my project: "The blues and black vernacular tradition in general both inspire and silence black women; they authorize articulations of self yet too often demean the individual woman who finds the courage to speak" (16).

12. See also Lordi, *Black Resonances*, on Baldwin, Bessie Smith, and Billie Holiday (99–136).

13. See Zaborowska, *James Baldwin's Turkish Decade*, 250–55.

14. See Stuart Hall's definition of diaspora: while "conjuring up a kind of imagined community that would cut across the configurations of cultural nationalism . . . *[it] has been [also] the site of some of the most closed narratives of identity known to human beings*." Hall's warning is that it must not "lodge . . . there for a people who are not going to change, who sat on top of sacred text and erected the barriers, and who then wanted to make the return exactly to the place where they came from. And who have gone back and sat on the head of all the other people who were there, too. If you open yourself to the politics of cultural difference, there is no safety in terminology" ("Subjects in History," 299, emphasis added). See also Édouard Glissant on the "difference between the transplanting (by exile or dispersion) of the people who continue to survive elsewhere and the transfer (by the slave trade) of a population to another place where they *change into something different, into a new set of possibilities*" (Glissant, *Caribbean Discourse*, 13–14, emphasis added).

15. This stance anticipates memoirs of transgender identity, such as Janet Mock's *Redefining Realness*, or ethnographies of black queer domestic life in the South in E. Patrick Johnson's *Sweet Tea*.

16. Auchincloss and Lynch, "Disturber of the Peace"; see also Field, *All Those Strangers*.

17. See Mumford, "Opening the Restricted Box"; Anderson, "Lorraine Hansberry's Letters"; Wright, "Lorraine Hansberry's Gay Politics"; Clements, "The Private Life of Lorraine Hansberry." Clements quotes from an important, unpublished 1961 essay by Hansberry titled "On Homophobia, the Intellectual Impoverishment of Women and a Homosexual 'Bill of Rights,'" which resonates with Baldwin's views on

male homosexuality and American otherness, though he never acknowledged that he knew of her lesbian desire: "I have suspected for a good time that the homosexual in America would ultimately pay a price for the intellectual impoverishment of women. Men continue to misinterpret the second-rate status of women as implying a privileged status for themselves; heterosexuals think the same way about homosexuals; gentiles about Jews; whites about blacks; haves about have-nots."

18. In *No Name, Beale Street*, and his stage version of *Fortune and Men's Eyes* in Istanbul (see Zaborowska, *James Baldwin's Turkish Decade*), Baldwin anticipates recent discussions on the prison-industrial complex in A. Davis, *Are Prisons Obsolete?*; Alexander, *New Jim Crow*; and Gilmore, *Golden Gulag*.

19. See also hooks and Mesa-Bains, *Homegrown*, wherein hooks claims that, after the indigenous people, "African Americans were the first 'homeless' people in this nation" (72); hooks recalls her childhood limited by fundamentalist Christian beliefs: "On Sunday girls couldn't wear pants, we couldn't play music, and we couldn't walk across the pulpit. The pulpit was considered a sacred space that a female—of any age—could not walk across, because she would defile it" (5).

20. Glissant, *Caribbean Discourse*, 196.

21. "Theatrical expression is necessary. . . . In its critical dimension: in order to help destroy alienated forms of representation . . . [and] whereby a people escapes the limitations of the folkloric expression to which it has been reduced" (Glissant, *Caribbean Discourse*, 209).

22. This box as a precious artifact disappeared sometime between 2014 and 2017; on my last visit, in June 2017, its contents were stored in a covered plastic bin.

23. The images may have been taken during either French or Swiss interviews that Baldwin gave in 1971 and 1972 with Pierre Dumayet ("James Baldwin Chez Pierre Dumayet—Lecture Pour Tous (1971)") and with Catherine Charbon ("James Baldwin—L'entretien Suisse—16 Novembre 1972").

24. See Zaborowska, *James Baldwin's Turkish Decade*, 199–201; Leeming and Zaborowska, "Remembering Sedat Pakay."

25. See the useful discussion of how the need for "queer" to combat normativity, or disrupt or otherwise explode it, locks the terms into a binary struggle in Brim, *James Baldwin and the Queer Imagination*.

26. Baldwin's refusal to be labeled brings to mind the widespread, sometimes contested, deployment of "queer," in academic discourses—literary, performance, black queer, and "queer of color" studies—and in the mainstream media. This makes some scholars, for example, Lisa Duggan, worry about its overuse and deployment in the service of "homonormativity." See Duggan, "New Homonormativity."

27. See also Ross, "Some Glances at the Black Fag," 153–73.

28. Christian, "Race for Theory," 78.

29. Duberman confirms the reluctance or inability to understand this when discussing Essex Hemphill's struggle with homophobia in black, as well as white, gay racism in *Hold Tight Gently* (80–83).

30. See Reid-Pharr, *Once You Go Black*: "The privacy and sacredness of the individual and the individual's body must be maintained even and especially at the

moment at which that individual offers up his own life story as a potent metaphor for the reality and the promise of the human condition" (115).

31. See also Dixon, *Ride Out the Wilderness*, 133. Also Griffin, in *"Who Set You Flowin'?,"* saw Baldwin sharing Wright's vision of "the stifling nature of black life" (11). Griffin sees him as a transitional figure, ahead of his time in narrative portrayals of the African American migration (37).

32. See Traub, "New Unhistoricism." I am with her on the fact that "there remain ample reasons to practice a queer historicism dedicated to showing how categories, however mythic, phantasmic, and incoherent, came to be" (33).

33. See Butler, *Gender Trouble*; Johnson, *Appropriating Blackness* and *Sweet Tea*; Nash, *Black Body in Ecstasy*.

34. Williams immediately became the target of racist hatred, which included death threats, after she had been stripped of her title, following unauthorized publication of nude photos of her with a white female model. She received a formal apology during the 2015 pageant, where she served as the head judge. See also Miller-Young, *Taste for Brown Sugar*, xi, 101; Goldsby, "Queen for 307 Days."

35. For an eloquent articulation of this issue in academic discourse, see McBride, "Can the Queen Speak?"

36. Max C. Smith, "By the Year 2000," in Beam, *In the Life*, 226.

37. See also Field, "Looking for Jimmy Baldwin"; Ross, "White Fantasies of Desire"; McBride, "Can the Queen Speak?"; Brody and McBride, "Plum Nelly."

38. Nicholas Delbanco mentioned in an interview with me in 2014 that many in literary circles wondered if Baldwin's own illness might have been caused by HIV. See also Woubshet, *Calendar of Loss*.

39. Woubshet, *Calendar of Loss*, 44.

40. See Zaborowska, *Other Americans, Other Americas*; Clark, *Black Manhood*.

41. See a similar vision of humanity in E. Patrick Johnson's *Sweet Tea* and in Marlon Ross's "sexual-identity theory attuned to the realities and representations of racialized cultures," one that "the current (white) queer theory seems not fully capable of handling" ("Beyond the Closet," 184). See also Reid-Pharr, *Black Gay Man*.

42. Beam, "Brother to Brother," 236–37.

43. Beam, "Brother to Brother," 230.

44. See also McBride, "Can the Queen Speak?," on essentialized approaches to blackness/race. "Any understanding of black oppression that makes it possible, and worse permissible, to endorse at any level sexism, elitism or heterosexism is a vision of black culture that is finally not politically consummate with liberation. We can no more excuse black homophobia than black sexism. One is as politically and, dare I say, morally suspect as the other" (367). (See also introduction note 47, this volume.)

45. See Douglas, *Feminization of American Culture*; Kaplan, "Manifest Domesticity"; McKittrick, *Demonic Grounds*; Tate, *Domestic Allegories of Political Desire*; Reid-Pharr, *Conjugal Union*.

46. See Zaborowska, *James Baldwin's Turkish Decade*, 21–22; and Brim, *James Baldwin and the Queer Imagination*, and his deployment of "paradox as a pointed tool for thinking about queerness" to get away from the unhelpful queer/normative

binary (5, 3–6). (As my colleague Vincent Mendoza recently remarked during a doctoral examination, he was stunned to realize that "queer" was being used so widely and frequently those days that it was becoming a "hegemonic" term.)

47. Johnson, *No Tea, No Shade*, 2. See also Somerville, *Queering the Color Line*, on "compulsory heterosexuality . . . as not simply parallel to discourses of racial segregation but integral to its logic," and what I see as Baldwin's lifelong theoretical project, that "disrupting the naturalized constructions of racial difference involves simultaneously unsettling one's relationship to normative constructions of gender and sexuality" (137).

48. Ahmed, *Willful Subjects*, 11.

49. Ahmed, *Queer Phenomenology*, 1–2, 9–11. See also Ferguson, *Aberrations in Black*; Mendoza, *Metroimperial Intimacies*; Johnston and Longhurst, *Space, Place, and Sex*; Nero, "Queering the Souls of Black Folk" and "Reading Will Make You Queer."

50. See Dixon, *Ride Out the Wilderness*, on "the *discourse on love and shelter*" in *Go Tell It on the Mountain* (124, emphasis added).

51. See also Reid-Pharr, *Once You Go Black*: "The privacy and sacredness of the individual and the individual's body must be maintained even and especially at the moment at which that individual offers up his own life story as a potent metaphor for the reality and the promise of the human condition" (115).

52. The title of this section is taken from Troupe, "Last Interview (1987)," 191.

53. See Zaborowska, *James Baldwin's Turkish Decade*, 260–62.

54. Leeming, *James Baldwin*, 316.

55. Baldwin, "To Crush the Serpent," 70.

56. Baldwin, "To Crush the Serpent," 70. See also Appiah, *Cosmopolitanism*; Doku, *Cosmopolitanism in the Fictive*; Friedel, *Racial Discourse*; Nwankwo, *Black Cosmopolitanism*.

57. Baldwin, "To Crush the Serpent," 70.

58. See also Zaborowska, "'In the Same Boat.'"

59. Standley and Pratt, *Conversations*, 200, emphasis added. See also Lowe on "intimacies" and conceptions of domesticity in the colonial world in *Intimacies of Four Continents*. Again, it is interesting to note that Baldwin's late works articulate already many of the transnational connections that Lowe explores in this study (28–41).

60. See Vlach, *Back of the Big House*, on how slaves were not mere victims, but exercised their agency in a "black system of place definition," to claim "an arena in which they could begin to piece back together their shattered lives" (14, 16).

61. Rifkin, *Manifesting America*, 23.

62. For example, Jacobson, *Whiteness of a Different Color* (1999); Roediger, *The Wages of Whiteness* (1991); Zaborowska, *How We Found America* (1995); Guglielmo, *White on Arrival* (2004); Deloria, *Playing Indian* (1999) and *Indians in Unexpected Places* (2004); Dowd, *War under Heaven* (2004); Mendoza, *Metroimperial Intimacies* (2015); Miles, *Ties That Bind* (2006) and *The House on Diamond Hill* (2012).

63. Rifkin, *Manifesting America*, 23. I support Rifkin's argument concerning the binary model of imperial power in Kaplan's *Anarchy of Empire*. I am grateful to the Ph.D. candidate Michael Pasquale for drawing my attention to this work in our seminar, AC 850 "Advanced Research Colloquium: Professionalization in American Studies" (University of Michigan, Winter 2016).

64. Hall, "Subjects in History," 299. See also Carby, "Becoming Modern Racialized Subjects."

65. Baldwin compares the United States to a house repeatedly throughout his works. As he describes it in "Encounter," that structure is deeply divided between a superficial façade and hidden interior; myth and pretense provide its superficial vision rather than a view of deep history, "each generation greeting with short-lived exultation yet more dazzling additions to our renowned façade" (PT, 39).

66. See Lusane, *Black History of the White House*.

67. Beam, "Making Ourselves from Scratch," 79, in Gross and Woods, *Columbia Reader*. In this work, Beam mentions "powerful people, mentors . . . Audre Lorde, James Baldwin, John Edgar Wideman, Essex Hemphill, Lamont Steptoe, Judy Grahn, Tommi Avicolli, Charles Fuller, Toni Morrison, and Barbara Smith . . . of local and international fame . . . connected by their desire to create images by which they could survive as gays and lesbians, as blacks, and as poor people. Their presence . . . bespeaks what . . . Samuel Delaney, calls 'the possibility of possibilities'" (79–80).

68. See the "Writer's Room" profiles in the *New York Times Style Magazine*, by both Colson Whitehead (February 16, 2014) and Kevin Young (April 17, 2016).

69. Tal, *Worlds of Hurt*, 247.

70. Finney, introduction to Baldwin, *Jimmy's Blues*, ix, xv, xxi.

71. Reid-Pharr, *Conjugal Union*, 131.

72. Reid-Pharr, *Conjugal Union*, 3, 6. On race being first used in the legal discourse in 1640, see *Slavery: The Making of America*.

73. Reid-Pharr, *Conjugal Union*, 131–32, emphasis added.

74. Hatton, "James Baldwin."

75. Troupe, *James Baldwin: The Legacy*, 78.

76. Troupe, *James Baldwin: The Legacy*, 76.

77. Troupe, *James Baldwin: The Legacy*, 78.

2. HOME MATTER

1. Professor Boris Veydovsky, University of Lausanne, kindly hosted my interview with Happersberger.

2. See also Als, "Family Secrets," for insights on the Baldwin-Happersberger relationship.

3. Correspondence with the author, 2009.

4. Reproduced in Leeming, *James Baldwin*, and in Wells, "Brief Musings on Beauford and James Baldwin."

5. I include both dates, as Happersberger seemed unsure which one was correct.

6. Johnson, *Appropriating Blackness*.

7. See Woubshet, "James Baldwin and the Question of Privacy."
8. Holloway, "When a Pariah Becomes a Celebrity," 6.
9. Holloway, "When a Pariah Becomes a Celebrity," 8.
10. Leeming, *James Baldwin*, 345.
11. Baldwin, letter to David Baldwin, February 6, 1979.
12. Leeming, *James Baldwin*, 345.
13. Traylor, "I Hear Music in the Air . . . ," 95–96.
14. Scott, *James Baldwin's Later Fiction*, 129. See Reid-Pharr, "Alas Poor Jimmy," in *Once You Go Black*, 96–118.
15. Scott, *James Baldwin's Later Fiction*, 126.
16. I made this point in *James Baldwin's Turkish Decade* and in an early chapter on *Giovanni's Room* in *Other Americans, Other Americas*. It has been repeated by numerous scholars, most recently, Matt Brim in *James Baldwin and the Queer Imagination*.
17. Henderson and Johnson, *Black Queer Studies*, 7.
18. The etymology and genealogy of "transnational" cut across disciplines and require a separate study. See its first use in Randolph Bourne's "Transnational America" in the *Atlantic Monthly* in July 1916. See also Grewal, *Transnational America*.
19. See Halberstam, *In a Queer Time and Place*; Retter, Bouthillette, and Ingram, *Queers in Space*; Betsky, *Queer Space*.
20. See Zaborowska, *James Baldwin's Turkish Decade*; Brenda Rein, in discussion with the author, May 2007.
21. David Baldwin and David Leeming had a plan to convert the house into a writers' colony, with an investor and an academic institution lined up to purchase and preserve the property.
22. The naming of "James Baldwin Place" is a symbolic gesture, unrelated to a writing space in the sense that, for example, Witold Rybczynski defines it in *Home: A Short History of an Idea*. For a list of American writers' houses, see Trubek, *Skeptic's Guide to Writers' Houses*, 5.
23. See Wilson, *Negro Building*. See also Wilson's definition of "the black counterpublic sphere" and revision of Habermas's theory on pp. 8–10. See also Fields, *Architecture in Black*; Lokko, *White Papers, Black Marks*.
24. Fields, *Architecture in Black*, x.
25. Fields, *Architecture in Black*, 107.
26. Morrison, "Home."
27. Morrison, "Home," 4.
28. Fields, *Architecture in Black*, 194. Fields imagines a house for the artist Kara Walker, linking discourses of blackness in architecture to her art of the silhouette.
29. Morrison, "Home," 12.
30. Bachelard, *Poetics of Space*, xxxvi. Besides Bachelard, I've looked to Walter Benjamin, Michel Foucault, Henri Lefebvre, Leslie Kanes Weisman, Dolores Hayden, and James Chafers, to name only the most important. See also Benjamin, *Arcades Project*; Lefebvre, *Production of Space*; Weisman, *Discrimination by Design*.
31. McKittrick, *Demonic Grounds*, xi. See also Wilkins, *Aesthetics of Equity*, especially 21–26.

32. The genre of the photo-text is best represented by Baldwin's collaboration with Richard Avedon in *Nothing Personal*. See also Blair, *Harlem Crossroads*; Joshua Miller, "Discovery of What It Means to Be a Witness."

33. Holloway, "When a Pariah Becomes a Celebrity," 2. See Leeming, "An Interview with James Baldwin on Henry James."

34. Fuss, *Sense of an Interior*, 1.

35. I echo here wide expanses of Euro-American literary and cultural studies scholarship from Bachelard's aforementioned work, through Derrida's *Specters of Marx*, Warner's *Phantasmagoria*, through Ball's *Traveling Concepts in the Humanities*, to Bennett's *Vibrant Matter*.

36. I return to this in chapter 5.

37. Trubek, *Skeptic's Guide to Writers' Houses*, 5.

38. Trubek, *Skeptic's Guide to Writers' Houses*, 45.

39. Leeming, *James Baldwin*, 313. Thanks to Coleman A. Jordan, my erstwhile partner, for assisting me during that trip.

40. For more information, see Musée et Office de Tourisme, "James Baldwin." See also the French interview "James Baldwin à propos de son enfance à Harlem" and http://savejimmyshouse.blogspot.com/; see also "Disparition de l'écrivain James Baldwin dans sa maison de Saint-Paul de Vence en 1987" for a short French television documentary that aired after Baldwin's death.

41. I took chrome slides then for the best-quality images.

42. Our meetings took place on June 16–18, 2014, at the storage space and Jill's house in Vence. I reconstruct our conversation on the basis of notes and photographs, as Jill preferred not to be video- or audio-recorded.

43. Fabre, *From Harlem to Paris*, 202.

44. Fabre mentions Hassell's lover, the "white American painter Richard Olney" (*From Harlem to Paris*, 202).

45. Leeming, *James Baldwin*, 327.

46. Delbanco, *Running in Place*, 166.

47. Zaborowska, *James Baldwin's Turkish Decade*, 256–58.

48. Hélène Roux Jeandheur, interview with author, August 28, 2017.

49. See Downs, "Not a Dream Deferred." For images of Baldwin's house, see the website for a course at New York University, "James Baldwin: Race, Sexuality, and American Culture," offered by Professor Nicholas Boggs, at https://nyuqueerlit.wordpress.com/. See also the *Huffington Post* tribute by Trevor Baldwin (James's nephew), "James Baldwin: My Uncle and His Love Life."

50. I was told that the estate halted all efforts to produce Baldwin's works after his death, to David's great frustration, as the house needed money for upkeep. David was forced to sell some (signed) first editions of James's books in order to pay the bills.

51. The "dungeon" description is from Leeming, *James Baldwin*, 379. Georges Braque was an important twentieth-century French modernist painter who aided in developing the Fondation Maeght for the arts in St. Paul-de-Vence in the 1960s.

52. Baldwin met Styron before leaving for Turkey, and he used his guesthouse as a writing haven while struggling with early drafts of *Another Country*.

53. The letter also mentions "circling around" *Just above My Head*; meeting Yoran Cazac in Paris about *Little Man, Little Man*; and a project entitled "All My Trials," for which he has "finished home-work."

54. Leeming, *James Baldwin*, 327.

55. Leeming, in discussion with the author, November 2012.

56. Trubek, *Skeptic's Guide to Writers' Houses*, 31.

57. Trubek, *Skeptic's Guide to Writers' Houses*, 33.

58. Fuss, *Sense of an Interior*, 151.

59. See the recently available James Baldwin Collection at the Smithsonian Institution's National Museum of African American History and Culture, which includes letters to his mother, Berdis Baldwin, and youngest sister, Paula Maria: https://transcription.si.edu/project/7660.

60. Fuss, *Sense of an Interior*, 151.

61. See the Bookends section of the *New York Times Book Review*, "Does Fiction Have the Power to Sway Politics?," February 22, 2015, 35.

62. Traylor, "I Hear Music," 97.

63. There are more than incidental links between *À la recherche du temps perdu* and *Just above My Head*, but that would require a separate study.

64. Fuss, *Sense of an Interior*, 152–53.

65. See Farber, *James Baldwin*, for unique photographs of Baldwin's social life.

66. Leeming, *James Baldwin*, 378–86.

67. Fuss, *Sense of an Interior*, 213–14.

68. D. Miller, *Stuff*, 109.

69. Sousanis, *Unflattening*, 150.

70. D. Miller, *Stuff*, 5.

71. Sent by insured certified mail to the United States; conversation with David Leeming, June 7, 2014, Montpellier, France. Right before Baldwin's death, Leeming was discussing with him, and with Howard Dodson of the Schomburg Center, depositing all of the writer's papers at the Schomburg.

72. Bachelard, *Poetics of Space*, 46–47.

73. hooks, *Outlaw Culture*, 98.

74. Farber, *James Baldwin*, 185.

75. Bachelard, *Poetics of Space*, 46–47.

76. Leeming, *James Baldwin*, 379. See also Farber, *James Baldwin*, 35.

77. Troupe, who was also a performer, playwright, and nonfiction writer, was part of the Black Arts Movement.

78. Troupe, *James Baldwin: The Legacy*, 11. See also the new edition of "The Last Interview," in JB.

79. See Leeming, *James Baldwin*, on letters written to Walter Dallas and Cyndie Packard: "These communications served as a means of facing the reality of death and the meaning of his life" (378).

80. Baldwin and Stein, *Native Sons*, 96.

81. Baldwin and Stein, *Native Sons*, 96–97.
82. Baldwin and Stein, *Native Sons*, 97.
83. Many scholars disagree with my designation of Baldwin's life abroad as "exile," but I stand by it, especially given Baldwin's late rhetoric on it as "saving" his life, and on the national "house of bondage."
84. The captions' authorship is unattributed, and it may be Baldwin's.
85. See Zaborowska, "Domesticating Baldwin's Global Imagination."
86. K. Thomas, "'Ain't Nothin' Like the Real Thing,'" 116.
87. K. Thomas, "'Ain't Nothin' Like the Real Thing,'" 117, 119, 123. Thomas's argument about Baldwin's desexualization resonates with Fuss's on Proust.
88. Holloway, "When a Pariah Becomes a Celebrity," 1.
89. David Leeming, in discussion with the author, March 2004.
90. Leeming, *James Baldwin*, 377.
91. Brenda Rein, in discussion with the author, May 2007.
92. Mea culpa: I misspelled Reading's name in *James Baldwin's Turkish Decade*. So did David Leeming in his biography.
93. Leeming, *James Baldwin*, 377.
94. Leeming, *James Baldwin*, 377.
95. Farber, *James Baldwin*, 37.
96. Hélène Roux Jeandheur, interview with author, August 28, 2017. See also "James Baldwin, St Paul de Vence—Save His Home," a video posted on YouTube, on her efforts to save Baldwin's house. Neither of Yvonne Roux's translations has been published.
97. Farber, *James Baldwin*, 38.
98. See Farber's house descriptions in *James Baldwin*, 33–35.
99. Farber, *James Baldwin*, 41. See also Gates, *Thirteen Ways*, 4–6. At the 2014 International James Baldwin Conference, "James Baldwin: Transatlantic Commuter," in Montpellier, France, Cecil Brown shared his recollections about his visit to Baldwin's house; see C. Brown, "James Baldwin, Digitally Yours."
100. Letter to David Baldwin from St. Paul-de-Vence, April 3, 1986, Schomburg Center for Research in Black Culture. The house in New York was never sold. Jill Hutchinson and Pitou Roux told me David made the final payment on the property after James's death.
101. Farber, *James Baldwin*, 38. In our 2014 interview, Hutchinson confirmed that David Baldwin paid whatever was still owed by James.
102. Hélène Roux Jeandheur, interview with author, August 28, 2017.
103. Farber, *James Baldwin*, 39. Farber describes the abundant gardens at Chez Baldwin as full of "almond and peach orchards, vineyards, fields of wild strawberries and asparagus . . . pines . . . hazel nut trees . . . thyme, and massive rosemary bushes . . . olives, figs, bananas, lemons, and pears" (39).
104. Leeming, *James Baldwin*, 314.
105. Leeming, *James Baldwin*, 313.
106. See also Delbanco, *Running in Place*: "Jimmy's acolytes believed the process . . . sacramental, as if behind his workroom door strange rituals took place. He would

shut himself into his study at midnight and somehow produce an object to which accrued money and fame" (163). In a letter from October 1975 to his brother David, as Ed Pavlić reports, Baldwin "describes the deeply affirming and yet troubling connections between his family and the characters in *Just above My Head*, a connection he'd never attempted before," and one that, perhaps, his safe haven helped him to make (Pavlić, "Come on Up, Sweetheart").

107. Interview at La Colombe d'Or with the author, June 2000.

108. See Baldwin's photograph with the owners of La Colombe d'Or (César and Yvonne Roux) in Buchet, *Taste of Provence*, 28.

109. See D. Q. Miller, "Going to Meet James Baldwin in Provence," 141.

110. Field, "On Breaking into James Baldwin's House."

111. Private correspondence with the author, June 2014.

112. I learned from a local real estate agency that the house was lost to a developer several years after David Baldwin's illness forced him to abandon it.

113. See Zaborowska, *James Baldwin's Turkish Decade*.

114. Morrison, "The Site of Memory," 92–93.

115. Trinh, "Other Than Myself / My Other Self," 9.

116. See Kaplan, "Manifest Domesticity," where national American domesticity excludes Blacks and queers. See also Floyd and Bryden, *Domestic Space*; Cieraad, *At Home*.

117. An artist-activist started a campaign to save the house in the summer of 2016; see the website and blog by Shannon Cain, *His Place in Provence*, http://hisplaceinprovence.org/.

3. LIFE MATERIAL

1. I met Trevor Baldwin and Aisha Karefa-Smart in New York City in 2013–14 for informal interviews in person and by telephone. Thanks to James Campbell, pers. comm., December 2017, on Wilmer as "Lover."

2. The white-dominated media's pitching of the two black male writers against each other reflected the approach of the time. Negative reactions of black critics to Baldwin's essay could be read as either pandering to the politics of respectability, or refusing to see legitimate reasons behind Baldwin's anti-essentialist argument linking Wright's and Stowe's novels' penchant for racialized stereotypes. See also Field, *All Those Strangers*, 29–32.

3. Muñoz, *Disidentifications*, 5.

4. See Field, *All Those Strangers*; Campbell, *Talking at the Gates* and *Exiled in Paris*. Leeming's biography confirms this, too, as does Farber. Leeming, interview with the author, November 2013.

5. See White, "Evidence of Things Not Seen," 240, 251–58, on the "price Baldwin had to pay for daring to break the silence on black homosexuality."

6. See S. Smith and Walker, *Where I'm Bound*; S. Smith and Watson, *Reading Autobiography*; Eakin, *Fictions in Autobiography* and *Touching the World*; Olney, *Memory and Narrative* and *Autobiography*.

7. *Esquire* symposium, "Role of the Writer in America," October 22, 1960.

8. Muñoz, *Disidentifications*; Butler, *Gender Trouble* and *Undoing Gender*; Fuss, *Essentially Speaking*; Johnson, *Appropriating Blackness*.

9. See Cvetkovich, *Archive of Feelings*; K. Stewart, *Ordinary Affects*; Massumi, *Politics of Affect*. Chapter 4 delves deeper into this theme.

10. See Crenshaw, "Demarginalizing the Intersection of Race and Sex."

11. See Ta-Nehisi Coates on the "Dream" in *Between the World and Me*, which neither fully recognizes nor acknowledges borrowing from *The Fire Next Time*.

12. See Rusk, *The Life Writing of Otherness*, where Baldwin appears as a "writerly" author in the company of such women writers as Woolf, Kingston, and Winterson.

13. I refer to the most recent published version of this interview (in JB).

14. Chekhov, *Three Sisters*, front matter.

15. I mean the copies I have obtained from Harvard and from the Schomburg. The copy that Walter Dallas has shared with me is nearly identical with the latter.

16. See Zaborowska, *James Baldwin's Turkish Decade*.

17. See Mock, *Redefining Realness*.

18. See R. Williams, "The Structures of Feeling," in *Long Revolution*.

19. See Zaborowska, *Other Americans, Other Americas*, for a detailed account of this theme.

20. See Ross, "Camping the Dirty Dozens," especially his discussion of "cultural *identification* as a *temporal* process that enables and constrains subjectivity" (291).

21. "James Baldwin—Reflections of a Maverick," in JB, 46.

22. See Ross, "Anatomy of the Straight Black Sissy," 41–45; Ross, "'What's Love but a Second Hand Emotion?'"

23. Muñoz, *Disidentifications*. Muñoz argues for "a certain survival strategy . . . made possible by this visual disidentification with . . . Davis and her freakish beauty . . . while simultaneously positioning himself within and outside of the image of the movie star" (18).

24. Muñoz, *Disidentifications*, 18.

25. Muñoz, *Disidentifications*, 31.

26. See also Zaborowska, *James Baldwin's Turkish Decade*, 21, 22, 252, 327. Jill Hutchinson, interview with author, Vence, France, June 19, 2014. Baldwin refuses any "pegged" (patriarchal-phallic, pun clearly intended) subject position on either side of the binary equation of gay-straight, or even the more ambivalent category of "bi." On the "black girl" Baldwin almost married, see Farber, *James Baldwin*, 186–87.

27. Leeming, *James Baldwin*, 332. See also chapter 4 of Zaborowska, *James Baldwin's Turkish Decade*. *The Devil Finds Work* made the list of "The Greatest Queer Books Ever Written" in the online *OUT* magazine, July 20, 2016, http://www.out.com/art-books/2016/7/20/greatest-queer-books-ever-written#slide-12.

28. The title of this section, "Congo Square," may link Crawford's dancing in that first film Baldwin saw to minstrelsy, and "jazz" in its sexualized and racialized meaning. The original Congo Square (Place de Nègres), part of the Jazz National Historic Park named after Louis Armstrong in New Orleans, commemorates the historic space of slave gatherings that took place on Sundays. Baldwin is moving here from

white movie stars and genres—Tom Mix, Bette Davis, Spencer Tracy—to Canada Lee in *Native Son* and Orson Welles's all-black-cast *Macbeth*.

29. Leeming, *James Baldwin*, 332, 333.

30. Lynn Orilla Scott on Baldwin's struggles with his gender identity. Interview with the author, May 20, 2013.

31. The Orilla "Bill" (Miller) Winfield–James Baldwin letters are currently available at the Beinecke Library at Yale University. The letters were donated by Winfield's son, Ken, and her niece, Lynn. I am grateful to Scott for sharing them with me, and to her and Ken Winfield for permitting me to use them and our interview in this project. All subsequent citations from this collection are noted as "Baldwin–Bill Miller letters."

32. The joint presentation occurred at Université Paul-Valery, Montpellier, France, June 5–7, 2014. Lynn and Ken's presentation was on June 6.

33. See John Miller, "John Miller Writes."

34. See also Leeming, *James Baldwin*, 14–20.

35. Lynn Orilla Scott, interview with the author, May 20, 2013. See also the preface to Scott's book for biographical information on Orilla Miller.

36. Scott, *James Baldwin's Later Fiction*, viii–ix.

37. Scott, *James Baldwin's Later Fiction*, viii.

38. Scott, *James Baldwin's Later Fiction*, ix.

39. Baldwin, "Me and My House," 55.

40. Scott, *James Baldwin's Later Fiction*, ix.

41. Ken Winfield and Lynn Orilla Scott, interview with the author, June 6, 2014.

42. Scott, *James Baldwin's Later Fiction*, vii.

43. Scott, *James Baldwin's Later Fiction*, ix.

44. See Zaborowska, *James Baldwin's Turkish Decade*.

45. For images of the design of this garment, which Cleaver marketed, having savaged Baldwin's private parts in *Soul on Ice*, see "The 1970s Political Activist Who Invented Penis Pants."

46. James Baldwin to Orilla (Bill) Winfield, December 27, 1984, Baldwin–Bill Miller letters.

47. James Baldwin to Orilla (Bill) Winfield, December 27, 1984, Baldwin–Bill Miller letters.

48. This quotation from the second volume of Edel, *Henry James's Letters*, is more a paraphrase than an exact copy of a longer passage. See page 424.

49. Field brought to my attention the many variations of Baldwin's letter signatures during a James Baldwin symposium at Amherst College, March 28, 2015.

50. Orilla (Bill) Winfield to James Baldwin, December 8, 1981, Baldwin–Bill Miller letters.

51. James Baldwin to Orilla (Bill) Winfield, July 5, 1982, Baldwin–Bill Miller letters.

52. Humphrey Bogart played Baby-Face Martin in the 1937 film *Dead End*, which also featured Baldwin's favorite, Sylvia Sidney.

53. Coincidentally, the subheading to this section echoes Field's *All Those Strangers*; this part of "Me and My House" was written before its publication.

54. As related in the "About the Author" note included on the back jacket flap of *Tell Me How Long the Train's Been Gone*, Baldwin also wrote a dramatization of his second novel, *Giovanni's Room*, which was staged by the Actors Studio in New York in 1958. This manuscript was not published but should be counted, thus numbering the second, in between *The Amen Corner* and *Blues for Mister Charlie*, with *The Welcome Table* being the fourth.

55. See Henderson and Thomas, *James Baldwin: Challenging Authors*.

56. This manuscript does not include a date, but it seems to be an earlier version of the one held at Schomburg. The file I have received also contained the following: several handwritten notes on what look like the play's revisions; two typewritten pages entitled "draft" relating an arrival in Tel Aviv; a handwritten draft as well as several typed copies of the epilogue to NNS; "Who Has Believed Our Report?," dated "Sept 6, 1971, St. Paul"; a letter to "Don," possibly the editor of NNS, informing him about an enclosed, final version of the epilogue; a note meant for Bernard from November 4 with no date, informing him about forthcoming money for the house payment and for what is owed him; handwritten notes on the Nobel Prize; one page with several lines in French, ending with "Et je t'aime," with no signature; and a loose page with a brief draft of a poem.

57. *The Welcome Table*, Harvard University manuscript, 9. These words are missing from the apparently trimmed drafts that I also obtained from Walter Dallas and from the Schomburg Center library.

58. Russian or East European literary forms are not part of the "western tradition" in the way that American readers often imagine it, though they, like all other literary traditions, must be approached in the comparative contexts of traveling ideas and influences. Similarly, the notion of "European," often approached as a uniform concept of continental cultural belonging, does not simply denote peoples that Americans define as indistinguishably "white." I refer to national and regional traditions, and I approach Europeanness in the complex way that Baldwin understood it when he spoke of the "European color wheel," or hierarchies of racialized ethnicities and nationalities stretching both north and south and east and west in *The Fire Next Time* and in his interview with Sedat Pakay in Istanbul in 1970.

59. Leeming, *James Baldwin*, 374. I refer here to the 1987 manuscript of the play, annotated by Baldwin, which Walter Dallas kindly shared with me in 2006. As with the rest of the Baldwin papers, direct quotations are not permitted by the estate.

60. Leeming, *James Baldwin*, 376.

61. See Zaborowska, *James Baldwin's Turkish Decade*.

62. See Zaborowska, *James Baldwin's Turkish Decade*. The play's original title, inspired by a Shakespearean sonnet, was translated into Turkish as *Düşenin Dostu*, or "friend of the fallen."

63. See Zaborowska, *James Baldwin's Turkish Decade*, and more in-depth in Zaborowska, "From Istanbul to St. Paul-de-Vence."

64. Beam, "Not a Bad Legacy, Brother," 186.

65. For information about the masque, see Berkowitz, *American Drama of the Twentieth Century*; Glassberg, *American Historical Pageantry*; M. Sedgwick, *Against*

the Modern World; Martindale, Ovid Renewed; Barthelemy, Black Face, Maligned Race; and Hamalian and Hatch, Roots of African American Drama.

66. Interview with the author, September 2014.

67. Interview with the author (by phone), September 23, 2014. See Uno and Burns, Color of Theater.

68. James Baldwin to David Moses, July 6, 1982, and March 10, 1983, Manuscript, Archives, and Rare Book Library, Emory University, Atlanta.

69. Leeming, James Baldwin, 356.

70. The play was made into a film, starring Bette Davis, in 1945. Davis also appeared in a musical adaptation in the late 1970s, with the context moved to the Deep South. Baldwin must have seen at least one of those versions before it made it into his novel.

71. Leeming, James Baldwin, 278–79.

72. The Welcome Table, Harvard University manuscript, 11.

73. I've read the play in three manuscript versions: one available at the Schomburg Center for Research in Black Culture; another, much the same, provided to me by Walter Dallas; and what seems to be an earlier version, recently made available at Harvard University. None of these have been published or made accessible to nonscholarly readers. The estate turned down my request to edit and publish—in an annotated edition—the final manuscript, which Dallas told me was ready to be issued and staged.

74. As the estate does not allow direct quotations from the play, I have to drastically limit my references to this text. Baldwin, The Welcome Table, manuscript, n.p. This copy is available at the Schomburg Center for Research in Black Culture.

75. This sense of self-worth and having become artistic aristocracy resonates in Rankine, "Meaning of Serena Williams."

76. In the "Characters" section of the Harvard manuscript and the two other versions I have read, she is not given a last name and appears simply as "EDITH, actress-singer/star: Creole, from New Orleans." The apparently later versions, or the Schomburg and Dallas manuscripts, as I refer to them, also include a section detailing the scenery, "Welcome Table Set," which lists "vivid paintings" hung on the walls and "pieces of sculpture, genuine, probably African." Subsequent references to the content of the play will come from the latter two, nearly identical, manuscripts. I comment on the Harvard one when it is important for understanding the development of the characters and action.

77. Baldwin, The Welcome Table, Schomburg manuscript, n.p., 5, 9.

78. These letters, Baldwin's only, including some press clippings and copies of the pieces he authored, can be accessed at the Beinecke Library at Yale University.

79. Gates, "Welcome Table," 318.

80. Leeming, James Baldwin, 377–78. In the late 1970s, Baldwin ran into an "old school and . . . Paris friend in Greenwich Village who had been bisexual but had not 'come out.'" The male friend was married and had a child but was considering a sex-change operation, to which Baldwin reacted angrily, suggesting that his friend needed to face himself as he was, "a combination, like everyone, of male and female" (Leeming, James Baldwin, 377–78).

81. See Zaborowska, *James Baldwin's Turkish Decade*.

82. Baldwin, *Perspectives*.

83. S. M. Smith, *At the Edge of Sight*, 16, 21. See also McKittrick, *Sylvia Wynter*, 25–26.

84. This summary refers to the manuscript marked "draft" on the title page, available at the Schomburg. The manuscript provided to me by Walter Dallas contained no markings other than the author's name and play's title on the first page, and it contains two extra pages with detailed stage-set descriptions. Both seem to be the same play version. I cannot be completely sure whether it *is* the final version that Baldwin worked on through late July 1987 and mentions in his letter to Dallas from July 24, 1987, which specifies that he has sent the manuscript "under separate cover" and that he cut the text by twenty pages while retyping it "without realizing it."

85. The Harvard manuscript reads, instead, "a genuine born again Black revolutionary" (8).

86. In the Harvard version, the line about David being shy is missing.

87. Leeming, *James Baldwin*, 276.

88. Leeming, *James Baldwin*, 375–76.

89. Leeming, *James Baldwin*, 376.

90. Jill Hutchinson, interview with the author, Vence, France, June 19, 2014; Happersberger, interview with the author, Switzerland, June 2007.

91. Baldwin, *The Welcome Table*, Schomburg manuscript, 26.

92. Leeming, *James Baldwin*, 376.

93. In the Harvard copy of the manuscript of *The Welcome Table*, there are a few pages of Baldwin's handwritten notes; one of them has Edith complain that LaVerne talked about her as "being too dark to pass the paper bag test" (n.p.).

94. Leeming, *James Baldwin*, 335–36.

95. Chekhov, *Three Sisters*, 112.

96. Leeming, *James Baldwin*, 378.

97. Interview with the author, November 14, 2005. Dallas told me the play was staged in London, but he was unable to give more detailed information.

98. Interview with Walter Dallas, June 20, 2006, Freedom Theater, Philadelphia.

99. James Baldwin, letter to Walter Dallas, July 24 (or 27), 1987.

100. Baldwin, *The Welcome Table*, Walter Dallas's copy, 10. It would have been Cleaver, given his well-publicized dabbling in phallic fashions.

101. Leeming, *James Baldwin*, 376.

102. Henry Louis Gates Jr. describes Baldwin's table in a series of essays based on his 1973 interview with Baldwin and Josephine Baker. See Zaborowska, *James Baldwin's Turkish Decade*. See also Leeming, *James Baldwin*, 374.

103. Leeming, *James Baldwin*, 374.

104. Leeming, *James Baldwin*, 378.

105. See also Butler, *Gender Trouble* and *Bodies That Matter*; Garber, *Vested Interests* and *Vice-Versa*; and Halberstam, *In a Queer Time and Place*.

106. See also Ferguson, *Aberrations in Black*; and Gerstner, *Queer Pollen*.

107. Mock takes the epigraph for her book's first chapter from *The Evidence of Things Not Seen* (86).

108. Mock, *Redefining Realness*, xvii.

109. The illustration in *Playboy* was created by Dennis Mukai.

110. Its conceptual and theoretical framing and narrative structure locate Baldwin's interest in gender and sexuality in one of his earliest published pieces, an essay entitled "Preservation of Innocence," first issued in the Paris literary magazine *Zero* in 1949. This essay's opening sentence makes an unequivocal and revolutionary statement that the "love that dare not speak its name" is Baldwin's central subject: "The problem of the homosexual, so vociferously involved with good and evil, the unnatural as opposed to the natural, has its roots in the nature of man and woman and their relationship to one another" (*James Baldwin: Collected Essays*, 594).

4. BUILDING METAPHORS

The interview quoted within the epigraph for this chapter can be heard at https://www.youtube.com/watch?v=dua3dtrvq84. Baldwin talks about writing essays to "clarify . . . reality" and to "feed" his fiction; this is a response to critics' opinions that he is a better essayist than novelist. See also "James Baldwin Reads from *Just above My Head*" (this recording is from April 1984, when he was teaching at Amherst).

1. A YouTube video from French television announcing Baldwin's death in 1987 shows a glimpse of him at work, typing in his study: "Disparition de l'écrivain James Baldwin dans sa maison de Saint-Paul de Vence en 1987."

2. Recorded in London, England, on November 4, 1971, and shown in the United States on WNET in two installments, on December 15 and 22, 1971. The book is based on the transcript, with Baldwin's and Giovanni's "slight revisions and corrections," according to the editor's note. See also "*Soul!* Episode List, 1968–1973."

3. Standley and Pratt, *Conversations*, 93.

4. Bill Mullen mentioned this Arab connection as well in his keynote at the International James Baldwin Conference at the American University in Paris on May 28, 2016. See also Raoul Peck's art film on Baldwin, *I Am Not Your Negro* (2016), whose screenplay he claims to have based on the manuscript, or treatment, of "Remember This House" that Baldwin left among his papers. Peck was granted access to this document by the estate, a privilege that I have been denied. See also the book version, *I Am Not Your Negro* by James Baldwin and Raoul Peck (New York: Vintage, 2017).

5. See the C-SPAN clip with Amiri Baraka: "James Baldwin's Literary Legacy."

6. See, for example, D. Q. Miller, *Re-viewing James Baldwin*; Balfour, *Evidence of Things Not Said*; White, "Evidence of Things Not Seen." This text is also echoed in Morrison's "Unspeakable Things Unspoken: The Afro-American Presence in American Literature," which later became *Playing in the Dark*.

7. I argue as well that Baldwin was not only deeply versed in local and international literary pasts but also well ahead of his time in applying theoretical con-

cepts of identity in his works, for example, what Sedgwick terms "nondualistic" approaches to identity. See Sedgwick and Frank, *Touching Feeling*, especially her discussion of "affect and texture" (13–22). See also "Black Spatial Humanities: Theories, Methods, and Praxis in Digital Humanities," which brings together the scholars Kim Gallon, Angel David Nieves, Bryan Carter, Jessica Johnson, Scott Nesbit, and David J. Kim, Digital Humanities 2017, Montreal, August 8–11, 2017, abstract available at https://dh2017.adho.org/abstracts/285/285.pdf.

8. See also Field's rich chapter "James Baldwin's Religion" in *All Those Strangers* (82–112), and especially his comments on Baldwin's writing and music (92–95).

9. See the first, unnumbered note for this chapter.

10. D. Q. Miller, *Criminal Power*, 159–60. Here, Miller quotes Richard Schur's "Unseen or Unspeakable? Racial Evidence in Baldwin and Morrison's Nonfiction."

11. D. Q. Miller, *Criminal Power*, 160.

12. Michel Foucault, "Of Other Spaces," 422. This essay was originally published in French in 1967 and translated by Jay Miskowiec.

13. Wilkins develops Foucault's ideas brilliantly in his rewriting of them in *The Aesthetics of Equity*, a theme I return to in my examination of *Just Above*.

14. See the closing line, clearly an inspiration for Baldwin: "I have but one passion: to enlighten those who have been kept in the dark, in the name of humanity which has suffered so much and is entitled to happiness. My fiery protest is simply the cry of my very soul. Let them dare, then, to bring me before a court of law and let the enquiry take place in broad daylight! I am waiting." Zola, "Letter to the President of the Republic: I Accuse!"

15. See note 2.

16. See Wald, *It's Been Beautiful*; Reynolds, "'Soul!'"

17. Baldwin and Giovanni, *Dialogue*, 14.

18. Baldwin and Giovanni, *Dialogue*, 14.

19. Interview with the author, December 3–4, 2009, Blacksburg, VA. I am grateful to Giovanni and her then partner, Ginny Fowler, for their generosity in hosting me in their home, sharing books and recordings of *Soul!*, and telling me stories I will never forget.

20. Wald, *It's Been Beautiful*, 156, 159.

21. Wald, *It's Been Beautiful*, 159.

22. Wald, *It's Been Beautiful*, 160.

23. See Ross's critique, in "White Fantasies of Desire," of bringing up black homophobia whenever one discusses queerness; Ross lists many safe spaces for African American queers.

24. One wonders whether she was aware of Haizlip's sexuality.

25. Wald, *It's Been Beautiful*, 94, 63.

26. Baldwin and Giovanni, *Dialogue*, 89, 95. I agree with Wald that their "dramatization of a couple is predicated on the unspoken fact of Baldwin's homosexuality," but I do not agree with her blaming him for his silence about his sexuality on the show (*It's Been Beautiful*, 161–62).

27. Baldwin and Giovanni, *Dialogue*, 16.

28. Giovanni confirmed this in our interview. Interview with the author, Blacksburg, VA, 2009.

29. Interview with the author, Blacksburg, VA, 2009.

30. James Baldwin, "National Press Club speech."

31. Baldwin and Giovanni, *Dialogue*, 8, emphases added.

32. See Ida Lewis's foreword to Baldwin and Giovanni, *Dialogue*, and her autobiographic recollections concerning the "gap between the black man and woman" (5–7).

33. Standley and Pratt, *Conversations*, 97. Baldwin's characters of Arthur, and especially Peanut, murdered by white racists in the South, in *Just above My Head*, and Fonny, Daniel, and Frank, who ends his own life, in *Beale Street*, echo such victimized men to various degrees, and they reflect Baldwin's rethinking of his earlier black male characters, such as John and Gabriel from *Go Tell It*, Rufus from *Another Country*, and Leo and Black Christopher from *Tell Me*. In *No Name*, he describes the tribulations of an unjustly imprisoned friend, Tony Maynard, and interrogates heteronormative black and white masculinities as spectacles weighted with regional race relations, and always menaced by violence—"something . . . I began to see, watching black men in the South and watching white men watching them." In such a mad, racist, homosocial staring contest, identity translates into fantasies of racialized sexual equipment, as each black man is judged by "the weight he carries between his legs" (PT, 482–83). He also mentions more publicly visible figures such as Eldridge Cleaver, who troubles him, and Malcolm X, whose death he mourns deeply, but begins to move toward much more ambiguous and queer ones in *Just Above* and *The Welcome Table*, whose female and queer characters and sexualities become his central focus.

34. Indeed, so is *Rap on Race* with Mead.

35. The statement of the Combahee River Collective is available online at http://americanstudies.yale.edu/sites/default/files/files/Keyword%20Coalition_Readings.pdf.

36. Some of the ideas and passages from this section were first rehearsed in Zaborowska, "Harlem Streets Can Talk."

37. See Gilroy, *Black Atlantic*; S. Hall, *Representations*; West, *Race Matters*; Fuss, *Essentially Speaking*. Baldwin came back to this theme multiple times throughout his career, especially in a 1967 essay published in the *New York Times*, "Negroes Are Anti-Semitic Because They're Anti-White."

38. Standley and Pratt, *Conversations*, 26.

39. Standley and Pratt, *Conversations*, 275.

40. I am aware of the gendered implications of the term "disorderly conduct" and its historical and disciplinary roots in the studies of nineteenth-century white women's culture. See Smith-Rosenberg, *Disorderly Conduct*; Kelley, *Private Woman, Public Stage* and "Need of Their Genius."

41. See also Catherine Rottenberg's discussion on black-Jewish encounters in *Performing Americanness*. Her discussions of "the ways in which the black-and-white divide has operated" and the "uncertainty surrounding the racial position of the Jew

at the turn of the century" (74) are especially helpful to situating this chapter's argument within a historical and literary historical context.

42. Baldwin's interest and investment in the complicated relationship between African Americans and Jews stemmed also from his close personal friendships with artists and intellectuals he met at the DeWitt Clinton High School in the Bronx, especially with Sol Stein and Richard Avedon. See Avedon and Baldwin's famous collaboration, *Nothing Personal*, and the one, posthumously published, with Stein, *Native Sons*.

43. See Harold Bloom's assessment of Baldwin's rhetoric in *James Baldwin*: "Like Carlyle (and a single aspect of the perspectivizing Nietzsche), Baldwin is of the authentic lineage of Jeremiah, most inward of prophets" (1).

44. See the racialized portrayals of Blacks making anti-Semitic comments and Jews exhibiting racist and sexist behavior by, for example, the characters Steve Ellis in *Another Country* and Fonny's friend Daniel in *Beale Street*.

45. For a thorough examination of the in-between street/church queer spaces, see E. Patrick Johnson's magisterial *Appropriating Blackness*.

46. "Walking disorderly" is a church idiom signifying straying off the path in both spiritual and sexual terms; Baldwin uses it to describe Ella Mae and Elisha's erotic friendship, which was publicly exposed and squelched by the church elders.

47. Leeming, *James Baldwin*, 11.

48. See also Sara Blair on Baldwin's photographic collaborations on Harlem in *Harlem Crossroads*.

49. Like Baldwin in his teens, in *Go Tell It*, the gimmick that changed John Grimes's life was becoming a youth preacher. For Rufus and Ida, it was jazz, the black music adored by white America. But for Peter and Ruth, who may be read as companion characters to the siblings from *Another Country*, an escape route seems unattainable. Similarly to the young protagonist of another short story set in Harlem, "The Rock Pile" (1965), they dream of running away but are held back by realities of race, class, and gender that they feel curtail their dreams and aspirations.

50. See Nicholas Boggs, "The Critic and the Little Man: On African American Literary Studies in the Post–Civil Rights Era" (Ph.D. diss., Columbia University, 2005). See also Boggs's "Of Mimicry and (Little Man Little) Man."

51. In his "An Open Letter to My Sister, Angela Davis," dated November 19, 1970, included in Davis's *If They Come in the Morning*, Baldwin describes the photograph of an activist in chains on the cover of *Newsweek* by referencing the Holocaust: "You look exceedingly alone—as alone, say, as the Jewish housewife in the boxcar headed for Dachau, or as any one of our ancestors, chained together in the name of Jesus, headed for a Christian land" (13). Having thus put the extermination of European Jews side by side with the death toll of the Middle Passage, he also compares the social histories of Germany and the United States, claiming that "since we live in an age in which silence is not only criminal but suicidal, I have been making as much noise as I can, here in Europe, on radio and television—in fact, have just returned from a land, Germany, which was made notorious by a silent majority not so very

long ago" (13). This letter shows his growing interest in black women's activism, as do his references to women in NNS, especially Dorothy Counts and her heroic walk to desegregate a high school.

52. See, for example, T. Edwards, "Can You Go Home Again?" See also Oates, "If Beale Street Could Talk."

53. Leeming, *James Baldwin*, 323. See also Zaborowska, *James Baldwin's Turkish Decade*.

54. D. Q. Miller, "Going to Meet James Baldwin in Provence," 142; Harris, *Black Women in the Fiction of James Baldwin*, 128–30.

55. Randall Kenan has assessed this text as concerning primarily "the precariousness of the American judicial system for black men . . . [and] love," as well as Baldwin's "mounting anger toward his homeland"; "James Baldwin, 1924–1987: A Brief Biography," 54. Like Harris, Clarence E. Hardy III sees it as another proof of Baldwin's commitment to demonstrating the spiritual and redemptive power of erotic love in challenging and transcending social divisions and norms. To Tish and Fonny, "sex holds a sacramental power over lovers, bodily cementing various partners across sex and gender." Hardy also sees Baldwin's deployment of religious language in this novel as "suggest[ing] the mystery at the core of all human relationships and the instability that marks all sexual (and racial) identities" ("James Baldwin as Religious Writer," 64–65). Darryl Pinckney wrote about *If Beale Street Could Talk* as echoing Balzac in its hatred of oppression and as Baldwin's unequivocal "return to the Harlem family" to celebrate its bonds and survival in "James Baldwin: The Risks of Love." Like Pinckney's, assessments published in the last decade tend to distance themselves from angry and emotional reactions of critics in the 1970s, such as those of Mary Fair Burks, whose religious sensibilities and notions of literary decorum were offended by the book's explicit sex scenes (in "James Baldwin's Protest Novel"), or Thomas R. Edwards, who felt unconvinced by the descriptions of Harlem because they did not correspond to his own perceptions of social realities of race, not to mention his conceptions of literary realism: "I unhappily suggest that an important and honorable writer has failed to make us believe in his vision of horrors that surely do exist, but outside his book" ("Can You Go Home Again?").

56. Despite this view, much like Gwendolyn Brooks illuminates Chicago and the domestic spaces of lower-class Blacks in *Maud Martha*, Baldwin sometimes shows Harlem as a place of new beginnings, especially for his female narrators and characters, of whom Tish is the most resilient. Like Brooks's Chicago or Ann Petry's New York in *The Street*, Baldwin's representations of his hometown as the "house of bondage" reveal the roots of the pre–Civil Rights Movement's gendered riffs in the black community in the late 1940s and 1950s.

57. See Zaborowska, "Mapping Transcultural Masculinities."

58. See also Michael Cobb's critique of binary regimes of representation that assume the "interrogated supremacy of the couple" (*Single*, 25–26).

59. On the ambivalence of home, see also Sharon P. Holland's foreword to Henderson and Johnson, *Black Queer Studies*, where she says, "Home *is* a four-letter word." Holland writes in a style that echoes the unmistakably Baldwinian mix of

autobiographical and critical musing, and she concludes about the emergent academic field that "the practice of black queer/quare studies embodies all of its [home's] double meanings" (xii).

60. DuCille, "Blues Notes on Black Sexuality," 419. See also Lordi, *Black Resonances*, especially 99–136.

61. The essay opens with a reference to Henry James, "It is a complex fate to be an American," which comes from a February 4, 1872, letter to Charles Eliot Norton.

62. Standley and Pratt, *Conversations*, 14, 23, emphases added.

63. See also Zaborowska, *James Baldwin's Turkish Decade*.

64. Baldwin told Giovanni that she served as an inspiration for the character of Tish. Interview with the author, Blacksburg, VA, 2009. See also Wall, *Worrying the Line*, on the ways in which black women writers in the late twentieth century were caught up in the conflicting and exclusionary "web of tradition . . . enmeshed in their intersecting lines" (11).

65. Harris, *Black Women in the Fiction of James Baldwin*, 206.

66. After Clough and Halley in *The Affective Turn*, I refer to affect as relating not only to the human body but also to technologies of representation the body might produce, i.e., to Tish's production of her narrative.

67. Burks chastised Baldwin for this portrayal and racialized Hayward as "the liberal Jewish lawyer," calling him "a new Baldwinian stereotype" ("James Baldwin's Protest Novel," 86).

68. Baldwin also mentions other hated establishments in Harlem run by Jews: "The grocer was a Jew . . . the butcher was a Jew. . . . We brought our clothes from a Jew . . . and the pawnbroker was a Jew—perhaps we hated him most of all. . . . Not all of these white people were cruel—on the contrary, I remember some who were as thoughtful as the bleak circumstances allowed—but all of them were exploiting us, and that was why we hated them" (PT, 425–26).

69. Chronologically, the meeting with Levy precedes the one with Hayward given that it has taken place before the meeting with the racist cop and Fonny's subsequent conviction, but Tish's narrative, interweaving recollections and current events, places them in reverse order.

70. Baldwin makes this encounter reflect the views on black-Jewish relationships he expressed in the essay "Negroes Are Anti-Semitic Because They're Anti-White," in which, as if echoing Du Bois's local-to-global perspective on the "color line" from *The Souls of Black Folk* (1903), he states, "The root of anti-Semitism among Negroes is, ironically, the relationship of colored peoples—all over the globe—to the Christian world. This is a fact that may be difficult to grasp, not only for the ghetto's most blasted and embittered inhabitants, but also for many Jews, to say nothing of many Christians" (PT, 427).

71. While "Jaime" is a common Hispanic name, it also may refer to Baldwin, who often signed letters to his family and lovers with that name, transliterating the French *j'aime*. See Pavlić, "Come on Up, Sweetheart."

72. Leeming told me that Ernestine was inspired by Tony Maynard's sister.

73. *Favela* is a Portuguese word that originates in Brazil, specifically in Rio de Janeiro. It has been used with increased frequency as a synonym for a slum or what in Spanish would be called a barrio.

74. See Norman, "James Baldwin's Confrontation." See also D. Q. Miller, *Criminal Power*; Balfour, *Evidence of Things Not Said*.

75. Norman, "Crossing Identitarian Lines," 244; Norman, "James Baldwin's Confrontation," 120.

76. The lack of affective connection between Sharon and Victoria in this scene points at Baldwin's skepticism concerning the limits of cross-ethnic sisterhood, of seeing blackness as uniform outside of the United States.

77. The presence of Puerto Rican and Caribbean contexts in the novel echoes Baldwin's trip to Puerto Rico in 1963, for a working vacation with Lucien Happersberger. See also Norman, "James Baldwin's Confrontation," 123.

78. Norman, "James Baldwin's Confrontation," 120.

79. Baraka, "Black Woman," 8.

80. Baraka, "Black Woman," 8.

81. Baraka, "Black Woman," 8.

82. K. Stewart, *Ordinary Affects*, 3.

83. See R. Williams, *Long Revolution*: the "methods of analysis which, over a range from literature to social institutions, can articulate actual *structures of feeling*—the meanings and values which are lived in works and relationships—and clarify the processes of historical developments through which these structures form and change" (319, emphasis added). I am particularly interested in how we can interpret the focus on what Williams refers to as the "created and creative meanings—which our inherited reality teaches and through which new reality forms and is negotiated" (319). See also Stuart Hall's approach to literary texts and "structures of feeling" as referring to "interactions between all these practices and patterns [and how they] are lived and experienced as a whole, in any particular period" (*Culture, Media, Language*, 223). I also find the deployment of Williams's term useful for understanding the impact of social space and locality in Taylor, Evans, and Fraser's *A Tale of Two Cities*, 5–6. Particularly useful is their focus on the "impact of local place on individual personality formation, personal biography, and 'orientation to the world' or 'affect' (all of which contribute to what we mean by 'local identity')" (6). For more on how structures of feeling are carried by "documentary culture," such as literature and the arts, see also Raymond Williams, in Storey, *Cultural Theory and Popular Culture*, 53.

84. See also Daniels, "James Baldwin, Eloquent Writer."

85. Oates, "If Beale Street Could Talk," 376.

86. This speech is available for viewing at https://www.youtube.com/watch?v=CTjY4rZFY5c ("National Press Club Speech").

87. Holloway, "When a Pariah Becomes a Celebrity," 4.

88. Holloway, "When a Pariah Becomes a Celebrity," 9.

89. Holloway, "When a Pariah Becomes a Celebrity," 9. See also Phil Donahue's talk show from 1989, *Black Women Writers*, which contextualizes these debates

through interviews with Alice Walker, Michele Wallace, Angela Davis, Maya Angelou, and Ntozake Shange.

90. Elijah Muhammad's NOI publication, dating to 1960.

91. The more accurate term to describe the narrative point of view here would be the aforementioned "third-person limited," which deliberately mixes the narrative consciousness of a character with that of the author. Listing all the examples of TJ's narrative unreliability is beyond the scope of this chapter, so I cite a couple: TJ seems to know how to read complicated construction-site signs (LM, 71); his psychological interpretation of Mr. Man in the postaccident basement scene (85).

92. Crawford, "James Baldwin's Side-View Mirror"; Boggs, "Baldwin and Yoran Cazac's 'Child's Story for Adults.'"

93. Boggs, "Of Mimicry and (Little Man Little) Man," 122; Zaborowska, *James Baldwin's Turkish Decade*, 108–9.

94. Standley and Pratt, *Conversations*, 235–36.

95. Baldwin spoke to Goldstein about once wanting to have children; he also mentioned this desire to his Turkish friends Sedat Pakay, Engin Cezzar, and Oktay Balamir, all of whom I interviewed. See also *house hold: four stories of kinship and curiosity*, a documentary by Craig Saddlemire (DVD; Round Point Movies, 2013).

96. Harlem is also the place where Arthur gets sexually assaulted as a child. This event launches his brother's narrative of his life as a black queer artist; I return to this theme later on.

97. See Bhabha's chapter "The World and the Home," with a discussion about how "the image of the house has always been used to talk about the expansive, mimetic nature of the novel. . . . Dickens is the novelist of home par excellence," in Briganti and Mezei, *Domestic Space Reader*, 358–59.

98. Kilpeläinen, "'Like the Sound of a Crumbling Wall,'" 109; Scott, *James Baldwin's Later Fiction*, 123. Kilpeläinen complicates Foucault's heterotopia with that of Mary Louise Pratt's "contact zone," working out an important context for regarding postcoloniality in the sexual encounter between Arthur and Guy.

99. Scott, *James Baldwin's Later Fiction*, 121, 123.

100. Harris, *Black Women in the Fiction of James Baldwin*, 211.

101. Kilpeläinen, "'Like the Sound of a Crumbling Wall,'" 121.

102. Wilkins, *Aesthetics of Equity*, 107.

103. Regardless of whether or not he read Foucault (though given his tremendous erudition and fluency in French, it is likely that he did).

104. Foucault, "Of Other Spaces," 422–25.

105. Wilkins, *Aesthetics of Equity*, 107–8. See this work also on hip-hop culture modifying architecture with the "sound" element (97–115).

106. Wilkins, *Aesthetics of Equity*, 113–15. Wilkins also develops the notion of "celebratory heterotopias"—which he defines as the "latest manifestation of this tradition of makin' space . . . the center of some new flava'. A [celebratory heterotopia] . . . is a space made by the peeps themselves, for themselves, in a kinda 'kiss-my-ass, we-don't-want-'cha-space' challenge. It is a way to kinda define space

how they damn well please to make it livable—and to hell wid' what other folks say" (115). This approach certainly echoes Baldwin's on artistic freedom. Ed Pavlić's recent book, *Who Can Afford to Improvise?*, describes a space somewhat akin to Wilkins's definition, albeit more poetic and literary, infused with music, "a lyric's space" capable of ushering in "the possibility of joy" (161).

107. Standley and Pratt, *Conversations*, 91.

108. Standley and Pratt, *Conversations*, 92.

109. Standley and Pratt, *Conversations*, 92.

110. Standley and Pratt, *Conversations*, 169, emphases added.

111. Reid-Pharr, *Once You Go Black*, 107–8. See also Butler, *Bodies That Matter*; Scarry, *Body in Pain*; P. Brooks, *Body Work*; Reid-Pharr, "Dinge," 75–76, 84.

112. Scott, *James Baldwin's Later Fiction*, 137.

113. Scott, *James Baldwin's Later Fiction*, 127.

114. In the *Bookstand* BBC Television interview with Peter Duval Scott, recorded on April 16, 1963, in England, Baldwin talks about the "literal" autobiographical influences in his novels concerning places he has lived.

115. I agree here with Reid-Pharr, *Once You Go Black*, 108.

116. Harris, *Black Women in the Fiction of James Baldwin*, 170.

117. This echoes Baldwin's deeply fraught and unsuccessful collaboration with Columbia Pictures over a script for a feature film on Malcolm X inspired by Alex Haley's book.

118. See also Harris, *Black Women in the Fiction of James Baldwin*, where she compares him to "Keats's drooling little boy, with his nose pressed firmly against the sweet-shop window of life, gazing at the life he really wishes to live" (167).

119. Also, passing through a bridge changes the perspective and view of the one crossing it; the activity of that passing is contained in a specific period of time (thus again evoking Foucault's fourth, heterochronic or time-bound space).

120. See also Edelman's chapter on *Just Above*, "The Part for the (W)hole: Baldwin, Homophobia, and the Fantasmatics of 'Race,'" in *Homographesis*, 42–74. I do not side with the psychoanalytic reading of race-sex in this chapter, for I find it missing key materialist approaches to black identities, a lack that mars Foucault's text in a similar manner. Still, I find Edelman's explication of Hall's allowing Jimmy's narrative at the end of the novel to "penetrate" his story as helpful.

121. I have corroborated this information with the biographer, David Leeming. Interview with the author, November 2012.

122. Standley and Pratt, *Conversations*, 78, 77.

123. Tal, *Worlds of Hurt*, 137.

124. Foucault, "Of Other Spaces," 423–24.

125. Standley and Pratt, *Conversations*, 83, 92.

126. Standley and Pratt, *Conversations*, 245–46.

127. Standley and Pratt, *Conversations*, 250–51.

128. Scott proposes a similar reading of the two novels, seeing *Just Above* as "a more nuanced treatment of the individual's relationship to his or her cultural legacy" than *Beale Street* (*James Baldwin's Later Fiction*, 121). See also Woubshet, *Calendar of Loss*.

129. See Scott, *James Baldwin's Later Fiction*; Reid-Pharr, *Once You Go Black*.

130. Harris, *Black Women in the Fiction of James Baldwin*, 179.

131. Bonetti, "Interview with James Baldwin." See the unnumbered note at the beginning of this chapter. See also Pirandello, *Six Characters in Search of an Author*.

132. Harris, *Black Women in the Fiction of James Baldwin*, 170, 175. See Harris's chapter on Julia for all the important elements of her story, which provides ample evidence for this reading, showing how Julia's father's economic aspirations and her mother's weakness ruin their daughter's chances to learn boundaries and respect for elders that could have saved her, and their household, from calamity.

133. Scott, *James Baldwin's Later Fiction*, 135.

134. Harris, *Black Women in the Fiction of James Baldwin*, 203.

135. Leeming, *James Baldwin*, 345. Leeming also erroneously gives the number of books in *Just Above* as six, not five (348).

136. Leeming, *James Baldwin*, 346.

137. I'm fully aware that the "world" that Baldwin refers to here does not include countries that are as homophobic as the United States. He clearly never investigated that issue in the Soviet Union or Poland or a myriad other places around the globe. Given his experience in France, Germany, Turkey, or England, however, he has every right to that claim.

138. See also Edelman's use of the same quotation in his chapter on *Just Above* in *Homographesis* (74–75).

139. Wole Soyinka, foreword, in Troupe, *James Baldwin: The Legacy*, 17.

140. Soyinka, in Troupe, *James Baldwin: The Legacy*, 16–17.

141. Yasmin De-Gout and Brian Norman have introduced these themes already. See also Zaborowska, *James Baldwin's Turkish Decade*, 338.

142. I am aware this list does not exhaust the topic; I limit it to the most pertinent aspects thereof for the project.

143. Scholars and writers who theorized these themes are too numerous to mention all here. They include Alice Walker, bell hooks, Nina Baym, Annette Kolodny, Julia Kristeva, Hortense Spillers, Deborah McDowell, Barbara Christian, Cheryl Wall, Nancy Miller, Kate Millet, and Carolyn Heilbrun. Also important for my argument is June Howard's "What Is Sentimentality?" See also what Laura Wexler in *Tender Violence* has termed the "Douglas-Tompkins debate," after the names of two feminist scholars who disagreed on the importance of domestic fiction.

144. Brim, *James Baldwin and the Queer Imagination*, 31.

145. Standley and Pratt, *Conversations*, 278.

146. Standley and Pratt, *Conversations*, 278, emphases added.

5. BLACK LIFE MATTERS OF VALUE

1. See Baldwin's interview with Peter Duval Smith for the BBC Television *Bookstand* program, April 16, 1963.

2. Standley and Pratt, *Conversations*, 250.

3. Standley and Pratt, *Conversations*, 278.

4. Rich, "The Baldwin Stamp," 55–56.

5. See B. Brown, *Other Things*; McPherson, "Post-archive."

6. See T. Morton, *Hyperobjects*; Grosz, "Feminism, Materialism, and Freedom"; Coole, "Inertia of Matter."

7. Schuessler, "Inside an Author's Oddball Trove of Artifacts."

8. See McGrane, "Saved from Demolition"; Papenfuss, "What Is Rosa Parks' House Doing in Berlin?"

9. See Brent Edwards's "The Taste of the Archive": "Orchestrated fragments echo the fragmentation of the archive itself. They are meant as a reminder that the distribution of archival artifacts into a historical narrative cannot deliver the past in a manner that would be seamless, much less exhaustive" (961), as well as his concept of "a *queer practice of the archive*: an approach to the material preservation of the past that deliberately aims to retain what is elusive, what is hard to pin down, what can't quite be explained or filed away according to the usual categories" (970). See also Hartman, "Venus," on "critical fabulation" as appropriate for approaching archives critically, and on archive as an "open casket" (5–8); see also Lowe, *Intimacies of Four Continents*.

10. Gayle, "Defense of James Baldwin"; Gayle, "Function of Black Criticism at the Present Time."

11. There have been efforts to save the remnants of the house in St. Paul-de-Vence that met with surprisingly unfriendly responses; ironically, these responses revive the very reductive binaries of essentialized "whiteness" and "blackness" that Baldwin so eloquently opposed, and so passionately wanted us to dismantle. See Donadio, "Battling to Save James Baldwin's Home"; Cain, *His Place in Provence*; Centre LBGT Côte d'Azur, "Maison de James Baldwin à Saint-Paul-de-Vence"; The James Baldwin Collective in Paris, France, "Let's Save James Baldwin's House" (multilingual petition), accessed August 25, 2017, https://www.change.org/p/minist%C3%A8re-de-la-culture-let-s-save-james-baldwin-s-house.

12. As Gallon, "Making a Case," argues, Digital Humanities needs to pay closer attention to issues of race, gender, and sexuality, or how "the digital comes to bear on blackness and vice versa." See also Posner, "What's Next"; Noviskie, "Resistance in the Materials."

13. Christine Wilson describes "animated haunted house stories," from Poe's "The Fall of the House of Usher" (1839) and Hawthorne's *The House of the Seven Gables* (1851), through James's *The Turn of the Screw* (1898) and Morrison's *Beloved* (1987). See "Haunted Habitability," in Pereen and Blanco, *Popular Ghosts*. My experience deals with more contemporary and immediate phenomena, or what the editors of *Popular Ghosts* see as a revival of interest in things ghostly that can be also digital: "Whether in rock songs, Internet news feeds, or museum exhibits, we appear to have entered an era that has reintroduced the vocabulary of ghosts and haunting" (ix). See also Holland, "Foreword," which speaks to some of the same issues, though in different terms from mine.

14. See Parham, *Haunting and Displacement*.

15. See B. Brown, *Sense of Things*; Schwenger, *Tears of Things*; Caws, *Surrealist Look*.

16. See Freud, *Uncanny*; de Certeau, *Practice of Everyday Life*; Derrida, *Specters of Marx*; Warner, *Phantasmagoria*.

17. Roberts, "Geography and the Visual Image," 386–87. See also Shawn Michelle Smith's exploration of spirit photography in *At the Edge of Sight* and Jane Bennett's *Vibrant Matter* on the life of objects and their affective qualities.

18. Pereen and Blanco, *Popular Ghosts*, ix, xiii.

19. Roberts, "Geography and the Visual Image," 386–87.

20. Gordon, *Ghostly Matters*, 23.

21. Gordon, *Ghostly Matters*, 22–23.

22. Warner, *Phantasmagoria*, 381.

23. Holland, "Foreword," xi.

24. Holland, "Foreword," xii.

25. Botton, *Architecture of Happiness*, 107.

26. See S. Smith, *Manifesto for the Humanities*; Burdick, *Digital Humanities*; Alexander and Nieves, *We Shall Independent Be*.

27. Bennett, *Vibrant Matter*, xiii, xv. Bennett relies on Spinoza's notion of affect, or the "capacity of any body for activity and responsiveness" (xii). See also Weheliye, *Habeas Viscus*, on assemblages and racism.

28. See Ball, *Traveling Concepts in the Humanities*.

29. Pinto, *Difficult Diasporas*, 9, 13.

30. Pinto, *Difficult Diasporas*, 9, 10.

31. Cazmir's first Baldwin book was *Little Man, Little Man*.

32. Standley and Pratt, *Conversations*, 268.

33. See Gaye, "Trump's Hate"; Black, "White Nationalist American History."

34. Standley and Pratt, *Conversations*, 250.

35. Standley and Pratt, *Conversations*, 277–78.

36. Standley and Pratt, *Conversations*, 254, emphasis added.

BIBLIOGRAPHY

Ahmed, Sara. "Affective Economies." *Social Text* 22.79 (2004): 117–39.
———. *Queer Phenomenology: Orientations, Objects, Others.* Durham, NC: Duke University Press, 2006.
———. *Willful Subjects.* Durham, NC: Duke University Press, 2014.
Aldridge, John. "The Fire Next Time?" *Saturday Review*, June 15, 1974, 20–24.
Alexander, Leslie M., and Angel David Nieves. *We Shall Independent Be: African American Place Making and the Struggle to Claim Space in the United States.* Boulder: University Press of Colorado, 2008.
Alexander, Michelle. *The New Jim Crow: Mass Incarceration in the Age of Colorblindness.* New York: New Press, 2010.
Als, Hilton. "Family Secrets." *PEN America*. March 28, 2016. http://www.pen.org/nonfiction-essay/family-secrets.
———. "Snaps: 1955–1965." *New Yorker*, February 23 and March 2, 2015.
American Masters. James Baldwin—the Price of the Ticket. WETA-TV, 1989.
Anderson, Melissa. "Lorraine Hansberry's Letters Reveal the Playwright's Private Struggle." *Village Voice*, February 26, 2014. http://www.villagevoice.com/arts/lorraine-hansberrys-letters-reveal-the-playwrights-private-struggle-7187630.
Appiah, Kwame A. *Cosmopolitanism: Ethics in a World of Strangers.* New York: W. W. Norton, 2007.
———. *The Ethics of Identity.* Princeton, NJ: Princeton University Press, 2005.
Armengol, Josep M. "In the Dark Room: Homosexuality and/as Blackness in James Baldwin's *Giovanni's Room.*" *Signs: Journal of Women in Culture and Society* 37.3 (2012): 671–93.
Auchincloss, Eve, and Nancy Lynch. "Disturber of the Peace: James Baldwin—An Interview." In *Conversations with James Baldwin*, edited by Fred L. Standley and Louis H. Pratt. Jackson: University Press of Mississippi, 1989. 64–82.
Avedon, Richard, and James Baldwin. *Nothing Personal.* New York: Atheneum, 1964.
Avilez, GerShun. "Housing the Black Body: Value, Domestic Space, and Segregation Narratives." In *Representing Segregation: Towards an Aesthetics of Living Jim Crow, and Other Forms of Racial Division*, edited by Brian Norman and Piper Kendrix Williams. Albany: SUNY Press, 2010. 131–47.
Bachelard, Gaston. *The Poetics of Space.* Boston: Beacon, 1994. Orig. pub. 1958.
Baker, Houston A. *Blues, Ideology, and Afro-American Literature: A Vernacular Theory.* Chicago: University of Chicago Press, 1987.

———. "The Embattled Craftsman: An Essay on James Baldwin." *Journal of African-Afro-American Affairs* 1.1 (1977): 28–51.

———. *Turning South Again: Re-thinking Modernism/Re-reading Booker T.* Durham, NC: Duke University Press, 2001.

Baldwin, James. *The Amen Corner*. New York: Dial, 1968; repr. New York: Vintage, 1996. Orig. pub. as excerpt (Act I) in *Zero*, 1954.

———. *Another Country*. New York: Dial, 1962.

———. "*Architectural Digest* Visits: James Baldwin." *Architectural Digest* (August 1987).

———. "As Much Truth as One Can Bear." *New York Times Book Review*, January 14, 1962, 120, 148.

———. *Blues for Mister Charlie*. New York: Dial, 1964.

———. *The Cross of Redemption: Uncollected Writings*. New York: Vintage, 2011.

———. *The Devil Finds Work*. New York: Dial, 1976.

———. "The Discovery of What It Means to Be American." In NKMN, 3–12.

———. "Encounter on the Seine: Black Meets Brown." In NNS, 117–23.

———. *The Evidence of Things Not Seen*. New York: Holt, Rinehart and Winston, 1985.

———. *The Fire Next Time*. New York: Dial, 1963.

———. "Freaks and the American Ideal of Manhood." *Playboy* (January 1985). In PT as "Here Be Dragons," 677–90.

———. *Giovanni's Room*. New York: Dial, 1956.

———. *Going to Meet the Man*. New York: Dial, 1965.

———. *Go Tell It on the Mountain*. New York: Knopf, 1953.

———. "'Go the Way Your Blood Beats': An Interview with Richard Goldstein." In *James Baldwin: The Legacy*, edited by Quincy Troupe. New York: Touchstone, 1989. 173–85.

———. "Here Be Dragons." In PT, 677–90.

———. *If Beale Street Could Talk*. New York: Dial, 1974.

———. *James Baldwin: Collected Essays*. Edited by Toni Morrison. New York: Library of America, 1998.

———. *James Baldwin: The Last Interview and Other Conversations*. Brooklyn: Melville House, 2014.

———. James Baldwin to Orilla (Bill) Winfield, December 27, 1984. Collection of Lynn Orilla Scott, now at Yale University's Beineke Library. Used by permission.

———. *Jimmy's Blues: Selected Poems*. New York: St. Martin's, 1985.

———. *Just above My Head*. New York: Dial, 1979.

———. Letter to David Baldwin, February 6, 1979. Schomburg Center for Research in Black Culture.

———. *Little Man, Little Man: A Story of Childhood*. New York: Dial, 1976.

———. "Me and My House." *Harper's* (November 1955): 54–61.

———. "National Press Club Speech." Washington, D.C., 1986. YouTube, posted December 22, 2014. https://www.youtube.com/watch?v=CTjY4rZFY5c.

———. "The Negro Assays the Negro Mood." *New York Times Sunday Magazine*, March 12, 1961, 25–26, 103.
———. "Negroes Are Anti-Semitic Because They're Anti-White." *New York Times*, April 9, 1967, 26–27, 135.
———. "The New Lost Generation." In PT, 305–13.
———. *Nobody Knows My Name: More Notes of a Native Son*. New York: Dial, 1961.
———. *No Name in the Street*. New York: Dial, 1972.
———. *Notes of a Native Son*. Boston: Beacon, 1955.
———. "Notes on the House of Bondage." *The Nation* (1980): 440–43.
———. *One Day, When I Was Lost: A Scenario Based on "The Autobiography of Malcolm X."* New York: Dial, 1972.
———. *Perspectives: Angles on African Art*. Interview with Michael John Weber. Center for African Art, New York, December 1987.
———. *The Price of the Ticket: Collected Nonfiction, 1948–1985*. New York: St. Martin's, 1985.
———. "Sweet Lorraine." Introduction to Lorraine Hansberry, *To Be Young, Gifted, and Black: An Informal Autobiography*. New York: Signet, 1970. xi–xv. In PT, 443–47.
———. *Tell Me How Long the Train's Been Gone*. New York: Dial, 1968.
———. "To Crush the Serpent." *Playboy* (January 1987): 66–70.
Baldwin, James, and François Bondy. "James Baldwin, as Interviewed by François Bondy." *Transition* 12 (1964): 12–19.
Baldwin, James, and Nikki Giovanni. *A Dialogue*. Philadelphia: Lippincott Williams & Wilkins, 1973.
Baldwin, James, and Margaret Mead. *A Rap on Race*. Philadelphia: J. B. Lippincott, 1971.
Baldwin, James, and Sol Stein. *Native Sons: A Friendship That Created One of the Greatest Works of the 20th Century: Notes of a Native Son*. New York: One World, 2004.
Baldwin, T. Better. "James Baldwin: My Uncle and His Love Life." *Huffington Post*, July 30, 2014 (updated September 29, 2014). http://www.huffingtonpost.com/t-better-baldwin/james-baldwin-my-uncle-an_b_5634524.html.
Balfour, Katharine Lawrence. *The Evidence of Things Not Said: James Baldwin and the Promise of American Democracy*. Ithaca, NY: Cornell University Press, 2001.
Ball, Mieke. *Traveling Concepts in the Humanities*. Toronto: University of Toronto Press, 2010.
Baraka, Amiri. "Black Woman." *Black World* (July 1970): 7–11.
———. "Jimmy! Amiri Baraka's Discussion of Writer James Baldwin." *Black Renaissance/Renaissance Noire* 9.2–3 (2009): 242.
Barthelemy, Anthony Gerard. *Black Face, Maligned Race: The Representation of Blacks in English Drama from Shakespeare to Southerne*. Baton Rouge: Louisiana State University Press, 1987.
Baym, Nina. "Melodramas of Beset Manhood." *American Quarterly* 33.2 (1981): 123–39.

Beam, Joseph. "Brother to Brother: Words from the Heart." In *In the Life: A Black Gay Anthology*, edited by Joseph Beam. Boston: Alyson, 1989. 230–42.

———, ed. *In the Life: A Black Gay Anthology*. 2nd ed. Washington, DC: RedBone, 2008.

———. "Not a Bad Legacy, Brother." In *Brother to Brother: New Writings by Black Gay Men*, edited by Essex Hemphill. Boston: Alyson, 1991. 184–88.

Bell, David, and Gil Valentine, eds. *Mapping Desire: Geographies of Sexuality*. New York: Routledge, 1995.

Benjamin, Walter. *The Arcades Project*. Translated by Howard Eiland and Kevin McLaughlin. Edited by Rolf Tiedemann. Cambridge, MA: Belknap Press of Harvard University Press, 1999.

———. *Illuminations*. New York: Schocken, 1968.

Bennett, Jane. *Vibrant Matter: A Political Ecology of Things*. Durham, NC: Duke University Press, 2009.

Benstock, Shari. *The Private Self: Theory and Practice of Women's Autobiographical Writings*. Chapel Hill: University of North Carolina Press, 1988.

Berkowitz, Gerald M. *American Drama of the Twentieth Century*. Longman Literature in English. New York: Longman, 1992.

Betsky, Aaron. *Queer Space: Architecture and Same-Sex Desire*. New York: William Morrow, 1997.

Bigsby, C. W. E. "The Divided Mind of James Baldwin." *Journal of American Studies* 13.3 (1979): 325–42.

Birmingham, Kevin. "No Name in the South: James Baldwin and the Monuments of Identity." *African American Review* 44.1 (2011): 221–34.

Black, Derrek R. "White Nationalist American History." *New York Times* Sunday Review, August 20, 2017, 6–7.

Blair, Sara. *Harlem Crossroads: Black Writers and the Photograph in the Twentieth Century*. Princeton, NJ: Princeton University Press, 2007.

Bloom, Harold. *James Baldwin*. New York: Chelsea House, 1986.

Blunt, Alison, and Gillian Rose, eds. *Writing Women and Space: Colonial and Postcolonial Geographies*. New York: Guilford Press, 1994.

Bobia, Rosa. *The Critical Reception of James Baldwin in France*. New York: Peter Lang, 1998.

———. "*If Beale Street Could Talk*: The French and American Criticism of James Baldwin's 'Prison Parable' / *If Beale Street Could Talk*: La critique française et américaine de la "parabole carcérale' de James Baldwin." *Revue LISA / LISA e-journal* (January 2005). http://lisa.revues.org/609.

Boggs, Nicholas. "Baldwin and Yoran Cazac's 'Child's Story for Adults.'" In *The Cambridge Companion to James Baldwin*, edited by Michele Elam. New York: Cambridge University Press, 2015. 118–32.

———. "'James Baldwin: The Last Interview and Other Conversations' by James Baldwin" (review). *Lambda Literary Newsletter*, February 28, 2015. http://www.lambdaliterary.org/reviews/02/28/james-baldwin-the-last-interview/.

———. "Of Mimicry and (Little Man Little) Man: Toward a Queersighted Theory of Black Childhood." In *James Baldwin Now*, edited by Dwight A. McBride. New York: New York University Press, 1999. 122–60.

Bonetti, Kay. "Interview with James Baldwin." Amherst College, 1984. YouTube, posted October 21, 2015. https://www.youtube.com/watch?v=dua3dtrvq84.

Botton, Alain de. *The Architecture of Happiness*. New York: Vintage International, 2006.

Bourne, Randolph. "Transnational America." *Atlantic Monthly* (July 1916). https://www.theatlantic.com/magazine/archive/1916/07/trans-national-america/304838/.

Boyce-Davies, Carole. *Black Women, Writing, and Identity: Migrations of the Subject*. London: Routledge, 1994.

Boyd, Herb. *Baldwin's Harlem: A Biography of James Baldwin*. New York: Atria Books, 2008.

Bozkurt, Saadet. "Harmony Within and Without: James Baldwin's Quest for Humanity." *American Studies International* 20.1 (1981): 45–51.

Brandon, Gordon. "Physical Sympathy: Hip and Sentimentalism in James Baldwin's *Another Country*." *Modern Fiction Studies* 57.1 (2011): 75–95.

Brendese, P. J. "The Race of a More Perfect Union: James Baldwin, Segregated Memory and the Presidential Race." *Theory & Event* 15.1 (2012).

Briganti, Chiara, and Kathy Mezei, eds. *The Domestic Space Reader*. Toronto: University of Toronto Press, 2012.

Brim, Matt. *James Baldwin and the Queer Imagination*. Ann Arbor: University of Michigan Press, 2014.

———. "James Baldwin's Queer Utility." *ANQ* 24.4 (2011): 209–16.

———. "Papas' Baby: Impossible Paternity in 'Going to Meet the Man.'" *Journal of Modern Literature* 30.1 (2006): 173–98.

Brody, Jennifer DeVere, and Dwight A. McBride. "Plum Nelly: New Essays in Black Queer Studies: Introduction." *Callaloo* 23.1 (2000): 285–88.

Brooks, Gwendolyn. *Maud Martha*. Chicago: Third World Press, 1953.

Brooks, Peter. *Body Work: Objects of Desire in Modern Narrative*. Cambridge, MA: Harvard University Press, 1993.

Brown, Bill. *Other Things*. Chicago: University of Chicago Press, 2015.

———. *A Sense of Things: The Object Matter of American Literature*. Chicago: University of Chicago Press, 2003.

Brown, Cecil. "James Baldwin, Digitally Yours." *Counterpunch*, June 17, 2014. https://www.counterpunch.org/2014/06/17/james-baldwin-digitally-yours/.

Brown, Jayna. *Babylon Girls: Black Women Performers and the Shaping of the Modern*. Durham, NC: Duke University Press, 2008.

Brown, Stephanie, and Keith Clark. "Melodramas of Beset Black Manhood?" *Callaloo* 26.3 (2003): 732–37.

Broyard, Anatole. "No Color Line in Cliches." *New York Times*, May 17, 1974, 37. http://www.nytimes.com/1974/05/17/archives/no-color-line-in-cliches-books-of-the-times-sentimental-love-story.html?_r=0.

Buchet, Martine. *The Taste of Provence: The Colombe d'Or at Saint Paul de Vence*. Paris: Editions Assouline, 1993. English translation, 1995.

Burdick, Anne. *Digital Humanities*. Cambridge, MA: MIT Press, 2016.

Burks, Mary Fair. "James Baldwin's Protest Novel: *If Beale Street Could Talk*." *Negro American Literature Forum* 10.3 (1976): 83–95.

Butler, Judith. *Bodies That Matter: On the Discursive Limits Of "Sex."* Routledge Classics. New York: Routledge, 1993.

———. *Gender Trouble: Feminism and the Subversion of Identity*. Thinking Gender. New York: Routledge, 1990.

———. *Undoing Gender*. New York: Routledge, 2004.

Cain, Shannon. "Artist Statement." *His Place in Provence* (blog), June 28, 2016. http://hisplaceinprovence.org/the-squat/artists-statement/.

Campbell, James. *Exiled in Paris: Richard Wright, James Baldwin, Samuel Beckett, and Others on the Left Bank*. New York: Scribner, 1995.

———. *Talking at the Gates: A Life of James Baldwin*. New York: Viking, 1991.

Camus, Albert. *L'Étranger* (*The Stranger*). Paris: Gallimard, 1942.

Carby, Hazel V. "Becoming Modern Racialized Subjects." *Cultural Studies* 23.4 (2009): 624–57.

———. *Reconstructing Womanhood: The Emergence of the Afro-American Woman Novelist*. New York: Oxford University Press, 1987.

Caws, Mary Ann. *The Surrealist Look: An Erotics of Encounter*. Cambridge, MA: MIT Press, 1997.

Cederstrom, Lorelei. "Love, Race and Sex in the Novels of James Baldwin." *Mosaic* 17.2 (1984): 175–88.

Centre LBGT Côte d'Azur. "Maison de James Baldwin à Saint-Paul-de-Vence: Le Centre LGBT Côte d'Azur monte au créneau pour éviter sa destruction." March 31, 2016. http://centrelgbt06.fr/wp/maison-de-james-baldwin-a-saint-paul-de-vence-le-centre-lgbt-cote-dazur-monte-au-creneau-pour-eviter-sa-destruction/.

Chametzky, Jules, ed. *A Tribute to James Baldwin: Black Writers Redefine the Struggle*. Amherst, MA: Institute for the Advanced Study in the Humanities, 1989.

Chapman, Tony, and Jenny Hockey, eds. *Ideal Homes? Social Change and Domestic Life*. New York: Routledge, 1999.

Chauncey, George. *Gay New York: Gender, Urban Culture, and the Making of the Gay Male World, 1890–1940*. New York: Basic Books, 2003.

Chekhov, Anton. *Three Sisters: An Authoritative Text Edition*. Translated by Tyrone Guthrie and Leonid Kipnis. New York: Avon, 1965.

Christian, Barbara. *Black Feminist Criticism: Perspectives on Black Women Writers*. The Athene Series. New York: Teachers College Press, 1997.

———. "The Race for Theory." *Feminist Studies* 14.1 (1988): 67–79.

Christian, Barbara, and Gloria Bowles, eds. *New Black Feminist Criticism, 1985–2000*. Urbana: University of Illinois Press, 2007.

Cieraad, Irene. *At Home: An Anthropology of Domestic Space*. Space, Place, and Society. Syracuse, NY: Syracuse University Press, 1999.

Clark, Keith. *Black Manhood in James Baldwin, Ernest J. Gaines, and August Wilson.* Champaign: University of Illinois Press, 2002.

Clemens, Walter, Jr. *Can Russia Change? The USSR Confronts Global Interdependence.* New York: Routledge, 2011. Orig. pub. 1990.

Clements, Alexis. "The Private Life of Lorraine Hansberry: Letters, Lists, and Conversations." *Hyperallergic*, January 29, 2014. https://hyperallergic.com/104946/the-private-life-of-lorraine-hansberry-letters-lists-and-conversations/.

Clines, Francis X. "Peter Ustinov Talks of Gorbachev's Chat." *New York Times*, October 30, 1986. http://www.nytimes.com/1986/10/30/world/peter-ustinov-talks-of-gorbachev-chat.html.

Clough, Patricia Ticineto, and Jean O'Malley Halley. *The Affective Turn: Theorizing the Social.* Durham, NC: Duke University Press, 2007.

Coates, Ta-Nehisi. *Between the World and Me.* New York: Spiegel and Grau, 2015.

Cobb, Michael L. *Single: Arguments for the Uncoupled.* New York: New York University Press, 2012.

Combahee River Collective. *The Combahee River Collective Statement: Black Feminist Organizing in the Seventies and Eighties.* Albany, NY: Kitchen Table Women of Color Press, 1986.

Coole, Diana. "The Inertia of Matter and the Generativity of Flesh." In *New Materialisms: Ontology, Agency, and Politics*, edited by Diana Coole and Samantha Frost. Durham, NC: Duke University Press, 2010. 92–115.

Crawford, Margo. "James Baldwin's Side-View Mirror: The Black Arts Movement." Paper presented at the American Studies Association Convention, Toronto, October 8–11, 2015.

Crenshaw, Kimberlé. "Demarginalizing the Intersection of Race and Sex: A Black Feminist Critique of Antidiscrimination Doctrine, Feminist Theory, and Antiracist Politics." *University of Chicago Legal Forum* 140.1 (1989): 139–67.

Crouch, Stanley. *Notes of a Hanging Judge: Essays and Reviews, 1979–89.* Oxford: Oxford University Press, 1990.

Cvetkovich, Ann. *An Archive of Feelings: Trauma, Sexuality, and Lesbian Public Cultures.* Series Q. Durham, NC: Duke University Press, 2003.

Daniels, Lee A. "James Baldwin, Eloquent Writer in Behalf of Civil Rights, Is Dead." *New York Times*, December 2, 1987. http://www.nytimes.com/books/98/03/29/specials/baldwin-obit.html.

Davis, Angela Y. *Are Prisons Obsolete?* Open Media Book. New York: Seven Stories Press, 2003.

———. *Blues Legacies and Black Feminism: Gertrude "Ma" Rainey, Bessie Smith, and Billie Holiday.* New York: Vintage, 1999.

———. *If They Come in the Morning: Voices of Resistance.* New York: Third Press, 1971.

Dayson, Sion. "Another Country: James Baldwin at Home and Abroad." In *James Baldwin: Challenging Authors*, edited by A. Scott Henderson and P. L. Thomas. Boston: Sense Publishers, 2014. 77–89.

de Certeau, Michael. *The Practice of Everyday Life.* Berkeley: University of California Press, 1984.

DeGout, Jasmin Y. "Dividing the Mind: Contradictory Portraits of Homoerotic Love in Giovanni's Room." *African American Review* 26.3 (1992): 425–35.

Delbanco, Nicholas. *Running in Place: Scenes from the South of France*. New York: Atlantic Monthly Press, 1989.

Deloria, Philip. *Indians in Unexpected Places*. Lawrence: University Press of Kansas, 2004.

———. *Playing Indian*. New Haven, CT: Yale University Press, 1999.

Derrida, Jacques. *Specters of Marx*. New York: Routledge, 1993.

DeSalvo, Louise. *On Moving: A Writer's Meditation on New Houses, Old Haunts, and Finding Home Again*. London: Bloomsbury, 2009.

Detweiler, Robert. "Blues Lament: A Review of *If Beale Street Could Talk* by James Baldwin." *Christian Century* 91.27 (1974). Available on *Chicken Bones: A Journal for Literary and Artistic African American Themes*, accessed August 25, 2017. http://www.nathanielturner.com/ifbealestreetcouldtalk.htm.

De Waal, Edmund. *The Hare with Amber Eyes: A Hidden Inheritance*. New York: Picador, 2010.

Dickstein, Morris. *James Baldwin*. Critical Insights. Pasadena, CA: Salem Press, 2011.

"Disparition de l'écrivain James Baldwin dans sa maison de Saint-Paul de Vence en 1987." YouTube, posted February 11, 2013. https://www.youtube.com/watch?v=8pE_Kp8aLW4.

Dixon, Melvin. *Ride Out the Wilderness: Geography and Identity in Afro-American Literature*. Urbana: University of Illinois Press, 1987.

Doku, Samule O. *Cosmopolitanism in the Fictive Imagination of W. E. B. Du Bois: Toward the Humanization of the Revolutionary Art*. London: Rowman and Littlefield, 2015.

Donadio, Rachel. "Battling to Save James Baldwin's Home in the South of France." *New York Times*, April 4, 2017. https://www.nytimes.com/2017/04/04/arts/battling-to-save-james-baldwins-home-in-the-south-of-france.html.

Donahue, Phil. *Black Women Writers*. VHS. Princeton Films for Humanities, 1992.

Douglas, Ann. *The Feminization of American Culture*. New York: Knopf, 1977.

Dowd, Gregory E. *Groundless: Rumors, Legends and Hoaxes on the Early American Frontier*. Baltimore: Johns Hopkins University Press, 2004.

———. *War under Heaven: Pontiac, the Indian Nations, and the British Empire*. Baltimore: Johns Hopkins University Press, 2015.

Downs, Jim. "Not a Dream Deferred: The Photography of Kali-Ma Nazarene." *Huffington Post*, January 16, 2012. http://www.huffingtonpost.com/jim-downs/kali-ma-nazarene-photography_b_1096359.html.

Dragulescu, Luminita M. "Into the Room and Out of the Closet: (Homo)Sexuality and Commodification in James Baldwin's *Giovanni's Room*." *Gender Forum* 16.1 (2006).

Duberman, Martin. *Hold Tight Gently: Michael Callen, Essex Hemphill, and the Battlefield of AIDS*. New York: New Press, 2014.

Du Bois, W. E. B. *The Souls of Black Folk*. Chicago: A. C. McClurg, 1903.

Du Bois, W. E. B., H. L. Gates, and T. H. Oliver. *The Souls of Black Folk: Authoritative Text, Contexts, Criticism*. New York: W. W. Norton, 1999.

duCille, Ann. "Blues Notes on Black Sexuality: Sex and the Texts of Jessie Fauset and Nella Larsen." *Journal of the History of Sexuality* 3.3 (1993): 418–44.

Duffy, Martha. "Book Review: All in the Family." *Time*, June 10, 1974, 94–96.

Duggan, Lisa. "The New Homonormativity: The Sexual Politics of Neoliberalism." In *Materializing Democracy: Toward a Revitalized Cultural Politics*, edited by Russ Castronovo and Dana Nelson. Durham, NC: Duke University Press, 2002. 175–94.

Dunning, Stefanie. "Parallel Perversions: Interracial and Same Sexuality in James Baldwin's *Another Country*." *MELUS* 26.4 (2001): 95–112.

DuPlessis, Rachel Blau. *Writing beyond the Ending: Narrative Strategies of Twentieth-Century Women Writers*. Everywoman: Studies in History, Literature, and Culture. Bloomington: Indiana University Press, 1985.

Eakin, Paul John, ed. *The Ethics of Life Writing*. Ithaca, NY: Cornell University Press, 2004.

———. *Fictions in Autobiography: Studies in the Art of Self-Invention*. Princeton, NJ: Princeton University Press, 1985.

———. *Touching the World: Reference in Autobiography*. Princeton, NJ: Princeton University Press, 1992.

Eckman, Fern Marja. *The Furious Passage of James Baldwin*. New York: M. Evans, 1966.

Edel, Leon, ed. *Henry James Letters: 1875–1883, Vol. 2*. Cambridge, MA: Harvard University Press, 1975.

Edelman, Lee. *Homographesis: Essays in Gay Literary and Cultural Theory*. New York: Routledge, 1994.

Edwards, Brent. "The Taste of the Archive." *Callaloo* 35.4 (2012): 944–72.

Edwards, Thomas R. "Can You Go Home Again?" *New York Review of Books*, June 13, 1974, 37–38.

Elam, Harry Justin, and Robert Alexander, eds. *The Fire This Time: African-American Plays for the 21st Century*. New York: Theatre Communications Group, 2004.

Elam, Michele, ed. *The Cambridge Companion to James Baldwin*. New York: Cambridge University Press, 2015.

———. "Review of New York City's 'The Year of Baldwin.'" *James Baldwin Review* 1 (2015): 202–6.

Ellis, Clifton, and Rebecca Ginsburg, eds. *Cabin, Quarter, Plantation: Architecture and Landscapes of North American Slavery*. New Haven, CT: Yale University Press, 2010.

Ellison, Ralph. *Invisible Man*. New York: Random House, 1952.

———. *Shadow and Act*. New York: Random House, 1964.

Engels, Friedrich, and Ernest Untermann. *The Origin of the Family, Private Property and the State*. Chicago: C. H. Kerr, 1902.

Fabre, Michel. *From Harlem to Paris*. Champaign: University of Illinois Press, 1993.

Farber, Jules B. *James Baldwin: Escape from America, Exile in Provence*. Gretna, LA: Pelican Publishing, 2016.

Faulkner, William. "Dry September." *Scribners* (January 1931): 49–56.

Feldman, Keith P. "Representing Permanent War: Black Power's Palestine and the End(s) of Civil Rights." *CR: The New Centennial Review* 8.2 (2008): 193–231.

Ferguson, Roderick A. *Aberrations in Black: Toward a Queer of Color Critique*. Minneapolis: University of Minnesota Press, 2004.

Field, Douglas. *All Those Strangers: The Art and Lives of James Baldwin*. New York: Oxford University Press, 2015.

———, ed. *A Historical Guide to James Baldwin*. Historical Guides to American Authors. Oxford: Oxford University Press, 2009.

———. *James Baldwin*. Writers and Their Work. Tavistock, UK: Northcote House / British Council, 2011.

———. "Looking for Jimmy Baldwin: Sex, Privacy, and Black Nationalist Fervor." *Callaloo* 27.2 (2004): 457.

———. "On Breaking into James Baldwin's House." *Times Literary Supplement*, July 30, 2014. http://www.the-tls.co.uk/articles/public/freelance-102/.

Fields, Darell Wayne. *Architecture in Black: Theory, Space, and Appearance*. New York: Bloomsbury Academic, 2015. Orig. pub. 2000.

Finney, Nikky. Introduction to James Baldwin, *Jimmy's Blues and Other Poems*. Boston: Beacon, 2014. ix–xxi.

Floyd, Janet, and Inga Bryden, eds. *Domestic Space: Reading the Nineteenth-Century Interior*. Manchester: Manchester University Press, 1999.

Foucault, Michel. "Of Other Spaces: Utopias and Heterotopias." In *Architecture Culture 1943–1968*, edited by Joan Ockman. New York: Rizzoli International, 1993. 420–26.

Foucault, Michel, and Jay Miskowiec. "Of Other Spaces." *Diacritics* 16.1 (1986): 22–27.

Freeburg, Christopher. "James Baldwin and the Unhistoric Life of Race." *South Atlantic Quarterly* 112.2 (2013): 221–39.

Freud, Sigmund. *The Uncanny*. London: Penguin, 1919.

Friedel, Tania. *Racial Discourse and Cosmopolitanism in Twentieth-Century African American Writing*. New York: Routledge, 2012.

Fuss, Diana. *Essentially Speaking: Feminism, Nature and Difference*. New York: Routledge, 1990.

———. *The Sense of an Interior: Four Writers and the Rooms That Shaped Them*. New York: Routledge, 2004.

Gallon, Kim. "Making a Case for the Black Digital Humanities." In *Debates in the Digital Humanities 2016*, edited by Matthew K. Gold and Lauren F. Klein. Minneapolis: University of Minnesota Press, 2016. 42–49.

Garber, Marjorie. *Vested Interests: Cross Dressing and Cultural Anxiety*. New York: Routledge, 1992.

———. *Vice-Versa: Bisexuality and the Eroticism of Everyday Life*. New York: Simon and Schuster, 1996.

Gates, Henry Louis, Jr. "From the Stacks: 'The Fire Last Time'" (June 1, 1992). *New Republic*, August 2, 2013. https://newrepublic.com/article/114134/henry-louis-gates-james-baldwin-fire-last-time.

———. *The Signifying Monkey: A Theory of African American Literary Criticism*. Oxford: Oxford University Press, 1988.

———. *Thirteen Ways of Looking at a Black Man*. New York: Vintage Books, 1998.

———. "The Welcome Table: James Baldwin in Exile." In *Exile and Creativity: Signposts, Travelers, Outsiders, Backwards Glances*, edited by Susan Rubin Suleiman. Durham, NC: Duke University Press, 1996. 305–20.

Gaye, Roxanne. "Trump's Hate." *New York Times*, Sunday Review, August 20, 2017, 1, 6.

Gayle, Addison, Jr. "A Defense of James Baldwin." *College Language Association Journal* 10.3 (1967): 201–8.

———. "The Function of Black Criticism at the Present Time." In *Reading Black: Essays in the Criticism of African, Caribbean, and Black American Literature*, edited by Houston A. Baker Jr. Ithaca: Cornell University Press, 1976. 37–40.

Gerstner, David. *Queer Pollen: White Seduction, Black Male Homosexuality, and the Cinematic*. Champaign: University of Illinois Press, 2011.

Ghansah, Rachel Kaadzi. "The Weight of James Arthur Baldwin." *BuzzFeed*, February 29, 2016. http://www.buzzfeed.com/rachelkaadzighansah/the-weight-of-james-arthur-baldwin-203#.ehn5OjmDj.

Gibson, Donald B. *The Politics of Literary Expression: A Study of Major Black Writers*. Contributions in Afro-American and African Studies. Westport, CT: Greenwood, 1981.

Gilbert, Sandra M., and Susan Gubar, eds. *Norton Anthology of Literature by Women*. New York: W. W. Norton, 2007.

Gilmore, Ruth Wilson. *Golden Gulag: Prisons, Surplus, Crisis, and Opposition in Globalizing California*. American Crossroads. Berkeley: University of California Press, 2007.

Gilroy, Paul. *Black Atlantic: Modernity and Double Consciousness*. Cambridge, MA: Harvard University Press, 1995.

Glassberg, David. *American Historical Pageantry: The Uses of Tradition in the Early Twentieth Century*. Chapel Hill: University of North Carolina Press, 1990.

Gleason, William A. *Sites Unseen: Architecture, Race, and American Literature*. New York: New York University Press, 2011.

Glissant, Édouard. *Caribbean Discourse: Selected Essays*. Translated by J. Michael Dash. Charlottesville: University Press of Virginia, 1989.

Goldsby, Jackie. "Queen for 307 Days: Looking B(l)ack at Vanessa Williams and the Sex Wars." In *Afrekete: An Anthology of Black Lesbian Writing*, edited by Catherine E. McKinley and L. Joyce DeLaney. New York: Anchor Books, 1995. 165–88.

Gordon, Avery. *Ghostly Matters: Haunting and the Sociological Imagination*. Minneapolis: University of Minnesota Press, 2008.

Gorman-Murray, Andrew. "Queering Home or Domesticating Deviance? Interrogating Gay Domesticity through Lifestyle Television." *International Journal of Cultural Studies* 9.2 (2006): 227–47.

Green-Barteet, M. A. "The Loophole of Retreat: Interstitial Spaces in Harriet Jacobs's *Incidents in the Life of a Slave Girl*." *South Central Review* 30.2 (2013): 53–72.

Greenbaum, Vicky. "Expanding the Canon: Shaping Inclusive Reading Lists." *English Journal* 83.8 (1994): 36–39.

Grewal, Inderpal. *Transnational America: Feminisms, Diasporas, Neoliberalisms*. Durham, NC: Duke University Press, 2005.

Griffin, Farah Jasmine. *"Who Set You Flowin'?" The African-American Migration Narrative*. Race and American Culture. New York: Oxford University Press, 1995.

Gross, Larry P., and James D. Woods, eds. *The Columbia Reader on Lesbians and Gay Men in Media, Society, and Politics*. New York: Columbia University Press, 1999.

Grosz, Elizabeth. "Feminism, Materialism, and Freedom." In *New Materialisms: Ontology, Agency, and Politics*, edited by Diana Coole and Samantha Frost. Durham, NC: Duke University Press, 2010. 139–57.

———. *Volatile Bodies: Towards a Corporeal Feminism*. Bloomington: Indiana University Press, 1994.

Guglielmo, Thomas. *White on Arrival: Italians, Race, Power, and Color in Chicago 1890–1945*. Oxford: Oxford University Press, 2003.

Hakutani, Yoshinobu. "If the Street Could Talk: James Baldwin's Search for Love and Understanding." In *Critical Insights: James Baldwin*, edited by Morris Dickstein. Pasadena, CA: Salem Press, 2011. 283–304.

Halberstam, Judith [Jack]. *In a Queer Time and Place: Transgender Bodies, Subcultural Lives*. Durham, NC: Duke University Press, 2005.

Hall, John, and James Baldwin. "James Baldwin, a Transition Interview." *Transition* 41 (1972): 21–24.

Hall, Stuart. *Representations: Cultural Representations and Signifying Practices*. London: Sage, 1997.

———. "Subjects in History: Making Diasporic Identities." In *The House That Race Built: Original Essays by Toni Morrison, Angela Y. Davis, Cornel West, and Others on Black Americans and Politics in America Today*, edited by Wahneema Lubiano. New York: Vintage, 1988. 289–300.

Hall, Stuart, et al., eds. *Culture, Media, Language: Working Papers in Cultural Studies, 1972–79*. London: Hutchinson, 1980.

Hamalian, Leo, and James Vernon Hatch, eds. *The Roots of African American Drama: An Anthology of Early Plays, 1858–1938*. African American Life Series. Detroit, MI: Wayne State University Press, 1991.

Hansberry, Lorraine. *A Raisin in the Sun*. New York: Random House, 1959.

———. *To Be Young, Gifted, and Black: An Informal Autobiography*. New York: Signet, 1970.

Hansen, Karen Tranberg. *African Encounters with Domesticity*. New Brunswick, NJ: Rutgers University Press, 1992.

Harding, Vincent. "From Harlem, with Love: Reflections on James Baldwin—a Dark Brother of Light." *Sojourners* 17.2 (1988): 28–29.

Hardy, Clarence E., III. "James Baldwin as Religious Writer: The Burdens and Gifts of Black Evangelicalism." In *A Historical Guide to James Baldwin*, edited by Douglas Field. Oxford: Oxford University Press, 2009. 61–82.

———. *James Baldwin's God: Sex, Hope, and Crisis in Black Holiness Culture*. Knoxville: University of Tennessee Press, 2003.

Harris, Trudier. "Bearing the Burden of the Blues: *If Beale Street Could Talk*." In *Critical Insights: James Baldwin*, edited by Morris Dickstein. Pasadena, CA: Salem Press, 2011. 305–49.

———. *Black Women in the Fiction of James Baldwin*. Knoxville: University of Tennessee Press, 1985.

———. "The Eye as Weapon in *If Beale Street Could Talk*." MELUS 5.3 (1978): 54–66.

Hartman, Saidiya. "Venus in Two Acts." *Small Axe* 26.2 (2008): 1–14.

Hatton, Nigel. "James Baldwin: 'Poetic Experimentors' in a Chaotic World." In *Kierkegaard's Influence on Literature, Criticism, and Art: The Anglophone World*, edited by J. Stewart. London: Ashgate, 2012. 27–40.

Hayden, Dolores. *The Power of Place: Urban Landscapes as Public History*. Cambridge, MA: MIT Press, 1997.

Heims, Neil. "The Matter of Identity in Maya Angelou's *I Know Why the Caged Bird Sings* and James Baldwin's *If Beale Street Could Talk*." In *Critical Insights: I Know Why the Caged Bird Sings, by Maya Angelou*, edited by Mildred R. Mickle. Pasadena, CA: Salem Press, 2010. 52–65.

Hemmings, Clare. *Why Stories Matter: The Political Grammar of Feminist Theory*. Next Wave. Durham, NC: Duke University Press, 2011.

Hemphill, Essex, ed. *Brother to Brother: New Writings by Black Gay Men*. Boston: Alyson, 1991.

Henderson, A. Scott, and P. L. Thomas, eds. *James Baldwin: Challenging Authors*. Boston: Sense Publishers, 2014.

Henderson, Mae, and E. Patrick Johnson, eds. *Black Queer Studies: A Critical Anthology*. Durham, NC: Duke University Press, 2005.

Hirsch, E. D. *Validity in Interpretation*. New Haven, CT: Yale University Press, 1967.

Hodder, Ian. *Entangled: An Archaeology of the Relationships between Humans and Things*. Malden, MA: Wiley-Blackwell, 2012.

Hoffman, Eva. *Lost in Translation: A Life in a New Language*. New York: Penguin, 1990.

Holland, Sharon. "Foreword: 'Home' Is a Four-Letter Word." In *Black Queer Studies: A Critical Anthology*, edited by Mae Henderson and E. Patrick Johnson. Durham, NC: Duke University Press, 2005. ix–xiii.

Holloway, Clayton G. "When a Pariah Becomes a Celebrity: An Interview with James Baldwin." *Xavier Review* 7.1 (1985): 1–10.

Homans, Margaret. *Women Writers and Poetic Identity: Dorothy Wordsworth, Emily Brontë, and Emily Dickinson*. Princeton, NJ: Princeton University Press, 1980.

hooks, bell. *Outlaw Culture: Resisting Representations*. New York: Routledge, 2006.
hooks, bell, and Amalia Mesa-Bains. *Homegrown: Engaged Cultural Criticism*. Cambridge, MA: South End, 2006.
Howard, June. *Publishing the Family*. New Americanists. Durham, NC: Duke University Press, 2001.
———. "What Is Sentimentality?" *American Literary History* 11.1 (1999): 63–81.
Iloeje, Azubike. "The Dimensions of Captivity in James Baldwin's *If Beale Street Could Talk*." In *Black Culture and Black Consciousness in Literature*, edited by Chidi Ikonné, et al. Ibadan, Nigeria: Heinemann Educational, 1987. 187–96.
Jacobson, Matthew F. *Whiteness of a Different Color: European Immigrants and the Alchemy of Race*. Cambridge, MA: Harvard University Press, 1999.
James, Henry. *The Complete Letters of Henry James 1855–1872*. Vol. 1, edited by Pierre A. Walker and Greg W. Zacharias. Lincoln: University of Nebraska Press, 2007.
James, Jenny M. "Making Love, Making Friends: Affiliation and Repair in James Baldwin's *Another Country*." *Studies in American Fiction* 39.1 (2012): 43–60.
"James Baldwin à propos de son enfance à Harlem." INA, July 20, 1972. http://www.ina.fr/video/I09211837.
"James Baldwin Chez Pierre Dumayet—Lecture Pour Tous (1971)." YouTube, posted October 23, 2014. https://www.youtube.com/watch?v=euJ-yrZMf4k.
James Baldwin Collection. Smithsonian Institution National Museum of African American History and Culture. https://transcription.si.edu/project/7660.
"James Baldwin Interview: Black Man in America (1961) with Studs Terkel." YouTube, posted October 21, 2015. https://www.youtube.com/watch?v=Ke6G3sEdj-s.
"James Baldwin—Interview—Pt. 1." YouTube, posted July 31, 2009. https://www.youtube.com/watch?v=xb_NbdeE2zU.
"James Baldwin—L'entretien Suisse—16 Novembre 1972." YouTube, posted March 15, 2017. https://www.youtube.com/watch?v=37GAVA16UUQ.
"James Baldwin Reads from *Just above My Head*." April 1984, Amherst, MA. YouTube, posted December 27, 2015. https://www.youtube.com/watch?v=XxCV-_8Twoo.
"James Baldwin's Literary Legacy" (user-created clip). Panel with Amiri Baraka. *Book TV*, C-SPAN, July 19, 2008. https://www.c-span.org/video/?c2848533/clip-james-baldwins-literary-legacy.
"James Baldwin, St Paul de Vence—Save His Home." YouTube, posted December 28, 2016. https://www.youtube.com/watch?v=baevi9bTXOM.
JanMohamed, Abdul R., and David Lloyd. *The Nature and Context of Minority Discourse*. New York: Oxford University Press, 1990.
Jean-Paul, Rocchi. "Dying Metaphors and Deadly Fantasies: Freud, Baldwin and Race as Intimacy." *Human Architecture* 7.2 (2009): 159–78.
Johnson, E. Patrick. *Appropriating Blackness: Performance and the Politics of Authenticity*. Durham, NC: Duke University Press, 2003.
———, ed. *No Tea, No Shade: New Writings in Black Queer Studies*. Durham, NC: Duke University Press, 2016.

———. *Sweet Tea: Black Gay Men of the South*. Chapel Hill: University of North Carolina Press, 2008.

Johnson-Roullier, Cyraina E. "(an)Other Modernism: James Baldwin, *Giovanni's Room*, and the Rhetoric of Flight." *Modern Fiction Studies* 45.4 (1999): 932–56.

Johnston, Lynda, and Robyn Longhurst. *Space, Place, and Sex: Geographies of Sexualities*. Lanham, MD: Rowman and Littlefield, 2009.

Kaplan, Amy. *The Anarchy of Empire in the Making of U.S. Culture*. Convergences. Cambridge, MA: Harvard University Press, 2002.

———. "Manifest Domesticity." *American Literature* 70.3 (1998): 581–606.

Kaplan, Cora, and Bill Schwarz, eds. *James Baldwin: America and Beyond*. Ann Arbor: University of Michigan Press, 2011.

Kelley, Mary. "The Need of Their Genius: Women's Reading and Writing Practices in Early America." *Journal of the Early Republic* 21.8 (2008): 1–22.

———. *Private Woman, Public Stage: Literary Domesticity in Nineteenth-Century America*. Chapel Hill: University of North Carolina Press, 2002.

Kenan, Randall. *The Fire This Time*. Hoboken, NJ: Melville House, 2007.

———. *James Baldwin*. Lives of Notable Gay Men and Lesbians. New York: Chelsea House, 1994.

———. "James Baldwin, 1924–1987: A Brief Biography." In *A Historical Guide to James Baldwin*, edited by Douglas Field. Oxford: Oxford University Press, 2009. 21–60.

Kennedy, Liam. *Race and Urban Space in Contemporary American Culture*. Race and Urban Space in American Culture. Chicago: Fitzroy Dearborn, 2000.

Kent, George E. "Notes on the 1974 Black Literary Scene." *Phylon* 36.2 (1975): 182–203.

Kilpeläinen, Pekka. "'Like the Sound of a Crumbling Wall': Transcultural Spatiality in James Baldwin's *Just above My Head*." *Atlantic Studies* 15.1 (2014): 109–27. http://dx.doi.org/10.1080/14788810.2014.919086.

King, Lovalerie, and Lynn Orilla Scott. *James Baldwin and Toni Morrison: Comparative Critical and Theoretical Essays*. New York: Palgrave Macmillan, 2006.

Kinnamon, Kenneth. "Native Son: The Personal, Social, and Political Background." *Phylon* 30.1 (1969): 66–72.

Knapp, Steven, and Walter Benn Michaels. "Against Theory." *Critical Inquiry* 8.4 (1982): 723–42.

Kristeva, Julia. *Strangers to Ourselves*. New York: Columbia University Press, 1991.

Lawrence, D. H. *Studies in Classic American Literature*. New York: T. Seltzer, 1923.

Leeming, David Adams. "An Interview with James Baldwin on Henry James." *Henry James Review* 8.1 (1986): 47–56.

———. *James Baldwin: A Biography*. New York: Knopf, 1994.

Leeming, David Adams, and Magdalena Zaborowska. "Remembering Sedat Pakay 1945–2016." *James Baldwin Review* 3 (2017).

Lefebvre, Henri. *The Production of Space*. Translated by Donald Nicholson-Smith. Cambridge, MA: Wiley, 1991.

Légitimus, Samuel. "Collectif James Baldwin de Paris." https://www.facebook.com/collectifjamesbaldwin?hc_ref=SEARCH&fref=nf.

Lester, Julius. "James Baldwin: Reflections of a Maverick." *New York Times*, May 27, 1984.

Lewis, Oscar. *La Vida: A Puerto Rican Family in the Culture of Poverty—San Juan and New York*. New York: Random House, 1966.

Lokko, Lesley Naa Norle. *White Papers, Black Marks: Architecture, Race, Culture*. Minneapolis: Athlone Press of the University of Minnesota, 2000.

Lordi, Emily J. *Black Resonances: Iconic Women Singers and African American Literature*. New Brunswick, NJ: Rutgers University Press, 2013.

Lowe, Lisa. *The Intimacies of Four Continents*. Durham, NC: Duke University Press, 2015.

Lubiano, Wahneema, ed. *The House That Race Built: Original Essays by Toni Morrison, Angela Y. Davis, Cornel West, and Others on Black Americans and Politics in America Today*. New York: Vintage, 1988.

Lusane, Clarence. *The Black History of the White House*. Open Media Series. San Francisco: City Lights Books, 2011.

Lyne, Bill. "God's Black Revolutionary Mouth: James Baldwin's Black Radicalism." *Science and Society* 74.1 (2010): 12–36.

Marc, Lombardo. "James Baldwin's Philosophical Critique of Sexuality." *Journal of Speculative Philosophy* 23.1 (2009): 40–50.

Marshall, Paule. *Brown Girl, Brownstones*. New York: Feminist Press, 1959.

Martindale, Charles. *Ovid Renewed: Ovidian Influences on Literature and Art from the Middle Ages to the Twentieth Century*. New York: Cambridge University Press, 1988.

Massey, Anne, and Penny Sparke, eds. *Biography, Identity, and the Modern Interior*. Burlington, VT: Ashgate, 2013.

Massumi, Brian. *The Politics of Affect*. Cambridge: Polity, 2015.

Matthews, Glenna. *"Just a Housewife": The Rise and Fall of Domesticity in America*. New York: Oxford University Press, 1987.

McBride, Dwight A. "Can the Queen Speak? Racial Essentialism, Sexuality, and the Problem of Authority." *Callaloo* 21.2 (1998): 363–79.

———, ed. *James Baldwin Now*. New York: New York University Press, 1999.

McClatchy, J. D. *American Writers at Home*. New York: Library of America, 2004.

McClusky, John. "If Beale Street Could Talk." *Black World* (1974): 88–91.

McDowell, Deborah E. *"The Changing Same": Black Women's Literature, Criticism, and Theory*. Bloomington: Indiana University Press, 1995.

McGrane, Sally. "Saved from Demolition, Rosa Parks House Gets a Second Life." *New York Times*, May 2, 2017. https://www.nytimes.com/2017/05/02/world/europe/rosa-parks-house-berlin.html?_r=0.

McKinney, Caitlin. "Leibovitz and Sontag: Picturing an Ethics of Queer Domesticity." *Shift: Queen's Journal of Visual and Material Culture* 3 (2010): 1–25.

McKittrick, Katherine. *Demonic Grounds: Black Women and the Cartographies of Struggle*. Minneapolis: University of Minnesota Press, 2006.

———. "Plantation Futures." *Small Axe* 17.3 (2013): 1–15.

———. *Sylvia Wynter: On Being Human as Praxis*. Durham, NC: Duke University Press, 2015.

McKittrick, Katherine, and Clyde Woods. *Black Geographies and the Politics of Place*. ✓
    Cambridge, MA: South End, 2007.
McPherson, Tara. "Post-archive: The Humanities, the Archive, and the Database."
    In *Between Humanities and the Digital*, edited by Patrick Svensson and David
    Theo Goldberg. Cambridge, MA: MIT Press, 2015. 483–502.
Mendoza, Victor Román. *Metroimperial Intimacies: Fantasy, Racial-Sexual Governance, and the Philippines in U.S. Imperialism, 1899–1913*. Durham, NC: Duke
    University Press, 2015.
Meyer, Gerald. *James Baldwin's Harlem: The Key to His Politics*. Research Group on
    Socialism and Democracy. New York: Taylor and Francis, 2011.
Miles, Tiya. *The House on Diamond Hill: A Cherokee Plantation Story*. Chapel Hill:
    University of North Carolina Press, 2012.
———. *Ties That Bind: The Story of an Afro-Cherokee Family in Slavery and Freedom*. Berkeley: University of California Press, 2006.
Miller, D. Quentin. *A Criminal Power: James Baldwin and the Law*. Columbus:
    Ohio State University Press, 2012.
———. "Going to Meet James Baldwin in Provence." *James Baldwin Review* 1
    (2015): 140–51.
———, ed. *Re-viewing James Baldwin: Things Not Seen*. Philadelphia: Temple University Press, 2000.
Miller, Daniel. *Stuff*. Cambridge: Polity, 2010.
Miller, Elise. "The 'Maw of Western Culture': James Baldwin and the Anxieties of
    Influence." *African American Review* 38.4 (2004): 625–36.
Miller, John. "John Miller Writes of the Galva of 80 Years Ago." *Galva* (IL) *News*,
    June 28, 1934, 5.
Miller, Joshua. "The Discovery of What It Means to Be a Witness: James Baldwin's
    Dialectics of Distance." In *James Baldwin Now*, edited by Dwight A. McBride.
    New York: New York University Press, 1999. 331–59.
Miller-Young, Mireille. *A Taste for Brown Sugar: Black Women in Pornography*.
    Durham, NC: Duke University Press, 2014.
Mills, Nathaniel. "Cleaver/Baldwin Revisited: Naturalism and the Gendering of
    Black Revolution." *Studies in American Naturalism* 7.1 (2012): 50–79.
Mock, Janet. *Redefining Realness: My Path to Womanhood, Identity, Love and So
    Much More*. New York: Atria, 2014.
Morrison, Toni. *The Bluest Eye*. New York: Holt, Rinehart, and Winston, 1970.
———. "Home." In *The House That Race Built: Original Essays by Toni Morrison,
    Angela Y. Davis, Cornel West, and Others on Black Americans and Politics in
    America Today*, edited by Wahneema Lubiano. New York: Vintage, 1988. 3–12.
———. *Home*. New York: Vintage International, 2012.
———. *Playing in the Dark*. Cambridge, MA: Harvard University Press, 1992.
———. "The Site of Memory." In *Inventing the Truth: The Art and Craft of Memoir*,
    edited by William Zinsser. Boston: Houghton Mifflin, 1995. 83–102.
Morton, Donald, ed. *The Material Queer: A Lesbigay Cultural Studies Reader*. Queer
    Critique. Boulder, CO: Westview, 1996.

Morton, Timothy. *Hyperobjects: Philosophy and Ecology after the End of the World.* Minneapolis: University of Minnesota Press, 2013.

Mosher, Marlene. "James Baldwin's Blues." In *Critical Essays on James Baldwin,* edited by Fred L. Standley and Nancy V. Burt. Boston: G. K. Hall, 1988. 111–20.

Mumford, Kevin. "Opening the Restricted Box: Lorraine Hansberry's Lesbian Writing." OutHistory.org. Accessed August 29, 2017. http://outhistory.org/exhibits/show/lorraine-hansberry/lesbian-writing.

Muñoz, José Esteban. "Cruising the Toilet: Leroi Jones / Amiri Baraka, Radical Black Traditions, and Queer Futurity." *GLQ: A Journal of Lesbian and Gay Studies* 13.2 (2007): 353–67.

——. *Disidentifications: Queers of Color and the Performance of Politics.* Minneapolis: University of Minnesota Press, 1999.

Musée et Office de Tourisme, St. Paul-de-Vence. "James Baldwin." Accessed August 28, 2107. http://www.saint-pauldevence.com/en/history/personalities/james-baldwin.

Nash, Jennifer Christine. *The Black Body in Ecstasy: Reading Race, Reading Pornography.* Durham, NC: Duke University Press, 2014.

Naughton, Gerald David. "Confronting the 'Foreigner from Within': (Sexual) Exile and 'Indomitable Force' in the Fiction of James Baldwin and Colm Tóibín." In *Exploring Transculturalism: A Biographical Approach,* edited by Wolfgang Berg and Aoileann Ní Éigeartaigh. Wiesbaden: VS Verlag für Sozialwissenschaften, 2010. 131–45.

Naylor, Gloria. *The Women of Brewster Place.* New York: Viking, 1982.

Nelson, Emmanuel. "Critical Deviance: Homophobia and the Reception of James Baldwin's Fiction." *Journal of American Culture* 14.3 (1991): 91–96.

Nero, Charles. "Queering the Souls of Black Folk." *Public Culture* 17.2 (2005): 255–76.

——. "Reading Will Make You Queer." *Palimpsest* 2.1 (2013): 74–86.

Newman, Charles. "The Lesson of the Master: Henry James and James Baldwin." *Yale Review: A National Quarterly* 56 (1967): 45–59.

New York Public Library. "The Schomburg Center for Research in Black Culture Acquires Papers of Renowned Literary Icon James Baldwin." Accessed August 24, 2017. https://www.nypl.org/press/press-release/april-12-2017/schomburg-center-research-black-culture-acquires-papers-renowned.

Nfah-Abbenyi, Juliana Makuchi. *Gender in African Women's Writing: Identity, Sexuality, and Difference.* Bloomington: Indiana University Press, 1997.

Nicholson, Mavis. Interview with James Baldwin. *Mavis on Four,* UK [1984; re-aired 1987]. YouTube, posted November 1, 2014. https://www.youtube.com/watch?v=3Wht4NSf7E4.

"The 1970s Political Activist Who Invented Penis Pants." *MessyNessy,* June 9, 2015. http://www.messynessychic.com/2013/08/01/the-1970s-political-activist-who-invented-penis-pants/.

Norman, Brian. "Crossing Identitarian Lines: Women's Liberation and James Baldwin's Early Essays." *Women's Studies* 35.3 (2006): 241–64.

———. "James Baldwin's Confrontation with U.S. Imperialism in 'If Beale Street Could Talk.'" *MELUS* 32.1 (2007): 119–38.

Norman, Brian, and Piper Kendrix Williams, eds. *Representing Segregation: Towards an Aesthetics of Living Jim Crow, and Other Forms of Racial Division*. Albany: SUNY Press, 2010.

Norse, Harold. *Memoirs of a Bastard Angel*. New York: William Morrow, 1989.

Noviskie, Bethany. "Resistance in the Materials." In *Debates in the Digital Humanities 2016*, edited by Matthew K. Gold and Lauren F. Klein. Minneapolis: University of Minnesota Press, 2016. 176–83.

Nwankwo, Ifeoma Kiddoe. *Black Cosmopolitanism: Racial Consciousness and Transnational Identity in the Nineteenth-Century Americas*. Philadelphia: University of Pennsylvania Press, 2014.

Oates, Joyce Carol. "If Beale Street Could Talk." *New York Times*, May 19, 1974, 376.

Ockman, Joan, and Edward Eigen, eds. *Architecture Culture, 1943–1968: A Documentary Anthology*. Columbia University Graduate School of Architecture Planning and Preservation. New York: Rizzoli, 1993.

O'Daniel, Therman B. *James Baldwin, a Critical Evaluation*. Washington, DC: Howard University Press, 1977.

Ohi, Kevin. "'I'm Not the Boy You Want': Sexuality, 'Race,' and Thwarted Revelation in Baldwin's *Another Country*." *African American Review* 33.2 (1999): 261–81.

Olney, James. *Autobiography: Essays Theoretical and Critical*. Princeton, NJ: Princeton University Press, 1980.

———. *Memory and Narrative: The Weave of Life Writing*. Chicago: University of Chicago Press, 1998.

O'Reilly, David. "A Play This Time the Fire Has Not Dimmed for James Baldwin, Whose 1950s Work 'The Amen Corner' Opens at the Annenberg Center Tomorrow Night." *Philadelphia Inquirer*, December 2, 1986.

Ostriker, Alicia. *Stealing the Language: The Emergence of Women's Poetry in America*. Boston: Beacon, 1986.

Pakay, Sedat, dir. *James Baldwin: From Another Place*. 1973. Hudson Film Works, 2007.

Papenfuss, Mary. "What Is Rosa Parks' House Doing in Berlin?" *Huffpost*, April 10, 2017. http://www.huffingtonpost.com/entry/rosa-parks-home-berlin_us_58eb2463e4b00de1410454cb.

Parham, Marisa. *Haunting and Displacement in African American Literature and Culture*. New York: Routledge, 2009.

Parham, Marisa, and John Drabinski, eds. *Theorizing Glissant: Sites and Citations*. London: Rowman and Littlefield, 2015.

Pavlić, Edward M. "Come on Up, Sweetheart: James Baldwin's Letters to His Brother." *Boston Review*, October 14, 2015. http://bostonreview.net/books-ideas/ed-pavlic-james-baldwin-letters-brother.

———. *Who Can Afford to Improvise? James Baldwin and Black Music, the Lyric and the Listeners*. New York: Fordham University Press, 2016.

Pereen, Esther, and María del Pilar Blanco. *Popular Ghosts: The Haunted Spaces of Everyday Culture*. London: Bloomsbury, 2010.

Petry, Ann. *The Narrows*. Boston: Beacon, 1953.

———. *The Street*. Boston: Houghton Mifflin, 1946.

Phillips, Michelle H. "Revising Revision: Methodologies of Love, Desire, and Resistance in *Beloved* and *If Beale Street Could Talk*." In *James Baldwin and Toni Morrison: Comparative Critical and Theoretical Essays*, edited by Lovalerie King and Lynn Orilla Scott. New York: Palgrave Macmillan, 2006. 63–81.

Pinckney, Darryl. "James Baldwin: The Risks of Love." *New York Review of Books*, April 13, 2000. http://www.nybooks.com/articles/archives/2000/apr/13/james-baldwin-the-risks-of-love.

Pinto, Samantha. *Difficult Diasporas: The Transnational Feminist Aesthetic of the Black Atlantic*. New York: New York University Press, 2013.

Pirandello, Luigi. *Six Characters in Search of an Author*. New York: Signet Classic, 1998.

Porter, Horace A. *Stealing the Fire: The Art and Protest of James Baldwin*. Middletown, CT: Wesleyan University Press, 1989.

Posner, Miriam. "What's Next: The Radical, Unrealized Potential of Digital Humanities." In *Debates in the Digital Humanities 2016*, edited by Matthew K. Gold and Lauren F. Klein. Minneapolis: University of Minnesota Press, 2016. 32–41.

Powers, Lyall H. "Henry James and James Baldwin: The Complex Figure." *Modern Fiction Studies* 30.4 (1984): 651–67.

Powers, Peter Kerry. "The Treacherous Body: Isolation, Confession, and Community in James Baldwin." *American Literature* 77.4 (2005): 786–813.

Pryse, Marjorie, and Hortense J. Spillers. *Conjuring: Black Women, Fiction, and Literary Tradition*. Bloomington: Indiana University Press, 1985.

Rankine, Claudia. *Citizen: An American Lyric*. Minneapolis, MN: Graywolf Press, 2014.

———. "The Meaning of Serena Williams." *New York Times Magazine*, August 25, 2015. http://www.nytimes.com/2015/08/30/magazine/the-meaning-of-serena-williams.html?_r=0.

Reddinger, Amy. "'Just Enough for the City': Limitations of Space in Baldwin's *Another Country*." *African American Review* 43.1 (2009): 117–30.

Reed, Christopher. "Imminent Domain: Queer Space in the Built Environment." *Art Journal* 55.4 (1996): 64–70.

Reid-Pharr, Robert. *Black Gay Man: Essays*. Sexual Cultures. New York: New York University Press, 2001.

———. *Conjugal Union: The Body, the House, and the Black American*. Race and American Culture. New York: Oxford University Press, 1999.

———. "Dinge." *Women and Performance: A Journal of Feminist Theory* 8.2 (1996): 75–85.

———. *Once You Go Black: Choice, Desire, and the Black American Intellectual*. Sexual Cultures. New York: New York University Press, 2007.

Retter, Yolanda, Anne-Marie Bouthillette, and Gordon Brent Ingram, eds. *Queers in Space: Communities, Public Places, Sites of Resistance.* Seattle: Bay Press, 1997.

Reynolds, Mark. "'Soul!,' the Groundbreaking Public TV Show from the Black Power Era Is Rescued from the Archives." *Pop Matters*, April 22, 2015. http://www.popmatters.com/review/192291-its-been-beautiful-by-gayle-wald/.

Rich, Adrienne. "The Baldwin Stamp." *A Human Eye: Essays on Art in Society.* New York: Norton, 2009. 49–56.

Rifkin, Mark. *Manifesting America: The Imperial Construction of US National Space.* Oxford: Oxford University Press, 2009.

Roberts, Elisabeth. "Geography and the Visual Image: A Hauntological Approach." *Progress in Human Geography* 37.3 (2012): 386–402.

Roediger, David. *The Wages of Whiteness: Race and the Making of the American Working Class.* New York: Verso, 1991.

Rogoff, Irit. *Terra Infirma: Geography's Visual Culture.* New York: Routledge, 2000.

Ross, Marlon B. "The Anatomy of the Straight Black Sissy as Theoretical Intervention." In *Blackness and Sexualities*, edited by Michelle M. Wright and Antje Schuhmann. Berlin: Lit Verlag, 2007. 41–45.

———. "Baldwin's Sissy Heroics." *African American Review* 46.4 (2013): 633–51.

———. "Beyond the Closet as Raceless Paradigm." *BQS* (2005): 161–89.

———. "Camping the Dirty Dozens: The Queer Resources of Black Nationalist Invective." *Callaloo* 23.1 (2000): 290–312.

———. "Some Glances at the Black Fag: Race, Same-Sex Desire, and Cultural Belonging." In *The Black Studies Reader*, edited by Jacqueline Bobo, Cynthia Hudley, and Claudine Michel. London: Routledge, 2004. 151–73.

———. "'What's Love but a Second Hand Emotion?' Man-on-Man Passion in the Contemporary Black Gay Romance Novel." *Callaloo* 36.3 (2013): 669–87.

———. "White Fantasies of Desire: Baldwin and the Racial Identities of Sexuality." *James Baldwin Now* (1999): 13–55.

Rottenberg, Catherine. *Black Harlem and the Jewish Lower East Side: Narratives out of Time.* SUNY Series in Multiethnic Literature. Albany: State University of New York Press, 2012.

———. *Performing Americanness: Race, Class, and Gender in Modern African-American and Jewish-American Literature.* Hanover, NH: Dartmouth College Press, 2008.

Rusk, Lauren. *The Life Writing of Otherness: Woolf, Baldwin, Kingston, and Winterson.* London: Routledge, 2002.

Royal, Gabrielle. "Interview with Kali-Ma Nazarene." Contemporary Literature Series at New York University, 2013. http://nyu-cls.org/karefasmartnazarene.html.

———. "Kali-Ma Nazarene." NYU Queer Literature, March 7, 2013. https://nyuqueerlit.wordpress.com/2013/03/07/kali-ma-nazarene/.

Rybczynski, Witold. *Home: A Short History of an Idea.* New York: Penguin, 1986.

Said, Edward W. *Culture and Imperialism.* New York: Knopf, 1993.

Scarry, Elaine. *The Body in Pain.* Oxford: Oxford University Press, 1987.

Schlosser, J. A. "Socrates in a Different Key: James Baldwin and Race in America." *Political Research Quarterly* 66.3 (2013): 487–99.

Schuessler, Jennifer. "Inside an Author's Oddball Trove of Artifacts." *New York Times*, January 2, 2017. https://www.nytimes.com/2017/01/01/books/inside-jonathan-lethems-oddball-trove.html?mcubz=0.

Schur, Richard. "Unseen or Unspeakable? Racial Evidence in Baldwin and Morrison's Nonfiction." In *James Baldwin and Toni Morrison: Comparative Critical and Theoretical Essays*, edited by Lovalerie King and Lynn Orilla Scott. New York: Palgrave Macmillan, 2006. 205–21.

Schwenger, Peter. *The Tears of Things: Melancholy and Physical Objects*. Minneapolis: University of Minnesota Press, 2006.

Scott, Lynn Orilla. *James Baldwin's Later Fiction: Witness to the Journey*. East Lansing: Michigan State University Press, 2002.

Sedgwick, Eve Kosofsky, and Adam Frank. *Touching Feeling: Affect, Pedagogy, Performativity*. Series Q. Durham, NC: Duke University Press, 2003.

Sedgwick, Mark J. *Against the Modern World: Traditionalism and the Secret Intellectual History of the Twentieth Century*. Oxford: Oxford University Press, 2004.

Shah, Nyan. "Perversity, Contamination, and the Dangers of Queer Domesticity." In *Queer Studies: An Interdisciplinary Reader*, edited by Robert Corver and Stephen Valocchi. Oxford: Blackwell, 2003. 121–41.

Shannon, Janet Harrison. "Family and Community Secrets: Secrecy in the Works of James Baldwin." *Western Journal of Black Studies* 22.3 (1998): 174–81.

Shin, Andrew, and Barbara Judson. "Beneath the Black Aesthetic: James Baldwin's Primer of Black American Masculinity." *African American Review* 32.2 (1998): 247–61.

Showalter, Elaine. *Sister's Choice: Tradition and Change in American Women's Writing*. Oxford: Oxford University Press, 1991.

Shulman, George M. *American Prophecy: Race and Redemption in American Political Culture*. Minneapolis: University of Minnesota Press, 2008.

Singley, Allison Chandler. "'Spurious Delusions of Reward': Innocence and United States Identity in the Caribbean of William Faulkner, Toni Morrison, James Baldwin, and Russell Banks." Ph.D. dissertation, University of Connecticut, 2004.

Slavery: The Making of America. PBS, July 12, 2014.

Slevin, James F., Art Young, and National Council of Teachers of English. *Critical Theory and the Teaching of Literature: Politics, Curriculum, Pedagogy*. Urbana, IL: National Council of Teachers of English, 1996.

Smith, Barbara. "Toward a Black Feminist Criticism." *Women's Studies International Quarterly* 2.2 (1979): 183–94.

Smith, Shawn Michelle. *At the Edge of Sight: Photography and the Unseen*. Durham, NC: Duke University Press, 2013.

Smith, Sidonie. *Manifesto for the Humanities: Transforming the Humanities in Good Enough Times*. Ann Arbor: University of Michigan Press, 2016.

Smith, Sidonie, and Robert H. Walker. *Where I'm Bound: Patterns of Slavery and Freedom in Black American Autobiography*. Westport, CT: Praeger, 1974.

Smith, Sidonie, and Julia Watson. *Reading Autobiography: A Guide for Interpreting Life Narratives*. Minneapolis: University of Minnesota Press, 2010.
Smith, Valerie. *Not Just Race, Not Just Gender: Black Feminist Readings*. New York: Routledge, 1998.
Smith-Rosenberg, Carroll. *Disorderly Conduct: Visions of Gender in Victorian America*. New York: Knopf, 1985.
Somerville, Siobhan B. *Queering the Color Line: Race and the Invention of Homosexuality in American Culture*. Series Q. Durham, NC: Duke University Press, 2000.
"*Soul!* Episode List, 1968–1973." *Thirteen: Media with Impact*. Accessed August 25, 2017. http://www.thirteen.org/soul/soul-episode-guide-1968-1973/.
Sousanis, Nick. *Unflattening*. Cambridge, MA: Harvard University Press, 2015.
Spender, Stephen. "James Baldwin: Voice of a Revolution." *Partisan Review* 30 (1963): 256–60.
Spillers, Hortense. *Comparative American Identities: Race, Sex, and Nationality in the Modern Text*. New York: Routledge, 1991.
———. "Mama's Baby." *Diacritics* 17.2 (1987): 65–81.
———. "The Politics of Intimacy: A Discussion." In *Sturdy Black Bridges: Visions of Black Women in Literature*, edited by Roseann P. Bell, Bettye J. Parker, and Beverly Guy Sheftall. Garden City, NY: Anchor, 1979. 87–106.
Standley, Fred L., and Nancy V. Burt, eds. *Critical Essays on James Baldwin*. Boston: G. K. Hall, 1988.
Standley, Fred L., and Louis H. Pratt, eds. *Conversations with James Baldwin*. Literary Conversations Series. Jackson: University Press of Mississippi, 1989.
Stewart, Jon. *Kierkegaard's Influence on Literature, Criticism, and Art*. Kierkegaard Research. Burlington, VT: Ashgate, 2012.
Stewart, Kathleen. *Ordinary Affects*. Durham, NC: Duke University Press, 2007.
Storey, John. *Cultural Theory and Popular Culture: A Reader*. Chicago: University of Chicago Press, 1998.
Suleiman, Susan Rubin. *Exile and Creativity: Signposts, Travelers, Outsiders, Backward Glances*. Durham, NC: Duke University Press, 1998.
Sundquist, Eric J. *To Wake the Nations: Race in the Making of American Literature*. Cambridge, MA: Harvard University Press, 1993.
Sylvander, Carolyn Wedin. *James Baldwin*. New York: Frederick Ungar, 1980.
Tal, Kalí. *Worlds of Hurt: Readings the Literatures of Trauma*. Cambridge: Cambridge University Press, 1995.
Tate, Claudia. *Domestic Allegories of Political Desire: The Black Heroine's Text at the Turn of the Century*. New York: Oxford University Press, 1992.
Taylor, Douglas. "Three Lean Cats in a Hall of Mirrors: James Baldwin, Norman Mailer, and Eldridge Cleaver on Race and Masculinity." *Texas Studies in Literature and Language* 52.1 (2010): 70–101.
Taylor, Ian R., Karen Evans, and Penny Fraser. *A Tale of Two Cities: Global Change, Local Feeling, and Everyday Life in the North of England*. New York: Routledge, 1996.
Terkel, Studs. *Giants of Jazz*. New York: Crowell, 1957.

---. "An Interview with James Baldwin." In *Conversations with James Baldwin*, edited by Fred L. Standley and Louis H. Pratt. Jackson: University Press of Mississippi, 1989. 3–23.

Terkel, Studs, and Milly Hawk Daniel. *Giants of Jazz*. Rev. ed. New York: Crowell, 1975.

---. *Giants of Jazz*. Rev. and updated ed. New York: New Press, 2002.

Thomas, Kendall. "'Ain't Nothin' Like the Real Thing': Black Masculinity, Gay Sexuality, and the Jargon of Authenticity." In *The House That Race Built: Original Essays by Toni Morrison, Angela Y. Davis, Cornel West, and Others on Black Americans and Politics in America Today*, edited by Wahneema Lubiano. New York: Vintage, 1988. 116–35.

Thomas, Piri. *Down These Mean Streets*. New York: Knopf, 1967.

Thorsen, Karen, dir. *James Baldwin: The Price of the Ticket*. Nobody Knows Production, 1989.

---. "The James Baldwin Project." http://jamesbaldwinproject.org/.

Tomlinson, Robert. "'Payin' One's Dues': Expatriation as Personal Experience and Paradigm in the Works of James Baldwin." *African American Review* 33.1 (1999): 135–48.

Tongson, Karen. *Relocations: Queer Suburban Imaginaries*. New York: New York University Press, 2011.

Traub, Valerie. "The New Unhistoricism in Queer Studies." *PMLA* 126.1 (2013): 21–39.

Traylor, Eleanor W. "I Hear Music in the Air . . ." In *James Baldwin: The Legacy*, edited by Quincy Troupe. New York: Simon and Schuster, 1989. 95–96.

Trinh T. Minh-ha. "Other Than Myself / My Other Self." In *Travelers' Tales: Narratives of Home and Displacement*, edited by George Robertson. New York: Routledge, 1994. 9–26.

Troupe, Quincy, ed. *James Baldwin: The Legacy*. New York: Simon and Schuster, 1989.

---. "The Last Interview (1987)." In *James Baldwin: The Legacy*, edited by Quincy Troupe. New York: Simon and Schuster, 1989. 186–212.

Trubek, Anne. *A Skeptic's Guide to Writers' Houses*. Philadelphia: University of Pennsylvania Press, 2011.

Truszczyńska, Dominika. "Widoczki znane też jako sekrety" [Vitrines: Also known as secrets]. January 2, 2006. http://www.2b.art.pl/index.php?LANG=pl&struct=9_11&art_ID=62.

Ulf, Schulenberg. "'Speaking out of the Most Passionate Love'—James Baldwin and Pragmatism." *European Journal of American Studies* 2.2 (2007): 1–19.

Uno, Roberta, and Lucy Mae San Pablo Burns, eds. *The Color of Theater: Race, Culture, and Contemporary Performance*. New York: Bloomsbury Academic, 2005.

Vlach, John Michael. *Back of the Big House: The Architecture of Plantation Slavery*. Chapel Hill: University of North Carolina Press, 1993.

Wald, Gayle. *It's Been Beautiful: Soul! and Black Power Television*. Photographs by Chester Higgins. Durham, NC: Duke University Press, 2015.

Walker, Alice. *In Search of Our Mother's Gardens: Womanist Prose*. San Diego, CA: Harcourt Brace Jovanovich, 1983.

Wall, Cheryl A. *Changing Our Own Words: Essays on Criticism, Theory, and Writing by Black Women*. New Brunswick, NJ: Rutgers University Press, 1989.

---. "Extending the Line: From Sula to Mama Day." *Callaloo* 23.4 (2000): 149–63.

———. *Women of the Harlem Renaissance*. Women of Letters. Bloomington: Indiana University Press, 1995.

———. *Worrying the Line: Black Women Writers, Lineage, and Literary Tradition*. Chapel Hill: University of North Carolina Press, 2005.

Ward, Jesmyn. *The Fire This Time: A New Generation Speaks about Race*. New York: Scribner, 2017.

Warner, Marina. *Alone of All Her Sex: The Myth and the Cult of the Virgin Mary*. New York: Knopf, 1976.

———. *Phantasmagoria: Spirit, Visions, Metaphors, and Media into the Twenty-First Century*. Oxford: Oxford University Press, 2006.

Warren, Kenneth. *What Was African American Literature? The W. E. B. Du Bois Lectures*. Cambridge, MA: Harvard University Press, 2012.

Washington, Bryan R. *The Politics of Exile: Ideology in Henry James, F. Scott Fitzgerald, and James Baldwin*. Boston: Northeastern University Press, 1995.

Weatherby, William J. *James Baldwin: Artist on Fire: A Portrait*. New York: D. I. Fine, 1989.

Webster, Ivan. "If Beale Street Could Talk." Book Review. *New Yorker*, July 8, 1974.

Weheliye, Alexander G. *Habeas Viscus: Racializing Assemblages, Biopolitics, and Black Feminist Theories of the Human*. Durham, NC: Duke University Press, 2014.

Weisenburger, Steven. "The Shudder and the Silence: James Baldwin on White Terror." *ANQ: A Quarterly Journal of Short Articles, Notes and Reviews* 15.3 (2002): 3.

Weisman, Leslie Kane. *Discrimination by Design: A Feminist Critique of the Man-Made Environment*. Champaign: University of Illinois Press, 1994.

Wells, Monique Y. "Brief Musings on Beauford and James Baldwin." *Les Amis de Beauford Delaney* (blog), December 1, 2010. http://lesamisdebeauforddelaney.blogspot.com/2010/12/brief-musings-on-beauford-and-james.html.

West, Cornel. *Race Matters*. Boston: Beacon, 1994.

Wexler, Laura. *Tender Violence: Domestic Visions in an Age of U.S. Imperialism*. Cultural Studies of the United States. Chapel Hill: University of North Carolina Press, 2000.

White, E. Frances. "The Evidence of Things Not Seen: The Alchemy of Race and Sexuality." In *James Baldwin and Toni Morrison: Comparative Critical and Theoretical Essays*, edited by Lynn O. Scott and Lovalerie King. New York: Palgrave Macmillan, 2006. 237–60.

Wilkins, Craig L. *The Aesthetics of Equity: Notes on Race, Space, Architecture, and Music*. Minneapolis: University of Minnesota Press, 2007.

Williams, Raymond. *The Long Revolution*. Letchworth, UK: Broadview, 1961.

Williams, Terrie M. *Black Pain: It Just Looks Like We're Not Hurting. Real Talk for When There's Nowhere to Go but Up*. New York: Scribner, 2008.

Williams, Thomas Chatterton. "Breaking into James Baldwin's House." *New Yorker*, October 28, 2015. http://www.newyorker.com/news/news-desk/breaking-into-james-baldwins-house.

Wilson, Mabel. *Negro Building: Black Americans in the World of Fairs and Museums*. Berkeley: University of California Press, 2012.

Woubshet, Dagmawi. *The Calendar of Loss: Race, Sexuality, and Mourning in the Early Era of AIDS*. Callaloo African Diaspora Series. Baltimore, MD: Johns Hopkins University Press, 2015.

———. "James Baldwin and the Question of Privacy." Paper presented at the American Studies Association Convention, Los Angeles, November 8, 2014.
Wright, Kai. "Lorraine Hansberry's Gay Politics." *The Root*, March 11, 2009. http://www.theroot.com/lorraine-hansberrys-gay-politics-1790869060.
Yaeger, Patricia. *Honey-Mad Women: Emancipatory Strategies in Women's Writing*. Gender and Culture. New York: Columbia University Press, 1988.
Zaborowska, Magdalena J. "Being James Baldwin, or Everything Is Personal." *New Centennial Review*, special issue, edited by John Drabinski and Grant Farred, 16.2 (2016): 47–64.
———. "Domesticating Baldwin's Global Imagination." In *The Cambridge Companion to James Baldwin*, edited by Michele Elam. New York: Cambridge University Press, 2015. 211–26.
———. "From Baldwin's Paris to Benjamin's: The Architectonics of Race and Sexuality in *Giovanni's Room*." In *Walter Benjamin and Architecture*, edited by Gevork Hartoonian. London: Routledge, 2010. 51–73.
———. "From Istanbul to St. Paul-de-Vence: James Baldwin's *The Welcome Table*." In *James Baldwin: America and Beyond*, edited by Bill Schwartz and Cora Kaplan. Ann Arbor: University of Michigan Press, 2011. 188–208.
———. "Harlem Streets Can Talk: Affective Disorders of Characterization in the Fiction of James Baldwin." In *Black Harlem and the Jewish Lower East Side: Narratives out of Time*, edited by Catherine Rottenberg. New York: SUNY Press, 2013. 133–59.
———. *How We Found America: Reading Gender through East European Immigrant Narratives*. Chapel Hill: University of North Carolina Press, 1995.
———. "'In the Same Boat': James Baldwin and the Other Atlantic." In *Historical Guide to James Baldwin*, edited by Douglas F. Field. Oxford: Oxford University Press, 2009. 177–211.
———. "James Baldwin." In *Oxford Bibliographies in African American Studies*, edited by Gene Jarrett. New York: Oxford University Press, 2016. http://www.oxfordbibliographies.com.
———. *James Baldwin's Turkish Decade: Erotics of Exile*. Durham, NC: Duke University Press, 2009.
———. "Mapping Transcultural Masculinities: James Baldwin's Innocents Abroad, or *Giovanni's Room* Revisited." In *Other Americans, Other Americas: The Politics and Poetics of Multiculturalism*, edited by Magdalena J. Zaborowska. Aarhus: Aarhus University Press, 1998. 119–31.
———, ed. *Other Americans, Other Americas: The Politics and Poetics of Multiculturalism*. Aarhus: Aarhus University Press, 1998.
Zinsser, William, ed. *Inventing the Truth: The Art and Craft of Memoir*. Boston: Houghton Mifflin, 1995.
Zola, Emile. "Letter to the President of the Republic: I Accuse!" January 13, 1898. Accessed August 28, 2017. https://www.marxists.org/archive/zola/1898/jaccuse.htm.

INDEX

aesthetics, 11, 36, 39, 45, 74, 183, 195, 265, 301; Baldwin's domestic, 32; Baldwin's late literary, 47, 48, 56; black, 33; of black domesticity in Baldwin's works, 18; of identity, 310

affect, affection, affective, 3, 27, 36, 43, 52, 66, 72, 78, 86, 104, 116, 128, 145–211, 219, 222, 234–55, 256, 265, 289, 301, 306, 310, 338n7, 344n76, 344n83, 349n17; affect theory, 343n66; haunting, 304–15

African (Black) Diaspora, 23, 29, 246, 251, 296, 310; artists, intellectuals, and writers, 24, 36, 59, 98, 112, 264, 291

age, aging, 52, 68, 72, 75, 124, 125, 146, 192, 193, 219, 281; coming of age, 26, 46, 47, 57, 66, 146, 239, 244, 246, 284, 290

Ahmed, Sara, 71

"Alas, Poor Richard" (Baldwin), 148

Algeria, 130, 193, 199, 200, 202, 203

Als, Hilton, 34–35, 155

Amen Corner, The (Baldwin), 14, 90, 163, 181, 185, 187, 204, 238

American Poets' Corner (New York City), 7

American South, 14, 17, 22, 54, 72, 81, 115, 164, 181, 184, 201, 222, 226, 259, 261, 265, 267; and groping incident, 313

American Writers Museum (Chicago), 32

Amherst, Massachusetts, 187, 217

Angelou, Maya, 36, 75, 82, 108, 128, 230, 255, 257, 289, 298; *I Know Why the Caged Bird Sings*, 255

Another Country (Baldwin), 7, 14, 38, 45, 72, 80, 81, 106, 163, 194, 238, 243, 277, 309, 330n52, 340n33, 341n44, 341n49

Any Bootlegger (Baldwin), 125

Anzaldúa, Gloria, 289

"*Architectural Digest* Visits: James Baldwin," 48, 98, 102, 103, 104, 111, 120, 121, 122–28, 142, 298, 304, 310

architecture, 24, 45, 98, 101, 104, 186, 254, 273, 283, 345n105; Harlem, 235; and identity, 31–32; of literary spaces, 103, 302; and literature, 32, 101, 142, 306, 320n40

Architecture in Black (Fields), 101, 328n28

archive, archiving, 41, 48, 57, 109, 112, 119, 210, 298, 300, 301, 309, 348n9; Chez Baldwin, 37, 41, 45, 61, 64, 65–66, 69, 73, 84, 103, 104, 117, 118, 120, 131, 133, 141, 151, 241, 299, 301, 304, 305, 309, 310; Jonathan Lethem, 48, 300; Lynn Scott, 167

artifacts, 48, 103, 109, 299, 300, 302, 306, 309, 348n9

artistic practice, 74, 95

Atlanta, Georgia, 17, 80, 204, 217, 221, 224, 279

Austen, Jane, 258; *Pride and Prejudice*, 117

authority, 13, 171, 197, 227, 278, 317n1

authors, authorship: African American male-female relationships and, 219; authorial anguish, 57; authorial comment, 25; authorial confession, 285;

authors, authorship (*continued*)
authorial experience, 15; authorial prerogative, 265; authorial redemption, 16; authorial stature, 29; authorial vantage point, 5; Baldwin and, 17, 46, 153, 181, 184, 206, 234, 246, 302; development, 219; dialogue between, 232; and documents, 119; domestic space, 98, 122, 274; dreamscape, 267; femininity, 189; freedom of, 150; home, 76, 305; homemaker and, 117; identity and, 149; identity politics, 229; imagination, 141; imperative, Toni Morrison's authorial, 101; insecurities, 111; interest in domesticity, 54; labor, 96; life, 276; of life story, 26, 54; international, 229; masquerade, 187; mastery, 35; names given to characters, 96; narrative, 246; national, 229; new modes of dwelling through, 27; occupation, 268; parties, 127; persona, 47, 66, 157; personal choices of, 150; personal experience of, 237; physical terrain, 304; powers, 91, 217; queer, 220, 233; and sexual persona, 71; style of, 35; theorization of *disidentification*, 154; unfulfilled plans, 210; U.S., 228; and works, 57. *See also* Austen, Jane; Baldwin, James; Devrim, Shirin; Faure, Jeanne; Lethem, Jonathan; Mock, Janet; Wharton, Edith

"Autobiographical Notes" (Baldwin), 27

autobiography, autobiographical, 17, 48, 57, 58, 98, 103, 104, 340n32, 342–43n59; as Baldwin's unique style, 10, 31, 56, 82, 152, 158, 163, 186, 190, 217, 227, 261, 262, 277–79, 293, 301, 302; dialogue, 232; domestication, 217; as genre, 20, 25, 43, 129, 142, 154, 208, 232, 233, 256; masques, 202; of Maxim Gorky, 172–73; meanings, Baldwin's, 14; personae, 23; references, Baldwin's, 26. *See also* life writing

Avedon, Richard, 41, 329n32, 341n42

Bachelard, Gaston, 24, 101, 102, 115, 116, 120, 121, 306, 307, 308; *The Poetics of Space*, 101, 306–7, 328n30, 329n35

"Backwater Blues" (Smith), 18, 25, 27, 54–55, 58, 216, 285

Baker, Josephine, 56, 108, 129, 193, 198

Baldwin, Berdis, 75, 146, 148, 169, 175, 213, 277

Baldwin, Daniel, 41, 42, 108, 146

Baldwin, David (brother), 95, 146, 175, 204, 307, 328n11; and Chez Baldwin, 2, 39, 41, 44, 94, 96, 98, 105–6, 108–9, 111, 117, 122, 126, 131, 136, 141, 147, 206, 212, 214, 275, 286, 328n21, 329n50, 331nn100–101, 332n112

Baldwin, David (stepfather), 52, 277–78, 287

Baldwin, Helen Brody, 108

Baldwin, James: as an African American (black, Negro) writer, 7, 18, 26, 27, 33, 36, 46, 52, 63, 81, 98, 114, 127, 148, 150, 153, 160–61, 162, 181, 210, 223, 227–33, 245, 246, 281, 289, 298, 301; as an American, 63, 75, 156, 159, 162; bisexuality, 23, 28, 57, 65, 68, 71, 72, 184, 197, 198; as a black American, 20–21, 28, 31, 46, 57, 59, 79, 91, 92, 104, 154, 245; as a black queer, 12, 15, 16, 19, 32, 48, 54, 56, 70, 71, 75, 76, 78, 81, 85–144, 149, 151, 152, 172, 185, 209, 281; desire to memorialize, 4–5, 297–302; as director, 177, 183, 184; as exile, 7, 11, 12, 16, 18–19, 20, 21, 25, 34, 48, 56, 59, 71, 74, 75, 97, 125, 129, 133, 142, 157, 229, 230; and homelessness, 25, 46, 48, 54, 56, 121, 127, 133, 142, 157, 244; as homeowner, 17, 125, 127, 302; as intellectual, 19, 246; as a legend, 5, 75, 139; as nomad, 112, 125, 134, 302; racial identity of, 15, 20, 24, 28, 62, 153; sexual and gender identity of, 10–11, 15, 28, 33, 35, 56, 62, 63, 65, 66, 86, 126–27, 129, 153, 159, 163, 208; sexual molestation of, 275–76; as

transatlantic commuter, 5, 33, 53, 182, 191; the "writer's house," 3, 45, 100, 104, 114, 117, 136–38, 140, 141, 214, 302, 304, 305, 308. *See also individual works*
Baldwin, Trevor, 9, 108, 146, 329n49, 332n1
Baldwin, Wilmer ("Lover"), 108, 146
"Baldwin Stamp, The" (Rich), 296–98
"Ballad (for Yoran)" (Baldwin), 79
Baraka, Amiri (LeRoi Jones), 36, 38, 217, 254, 289; "Black Woman," 254
Beam, Joseph, 68, 70–71, 184, 291, 327n67; "Making Ourselves from Scratch," 80
Belafonte, Harry, 185
Beloved (Morrison), 291, 348n13
Berlin, Germany, 168; Rosa Parks's house as museum in, 301
Birdsong, Alexa, 291
black artist, 14, 25, 36, 59, 155, 246, 261. *See also* writers
Black Arts Movement, 228, 242, 244, 259
blackness, 15, 16–27, 28, 31, 46, 57, 65, 66, 72, 92, 97, 101, 156, 157, 159, 170–71, 221, 222, 228, 234, 244, 245, 249, 263, 266, 286, 302, 325n44, 328n28, 344n76, 348nn11–12; American, 246; fragmented, 62; national, 127; queer, 75. *See also home, blackness, and me / space, story,* and *self*
Black Panthers, 193, 196, 203, 205
Black Power, 23, 35, 75, 172, 230, 233, 244
black queers, queerness, 19, 32, 48, 57, 66, 70, 71–72, 78, 85–211, 159, 210, 220, 223, 231, 298, 308, 324n26, 345n96; American, 12, 15, 19, 54; artists, 48, 54, 56, 280; desire, 293; domesticity, 72, 81, 142, 219, 274, 323n15; heterotopias, 220, 222, 255–93; humanism, 31, 70–71, 76, 97, 296; literary life, 101; marginalization, 308; men, 16, 70, 75; movements, 291; spaces, 48, 222; studies, 71, 308; women, 56. *See also* Johnson, E. Patrick; "quare"
black space, 262–63
"Black Woman" (Baraka), 254
Bleak House (Dickens), 259
Blues for Mister Charlie (Baldwin), 14, 58, 130, 163, 181, 187, 188, 277–78
Bluest Eye, The (Morrison), 291
Boggs, Nicholas, 259, 329n49
Braque, Georges, 111, 135
Brim, Matt, 34, 291, 324n25, 325n46, 328n16
Brooks, Gwendolyn, 22, 36, 38, 229, 255, 291
Brown, Cecil, 36, 108, 193
Bullins, Ed, 289

Camus, Albert, 30, 31
Cathedral of St. John the Divine (New York City), 7, 82, 127
Cazac, Yoran, 240, 258–59, 330n53. *See also* "Ballad (for Yoran)"
Césaire, Aimé, 24
César, 130
Cezzar, Engin, 107, 184, 204
Chekhov, Anton, 154–55, 197, 204, 333n14, 337n95. *See also individual works*
Cherry Orchard, The (Chekhov), 183, 186, 192, 195, 204, 209
Chez Baldwin, 6, 17–18, 24, 37, 39, 44, 48, 51, 85–143, 154, 175, 193, 195, 212, 214, 292, 294, 297, 298, 304, 312, 313; archive, 64, 66, 69, 73, 84, 118, 241, 299, 301, 305, 310; as a character, 310; remnants of, 100, 117, 133, 135–38, 139, 140, 206, 306, 314; spatial elements of, 125; as "the spread," 124; as stage set for *The Welcome Table*, 154, 184, 191–93, 195–96, 206–8; the welcome table at, 182, 206–8. *See also* home, homes; house, houses; Zaborowska, Magdalena

Childhood of Maxim Gorky, The, 172–73
Christian, Barbara, 23, 60, 64, 289, 347n143
church, churches, 151, 161, 176, 178, 179, 208, 234, 237, 265, 313, 341nn45–46; Baldwin's family in, 223, 267; in Baldwin's works, 26, 35, 58, 72, 162, 177, 180, 181, 187, 188, 221, 224, 233, 238, 240, 241, 242, 243, 244, 247, 260, 262, 265, 267, 273, 277, 279; black, 14, 34, 95, 187, 236; Catholic, 91, 92; Harlem, 95, 181, 236, 262; vs. street, 247, 265
Civil Rights Movement, 7, 10, 17, 75, 115, 125, 184, 242, 244, 247, 261; Black Lives Matter as the new, 38
class, 164, 245; and age, 240; and black masculinity, 38; and colorism, 202; conflicts, 58; and culture, 169; and ethnicity, 237; and gender, 183, 238, 282, 341n49; influence on black lives, 230; and intersectional identity, 7, 19, 32, 58, 101, 127, 201, 219, 225, 262, 263, 290, 291; lines, 256; lower, 14, 38, 53, 57, 95, 342n56; and materialism, 24; middle, 21, 72, 126, 239, 280; and nationality, 208; and political power, 146; politics, 159; race and, 86, 97, 169, 171, 173, 208, 237, 240, 281, 341n49; and region, 21, 250; relations, 32; and religion, 21, 208; segregation, 238; and sexuality, 36; systems, 72
Cleaver, Eldridge, 36, 75, 172, 193, 205, 209, 334n45, 340n33
Coates, Ta-Nehisi, 35, 38, 291, 321n63
Cold War, 43, 47, 57, 173, 186, 192, 312
Cole, Teju, 291
Collected Essays (Baldwin), 223
Colombe D'Or, La, 57, 107, 108, 132, 133, 138, 139
colorism, 201, 247, 255; and class, 202
color lines, 15, 19, 23, 27–32, 58, 76, 149, 220, 247, 248; *Queering the Color Line*, 71

Color Purple, The (Walker), 70, 255, 291
"Come on Up, Sweetheart" (Pavlić), 332n106
"Come Out the Wilderness" (Baldwin), 238–39
community, communities, 30, 32, 54, 72, 76, 97, 117, 165, 209, 224, 225, 232, 290; black, 59, 162, 209, 221, 231, 232, 233, 247, 279, 281, 283, 284, 285; black gay, 70; of color, 225, 250; of men, 71; religious/as congregations, 181, 223, 224; in St. Paul-de-Vence, 124, 127; transnational, 182; urban, 181, 240; white gay, 68; of women, 290; of writers, 310
Coombs, Orde, 232–33
Cosby, Bill, 108, 139
Crawford, Margo, 259
creative process, 57, 120, 189, 308. *See also* authors, authorship; writing process
Cullen, Countee, 229

Dallas, Walter, 17, 155, 204–6, 330n79, 333n15, 335n57, 335n59, 336n73, 336n76, 337n84, 337n97, 337n99, 337n100. See also *Welcome Table, The*
Davis, Angela, 246, 323n9, 341n51
Davis, Miles, 39, 45, 108, 139
Delaney, Beauford, 45, 88, 107, 141, 174, 258, 259
Delbanco, Nicholas, 107, 108, 325n38, 331n106
Dempsey, Douglas, 8, 114, 144, 182, 191, 214–15, 275
Devil Finds Work, The (Baldwin), 10, 17, 45, 47, 56, 111, 129, 145, 146, 153, 155, 158, 162, 163, 164, 169, 170, 173, 175–76, 177, 179, 180, 223, 224, 241
Devrim, Shirin, 128
Dialogue, A (Baldwin and Giovanni), 70, 75, 217, 219, 232–33, 256
Dickens, Charles, 145, 146, 155, 166, 171, 175, 259, 261. *See also individual works*

"Discovery of What It Means to Be an American, The" (Baldwin), 244
disidentification, 47, 76, 145–212, 219, 265, 288. *See also* Muñoz, José
Dixon, Melvin, 22, 35, 72, 290, 319n35
domestic, domesticity, 10, 13, 14, 17, 19, 22, 23, 24, 26, 32, 36, 38, 47, 54, 55, 57, 72, 76, 77, 78, 86, 101, 115, 116, 119, 127, 134, 161, 189, 210, 220, 222, 227, 231, 242, 244, 259, 261, 263, 266, 267–69, 271, 274, 276, 277, 280, 285, 286, 288, 290, 291, 293, 319n32, 319n38, 320n40, 323n9; alternative, 47, 56, 57, 222; black, 18, 20, 32, 41, 47, 217, 233, 261, 262, 263, 267; black queer, 72, 85–143, 94–95, 142, 219, 323n15; at Chez Baldwin, 20, 24, 33, 41, 46, 47, 95, 97, 98, 100, 103, 104, 114, 116, 117, 126, 133, 141, 142, 196, 208, 298, 309; definitions of, 57, 262; feminine narrative of, 152, 155, 187, 347n143; life, 4, 5, 16, 19, 24, 45, 155, 210, 276, 279; maintenance, 124; nationalism, 76, 240; practices, 81; queer, 189–204; queer black, 85–144; scenery, 154; separating oneself from, 70; space, 11, 13, 14, 46, 48, 217, 222, 233, 265, 267, 270, 274, 279, 280, 283, 285, 286, 290, 304, 307, 310, 342n56; stability, 17, 131, 197; terrorism, 10, 161, 221, 226; traces, 117; tragedy, 266; work, 124, 155, 290. *See also* aesthetics; authors, authorship; imagination; material, materiality; nation, national; nationalism; queerness; race; sexuality; space; theater; writers
domestication, 18, 48, 49, 51–84, 153, 154, 157, 217, 265, 298, 310; of trauma, 313. *See also* autobiography, autobiographical
Douglass, Frederick, 22, 32, 59, 230; house/museum, 32
"Dream Deferred" (Hughes), 58

Du Bois, W. E. B., 15, 24, 27, 28, 59, 82, 101, 150, 343n70. *See also* color lines
Duggan, Lisa, 324n26
Dumas, Alexandre, 228
Dunbar, Paul Lawrence: "We Wear the Mask," 225
Düşenin Dostu (Baldwin), 177, 204

Edelman, Lee, 346n120
Edwards, Brent H., 301, 348n9
Ellison, Ralph, 14, 23, 35, 36, 229, 247, 257, 289, 321n60; *Invisible Man*, 14
"Encounter on the Seine: Black Meets Brown" (Baldwin), 21, 173
Engels, Friedrich, 22
"Equal in Paris" (Baldwin), 87
Equiano, Olaudah, 59, 229
Étranger, L' (Camus), 30
Evers, Medgar, 10, 125, 216
"Everybody's Protest Novel" (Baldwin), 148, 152, 161
"Every Good-Bye Ain't Gone" (Baldwin), 1, 11, 15–16, 18, 20, 27, 28–29, 30–31, 52
Every Good-Bye Ain't Gone (Njeri), 255
Evidence of Things Not Seen, The (Baldwin), 10, 17, 44, 45, 48, 56, 77, 78, 146, 153, 179, 209, 217, 218, 219, 221–27, 234, 237, 242, 261, 279, 305
exile, 7, 11, 12, 13, 16, 18, 19, 20, 48, 56, 59, 74, 75, 125, 133, 142, 157, 229, 230, 236, 242, 283, 331n83; in France, 21, 25, 34, 97, 130, 193, 208; in Turkey, 71, 97

Fabre, Michel, 107, 329n44
façade, 12, 51–84, 140. *See also* mask; masquerade; persona
faggot, 62, 76, 161, 209
Fanon, Frantz, 24
Farber, Jules B., 34, 120, 130, 132, 331n103
Faure, Jeanne, 2, 121, 130–31, 132, 193, 195, 215

female, 22, 38, 129, 152, 153, 158, 191, 210, 336n80; African American/black, 13, 56, 209, 219, 232, 244, 247, 254, 255, 284, 324n19; influence on/in Baldwin's work, 58, 75, 81, 82, 103, 133, 134, 151, 154, 160, 163, 181, 182, 184, 187, 189, 190, 194, 196, 198, 200, 209, 232, 233, 240, 243, 246, 256, 280, 284, 285, 286, 323n8, 340n33; male in, 70, 288; male to, 193; queer, 233; white, 325n34, 342n56

femininity, 31, 287, 290, 313; Baldwin as identified with, 158, 160; in Baldwin's works, 38, 163, 189, 191, 234–55, 279, 281, 289; black, 48, 56, 70, 129, 219, 233, 286; and domestic/home, 21, 36, 155, 163, 189; expatriate, 128; and genre, 14, 20, 256; and identity, 10–11, 14, 22, 56, 86, 153, 160, 162, 186, 192, 193, 194, 208, 210, 234, 246, 250, 254, 289, 291, 310; mode of writing, 20, 149, 189; white, 152

feminism, 75, 220, 228–33, 247, 250, 255, 290; and architecture, 31–32; black, 23, 64, 75, 219, 228–33, 323n9; of color, 291; feminist criticism, 20, 22, 33; men, 198; second-wave, 20, 152, 289; theory, 184, 301

Field, Douglas, 3, 33, 34, 141, 334n49, 334n53

Fields, Darell, 24, 101, 306; *Architecture in Black*, 101, 328n28

Fire Next Time, The (Baldwin), 7, 35, 46, 146, 173, 186, 226, 236, 239, 288, 289, 333n11, 335n58

"Fly in Buttermilk, A" (Baldwin), 53, 256

Foucault, Michel, 19, 24, 225–26, 262–63, 265, 280, 339n13, 345n98, 345n103, 346nn119–20. *See also* heterotopia

France, 18, 29, 31, 44, 52, 53, 56, 95, 97, 107, 125, 130, 131, 182, 197, 199, 202, 203, 222, 228, 244, 264; Baldwin on, 5, 11–12; Baldwin's critical reception in, 33; Baldwin's exile in, 21, 25, 97, 186; Baldwin's home in, 217; erasure of Baldwin's life in, 24, 302; Kali-Ma Nazarene in, 3; South of, 1, 17, 56, 95, 97, 103, 183. *See also* Baldwin, James; St. Paul-de-Vence

"Freaks and the American Ideal of Manhood" (Baldwin), 56, 57, 64, 65, 66, 68, 70, 71, 76, 152, 153, 154, 156, 157, 158, 184, 194, 197, 208, 209–10, 223, 231, 275–76, 277, 278, 288, 289. *See also* "Here Be Dragons"

Friedan, Betty, 289

Gates, Henry Louis, Jr., 101, 108, 193, 312, 337n102. *See also Signifying Monkey, The*

gender, 13, 19, 25, 26, 28, 32, 33, 47, 56, 58, 65, 68, 72, 76, 81, 103, 116, 117, 126, 127, 128, 129, 152, 158, 163, 164, 184, 189, 191, 196, 201, 208, 210, 211, 233, 238, 240, 243, 244, 247, 249, 251, 252, 257, 258, 262, 263, 282, 286, 287, 288; androgyny, 48, 56, 66, 70, 184, 186, 193, 194, 197, 201, 208, 209, 210, 231, 286, 288; bending, 181, 208; conflicts, 183; definitions, 199, 219, 230, 281; determinism, 293; difference, 30, 127, 202, 290; discrimination, 238; and domicile, 21, 72; equality, 246, 254; out-of-, 35; performance/performativity, 66, 129, 152, 157, 159, 183; personae, 152, 157, 187; politics of, 155, 310; and race, 247; racialized, 12, 59, 209, 219; representation of, 23, 247; roles, 23, 47, 56, 75, 128, 186, 232, 233, 235, 254, 280; and sexuality, 33, 47, 56, 59, 66, 101, 117, 126, 129, 163, 211, 219, 231, 262, 263, 326n47, 338n110, 348n12; and social space, 17, 58, 231, 265; studies, 33, 101, 184; trans-, 158, 186, 187, 192, 193, 209, 291, 323n15; transgression, 256; trauma and, 279. *See also* female; femininity; male; man; masculinity; woman, women

Ghansah, Rachel Kaadzi, 3
Giovanni, Nikki, 23, 36, 70, 75, 129, 214, 217, 219, 228–33, 246, 256, 257, 338n2, 343n64; *A Dialogue*, 70, 75, 217, 219, 232–33, 256
Giovanni's Room (Baldwin), 12–14, 70, 72, 157, 160, 199, 225, 239, 241, 244
Glissant, Édouard, 24, 59, 323n14, 324n21
"Going to Meet the Man" (Baldwin), 222
Going to Meet the Man (Baldwin), 239, 278
Goldstein, Richard, 63, 64, 153, 156, 157, 158, 159, 160, 161, 162, 291
Goodwin, Ruby Berkley, 73, 230
Gorbachev, Mikhail, 5, 192
Go Tell It on the Mountain (Baldwin), 14, 16, 38, 72, 80, 86, 90, 125, 148, 163, 178, 181, 194, 225, 230, 245, 277
Greenwich Village, 7, 45, 242, 244, 248, 249, 253, 260, 336n80; authorial location, 134, 158, 235; Baldwin's coming of age, 57, 63, 65, 152–53, 156, 159; 81 Horatio Street in, 7, 318n16
Greer, Germaine, 289
Grosvenor, Vertamae, 57, 128
Guillaumes, France, 141

Haizlip, Ellis, 214, 228; *Soul!*, 214, 227–33
Hall, Stuart, 78, 323n14, 344n83
Hammond, Jupiter, 59, 229
Hansberry, Lorraine, 38, 57–59, 82, 151, 321n70, 323n17. *See also individual works*
Haley, Alex, 346n117; house/museum, 32, 320n52
Happersberger, Lucien, 47, 86–94, 107, 120, 122, 198, 203, 327n1, 327n5, 344n77
Harlem, 11, 18, 34, 45, 47, 58, 88, 108, 112, 134, 213, 308; architecture, 235; as authorial location, 17, 38, 52, 54, 81, 92, 95, 152–53, 157, 158, 181, 211, 219, 222, 228, 233, 234, 235–64, 267–68, 278, 282, 342nn55–56, 345n96; as Baldwin's birthplace, 7, 52, 114; Baldwin's coming of age in, 26, 57, 114, 166, 169, 172, 223, 233, 313; Baldwin's elementary school in (P.S. 24), 9, 146, 166, 171, 172, 278; church, 233; as homophobic, 127, 14; Jews in, 235–37, 343n68; 1943 riots, 26, 237–38, 264, 278; police, 80, 153, 170, 175, 238
"Harlem Ghetto, The" (Baldwin), 219, 234–39, 241, 249, 256, 259
Harlem Renaissance, 35
Harlem Theater, 177
Harper, Frances, 59, 230
Hassell, Bernard, 2, 66, 84, 94, 107, 182, 193, 195, 212
Hemingway, Ernest, 32, 117
Hemphill, Ernest, 68, 70, 291
"Here Be Dragons" (Baldwin), 56, 62, 104, 152, 208. *See also* "Freaks and the American Ideal of Manhood"
heterotopia, 48, 213–94, 345n98, 345n106
Himes, Chester, 32; *If He Hollers Let Him Go*, 148
Hodder, Ian, 4
Home (Morrison), 38
home, blackness, and *me / space, story*, and *self*, 15, 16–20, 25, 26, 30, 32, 43, 117, 263
home, homes, 13, 14, 15–16, 25, 29, 31, 38, 54, 55, 58, 71, 75, 85–144, 154, 156, 175, 176, 187, 196, 203, 215, 216, 219, 223, 234, 239, 245, 246, 249, 252, 254, 267, 270, 274, 276, 277, 278, 280–81, 282, 283, 285, 290, 293, 296, 302, 304, 305, 311–12; African American (black), 14, 58, 59, 76, 259, 280; Baldwin's childhood, 23, 47, 57, 153, 168, 220, 223, 247, 313; Baldwin's last, 206; being at, 156–62, 191, 209, 220, 234, 245, 258, 271, 277, 293, 301, 308; black

INDEX 383

home, homes (*continued*)
queer, 96, 97; of black writers, 210; and community, 30; country, 3, 7, 11, 13, 26, 46, 52, 53, 57, 59, 78, 79, 81, 82, 130, 149; definitions, 11, 12, 24, 52, 56, 57, 59, 81, 210, 214, 222, 262, 263, 266, 268, 308, 342n59; exile from, 48, 75, 129, 130, 230; femininity and, 163; in France, 217; free, 217, 227–33; homelessness, 5, 13, 14, 16, 25, 46, 48, 52, 54, 56, 153, 211, 216, 217, 219, 222, 244, 301; home owner, 193, 302; house and, 21, 281; in literary legacy, 82, 286; loss of, 79, 127, 153, 234, 270; memories of, 223; national, 21, 48, 74; nomadic, 112; social space, 1–2, 5, 22, 72, 80, 152, 155, 191, 209, 221, 259, 264, 313, 320n40; terror and, 223; as trope in Baldwin's work, 146; women and, 22. *See also* Chez Baldwin; domestic, domesticity; house, houses

homophobia, homophobic, 10, 12, 153, 157–61, 287–89, 346n120, 347n137; critiques of Baldwin, 172, 209; and misogyny, 10, 157, 158, 159, 209, 287–89, 301, 311; and police, 114, 153; and poverty, 53; and racism, 53, 63, 70, 83, 114, 238, 301; and sexism, 83, 238. *See also* transphobia

hooks, bell, 23, 120, 263, 289, 324n19

house, houses, 1, 13, 20, 23, 26, 39, 48, 54, 55, 57, 58, 71, 78, 81, 85, 87, 91, 98, 100, 101, 120, 121, 122, 125–26, 129, 160, 190, 197, 199, 202, 203, 204, 214, 215, 216, 249, 254, 255, 260, 262, 267, 268, 273, 274, 275, 277, 279, 280–81, 283, 285, 286, 293, 296, 305, 327n65; African Diasporic, 266; American, 1–50, 74, 76, 210, 244, 301; Baldwin's, in St. Paul-de-Vence, 1–5, 17, 18, 24, 39, 41, 44, 45, 46, 60, 80, 95, 96, 97, 98, 100, 102–12, 117, 119, 120, 121, 122, 124, 125, 126, 127, 134–44, 160, 182, 191, 192, 193, 195, 196, 206, 210, 214, 217, 286, 289, 302, 309, 312, 315, 328n21, 329n50, 332n112, 332n117, 348n11; Baldwin's childhood, in Harlem, 7, 24, 146, 277; black, 14, 328n28; black queer, 83, 117; Coretta Scott King's, 204; haunted, 145–212; and home, 11, 21, 98, 281; household, 17, 72, 80, 81, 91, 97, 102, 107, 117, 120, 124, 154, 182, 191, 193, 195, 196, 199, 200, 260; housework, 124, 146; invisible, 295–315; literary-legacy-as-metaphor, 82, 206, 231, 233, 261; and literature, 116; loss of, 166; materiality of, 119, 121, 128; as metaphor, 10, 101, 102, 121, 157, 206, 213–94; the national, 10, 12, 13, 14, 16, 17, 18, 19, 22, 36, 38, 48, 58, 66, 68, 72, 75, 76, 77, 79, 101, 146, 156, 180, 208, 210, 217, 220, 221, 223, 226, 237, 250, 256, 257, 263–66, 277, 299, 301, 310, 312, 313, 319n38, 331n83; playing, 91; poetics, 120, 121, 308; the projects, 239; racial, 101; Rosa Parks's, 301; as theater, 304; virtual (house-museum), 48, 302; White House, 10, 79, 310, 312; women and, 128–33, 254; writers', 26, 32, 45–46, 98, 100, 104, 112–14, 116, 117, 137, 299, 300, 302, 304, 305, 308, 320n52, 328n22, 329nn37–38, 330nn56–57. *See also* Chez Baldwin; domestic, domesticity; home, homes

Hughes, Langston, 229; "Dream Deferred," 58

Hurston, Zora Neale, 35, 59, 65, 230, 255

Hutchinson, Jill, 42, 44, 100, 105–6, 108–9, 112, 133, 141, 198, 206, 207, 208, 307, 331n100

I Am Not Your Negro (Peck), 7, 10–11, 318n18, 338n4

If Beale Street Could Talk (Baldwin), 14, 17, 38, 45, 48, 56, 58, 81, 115, 130, 153, 189, 194, 203, 211, 217, 219, 220, 222, 225, 232, 233–61, 266, 281, 284, 305

If He Hollers Let Him Go (Himes), 148
I Know Why the Caged Bird Sings (Angelou), 255
imagination, 31, 34, 57, 66, 68, 82, 85, 101, 102, 112, 114, 142, 170, 173, 175, 178, 210, 221, 222, 291, 296, 299, 308; American, 208; American literary, 220, 229; black queer, 66; creative, 41; domestic, 41; humanistic, 227; lack of, 300; literary, 256; literary-critical, 2; phenomenology of, 101, 121; racist, 221; readers', 4, 204; writer's, 115, 141. *See also* Brim, Matt; Zaborowska, Magdalena
individual, individuality, 20, 22, 28, 36, 43, 54, 57, 58, 74, 76, 79, 109, 115, 150, 152, 154, 169, 170, 174, 239, 261, 262, 264, 289, 290; American, 10; identity, 127; imagination, 101; influence, 176; memory, 280; and privacy, 64; private, 19, 289; and social (space), 45, 151; trauma, 279; whiteness and self-understanding, 22
individualism, 57, 75, 70, 75, 76, 116, 159; and national identity, 46
Invisible Man (Ellison), 14
Istanbul, Turkey, 5, 44, 86, 107, 112, 128, 134, 149, 184, 197, 260, 264, 268

J'accuse (Zola), 226
Jackson, Michael, 208
Jacobs, Harriet, 22, 59, 229–30
James, C. L. R., 24
James, Henry, 33, 103, 175, 250, 255, 317n9
James Baldwin: A Biography (Leeming), 88, 95, 96, 121, 129, 132, 162, 184, 190, 199, 203, 206, 208, 240, 278, 286, 304, 313
James Baldwin: From Another Place (Pakay), 5, 59, 157
James Baldwin: The Legacy (Troupe), 122, 289. *See also* Soyinka, Wole
James Baldwin: The Price of the Ticket (Thorsen), 5, 8, 52, 80, 83, 88, 91, 92, 107, 109, 111, 114, 125, 127, 133, 144, 182, 191, 214–15, 275, 278, 318n17
"James Baldwin: *This* Time!" Festival, 7
James Baldwin Place (New York), 7, 9, 146
James Baldwin Project, The, 8, 114, 134, 144, 182, 191, 215, 275
James Baldwin Review, The, 7, 141
James Baldwin's Turkish Decade: Erotics of Exile (Zaborowska), 34, 71, 87, 134
Jeandheur, Hélène Roux, 109, 129–30, 331n96, 331n102
Jefferson, Margo: *Negroland*, 255
Jimmy's Blues and Other Poems (Baldwin), 72, 80, 81
Johnson, E. Patrick, 23, 71, 97, 150, 301, 323n15
Just Above My Head (Baldwin), 14, 17, 38, 45, 48, 54–55, 56, 58, 71, 72, 81, 85, 94–97, 101, 102, 114, 116, 126, 134, 153, 184, 186, 189, 203, 211, 217, 219, 220, 222, 223, 225, 232, 237, 240, 255–93, 304, 305, 313, 330n63, 340n33

Karefa-Smart, Gloria, 108, 146
Kazan, Elia, 190
Kenan, Randall, 38, 290, 291
Kierkegaard, Søren, 82, 103, 180
Kilpeläinen, Pekka, 261, 262
King, Coretta Scott, 204
King, Martin Luther, Jr., 10, 70, 75, 125, 217, 281
Kitt, Eartha, 128
Kristeva, Julia, 30, 320n44
Kuncewicz, Maria, 304

Ladd, Florence, 57, 75, 108, 128, 206
Larsen, Nella, 59, 230, 255
Lawrence, D. H., 74, 106
Leeming, David, 44, 75, 107, 119, 197, 328n21, 343n72, 347n135. *See also James Baldwin: A Biography*
Lefebvre, Henri, 24, 32, 102, 221, 262–63

Légitimus, Samuel (Collectif James Baldwin de Paris), 318n17
Lethem, Jonathan, archive, 48, 300
Levine, David, 64
Lewis, Ida, 232–33, 264, 281
life writing, 22, 25, 29, 47, 76, 80, 124, 146, 154, 180, 186, 209, 217, 220, 222, 224, 267, 274, 277, 296, 298, 301, 302, 313. *See also* autobiography, autobiographical
literary archeology, 142
Little Man, Little Man (Baldwin), 48, 58, 194, 258–60, 349n31
Löeche-les-Bains (Switzerland), 86, 88, 89–93, 120, 198
London, England, 48, 86, 96, 190, 213, 228, 266, 267, 268, 271, 272, 273, 289
Lorde, Audre, 23, 32, 36, 129, 246, 257, 289, 298, 301
Lowe, Lisa, 301

Mabanckou, Alain, 38, 291
Macbeth (Welles), 177–78, 179
"Making Ourselves from Scratch" (Beam), 80
Malcolm X, 10, 125, 215, 340n33, 346n117
male, 120, 151, 153, 161, 164, 210, 228, 232, 247, 255, 256, 287, 290, 336n80; androgyny, 197; black, 23, 27, 36, 54, 64, 68, 72, 146, 158, 160, 164, 187, 200, 205, 219, 222, 231, 246, 257, 286, 332n2, 340n33; female in, 70, 129, 158, 288; influence on/in Baldwin's works, 82, 116, 154, 189, 190, 191, 193; sex(uality), 88, 97, 172, 324n17; white, 13, 157, 159, 164, 209, 244
"Mama's Baby" (Spillers), 319n34, 347n143
man, 38, 60, 71, 77, 93, 98, 134, 137, 148, 158, 196, 197, 198, 199, 202, 242, 249, 260, 262, 275, 276, 283, 284–93, 313, 324n17, 325n40, 338n110; Arab, 30; Baldwin as, 34, 63, 74, 122, 126, 129, 130, 152, 159, 169, 174, 189, 223; Baldwin as race man, 10, 28; black, 13, 14, 26, 35, 57, 75, 80, 126, 138, 139, 153, 157, 161, 180, 201, 203, 227–33, 235, 246, 250, 251, 252, 253, 254, 282, 284, 340n32, 340n33; black queer, 70, 75, 152, 209, 281; and domestic space, 13, 26; elder statesman, 163; French, 28, 29, 30, 31, 106; gay, 80; Jewish, 193; of letters, 27; the Man, 70, 164, 222, 239; manhood, 12, 13, 56, 57, 95, 116, 129, 152, 161, 184, 188, 190, 208, 223, 246, 318n22, 320n46; mankind, 78, 226; as narrator, 54; police-, 175, 244; unmanly, 70, 185; white, 13, 22, 248, 340n33
Mandela, Nelson, 2, 39
Manifest Destiny, rhetoric of, 76–77, 159
mantelpiece arrangements, 2, 14, 39, 109, 120, 130, 214, 215
"Many Thousands Gone" (Baldwin), 148
Marshall, Paule, 36, 128, 257, 291, 298
masculinity, 189, 257, Baldwin's, 18; Baldwin's views on and attention to, 205, 246, 281; black/African American, 23, 38, 47, 56, 70–71, 75, 184, 219, 231, 233, 279, 340n33; domestic models of, 288; to feminine identity, 186; gendered, 287; hetero-, 116; names and pronouns, 164, 165, 166; national, 184, 277; opposed to femininity, 31; queer, 282; transcultural, 342n57; white, 152, 340n33
mask, 62, 186, 187, 225, 229, 236; Pascal's death, 44, 126. *See also* façade; masquerade; persona
masquerade, 154, 186, 187, 191, 199, 202, 223, 225, 264. *See also* façade; mask; persona
material, materiality, 3, 4, 5–46, 52, 58, 71, 98, 103, 112, 119, 120, 133, 142, 219, 220, 265, 274, 296, 306, 307, 309,

313; artifacts, 309; biographical, 298; body, 223, 308, 312; circumstances, 96, 265; commentary, 133; culture, 301; documentation, 309; domesticity, 14, 101, 102, 231; effects, 141, 306; erasure of Baldwin's life, 297–302; evidence, 98; houses, 121; legacy, 48, 298–300; life, 145–212; literary, 82, 92; memory, 100; as objects for the metaphorical, 5–46, 112, 117, 302; preservation, 348n9; profit, 55; reminders, 141; remnants, 46, 47, 48, 58, 83, 103, 218, 300; setting, 286; site, 4; spaces, 103, 121, 128, 231, 267; structures, 120, 121; teaching, 228; world, 57; writing process as, 120. *See also* objects
materialism, materialist, 47, 77, 102, 263, 309, 310
McBride, Dwight, 33, 325n44
McPherson, James, 257
Mead, Margaret, 75, 232. *See also individual works*
"Me and My House" (Baldwin), 25, 27, 29, 168, 237–38, 264, 334n53. *See also* "Notes of a Native Son"
Memoirs of a Bastard Angel (Norse), 63
Meriwether, Louise, 108, 128, 257
Middle Passage, 10, 22, 102
Miller, Daniel, 4, 119
Miller (Winfield), Orilla "Bill," 47, 52, 155, 162, 164–79, 259, 278, 334n31
misogyny, misogynist, 198; and heterosexism, 244; and homophobia, 10, 157, 158, 159, 209, 287–89, 301, 311; and Islamophobia, 301; and racism, 301; and transphobia, 301; and white supremacy, 10, 149
Mitterrand, François, 106, 132
Mock, Janet, 155–56, 291; *Redefining Realness*, 70, 156, 209
Mohammed (James Baldwin's gardener), 2, 193, 217
Montand, Yves, 108, 139
Moraga, Cherríe, 289

Morrison, Toni, 22, 23, 33, 36, 37, 38, 75, 101, 102, 108, 129, 142, 230, 257, 286, 291, 321n63; eulogy of Baldwin, 82–83. *See also individual works*
Moses, David, 170, 189
Muñoz, José, 47, 149, 150, 158–59, 209. *See also* disidentification
"My Dungeon Shook" (Baldwin), 38

nation, national, 11, 22, 28, 45, 49, 56, 57, 58, 59, 74, 75, 76, 77, 79, 81, 101, 180, 188, 210, 221, 222, 225, 226, 227, 228, 234, 237, 239, 244, 245, 253, 261, 262, 288, 290, 335n58; audience, 33; blackness, 127; Book Award, 35; borders, 76, 290; domestic space, 13; domesticity, 240; family, 21; house, 5, 10, 12, 13, 14, 16, 17, 18, 19, 22, 36, 38, 48, 66, 68, 72, 74, 75, 76, 77, 78, 79, 101, 146, 156, 180, 208, 210, 217, 219, 220, 221, 223, 226, 237, 250, 256, 257, 263–66, 277, 299, 301, 310, 312, 313, 319n38, 331n83; identity, 14, 17, 21, 47, 57, 58, 68, 75, 126, 149, 150, 152, 157, 162, 163, 184, 186, 191, 199, 219, 220, 222, 226, 246, 249, 250, 252, 254, 261, 288, 302, 310; literary canon and icons, 101, 117, 231; literature, 32, 81, 233; masculinity, 184; multiracial, 21; origins, 92, 200; otherness, 174, 208; pantheon, 116; revolution, 188; space, 25, 72, 221, 225; theater, 155; trauma, 291; whiteness, 233
nationalism, 230, 310, 311, 312; black, 36, 48, 56, 57, 134, 184, 210, 219, 220, 233, 263; Black Power, 23, 230; domestic, 76; heterosexist, 184, 219; racist, 256; white, 233
National Museum of African American History and Culture, 46, 93, 301, 302, 303, 304
Native Son (Wright), 148, 333–34n28
Nazarene, Kali-Ma, 3, 108
Negroland (Jefferson), 255

INDEX   387

neighborhood, 65, 81, 163, 233, 249, 267, 268; Black, 68; Greenwich Village, 45; Harlem (Baldwin's childhood), 7, 45, 237, 239, 240, 258, 259, 261; spaces, 233; widoczki around the, 43

"New Lost Generation, The" (Baldwin), 60, 74

New Materialism, 298

Newton, Huey, 205

New York City, 5, 7, 12, 14, 24, 45, 52, 54, 63, 72, 82, 86, 95, 108, 125, 127, 128, 131, 155, 166, 168, 175, 217, 222, 223, 234, 235, 238, 241, 249, 250, 260, 262, 266, 267, 268, 282; Police Department, 166. *See also* Greenwich Village; Harlem

New York Live Arts Theater, 7

Nicholson, Mavis, 14

Nobody Knows My Name (Baldwin), 115, 245–46

Njeri, Itabari: *Every Good-Bye Ain't Gone*, 255

No Name in the Street (Baldwin), 10, 45, 47, 53, 56, 68, 71, 74–75, 115, 117, 146, 149, 153, 162, 170, 184, 201, 205, 214, 219, 225, 237, 239, 241, 243, 278, 281, 324n18, 340n33; groping incident in, 80, 313, 321n58

No Papers for Mohammed (Baldwin), 193, 217

Norse, Harold: *Memoirs of a Bastard Angel*, 63

"Notes for a Hypothetical Novel" (Baldwin), 149, 151, 152, 153

"Notes for *The Amen Corner*" (Baldwin), 181

"Notes of a Native Son" (Baldwin), 25–26, 168, 237. *See also* "Me and My House"

Notes of a Native Son (Baldwin), 27, 80, 152, 321n63

"Notes on the House of Bondage" (Baldwin), 20, 21, 22, 39, 53, 78, 79, 221, 309

Oates, Joyce Carol, 240, 256

objects, 2, 39, 44, 45, 57, 80, 98, 106, 109, 112, 119, 120, 121, 133, 141, 154, 206, 220, 300, 301, 302, 304, 307, 309; art, 194; human entanglement and, 4, 41, 48, 57; of intellectual labor, 103

Oliver Twist (Dickens), 259

Oral, Zeynep, 128

out-of-gender, 35

Painter, Mary, 108, 128, 193, 199

Pakay, Sedat, 62, 318n18; *James Baldwin: From Another Place*, 5, 28, 59, 62, 157

Paris, 3, 12, 112, 134, 148, 157, 196, 213, 267, 273, 329nn43–44; Baldwin in, 11, 86–88, 91, 107, 128, 132, 198, 235, 260, 318n22, 330n53, 332n4; immigrant communities in, 72; Proust's bedroom in, 114; roots, 81. *See also Giovanni's Room*; Légitimus, Samuel (Collectif James Baldwin de Paris); *Just Above My Head*; *Welcome Table, The*

Paris Review James Baldwin interview, 281

Parks, Rosa, 301

Parks, Suzan-Lori, 38, 129, 291

Pavlić, Edward M., 34; visit to Chez Baldwin, 141–42. *See also individual works*

performance, performativity, 35, 66, 90, 101, 150, 157, 160, 164, 182, 194, 230–31, 266, 269, 270, 304, 308; of black masculinity, 71; blackness as, 28; camp, 117, 129; of the feminine, 48, 56, 158; gender, 75, 129, 152, 157, 159, 183, 187; of homosexual identity, 159; of memory, 223; racial, 183; screen, 180; singing, 54, 240; of straight identity, 282, 290; theatrical, 58, 96, 177–81, 185, 187, 194, 204–5, 231

persona, 122, 182, 223, 225, 310; androgynous, 201; authorial, 47, 66, 157; autobiographical, 23; Baldwin's queenly, 117; Bessie Smith's singing, 25,

388 INDEX

54–55, 285; black queer, 126; dramatis personae, 154, 186, 191, 193; gendered, 152, 157, 187; intersectional, 152; polyracial, 201; public, 19, 57; sexual, 71; symbolic, 237. *See also* façade; mask; masquerade

Perspectives: Angles on African Art (Baldwin), 194

Petry, Ann, 22, 36, 38, 65, 229, 255, 291

Phillips, Caryl, 36, 108, 139

Picasso, Pablo, 315

Playing in the Dark (Morrison), 286

Poetics of Space, The (Bachelard), 101, 306–7

Poitier, Sidney, 185

Poland, 43, 173, 201, 304, 311, 312, 347n137

politic, 10, 13, 25, 78, 80, 150, 159, 186, 192, 197, 200, 205, 236, 237, 256, 289–90, 305, 313; of affect, 9; American, 7, 20, 48, 155; Baldwin and, 36, 49, 52, 68, 132, 146, 169–70, 174, 219, 301; class and, 146, 159; culture and, 56, 319n38; of diaspora, 78; engagement with, 53; female participation in, 22, 183, 196, 246–47, 289–90; gay, 63; gender, 155, 252, 310; geopolitics, 29, 77, 78, 173, 221, 222, 226, 253; of home, 72, 121, 281; identity, 160, 229, 237, 244, 310; national, 210; of Orilla Miller, 166, 170; as personal, 10, 20, 80, 92, 116, 301; of place, 32; private and, 14, 151–52, 301; of race and sexuality, 7, 17, 63, 155, 252, 310; racial, 159; and religion, 187; of respectability, 57, 239, 276, 332n2; of social space, 17, 25, 72; sociopolitical, 163; spatial, 24, 102, 263; vocabulary, 53

preservation: of writers' literary estates, 41, 114, 149; of black vs. white writers' literary estates, 298–300

"Previous Condition" (Baldwin), 238

"Price of the Ticket, The" (Baldwin), 76, 77

Price of the Ticket, The (Baldwin), 11, 15, 16, 21, 26, 27, 29, 30, 38, 44, 52, 53, 65, 66, 68, 70, 74, 77, 78, 79, 80, 88, 90–91, 92, 148, 149, 150, 151–52, 153, 154, 155, 160, 163, 164, 165, 170, 171, 172, 176, 177, 178, 179, 180, 208, 210, 223, 236, 237, 238, 239, 245, 248, 256, 276, 277, 278, 288

Pride and Prejudice (Austen), 117

"Princes and Powers" (Baldwin), 173, 200

prison, prisoners, 13, 14, 54, 58, 115, 180, 201, 202, 203, 239–42, 243, 248, 249, 250, 254, 263, 284, 291; at home, 55; and homosexuality, 184; and literature, 34; metaphorical, 101, 256, 269, 283, 293; prison-industrial complex, 227, 250, 324n18

Proust, Marcel: bedroom in Paris, 114, 116, 117

Provence (Provençal), 86, 107, 109, 128, 192; Baldwin's house in, 17, 98, 104, 105, 289; style around, in, and of Baldwin's house, 121, 124, 126, 182, 186. *See also* Chez Baldwin; Farber, Jules B.; St. Paul-de-Vence

Puerto Rico, 86, 88, 115, 168, 222, 249, 250, 251, 252

Pushkin, Alexander, 228

"quare," 97, 184, 308

queen: Baldwin's persona, 117; belles-lettres, 158; diva and, 66, 191; "Martin Luther Queen," Baldwin as, 289

queerness, 28, 57, 62, 64, 71, 72, 75, 95, 96, 97, 117, 133, 151, 159, 160, 184, 193, 194, 197, 198, 199, 220, 232, 262, 280, 291, 293, 324nn25–26, 325n32, 325n46, 339n23, 340n33; authorship and, 233; black, 97, 222, 233; bodies and, 220; domestic, 189–203, 217; female, 222, 233; homelessness and, 14; households and, 260, 262; identity and, 158, 249; imagination and,

queerness (*continued*)
34, 291; intellectual, 19; male, 97; masculinity and, 282; parenting, 260; queer baiting, 36; queer male in black community, 231; queer studies, 33, 70, 184; race and, 298; sexuality and, 23, 192; women and, 233; world, 153, 158; young readers, 290. *See also* black queers, queerness; "quare"; queen

race, 7, 18, 19, 24, 25, 32, 33, 47, 56, 63, 68, 72, 81, 86, 88, 97, 101, 116, 157, 160, 161, 172, 236, 244, 258, 340n33, 340n37, 346n120; and affect, 243; and age, 240, 243; American relations, 243; and authorship, 228; and beauty standards, 163; and black feminism, 233; and citizenship, 211; and class, 19, 169, 171, 173, 101, 208, 230, 236–37, 240, 281, 291, 341n49; and colonialism, 225; and culture, 169, 190; and domesticity, 19, 210, 320n40; and ethnicity, 199, 219, 225, 236, 254; and gender, 13, 19, 47, 72, 101, 129, 164, 186, 196, 210, 230, 233, 243, 246, 247, 250, 252, 254, 263, 281, 291, 310, 341n49, 348n12; in *Giovanni's Room*, 13; global issues of, 5; hierarchies related to, 58; and identity, 262; and imperialism, 225; literary representation, 148; mixed-, 68; and national identity, 126, 186, 208, 210, 246, 250, 254; and nationalism, 233; as performative, 164; politics of, 7; and power, 35; and queerness, 293, 298; race man, 10, 28, 238; race studies, 34; racism, 10, 35, 38, 47, 53, 59, 63, 68, 70, 72, 74, 77, 79, 83, 88, 114, 115, 153, 156, 181, 187, 188, 199, 201, 202, 210, 219, 221–27; 228, 231, 234, 236, 243, 246, 251, 253, 256, 282, 288, 301, 311, 312, 324n29, 325n34, 340n33, 341n44; and religion, 19, 186, 208; riots, 26; and sexuality, 7, 13, 18, 19, 47, 72, 101, 116, 129, 148, 149, 152, 186, 196, 201, 210, 219, 263, 291; and social space, 19, 254, 263; for theory, 23, 60, 64; and transnational, 310. *See also* Christian, Barbara; *Rap on Race, A*

Raisin in the Sun, A (Hansberry), 58
Rankine, Claudia, 35, 38, 291
Rap on Race, A (Baldwin and Mead), 75, 232
Reading, Bertice, 57, 128
Redefining Realness (Mock), 70, 156, 209
Reid-Pharr, Robert, 23, 33, 81, 265
Rein, Brenda (Keith), 128, 149
"Remember This House" (Baldwin), 10, 215
Rich, Adrienne, 32, 38; "The Baldwin Stamp," 296–98
Riggs, Marlon, 291
Rodriquez, Richard, 290
Roux, Hélène. *See* Jeandheur, Hélène Roux
Roux, Pitou, 109, 138, 139
Roux, Tintine, 132
Roux, Yvonne, 57, 129–30, 139
Russia, 173, 186, 228

Said, Edward, 18
Sanchez, Sonia, 289
San Juan, Puerto Rico, 48, 213, 234, 250, 251, 252
Scott, Darieck, 290
Scott, Lynn Orilla, 33, 34, 96, 141, 165, 166, 167, 195, 261, 278
Seale, Bobby, 205
sexuality, 12, 13, 35, 59, 65, 97, 101, 127, 157, 161, 186, 196, 198, 219, 244, 256, 262, 276, 280; bisexuality, 65, 197–98; and class, 7, 36, 201; and domesticity, 13; and gender, 13, 25, 47, 101, 184, 199, 201, 208; and gender identity, 10; homosexuality, 12, 88, 116, 184, 230, 271, 286–88; manhood and, 161; and

morality, 7; and politics, 63; queer, 23; and race, 7, 13, 18, 19, 25, 33, 47, 62, 63, 101, 201; and social space, 47; studies of, 33
Signifying Monkey, The (Gates), 101
Signoret, Simone, 108, 132, 139
Simone, Nina, 45, 57, 108, 129, 139, 193
sissy, 35, 65, 116, 117, 153, 157, 158, 160, 164, 287, 313
"Site of Memory, The" (Morrison), 142, 257
slaves, slavery, 19, 22, 23, 29, 53, 59, 76, 77, 78, 91, 101, 102, 145, 146, 200, 227, 236, 242, 251, 291, 310, 312, 313, 326n60; African, 11, 59, 77; ex-slaves, 30, 31, 75, 79; slaveholding, 79, 102; transatlantic, 23, 77, 102; women, 200. *See also* Middle Passage
Smith, Bessie, 45, 54, 55, 92, 129, 151, 244–45, 262; "Backwater Blues," 18, 25, 27, 54–55, 58, 216, 285
Sordello, Valerie, 2, 132–34, 193
Soul!, 214, 227–33
Souls of Black Folk, The (Du Bois), 15, 343n70
Soyinka, Wole, 36, 122, 289
space, 12, 14, 15, 17, 18, 22, 25, 26, 29, 30, 31, 32, 41, 44, 48, 59, 65, 66, 70, 72, 80, 82, 92, 95, 100, 101–3, 106, 112, 114, 117, 120, 121, 134, 135, 141, 143, 162, 187, 200, 206, 215, 217, 219, 220, 221–27, 231, 233, 241, 242, 246, 263, 264–79, 280, 282, 286, 290, 293, 298, 301, 302, 305, 306, 310, 319n35, 328n22, 346n119; and abuse, 81; alternative, 81; artistic, 95; of authorial labor, 96, 214; black, 59, 217, 262, 263, 288; of the color line, 28; domestic, 11, 13, 14, 46, 48, 55, 57, 72, 77, 86, 95, 97, 98, 104, 114, 119, 142, 143, 217, 233, 267, 268, 274, 279, 280, 283, 285, 286, 290, 298, 304, 305, 307, 310, 342n56; familial, 14; geographic, 91; home, 14, 23, 38, 59, 72, 96, 97, 217, 305; imaginary, 49; of imprisonment, 242; liminal, 284; material, 121, 128; and matter, 43; narrative, 13; national, 72, 225; prison, 242; private, 11, 24, 38, 80, 313; production of, 32; public, 14, 46, 57, 46, 57, 86; racialized, 21; religious, 72, 95, 247; safe, 23, 55; and sex, 148; social, 12, 15, 17, 19, 21, 24, 25, 31, 38, 43, 45, 47, 58, 72, 76, 86, 91, 221, 225, 231, 235, 254, 260, 263, 265, 302, 310; street, 72, 247; time and, 28, 29; transnational, 250; white, 248; and women, 23, 189; writing, 117, 302. *See also* black queers, queerness; black space; *home, blackness,* and *me / space, story,* and *self*; queerness
Spillers, Hortense, 22, 23
Stein, Gertrude, 314
Stein, Sol, 124–25, 341n42
Steinem, Gloria, 289
Stowe, Harriet Beecher, 146, 149; *Uncle Tom's Cabin*, 146–48
St. Paul-de-Vence, 1, 3, 4, 5, 10, 17, 18, 20, 24, 35, 39, 41, 45, 46, 47, 56, 57, 60, 80, 81, 85–143, 154, 160, 162, 196, 206, 208, 209, 210, 214, 215, 217, 219, 266–67, 286, 289, 293, 305, 310, 312, 329n51, 348n11
Stranger, The (Camus), 30
"Stranger in the Village" (Baldwin), 79, 88, 90, 91, 92, 140, 160, 173
streets, 35, 58, 90, 91, 92, 93, 105, 134, 140, 158, 235, 238, 243, 244, 247, 258, 263, 265, 269, 273, 279, 282, 313
structures of feeling, 157, 220. *See also* Williams, Raymond
Styron, William, 111
Sula (Morrison), 291
Sururi, Gülriz, 128, 204
"Sweet Lorraine" (Baldwin), 58, 59, 82

Tale of Two Cities, A (Dickens), 145, 146, 166, 172, 174, 180
Tate, Claudia, 13, 23

Tell Me How Long the Train's Been Gone (Baldwin), 14, 35, 38, 45, 47, 72, 184–85, 189–90, 237, 278, 309, 335n54, 340n33

Terkel, Studs, 18, 25, 53, 54, 244, 246

theater, 34, 58, 91, 146, 153, 154, 155, 159, 166, 170, 177–12, 278; Baldwin directing performances, 96; Baldwin's friends in, 107; Baldwin's house as, 304; of composition (writer's homes), 103; domestic, 103; national, 155. *See also* New York Live Arts Theater

Thorsen, Karen, 5, 8, 88, 91, 92, 107, 111, 114, 125, 127, 134, 144, 182, 191, 214–15, 275, 278, 318nn17–18. See also *James Baldwin: The Price of the Ticket*

Three Sisters, The (Chekhov), 154–55, 183, 186, 192, 197, 204

To Be Young, introduction to, 38

To Be Young, Gifted, and Black (Hansberry), 57

"To Crush the Serpent" (Baldwin), 57, 65, 66, 76, 223

Torres, Justin, 290

trans, 10, 66, 70, 152, 158, 194, 209, 220, 291

transatlantic, 5, 13, 24, 33, 34, 47, 53, 76, 77, 102, 182, 191, 200, 302

transcultural, transculturation, 192, 261

transgender, 158, 186, 187, 192, 193, 209, 291, 323n15

transnationalism, 19, 47, 53, 57, 85–144, 154, 182, 183, 191, 221, 222, 250, 310, 326n59, 328n18

transphobia, 301

Traub, Valerie, 325n32

trauma, traumatic, traumatized, 54, 55, 96, 114, 115, 128, 160, 220, 250, 253, 255–93, 313; Baldwin's childhood, 56, 80, 81, 175; metaphors, 80; national, 291; society, 160, 291

Traylor, Eleanor, 96, 108, 116, 129, 261

Troupe, Quincy, 5, 35, 39, 41, 51, 78, 116, 121–22, 128, 130, 131, 132, 289, 330n77

Truth, Sojourner, 22

Turkey, 17, 25, 35, 44, 45, 53, 56, 72, 74, 75, 86, 95, 96, 97, 107, 112, 128, 129, 177, 183, 184, 186, 204, 206, 264, 347n137; Ankara, 134; Bodrum, 134; Taksim Square (Istanbul), 62. *See also* Istanbul

Uncle Tom's Cabin (Stowe), 146–48

United States, 264, 302, 311

vitrines, 1, 39, 43, 59, 309

Walker, Alice, 23, 36, 230, 257, 289, 298; *The Color Purple*, 70, 255, 291

Warwick, Dionne, 214, 215, 293

Welcome Table, The (Baldwin and Dallas), 2, 14, 17, 45, 47, 56, 102, 109, 114, 117, 122, 126, 128, 133, 134, 153–212, 217, 223, 261, 286, 335n54, 335n57, 336n74, 336n76, 337n93, 340n33

Welles, Orson, 177; *Macbeth*, 177–78, 179

"We Wear the Mask" (Dunbar), 225

Wharton, Edith, 258

Wheatley, Phyllis, 59, 229

whiteness, 14, 24, 31, 46, 57, 70, 74, 78–79, 102, 157, 161, 170, 172, 219, 220, 222, 229, 233, 234, 248, 249, 265, 286, 320n40, 348n11

Who Can Afford to Improvise? (Pavlić), 34

Wideman, John, 257

widoczek (widoczki), 43

Wilkins, Craig, 24, 262–63

Williams, Raymond, 220, 255

Williams, Thomas Chatterton, 3

Williams, William Carlos, 296, 298

Winfield, Ken, 165

woman, women, 20, 22, 23, 33, 35, 37, 41, 52, 54–57, 65, 68, 71, 75, 80, 90, 91, 103, 105, 106, 127, 128–33, 139, 148, 153, 154, 155, 157, 158, 160–66, 168, 169, 181–83, 185, 186–90, 192–94, 196–201, 204, 209, 210, 219, 222, 227–33,

238–41, 243, 244, 245, 248–58, 262, 266, 272, 278, 279–82, 284–93, 299, 313, 318n29, 319n36, 323n11, 323n17, 324n17, 333n12, 338n110, 340n32, 340n40, 342n54; black, 36, 38, 48, 54, 56, 70, 81, 108, 114, 115, 128, 129, 159, 211, 231, 241, 244, 246, 247, 249, 255, 257, 258, 272, 280, 284, 298, 310, 319, 312, 323n11, 342n51, 343nn64–65, 344n89, 345n100, 346n116, 346n118, 347n130, 347n132, 347n134. *See also* "Black Woman"

Wonder, Stevie, 139

World War II, 32, 168, 199, 201, 234, 238

Wright, Richard, 23, 36, 229, 247, 289, 325n31, 332n2; Baldwin's critique of, 148. See also *Native Son*

writers, 3, 5, 38, 80, 108, 118, 149, 150, 151, 234, 287, 293, 305, 313; African American, 18, 52, 98, 148, 245; African Diaspora, 98, 112; American, 4, 36, 98, 148, 230, 246; assumed male, 228; assumed white, 228, 229; black, 7, 18, 33, 36, 81, 148, 153, 160, 183, 228, 229–33, 289, 298, 301; black male, 158, 246, 257, 332n2; black queer, 32, 86, 294; black/African American women, 229–33, 255, 257, 258, 291, 298; colony, 328n21; writers of color, 32, 74; diasporic, 265, 291; and domestic (home) life, 45, 47, 104, 141, 310; and dwelling, 27, 32, 220; and exile, 25, 59, 186; feminist, 289; gay, 7, 33, 158; house/museums of, 32, 45, 56, 98, 100, 103, 105, 112–28, 134–40, 210, 214–17, 304, 308; landmark, 7; life and oeuvre, 7; male, 23, 247, 256, 290; Negro, 63, 148, 150, 180, 230; traumatized, 279; as a witness, 103; women, 20, 36, 37, 81, 128–29, 255, 257, 291. *See also* Baldwin, James

Writer's House and Museum for James Baldwin (digital archive), 302

writing process, 96, 97, 111, 114, 120, 124, 160, 264–65, 279. *See also* authors, authorship; creative process

Yonkers, New York, 227, 260, 267, 280

Young, Kevin, 80

Youngblood, Shay, 38, 129, 291

Zaborowska, Magdalena: visits to Chez Baldwin, 1–3, 41, 104–9, 112, 114–21, 134–43, 304–6. *See also individual works*

Zola, Emile, 226